# Overtourism and Cruise Tourism in Emerging Destinations on the Arabian Peninsula

Cruise tourism is one of the fastest growing sectors worldwide. This book is the first of its kind to provide in-depth insights into the emergence of mega-cruise tourism in destinations on the Arabian Peninsula and its impacts on local communities, their spaces, cultures, identities and tourist experiences.

It offers a micro-sociological analysis, calling for holistic, participatory, mindful approaches and to rethink current exploitative tourism planning and development. It assumes a high political, social and economic importance within globalization. It draws on a long-term field study in an under-researched region in Asia that developed large-scale tourism recently to diversify the economy. The book provides insights on the destination development from a state of continuous growth to a sudden fall in tourism activities due to a sudden shock, caused by the global health pandemic and its resilience. It explores the sociocultural, economic and spatial challenges faced in international tourism development and its power relations analysed from different perspectives and within time. It analyses time-space compression, overtourism, urban tourism, nature-based tourism, enclavization, social capital, imaginaries, Cultural Ecosystem Services, slow tourism as well as just tourism.

The book provides an innovative contribution to the planning and development of tourism destinations, communities and their spaces in which tourism operates at a fast pace. It will be of interest to academics, undergraduate and postgraduate students in the field of tourism and hospitality management, geography, sociology, anthropology, urban planning and environmental sciences. Moreover, the book will be useful for practitioners and policymakers around the globe, as well as all those interested in the fast emergence and the impacts of mega-cruise tourism.

**Manuela Gutberlet** is a critical tourism geographer. She is passionate about social and action research within communities. She is currently a Research Associate, University of Johannesburg, Department of Tourism and Hospitality, South Africa and a Research Associate at the Bavarian Centre for Tourism. Moreover, she has taught sustainable tourism and tourism planning in Germany. Manuela has earnt a degree in Business and Arabic and did her PhD in Cultural Geography at RWTH Aachen University, Germany. Her research was presented at numerous scientific conferences and was published in ranked journals. Her research interests include the impacts of globalisation on communities and their sociocultural environments. She has gained over twenty-five years of work experiences in the Middle East working in public relations, journalism, higher education and in tourism research.

**Routledge Insights in Tourism Series**
Series Editor: Anukrati Sharma, Head & Associate Professor
of the Department of Commerce and Management at the
University of Kota, India

This series provides a forum for cutting edge insights into the latest developments in tourism research. It offers high quality monographs and edited col-
lections that develop tourism analysis at both theoretical and empirical levels.

**Tourism, Safety and COVID-19**
Security, Digitization and Tourist Behaviour
*Salvatore Monaco*

**COVID-19 and the Tourism Industry**
Sustainability, Resilience and New Directions
*Edited by Anukrati Sharma, Azizul Hassan and Priyakrushna Mohanty*

**Management of Tourism Ecosystem Services in a Post Pandemic Context**
Global Perspectives
*Edited by Vanessa G. B. Gowreesunkar, Shem Wambugu Maingi and Felix
Lamech Mogambi Ming'ate*

**Tourism, Knowledge and Learning**
Conceptual Development and Case Studies
*Edited by Eva Maria Jernsand, Maria Persson and Erik Lundberg*

**Potentials, Challenges and Prospects of Halal Tourism Development in Ethiopia**
*Mohammed Jemal Ahmed and Atilla Akbaba*

**Diasporic Mobilities on Vacation**
Tourism of European-Moroccans at Home
*Lauren B Wagner*

**Overtourism and Cruise Tourism in Emerging Destinations on the Arabian
Peninsula**
*Manuela Gutberlet*

For more information about this series, please visit: www.routledge.com/
Routledge-Insights-in-Tourism-Series/book-series/RITS

# Overtourism and Cruise Tourism in Emerging Destinations on the Arabian Peninsula

**Manuela Gutberlet**

LONDON AND NEW YORK

First published 2024
by Routledge
4 Park Square, Milton Park, Abingdon, Oxon OX14 4RN

and by Routledge
605 Third Avenue, New York, NY 10158

*Routledge is an imprint of the Taylor & Francis Group, an informa business*

© 2024 Manuela Gutberlet

*British Library Cataloguing-in-Publication Data*
A catalogue record for this book is available from the British Library

*Library of Congress Cataloging-in-Publication Data*
Names: Gutberlet, Manuela, author.
Title: Overtourism and cruise tourism in emerging destinations on the Arabian Peninsula / Manuela Gutberlet.
Description: Abingdon, Oxon ; New York, NY : Routledge, [2023] |
Series: Routledge advances in tourism and anthropology |
Includes bibliographical references and index.
Identifiers: LCCN 2022056449 (print) | LCCN 2022056450 (ebook) |
ISBN 9781138354272 (hardback) | ISBN 9781032490519 (paperback) |
ISBN 9780429424946 (ebook)
Subjects: LCSH: Tourism--Arabian Peninsula. | Ocean travel--Arabian Peninsula. | Arabian Peninsula--Description and travel.
Classification: LCC G155.A67 G88 2023 (print) | LCC G155.A67 (ebook) |
DDC 338.4/79153--dc23/eng/20230505
LC record available at https://lccn.loc.gov/2022056449
LC ebook record available at https://lccn.loc.gov/2022056450

ISBN: 978-1-138-35427-2 (hbk)
ISBN: 978-1-032-49051-9 (pbk)
ISBN: 978-0-429-42494-6 (ebk)

DOI: 10.4324/9780429424946

Typeset in Times New Roman
by KnowledgeWorks Global Ltd.

# Contents

*List of figures*     vi
*List of tables*     viii
*Foreword by (Prof. Dr.) Dallen J. Timothy*     ix
*Acknowledgements*     xii

1   Introduction: Framing overtourism within time,
    space and society     1

2   Exploring concepts     18

3   The research setting     49

4   Methods     69

5   Results: Oriental imaginaries, tourist experiences and
    the local quality of life     89

6   The local community and their silent resistance: Tourist
    behaviours, culture clashes and the ethics of tourism     133

7   Fast and slow experiences in the desert and an oasis     175

8   Management and planning implications: Rethinking
    tourism: Towards more community and an ethics of care     209

9   Conclusions     223

*Index*     241

# Figures

1.1    A tourist bus at the entrance to Souq Muttrah, opposite
to the cruise terminal    9

1.2    Conceptualizing overtourism    12

3.1    Map of the district of Muttrah, including Souq Muttrah
and Port Sultan Qaboos    52

3.2    Map of the Sultanate of Oman including Sharqiyah Sands desert    53

3.3    The old souq area in Mudhairib    55

3.4    Lush greenery in the oasis in Al Mudhairib    55

3.5    A mega-cruise liner in the port of Muscat    61

4.1    During my fieldwork in Souq Muttrah    72

4.2    Guiding mega-cruise tourists through Muscat by bus.
German-speaking tour guides Alice, Daniela and myself
at the cruise port    73

5.1    AIDABlu in Muscat    90

5.2    The Corniche Road with Souq Muttrah, the residential
area Sur Al-Lawatia and its mosque    94

5.3    The main entrance of Souq Muttrah with its tower at the
Corniche road. The tower was built in the early 2000, prior
to the arrival of mega-ships    97

5.4    Map of the Bay of Muttrah including its souq area and
main tourist entrance as well as the residential district,
Sur Al-Lawatia    102

5.5    Tourists gather in front of the souq, Corniche road    103

5.6    Cruise tourists walking along the main, colourful street of
the souq, some vendors staring at them passing by    103

5.7    The attraction connects the individual and the group
tourist with the local community, whereas the cruise
tourist is connected with the attraction only    105

5.8    One of the first shops in the souq: the frankincense shop    107

5.9    An Omani tour guide "staging" at the frankincense shop in
front of his group of German-speaking cruise tourists    109

5.10    The main tourist street in Souq Muttrah when a mega-cruise
liner was in the port    115

5.11   Tourist souvenir shops along the main street of the souq           119
5.12   Tourist souvenirs, introduced on a larger scale in Souq
       Muttrah, with the arrival of more mega-cruise tourists
       from 2012 onwards                                                   120
5.13   New colourful glass windows were inserted in the ceilings
       of the souq, within the 'main tourist bubble'                      125
6.1    An Omani boy and his mother, in the periphery of Souq
       Muttrah, purchasing household items                                136
6.2    A cruise tourist wearing revealing clothes and other
       tourist wearing a local dishdasha and turban in the
       main street of Souq Muttrah                                        140
6.3    Tourists along the main street. Male cruise tourists in shorts
       and a loosely wrapped turban, staging an 'Oriental Other'
       at the entrance to the souq                                        146
6.4    An Omani shop selling items from Africa and Oman along
       the main street until 2014. One year later the shop converted
       into a tourist shop                                                150
6.5    The Omani shop was converted into a tourist shop in 2014           151
6.6    Dimensions of overtourism and local governance in Souq
       Muttrah                                                            154
6.7    A shop of the well-established trader community in Souq
       Muttrah                                                            156
6.8    Akshay's shop turned into a flashy textile, tourist shop with
       windows and an air conditioner, from 2016 onwards                  161
6.9    Framework of the dimensions of bonding and bridging
       social capital leading to a transnational community in
       Souq Muttrah                                                       165
6.10   In front of Souq Muttrah – an empty square where tourists
       gathered in the past                                               168
7.1    German-speaking cruise tourists leaving a mega-ship one
       early morning in Muscat                                            176
7.2    The constructed coffee break in the oasis                          184
7.3    Cruise tourists immerse themselves in the oasis                    188
7.4    Fast experiences in the desert landscape that transforms
       into a liminoid zone                                               195
7.5    A spiritual communion with nature, memorizing the sunset           200
7.6    Framework of aesthetic and spiritual ecosystem services in
       the desert and their importance for creating a new identity
       (for German-speaking tourists)                                     203
8.1    Management implications for emerging cruise destinations           212
9.1    A mega-cruise liner arriving in Muscat                             224
9.2    A local, expatriate tour guide explains the souq and its
       heritage to a small group of German tourists, at the
       frankincense shop in Souq Muttrah                                  230

# Tables

1.1   Gobal CLIA ocean cruise passengers in million                    5
3.1   Inbound tourists in Oman                                        58
3.2   Ocean cruise tourist arrivals in Oman (2009–2020)               64

# Foreword

Since the end of World War II, international tourism has grown at an exponential rate, exceeding 1 billion international trips in 2012 for the first time in history. A significant part of that growth is comprised of 'mass tourism', which is driven largely by the pursuit of pleasure, leisure, relaxation and fun. Mass tourism developed rapidly after the mid-20th century as transportation technology enabled more efficient aircrafts and modern cruise ships, globalization processes, the proliferation of inexpensive flights in the marketplace and as more destinations undertook mass marketing campaigns and global image development through massive branding programs. In the 1990s and 2000s, a number of low-cost airlines emerged, transporting masses of passengers cheaply and quickly to popular destinations for short stays and long weekends, especially in closely connected Europe, or for longer holidays elsewhere. These and other forces have seen certain destinations both flourish and languish due to the growth of mass tourism.

Mass tourism is often blamed for the social, cultural, economic and environmental ills associated with rapid tourism growth, and its participants are often seen as careless consumers who leave rubbish, graffiti, bad attitudes and frustrated destination residents in their wake. Opposite of mass tourism are special-interest forms of tourism that are sometimes seen to be less damaging to destination environments because they are smaller in scale and their participants exhibit more caring behaviours and are more interested in learning, pursuing a hobby and protecting destination assets. More sustainable ways of planning and carrying out tourism have emerged as an answer to mass tourism. Included in this category are community-based tourism, ecotourism and pro-poor tourism, which are not types of tourism per se but rather approaches to tourism development, with most kinds of tourism being able to adopt any of these sustainability paradigms. However, even special-interest tourisms are now massified and are becoming as much a part of the problem as they are a part of the triple-bottom-line solution.

The growth of mass tourism since the 1960s and the massification of special interest tourisms since the 1990s have affected many changes in many destinations, most of them less favourable. Today, this often manifests in what is known as 'overtourism', or too much tourism in which carrying capacities are exceeded, resulting in overcrowding, disrespect for local sociocultural norms, physical impacts on natural and built environments, and gentrification processes that crowd out the local population and create a deep sense of disdain for tourists and tourism. This has become a salient problem in locations such as Prague, Amsterdam, Rome, Florence, Barcelona, Bali and Machu Picchu. In some of these famous destinations, residents no longer welcome tourists with open arms, and many a tourist has expressed frustration with decreasing local hospitality and increased local hostility, resulting in less satisfying travel experiences.

Cruise tourism is one of the clearest manifestations of mass tourism and is a salient contributor to overtourism in many well-established destinations. Among the most prevalent cruise-specific cases today are many Caribbean ports, as well as Barcelona, Venice, Santorini, Dubrovnik and several other Mediterranean ports of call. Many of these places have experienced not only a rapid growth in cruise tourism and other forms of mass tourism but also a declining environment for local residents and tourists, causing their residents to question the true value of tourism.

New destinations have begun to appear on the cruise circuit, including the Arabian Peninsula, which only a quarter century ago, was thought to be of little interest to the cruise sector and many special interests because of the region's perceived religious conservatism, lack of tourism image and its sprawling Arabian Desert environment. Yet, in the past decade, the region has found favour among cruise passengers from Europe, North America and elsewhere, largely because of its storied mysticism and 'oriental otherness'. Ports of call in Qatar, Bahrain, Saudi Arabia and several localities in the United Arab Emirates and Oman are increasingly popular stops on Red Sea, Persian Gulf and Arabian Sea itineraries. Despite their increasing popularity, the cruise industry in this part of the world has received relatively little research attention, even though mass cruise tourism has the potential to impact the region as it has other parts of the world. Thus, overtourism is becoming a reality in places that heretofore have not been on the conventional cruise circuit.

The author of this volume is certainly correct in suggesting that there is a general lack of critical tourism studies in the Middle East. She has spent many years working in the region, collecting longitudinal data, entrenching herself into local social life and local tourism to remedy this dearth of knowledge. I wholeheartedly applaud the work of Manuela Gutberlet in shedding light on the growing trend of overtourism and the emerging cruise industry on the Arabian Peninsula and all of its multitudinous implications. This book is conceptually rich and theoretically sound. It is eruditely written and is chock full of empirical data based on the author's systematic surveys at Souq Muttrah in Oman but also on her years of embedded experience in the region, which lends a richness and depth to the study unparalleled by any other works I have read.

In this volume, Dr. Gutberlet examines a wide array of crucial concepts that manifest in emerging places facing overtourism. Conceptions such as authenticity; social capital; tourist performances; oriental imaginaries and stereotypes of exotic otherness; gendered spaces; bounded spaces of othering, exclusion and inclusion; and privileged tourist gazes offer a depth of theoretical analysis uncommon to research monographs on the Middle East and in tourism in general. It is rare to see such a splendid mix of ideas, concepts, and empirical insights in a single volume. I am thrilled to see how the author has succeeded in meticulously crafting a narrative of tourism and a voice of warning on the Arabian Peninsula that is broad yet specific, scholarly yet use-inspired and practical, and critical yet encouraging. This certainly lends breadth, depth and holistic clarity to a traditional off-the-beaten-path destination that is now a rooted part of mainstream tourism.

*Overtourism and Cruise Tourism in Emerging Destinations on the Arabian Peninsula* is essential reading for all students and scholars of tourism, geography, anthropology, sociology, sustainability and Middle East studies. Although its empirical material derives from the Arabian Peninsula, the work contained in this volume is cutting-edge, borderless and timely, and therefore applicable to any mass tourism setting in any part of the globe. The book is extremely valuable for tourism and development scholars in every discipline. Its pages come alive through Dr. Gutberlet's chronicled accounts of cruise passengers' behaviours and their impacts in an increasingly popular tourism region, which presently faces a critical time when planning decisions are needed to reap the rewards of tourism while simultaneously protecting the destination from the ravages of overtourism.

*Dallen J. Timothy*
*Professor and Senior Sustainability Scientist*
*Arizona State University, USA*

# Acknowledgements

My first thoughts go to The Sultanate of Oman – its land and its people. I have developed a deep belonging and a strong fascination for the country that I have called "my home" between 2004 and 2021. My research is a tribute to the country's diversity, its youth and its leaders; in particular late H.M. Sultan Qaboos bin Said Al Said. The diverse sociocultural and natural landscapes and the warm-hearted hospitality of the people create a rich, mesmerizing spirit many people get attracted to. My entire research presented in this book has been part of an inspiring and challenging journey. I enjoyed the opportunity to engage with diverse stakeholders of the local communities. Initially, my research developed from my interest in communities, travelling, writing and guiding tourists around the Arabian Peninsula. Without the support and encouragement extended by numerous people, my research would have been much more challenging.

My heartfelt thanks to Prof. Dr. Carmella Pfaffenbach (RWTH Aachen University) for her advice, support and encouragement from the outset of my research study. I would also like to thank Prof. Dr. Dieter Müller, University of Umea (Sweden) for his council and encouragement throughout the years. Thanks to Prof. Dr. Janos L. Urai and Prof. Dr. Peter Kukla, RWTH Aachen University for their support during the initial stage of my research. Moreover, I would like to thank Prof. Dr. Andreas Bürkert, Kassel University, who was the first academic to inspire me to think about a research project in Oman. He and his colleagues gave a workshop and an exhibition about the "Oases in Oman" at Sultan Qaboos University in 2006. Their project made me think about responsible tourism. As a journalist, I wrote newspaper articles on the preservation of the oases and I was producer for an ARTE TV documentary, "The Roses of the Desert", about life in Jebel Al Akhdar.

As for my entire fieldwork in Oman, which involved tremendous efforts and logistics, I would like to thank all tourists interviewed and local interviewees from the community in both locations. At times, it was difficult to gain access to mega-cruise ships that are typically off-limits to curious outsiders. Nevertheless, I was fortunate to have been able to gain access to German-speaking tourists from mega-ships. I especially thank my former colleagues in tourism, Anuj Bhandari, now general manager (Travco Oman), as well as Shankar Bose, former general manager (Bahwan Tourism) for their support. Sincere thanks to the management of AIDA Cruises and their on-board employees who were open to speak to me, as well as the other cruise liner brand that does not wish to be named. Thanks to Prof. Dr. Dallen Timothy, University of Arizona, and Prof. Dr. Kyle Maurice Woosnam, University of Georgia, who supported my path with valuable advice during the final stage of my book writing, as well Prof. Dr. Gerhard Platz. Furthermore, I would like to thank several professors attending the annual International Geographical Union (IGU) conferences for all the critical and encouraging feedback I received during those forums. The conferences were held in Cologne, Kyoto, Krakow, Moscow, Beijing, Québec and Washington between 2012 and 2019. I would like to acknowledge the advice of Prof. Dr. Jarkko Saarinen and Prof. Dr. Alan Lew, and I would like to thank Prof. Dr. Sanette Ferreira, as well as Prof. Dr. Joseph Cheer. I wish to thank Routledge employees Ruth Anderson, Nonita, Prachi and Faye Leerink, the corresponding editor whom I met during the AAG Washington in 2019.

Special thanks to my former employer, the German University of Technology in Oman (GUtech) and my past bosses. Thanks to my former colleagues, especially Rollo Desoutter and Terence Adby who were a great support for polishing the style and proofreading of my work. Moreover, my thanks go to Prof. Dr. Christian Rogerson and Prof. Dr. Jayne Rogerson who asked me during the IGU 2019 Washington to join the academic network of Tourism Research Associates at the University's Department of Hospitality and Tourism, Faculty of Business, University of Johannesburg, South Africa.

I would also like to thank all journalists who featured my research and helped inform the public. In particular, I thank Conrad Prabhu (Oman Daily Observer), Sarah MacDonald as well as Hassan Al Lawati (both former Times of Oman). I would like to thank the ARTE TV team that shot a documentary about Oman's economic diversification in October 2018. I was happy to walk with them through the souq while being interviewed. Moreover, I thank all government officials for responding to my interview requests. In particular, I wish to thank the former Minister of Tourism in Oman, H.E. Ahmed Al Mahrzi, whom I had the pleasure to meet three times. In February 2020, I was delighted to hear from him that my research was presented to the Council of Ministers and has created a policy debate. I would like to acknowledge the support received from high-ranking members of the Al Lawati community in Muttrah and for the assistance in connecting me to locals. Thanks as well to Mohammed Al Ajmi, Ministry of Environment and Water, as well as Dr. Abdulrahman Al Salmi, Ministry of Religious Affairs and Awqaf, for their support. My sincere gratitude goes to all interviewees: German-speaking tourists and local community members. In Muttrah, I would like to recognize the support received by Malik Al Hinai, former director of Bait Al Baranda Museum.

I extend a big thank you to all cultural mediators who agreed to be interviewed. I am convinced that especially tour guiding is one of the most important professions for establishing responsible tourism practices. I hope that the overall recognition of tour guiding will be enhanced in the eyes of the public. I also wish to thank my friend Bharat Khatri for his support throughout the research. Several former colleagues helped in distributing the survey forms. Special thanks to Sultan Al Maskari, who on several occasions agreed to help in mediating with the male community in Sharqiyah. I also thank my friends and neighbours in Muscat: Malika, Nasra and Bindhu who often supported me with their warm hospitality, a cup of spicy karak tea and delicious food that helped to navigate through my writing. Thanks as well to my friends who have shared my passion for sports in Muscat. I also thank my funny Omani cats Knuffi and Krispie. Knuffi was often lounging beside my laptop when I started writing this book. Then Krispie 'took over' his place in June 2020 – both became precious friends. Their purring has been like music to my ears and their relaxed posture inspired me to stay focused.

My final thoughts go to my grandparents and my parents who planted in me the seeds of curiosity about the world. They inspired me to learn languages, to be on the move, reach out and understand other people, cultures and nature from an early age.

I hope and wish that my research creates awareness and a debate about overtourism and that it drives a discussion in policymaking towards concrete action for the benefit of local people and their environment on the Arabian Peninsula. Any omissions from these acknowledgements are mine and they are unintentional.

# 1 Introduction

## Framing overtourism within time, space and society

Our current era we are living in is conceptualized as living 'on the go'. Individual experiences and tourist destinations are consumed on the spot through the moment and instantaneity that makes the current moment a quasi "immortal experience" (Bauman, 2000). Long-term has been replaced by short-term. Tourism practices in the destination are shaped by everyday socialities, practices and cultures. An urban destination like an "Oriental" marketplace creates an imaginary space while a remote, rural destination such as the desert and an oasis can create an impression of being within a vast, empty space, with little human interference and without physical borders or ownership like a space of freedom, thrill and liberty.

Time-space compression has increased dramatically due to modernization processes that our planet Earth has encountered since the Industrial Revolution in the 17th century, embedded in a neoliberal economic system and its extractivism (Harvey, 2020). Because of the acceleration of time in space, our mobilities have increased, changing the appreciation of the physical, natural and social environments (Urry, 1995). Tourism has been promoted by globalization and capitalism. One of the early male, European tourism scholars, Jost Krippendorf (1987, p. XIII), commented: "a restless activity has taken hold of the once sedentary human society". Initially, the introduction of rapid forms of transportation in the 19th century through trains and aeroplanes had changed the way people experience their environments, leading to different forms of sociability and the aesthetic appreciation of landscapes, of other places away from their homes as well as different societies and cultures (Urry, 1995). Time is speeded up, images, sounds and texts can now be transmitted instantaneously. Distances are extinguished since the end of 1980 and when globalization reached a "new level of hyper-capitalism and digital technology" between 1990 and 2020. During that time international travel became like a routine (Piketty, 2020, p. 649). Continuous physical and virtual mobilities have created the superficial impression of a physical and virtual *global village*. "Space no more sets limits to action and its effects, and counts little, or does not count at all ... differences between far away and close by are cancelled" (Bauman, 2000, p. 117).

DOI: 10.4324/9780429424946-1

These increasingly fast mobilities are changing the ways in which people experience the world. Moreover, since the development of mass tourism, tourism has been linked with impacts of colonialism and even compared to a military invasion or an economic penetration between the Global North and the Global South (Turner & Ash, 1975). MacCannell (1999) described tourism as a movement of the "Western Ego that wants to see it all, know it all, and take it all" (p. xxi). What tourists buy and wish to experience during their holidays is a certain *habitus* or lifestyle of other consumers (Urry, 1995). Tourism has been related to "the pursuit of the exotic" outside the everyday life (Turner & Ash, 1975), as an escape from our everyday life. "We are all missing something, something we believe we must be able to find somewhere elsewhere .... We purchase package tours that promise to lead us straight to it. It would, after all, be a shame to go all the way and somehow miss it. And whatever it is we believe we are missing, it must be something vastly important and irresistibly attractive" (Flusty, 2012, p. 1837). There has been a thirst to travel to exotic places away from home. This urge for mobility compensates for some of modernity's inauthentic lifestyles, taking tourists back to places and cultures having more originality and authenticity.

Worldwide 1.5 billion tourists travelled in 2019, compared to only 25 million in 1950. Due to the COVID-19 pandemic in 2020, the number of tourists fell to 402 million, which was the lowest figure since 1989 (Statista, 2021, 2022). In Oman, a total of 275 cruise ships arrived in the Sultanate during the tourist season from October 2019 to April 2020. A total of 283,488 cruise tourists arrived in Oman in 2019, compared to 193,467 tourists in 2018 (Ministry of Heritage and Tourism 2021a). With fewer visa restrictions, increased leisure time and a growth in income of the middle class worldwide, the "whole world" seemed on the move and travelling. A significant population growth worldwide and an exponential growth in the middle classes around the world and in particular in Asia mean there are more people with more money to spend on tourism and leisure. Cheaper airfares and the rise of affordable services like Uber and Airbnb have made travelling cheaper and easier. Due to the acceleration of our communication via social media, there has been a growth in global demand (Fyall, 2019). Travelling has become a lifestyle and an essential part of everyday life (Larsen, 2019; Salazar & Jayaram, 2016). For those who can afford to travel, it is in to tick off must-see destinations before one dies. Since the increase of mass tourism in the West during the 1960s and 1970s, tourism has been criticized by scholars as having negative impacts on communities and engendering a "creative destruction through liquid modernity" (Bauman, 2005) and a "massive destruction of nature" (MacCannell, 1992). Tourism has resulted in various sociocultural impacts, the exploitation of cultural heritage, nature and people leading to growing inequalities, biodiversity losses (Galvani et al., 2020), global warming as well as growing waste and the creation of "spaces of exception" (Büscher & Fletcher, 2016).

In addition to globalization and the outbreak of health pandemics, various other factors were predicted to influence international tourism. These were an increasing trend towards nostalgia, more elaborated, distinguished (sophisticated) leisure tastes, mobile devices, augmented reality and artificial intelligence (AI), leisure choices that are visual and authentic and a rising income of the middle class, creating a demand for sophisticated service, increased longevity and an ageing population, consumers who are sensitive to ethical issues as well as an interest of the tourist to showcase their social and cultural capital (Yeoman, 2013), e.g. while travelling with a cruise liner.

## The overaccumulation of people and places

My study presented in this book assumes a high political, social and economic importance within globalization impacting emerging tourist destinations on the Arabian Peninsula. It can be applied to similar emerging destinations worldwide developing from a state of continuous growth to a sudden fall in tourism activities due to a sudden shock, caused, e.g. by a global health pandemic. My research is unique; there is no existing long-term research that explores the linkages between tourism development, the ethics of tourism, tourist experiences and community well-being on the Arabian Peninsula. My book engages with mega-cruise tourism, its planning and development, the social and cultural impacts of cruise tourism as well as tourist experiences influenced by geopolitical imaginaries and Cultural Ecosystem Services of the landscape. The "overaccumulation" of people, places and services is conceptualized in mega-cruise tourism in a small, emerging destination on the Arabian Peninsula.

A critical inquiry into mega-cruise tourism and its planning and development in destinations as well as tourist experiences illuminates the underlying sociocultural context and understanding of overtourism. In particular, cruise ships have been described as "a refuge from liquid life" (Bauman, 2000; Vogel & Oschmann, 2013), while embodying an individualized and multi-optional consumerism. It has been argued that the development of a consumption-oriented society within "liquid modernity" and their quest for escape and nostalgia has facilitated the cruise industry to develop rapidly into a profitable mega-business (Vogel & Oschmann, 2013). Researchers have analysed spatial challenges facing cruise destinations with respect to overtourism, the physical and sociocultural carrying capacity. This is the overall ability to accommodate increasing larger numbers of tourists and mega-ships worldwide (Gutberlet, 2016a, 2019, 2020, 2022a; Milano et al., 2019; Renaud, 2017; Séraphin et al., 2018; Weeden et al., 2011). Mega-cruise tourism has been overcrowding city centres around the world, e.g. in Europe (Giuffrida, 2021), causing traffic congestion and disrupting local community life (Koens et al., 2018; Milano et al., 2019; Séraphin et al., 2018). Cruise tourism development in the Caribbean has promoted artificially created islands or "enclosed tourist bubbles", comparable to exclusive tourist resorts. Similar to the Caribbean, in Abu Dhabi (UAE) the first "cruise beach", Sir Bani Yas Cruise Beach, opened in December 2016 (Travel & Tourism News Middle East, 2017). In the Caribbean, which has been the top destination for cruise tourism worldwide and in many European cities, cruise ships have been perceived as disruptors, causing damage to local everyday-life, contributing to "overtourism" (Koens et al., 2019; Milano et al., 2019). Referring to the social exchange theory, host-communities will be more supportive of tourism development when they participate and benefit from tourism operations (Ap, 1992). Residents in popular European destinations such as Venice, Barcelona and Dubrovnik have raised their voices as a result of overtourism and against mega-cruise liners through social anti-tourism movements and "tourismphobia" (Milano et al., 2019), mentioned for the first time in the Spanish daily El Pays in 2008. The instability, uncertainty and disorientation accompanying "liquid modernity" (Bauman, 2000) have facilitated the continuous growth and success of the mega-cruise sector, which has been one of the fastest growing segments in global tourism until 2019.

## Challenges facing the cruise tourism sector

In the 1970s, my parents and grandparents took small ocean cruises to the fjords of Norway and in the Mediterranean. At that time, they travelled with a small ship carrying around 500 people that anchored in different destinations. Since the appearance of Disney Cruise Line and themed ships in the 1980s, the cruise liners have become bigger and bigger, developing into independent cities and a *playscape* or a pleasure destination on its own. The majority of these ships have a capacity of 3,000–5,000 passengers and more. The average passenger capacity has been 2,126 and the average duration of the cruise travel was seven days (CLIA, 2022). On board a mega-ship, all the senses are absorbed; a kind of *fantasy-island* or *bubble* where one can consume, play, eat and drink 24 hours a day. It seems the destination and its people have become rather secondary and serve more as a backdrop.

In 2019, as a result of the COVID-19 pandemic, there was a dramatic drop in tourist arrivals of 85% worldwide and in the Middle East by 83% in the first quarter of 2021, compared to 2019 (UNWTO, 2021). The standstill of tourism was followed by an economic slowdown in many countries, especially in the Global South. A "rebound in tourism" is expected in 2022 (UNWTO, 2021), although international tourism growth is expected to return to the 2019 level by 2024.

Globally, 29.7 million people travelled with cruise liners in 2019 (CLIA, 2021a). That year, the number of cruise ships worldwide increased (Table 1.1) by 10% to 500 ships compared to 2017 (CLIA, 2022). In 2019,

*Table 1.1* Gobal CLIA ocean cruise passengers in million

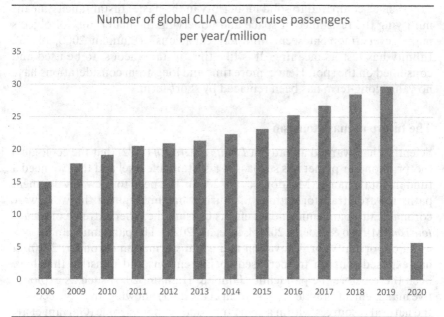

Number of global CLIA ocean cruise passengers
per year/million

Source: CLIA (2021a).

the global cruise revenue increased to over 27 billion US dollar (Statista, 2021a). One year later, in 2020, the number of passengers dropped to 5.7 million (CLIA, 2021a) due to the COVID-19 pandemic and international cruise revenues declined by 87.8% (Statista, 2021a). The United States with its coastlines and close access to ports in the tropical Caribbean has been the global leader in cruise revenue, followed by Germany.

A total of 2.5 million German passengers were travelling with an ocean and river cruise ship in 2019, compared to 14 million cruise passengers from North America. Due to the COVID-19 pandemic, the number dropped to 531,000 German passengers in 2021 (CLIA, 2021a).

After a global standstill of cruise operations for roughly one and a half years, in the spring and summer 2021, popular mega-cruise liners have relaunched their fleets with itineraries in Europe, North America and in the Caribbean (Cruise Adviser, 2021), which was followed by the relaunch of their itineraries around the Arabian Peninsula by the end of 2021.

My research contributes to the discussion on the political economy and the sociology of tourism. It questions the consumption and *overaccumulation* of people, places and services (Bauman, 2000; Harvey, 1989) and calls for more conscious, just, responsible and sustainable tourism. Within the sociology of tourism, Zygmund Bauman (2000, 2005, 2007) conceptualized the current era we are living in as "liquid modernity", living on the go, through the moment and instantaneity that makes the current moment an "immortal experience" compared to solid modernity in the past. "Instantaneity means nullifying the resistance of space and liquefying the materiality of objects makes every moment seem infinitely capacious" (Bauman 2000, p. 25). Infinity has lost its meaning. It is like time instantaneous, to be used and consumed on the spot. Hence, more time and long-term considerations have no value; long-term has been replaced by short-term.

## The future of mass tourism

Scientists had warned already in *Limits to Growth* (1972) that the ecological footprint on our planet has surpassed a sustainable level and that we need a fundamental change (Meadows et al., 2004). The need for new development paths towards transformations in tourism has highlighted the worldwide corona health pandemic and its effects causing the other extreme of *undertourism* (Milano & Koens, 2021; Lew et al., 2020). The pandemic can be seen as an opportunity for innovation and a transformation (Brouder, 2020). It has exposed tourism to increased social tensions and injustice that have been there before the pandemic (Jamal & Higham, 2021) such as exploitative management practices (Benjamin et al., 2021) allowing an easy access to the natural resources within a short time and to more people (Galvani et al., 2020) while increasing the gap between the Global North and the Global South.

Critical tourism research not only calls for more personal safety and security (Fotiadis et al., 2021) but for an overall change and a holistic transformation in tourism (Galvani et al., 2020; Ioannides & Gyimóthy, 2020; Jamal & Higham, 2021), claiming that a return to the previous *normal* will be extremely difficult. There are calls for a different approach to tourism "in the service of the people of destinations" (Higgins-Desbiolles, 2020), new ethics and a "new global consciousness of humankind" (Galvani et al., 2020) that operates beyond egoism and selfishness. This implies a different economic system, aiming towards an inclusive, "regenerative" tourism development (Cave & Dredge, 2020) and more mindfulness for our planet and its people, beyond pure economic objectives like employment and income generation. Tourism can be used as a tool to create a society that is more socially and environmentally responsible leading to a new human consciousness, empathy and towards a transformation of our planet (Benjamin et al., 2020; Galvani et al., 2020). There has been a demand for a paradigm shift towards *degrowth* in tourism and in other sectors, including the way tourism success is measured in economic terms as well as how it is operated and planned (Cheer et al., 2019; Koens et al., 2019; Milano & Koens, 2021; Milano et al., 2019; Séraphin et al., 2018). Séraphin et al. (2018, 2019) consider de-marketing strategies and the removal of popular, overcrowded cruise destinations like Venice and Amsterdam from tourism marketing and branding materials.

## A lack of critical tourism research in the Middle East

Similar to earlier tourism development in the Mediterranean (Bianchi & Sewlyn, 2018) and in the Caribbean (Sheller, 2003), tourism development on the Arabian Peninsula has been a tool to increase revenues – thus promoting capitalism while strengthening local identities through ideas and practices related to the state, nationhood and the aesthetic beauty of destinations. Tourism is an economic sector to boost and diversify the economy away from oil and gas and as an opportunity to create jobs for the growing, young population and to publicize the genuine hospitality of the local people.

Critical social studies and "action research" on overtourism and its impacts on local communities and their social and human capital have been non-existent in the Middle East and in particular on the Arabian Peninsula. Moreover, due to tight restrictions for researchers imposed by cruise companies, research on tourist experiences within enclosed holiday environments is extremely limited worldwide (Weaver, 2005a), analysing the often romanticized branding of a destination and the reality of the local community as well as the actual experience that tourists in overvisited destinations consume (Séraphin et al., 2019). Despite the growing importance of cruise tourism worldwide, especially qualitative research on the impacts on local communities and their tangible and intangible assets are scarce (Del Chiappa et al., 2018; MacNeill & Wozniak, 2008; Vega-Muñoz et al., 2019; Weeden et al., 2011; Williams & Lew, 2015). One of the main reasons for a lack of critical social tourism research is that social practices and cultural beliefs are difficult to quantify (Williams & Lew, 2015). They are very diverse and not easily separated from the impacts of other influences such as globalization and the internet (Bohn Gmelch, 2010).

On-site experiences of Western (European, North American) and Asian tourists in various places around the world have been studied extensively (Chronis, 2005; Edensor, 1998; Pearce et al., 2013; Quinlan Cutler et al., 2014; Rakić & Chambers, 2012; Rantala, 2010; Ryan, 1995; Tung & Ritchie, 2011; Wu et al., 2014). However, the social construction of imaginaries and performances of German-speaking mega-cruise tourists visiting an Oriental destination on the Arabian Peninsula, highlighting tourist and host perspectives have not been studied yet.

In my research, I followed previous researchers like Su et al. (2013) who studied how economic activities influence the moral norms of Chinese tourism entrepreneurs, compromising their moral sentiments with commercial profit-making (Su et al., 2013, p. 232). Jafari and Scott (2014) have stressed the conflict potential in tourism, referring to the Muslim and European value system. Stephenson and Ali-Knight (2010) called for an urgent need to examine the sociocultural impacts of tourism on the Emirati society. In particular, Western mass tourism that is characterized by "hedonism, permissiveness, lavishness, servitude, foreignness, with a lack of cross-cultural understanding and communication" (Din, 1989, p. 551). It is different from religious tourism, which promotes purposeful travel, spirituality, cross-cultural understanding and hospitality (Din, 1989, p. 559). Henderson (2003) already mentioned contradictions between Islamic values and Western requirements in tourism in Malaysia. He mentioned that commercial objectives aiming at maximizing revenue through providing a leisure environment based on the Western concept of the tourism industry may take precedence over Islamic values (Henderson, 2003). Belhassen et al. (2008) analysed the link between the tourists' belief, the action and the place during pilgrimages in Israel. Cooper et al. (2016) analysed the aesthetic and spiritual value of residents towards marine environments in the United Kingdom. They argued that a deeper understanding of the spiritual and aesthetic values of nature leads to increased moral responsibilities towards our environments.

My study is inductive; it aims at analysing the voices and perceptions of mainly German-speaking cruise tourists travelling with a mega-ship as well as German-speaking group tourists, individual tourists and local community members including shopkeepers, tour guides, tour operators, shipping agents, local residents, business owners and high-ranking government officials while applying a social-constructivist approach. Field-research including a pre-study was conducted in both destinations, in Souq Muttrah, in the Sharqiyah Sands desert and in an oasis between 2011 and 2015. Follow-up research was done between 2016 and 2019 and again in 2020/2021 in Souq Muttrah. The aim of my research has been to support policy and decision-making towards the well-being of local communities and the preservation of the local character of tourist destination on the Arabian Peninsula for future generations.

I conducted this research during the introductory phase of a large-scale tourism development: just before the start of the planned cruise port and the Waterfront Project in the bay of Muttrah in Muscat, which has been postponed for several years and has not been realized by autumn 2021, as well as the planned expansion of cruise tourism to other ports, from currently three ports to another four ports (Muscat Daily, 2018). Moreover, to boost cruise tourism, a Cruise Alliance between Oman, Dubai, Abu Dhabi, Bahrain and Qatar was created. These destinations have been competing with each other, pushed by Dubai the main home-port of the mega-cruise liners that are the topic of my research.

In the following paragraph, I will briefly introduce the urban research setting in Souq Muttrah (Figure 1.1).

*(My observation): One morning around eight large tourist buses stopped along the road, in front of the narrow entrance to the souq in Muttrah. The doors opened and tourists in colorful Western clothes, most of them wearing short or long trousers disembarked … Germans, Dutch, Austrians, French and Italians speaking in their own languages, stepped out and flocked into the souq in large groups of 20-48 people,*

*Figure 1.1* A tourist bus at the entrance to Souq Muttrah, opposite to the cruise terminal
Source: Gutberlet (March 2018).

*headed by a tour guide who was holding up a white signboard with the*
*bus number. To be recognized by the cruise staff and to remember their*
*bus, all tourists of different age groups were wearing small, colorful*
*stickers with their bus numbers on their shirts, similar to name badges.*
*It appeared a bit 'child-like'. The tourists then entered all together and*
*lined-up in a row, through the main gate. The tour guide gave them*
*some instructions and the majority of them were then seen walking or*
*strolling along the main streets of Souq Muttrah, which are the known,*
*secure and trusted paths.*

Such a scene inside Souq Muttrah, the popular marketplace, opposite the
cruise terminal in the Omani capital Muscat, repeated on a daily basis during the cooler seasons each year. During this period, mega-cruise liners
carrying large numbers of tourists anchor in the narrow bay of Muttrah,
located next to the Fish Market and the Corniche Road.

Referring to the continuous rise of large-scale circular, one-week, mega-
cruise tourism and the formation of constructed, "enclosed tourist bubbles,"
my book aims to fill a gap in cruise destination management, community-
based tourism and the tourist experiences on land, in an emerging destination in West Asia, on the Arabian Peninsula. My research in Souq Muttrah
aspires to deepen the local knowledge assets about tourist experiences and
the social capital in an emerging heritage destination by identifying local
narratives and life-stories. It also responds to research by Causevic and
Neal (2019) that call for illuminating some of the recent history of Souq
Muttrah, which is currently well hidden or veiled. The official, geopolitical

narrative of tourism marketing about the urban destination Souq Muttrah, being an ancient marketplace creates an impression of an "utopic space", or a "non-place" (Augé, 2010). As products of globalization and capitalism, destinations have transformed into tourist enclaves or "tourist bubbles" (Gutberlet, 2016a, 2019, 2022; Jaakson, 2004) that are commodified, touristified spaces based on outsider values and needs instead of the quality of life of local communities and their needs (Ioannides et al., 2019; Saarinen, 2021). A rural destination such as the desert and an oasis can create an impression of being within a vast, empty space, with little human interference and without physical borders or ownership, a space of freedom, thrill and liberty.

## Outline of the book

In the following paragraphs, I will outline the structure of my book. In Chapter 2, I briefly introduce the theoretical concepts used such as *mobility, overtourism, time-space compression, cruise tourism* and *Oriental imaginaries*. The chapter is followed by the research setting (Chapter 3), Souq Muttrah, Sharqiyah Sands desert and an oasis in the periphery. These are "Oriental" places from a European and Global North perspective. They are conceptualized within the historical, economic and geographical setting. In Chapter 4, I outline my quantitative and qualitative research methods used along with my research approach and thoughts about myself being a female, (white) European researcher within a male-dominated public space and society. When European tourists and the multi-ethnic, resident community on the Arabian Peninsula share the same space, sociocultural and spatial conflicts may arise. My research aims to answer the following questions:

- What are the local community's perceptions about mega-cruise tourism? Here the concept of "local community" includes cultural brokers, shop vendors, business owners, camp managers, tour operators, Omani and expatriate residents as well as high-ranking government officials and decision-makers like ministers.
- What are the cruise tourist's imaginaries of Oman?
- What are the tourists' embodied experiences and performances in both destinations visited?
- What are the impacts of mega-cruise tourism for the local community and their everyday lives in both places?
- What are the impacts of the corona pandemic on tourism and the local community in Souq Muttrah?

In Chapters 5, 6 and 7, I analyse the research results of my long-term research. Souq Muttrah is one of the cruise tourists' favourite destinations, an Arabian shopping site within walking distance from the port. In Chapter 5,

I elaborate on my findings developed around the concept of overtourism. These are conceptualized in overcrowding of the space, limited parking and an aggressive selling behaviour of expatriate vendors that are impacting the local community and the tourists alike (Gutberlet, 2016a, 2017, 2021). A lack of ethical, mindless tourist dress behaviour and low-spending have contributed to negative views about cruise tourists among the multi-ethnic community. As one result, well-established businesses, located within the tourist bubble relocate or close down, changing the sense of space, promoting a monoculture of businesses, similar to other places around the world. I then integrate the ethics of tourism in the study of the on-site behaviour of German-speaking mega-cruise tourists and group tourists visiting the souq or an oasis and the Sharqiyah Sands desert. In Chapter 6, I elaborate on the tourists' imaginaries and on-site experiences in the souq. My results show that the cruise tourists' main motivation is to experience a cliché of the Orient, an imaginative country of The Arabian Nights, consisting of colourful souqs, camels and sand dunes and to realize their own selves within a *cruise communita*. Their experience is visual: Tourists gaze at the locals and locals gaze at the tourists; there is little exchange between them (Gutberlet, 2019, 2022). Contradictions between local community values, the pre-travel information, the social construction of the media, and the tourists' on-site behaviour will be identified. Moreover, I consider local identities through life-stories and narratives of the diaspora community in Souq Muttrah. I consider local community perceptions about tourism and the importance of their bonding and bridging social capital for sustainable tourism development.

In Chapter 7, I analyse the cruise tourist experience in the desert and an oasis and local reactions. My results reveal that the tourist experience is rushed and superficial due to time-space compression and a lack of time in the places visited as well as little pre-travel information and preparation. Moreover, there is a lack of social interaction and exchange between hosts and guests and there are few benefits for the local community. I continue in Chapter 7 with slower, spiritual tourist experiences and their imaginaries from the desert and an oasis, experienced by German-speaking group tourists during their tour. Slowness enhances a more conscious, mindful travel and involvement with the environment. The chapter ends by arguing that cruise tourist experiences are highly commoditized. The tourists experience different customized "enclosed tourist bubbles" (Gutberlet, 2019, 2022). Time is sped up for the tourists to experience a "constructive authenticity" (Wang, 1999), or a "customized authenticity" (Wang, 2007) of the local culture in both destinations. My book closes in Chapters 8 and 9 with recommendations and conclusions for the planning and management of emerging destinations, highlighting that enclosed tourism enclaves are undesirable and unsustainable for long-term tourism development on the Arabian Peninsula, for local communities and for future generations.

In conclusion, my book examines social changes, representations and power relations predominantly through a stakeholder analysis and a

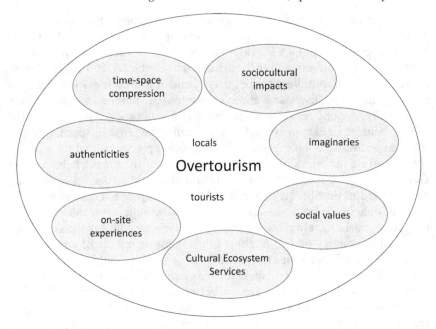

*Figure 1.2* Conceptualizing overtourism

Source: Gutberlet (2021).

social-constructivist approach, analysing tourist and community experiences, narratives and signs in a traditional marketplace in Muscat and in an oasis and the desert in the Interior of Oman (Figure 1.2). Both destinations are little-studied research locations on the Arabian Peninsula (Gutberlet, 2016a, 2016b, 2017, 2019, 2020, 2021, 2022). My aim is to fill a gap linking different disciplines: critical tourism geography, urban and regional planning, connecting them with cultural studies, sociology, business, ecology and anthropology. Students and academics in tourism, recreation, sociology, anthropology, urban planning and business studies as well as decision-makers, policymakers, urban and regional planners and destination marketing managers who wish to learn more about socio-cultural sustainability in emerging destinations, will find my research significant and insightful. Since there is no one size-fits-all solution for overtourism (Koens et al., 2019), the empirical and theoretical insights of my book make a significant contribution to the literature on morality and tourism in an emerging cruise destination in the Global South. My study aspires to enhance critical thoughts and challenge readers to reflect on their own travel behaviour and on-site experiences. It contributes to the literature by providing holistic insights into the dynamics of the social organization of tourist sites on the Arabian Peninsula while improving its planning towards a more mindful visitor behaviour and on-site tourism management.

# References

Ap, J. (1992). Residents' perceptions on tourism impacts. *Annals of Tourism Research*, *19*(4), 665–690.

Augé, M. (2010). *Nicht-orte*. Verlag C.H. Beck.

Bauman, Z. (2000). *Liquid modernity*. Polity Press.

Bauman, Z. (2005). *Liquid life*. Ebook for PC. Polity Press.

Bauman, Z. (2007). *Liquid times. Living in an age of uncertainty*. Ebook for PC. Polity Press.

Belhassen, Y., Caton, K., & Stewart, W. P. (2008). The search for authenticity in the pilgrim experience. *Annals of Tourism Research*, *35*(3), 668–689.

Benjamin, S., Dillette, A., & Alderman, D. H. (2020). "We can't return to normal": Committing to tourism equity in the post-pandemic age. *Tourism Geographies*, *22*(3), 476–483.

Bianchi, R., & Sewlyn, T. (2018). Politics and tourism in the Mediterranean region. *Routledge handbook of Mediterranean politics* (Kindle ed., pp. 279–291). Taylor and Francis.

Bohn Gmelch, S. (2010). Why tourism matters. In S. Bohn Gmelch (Ed.), *Tourists and tourism, a reader* (2nd ed., pp. 3–24). Weaveland Press.

Brouder, P. (2020). Reset Redux: Possible evolutionary pathways towards the transformation of tourism in a COVID-19 world. *Tourism Geographies*, *22*(3), 484–490.

Büscher, B., & Fletcher, R. (2016). Destructive creation: Capital accumulation and the structural violence of tourism. *Journal of Sustainable Tourism*, *25*(5), 651–667.

Causevic, S. & Neal, M. (2019). The exotic veil: Managing tourist perceptions of national history and statehood in Oman, *Tourism Management*, *71*, 504–517.

Cave, J., & Dredge, D. (2020). Regenerative tourism needs diverse economic practices. *Tourism Geographies*, *22*(3), 503–513.

Cheer, J., Milano, C., & Novelli, M. (Eds.). (2019). Afterword: Over overtourism or just the beginning? Overtourism: Excesses, discontent and measures in travel and tourism (pp. 227–232). CABI.

Chronis, A. (2005). Coconstructing heritage at the Gettysburg storyscape. *Annals of Tourism Research*, *32*(2), 386–406.

Cooper, N., Bradey, E., Steen, H., & Bryce, R. (2016). Aesthetic and spiritual values of ecosystems: Recognising the ontological and axiological plurality of cultural ecosystem 'services'. *Ecosystem Services*, *21*, 218–229.

Cruise Adviser (2021). Seattle marks restart of Alaska cruise season. Retrieved July 21, 2021, from https://cruise-adviser.com/seattle-marks-restart-of-alaska-cruise-season/

Cruise Lines International Association (CLIA) (2021a). CLIA Global Passenger Report 2020. Retrieved March 3, 2022, from https://cruising.org/en-gb/news-and-research/research/2021/june/clia-global-passenger-report-2020

Cruise Lines International Association (CLIA) (2022). CLIA State of the Cruise Industry Outlook 2022. Retrieved April 5, 2022, from https://cruising.org/en-gb/news-and-research/research/2022/january/state-of-the-cruise-industry-outlook-2022

Del Chiappa, G., Lorenzo-Romero, C., & Gallarza, M. (2018). Host community perceptions of cruise tourism in a homeport: A cluster analysis. *Journal of Destination Marketing & Management*, *7*, 170–181.

Din, K. (1989). Islam and tourism. *Annals of Tourism Research*, *16*, 542–563.

Edensor, T. (Ed.). (1998). Tourists at the Taj. *Performance and meaning at a symbolic site*. Routledge.

Flusty, S. (2012). The rime of the frequent flyer or what the elephant has in his trunk. In C. Minca & C. Oakes (Eds.), *Real tourism. Practice, care and politics in contemporary travel culture*. Routledge.

Fotiadis, A. K., Woodside, A. G., Del Chiappa, G., Séraphin, H., & Hansen, H. O. (2021). Novel coronavirus and tourism: Coping, recovery, and regeneration issues. *Tourism Recreation Research*, *46*(2), 144–147. https://doi.org/10.1080/02508281.2021.1919422

Fyall, A. (2019). *Too many tourists? The problem of overtourism – and how to solve it, Summer 2019, Pegasus*. The magazine of the University of Central Florida. Retrieved November 13, 2020, from https://www.ucf.edu/pegasus/too-many-tourists/

Galvani, A., Lew, A. A., & Sotelo Perez, M. (2020). COVID-19 is expanding global consciousness and the sustainability of travel and tourism. *Tourism Geographies*, *22*(3), 567–576. https://doi.org/10.1080/14616688.2020.1760924

Giuffrida, A. (2021). Monsters or a must? Venice tussles with return of cruise shops. *The Guardian*. Retrieved June 14, 2021, from https://www.theguardian.com/world/2021/jun/14/monsters-or-a-must-venice-tussles-with-return-of-cruise-ships

Gutberlet, M. (2016a). Socio-cultural impacts of large-scale cruise tourism in Souq Muttrah. *Fennia*, *194*(1), 46–63.

Gutberlet, M. (2016b). Cruise tourist dress behaviors and local-guest reactions in a muslim country. *Tourism Culture & Communication*, *16*, 15–32.

Gutberlet, M. (2017). Staging the Oriental Other: Imaginaries and performances of German-speaking cruise tourists. Published online first and in 2019 *in. Tourist Studies*, *19*(1), 110–137.

Gutberlet, M. (2018). *A tourist bus at the entrance to Souq Muttrah, opposite to the cruise terminal*.

Gutberlet, M. (2019). In a rush: Time-space compression and its impacts on cruise excursions, *Tourist Studies*, *19*(4), 1–29. Published online first, April.

Gutberlet, M. (2020). "They just buy a karak and leave" – Overtourism in Souq Muttrah, The Sultanate of Oman, *Zeitschrift für Tourismuswissenschaften*, 13 October, De Gruyter Oldenburg. https://doi.org/10.1515/tw-2020-0004

Gutberlet, M. (2021). Valuing social capital and a legacy: "The old shops are the beauty of the place. In J. Saarinen & J. Richardson (Eds.), *Change in tourism/tourism in change* (pp. 135–150). Routledge Publishing House.

Gutberlet, M. (2022a). Geopolitical imaginaries and cultural ecosystem services (CES) in the desert. *Tourism Geographies*, *24*, 4–5. https://doi.org/10.1080/14616688.2018.1545250

Gutberlet, M. (2022b). *Insight 288: Tourist bubbles and climate change in the GCC*. COP 27 and Climate Action in the Middle East, Middle East Institute, October 24, Singapore.

Harvey, D. (1989). *The condition of postmodernity*. Blackwell.

Harvey, D. (2020). Anti-capitalist politics in the time of COVID-19. Retrieved November 30, 2020, from www.davidharvey.com

Henderson, J. C. (2003). Managing tourism and Islam in peninsular Malaysia. *Tourism Management*, *24*, 447–456.

Higgins-Desbiolles, F. (2020). Socialising tourism for social and ecological justice after COVID-19. *Tourism Geographies: An International Journal of Tourism Space, Place and Environment*. https://doi.org/10.1080/14616688.2020.1757748

Ioannides, D., & Gyimóthy, S. (2020). The COVID-19 crisis as an opportunity for escaping the unsustainable global tourism path. *Tourism Geographies, 22*(3), 624–632. https://doi.org/10.1080/14616688.2020.1763445

Ioannides, D., Röslmaier, M., & van der Zee, E. (2019). Airbnb as an instigator of 'tourism bubble' expansion in Utrecht's Lombok neighbourhood. *Tourism Geographies, 21*(5), 822–840.

Jaakson, R. (2004). Beyond the tourist bubble? Cruise ship passengers in port. *Annals of Tourism Research, 31*(1), 44–60.

Jafari, J., & Scott, N. (2014). Muslim world and its tourisms. *Annals of Tourism Research* 44, 1–19.

Jamal, T., & Higham, J. (2021). Justice and ethics: Towards a new platform for tourism and sustainability. *Journal of Sustainable Tourism, 29*(2–3), 143–157.

Koens, K., Postma, A., & Papp, B. (2018). Is overtourism overused? Understanding the impact of tourism in a city context. *Sustainability*, 10.

Koens, K., Postma, A., & Papp, B. (2019). Management strategies for overtourism – From adaptation to system change. In H. Pechlaner, E. Innerhofer, & G. Erschbamer (Eds.), *Overtourism, tourism management and solutions*. Routledge.

Krippendorf, J. (1987). *The holiday makers*. Heinemann.

Larsen, J. (2019). Ordinary tourism and extraordinary everyday life: Re-thinking tourism and cities. In T. Frisch, N. Stors, L. Stoltenberg, & C. Sommer (Eds.), *Tourism and everyday life in the city*. Routledge.

Lew, A., Cheer, J. M., Haywood, M., Brouder, P., & Salazar, N. B. (2020). Visions of travel and tourism after the global COVID-19 transformation of 2020. *Tourism Geographies, 22*(3), 455–466. https://doi.org/10.1080/14616688.2020.1770326

MacCannell, D. (1992). *Empty meeting grounds: the tourist papers*. Routledge.

MacCannell, D. (1999). *The tourist – A new theory of the leisure class*. University of California Press.

MacNeill, T., & Wozniak, D. (2008). The economic, social and environmental impacts of cruise tourism. *Tourism Management, 66*, 387–404.

Meadows, D., Randers, J., & Meadows, D. (2004). *Limits to growth, the 30-year update*. Chelsea Green Publishing.

Milano, C., & Koens, K. (2021). The paradox of tourism extremes. Excesses and restraints in times of COVID-19. *Current Issues in Tourism*. https://doi.org/10.1080/13683500.2021.1908967

Milano, C., Novelli, M., & Cheer, J. M. (2019). Overtourism and degrowth: A social movements perspective. *Journal of Sustainable Tourism*. https://doi.org/10.1080/09669582.2019.1650054

Ministry of Heritage and Tourism (2021a, April). *Statistics on cruise tourism in Oman*. Department of Events, Cruises and Charter Flights.

Muscat Daily (2018, September 4). *Ministry of Tourism plans to extend cruise tourism to ports in Sohar, Sur, Duqm and Suwaiq*. Apex Press and Publishing.

Pearce, P. L., Mao-Ying, W., De Carlo, M., & Rossi, A. (2013). Contemporary experiences of Chinese tourists in Italy: An on-site analysis in Milan. *Tourism Management Perspectives, 7*, 34–37.

Piketty, T. (2020). *Capital and ideology* (Kindle ed.). Harvard University Press.

Quinlan Cutler, S., Carmichael, B., & Doherty, S. (2014). The Inca trail experience: Does the journey matter. *Annals of Tourism Research, 45*, 152–166.

Rakić, T., & Chambers, D. (2012). Rethinking the consumption of places. *Annals of Tourism Research, 39*(3), 1612–1633.

Rantala, O. (2010). Tourist practices in the forest. *Annals of Tourism Research*, *37*(1), 249–264.

Renaud, L. (2017). Résister au débarquement: Tourisme de croisière et dynamiques territoriales au québec et dans la caraïbe. *RITA* [online], N°10: Retrieved July 2017, from http://revue-rita.com/thema/resister-au-debarquement-tourisme-de-croisiere-et-dynamiques-territoriales-quebec-caraibe.html

Ryan, C. (1995). Learning about tourists from conversations: The over 55s in Majorca. *Tourism Management*, *16*(3), 207–215.

Saarinen, J. (2021). Tourism for change. Change management towards sustainable tourism development. In J. Saarinen & J. Richardson (Eds.), *Change in tourism/tourism in change* (pp. 135–150). Routledge Publishing House.

Salazar, N. B., & Jayaram, K. (2016). Keywords of mobility. Critical engagements. *Ebook for PC*. Berghahn Books.

Séraphin, H., Sheeran, P., & Pilato, M. (2018). Over-tourism and the fall of Venice as a destination. *Journal of Destination Marketing & Management*, *9*, 374–376.

Séraphin, H., Zaman, M., Olver, S., Bourliataux-Lajoinie, & Dosquet, F. (2019). Destination branding and overtourism. *Journal of Hospitality and Tourism Management*, *38*, 1–4.

Sheller, M. (2003). *Consuming the Caribbean. From Awaks to Zombies*. Routledge.

Statista (2021). Number of international tourist arrivals worldwide from 1950 to 2020. Retrieved November 13, 2021, from https://www.statista.com/statistics/209334/total-number-of-international-tourist-arrivals/

Statista (2021a). Cruise industry worldwide – statistics and facts. Statista Research Department. Retrieved January 15, 2022, from https://www.statista.com/topics/1004/cruise-industry/#dossierKeyfigures

Statista (2022). Anzahl er deutschen Hochseekreuzfahrtpassagiere von 1998 bis 2021, published on 14.03. 2022. Retrieved March 27, 2022, from https://de.statista.com/statistik/daten/studie/5240/umfrage/passagiere-von-hochseekreuzfahrten-in-deutschland-seit-1998/

Stephenson, M., & Ali-Knight, J. (2010). Dubai's tourism industry and its societal impact: Social implications and sustainable challenges. *Journal of Tourism and Cultural Change*, *8*(4), 278–292.

Su, X., Wang, H., & Wen, T. (2013). Profit, responsibility, and the moral economy of tourism. *Annals of Tourism Research*, *43*, 231–250.

Travel & Tourism News Middle East (TTN) (2017). *The region's cruise sector makes waves*, *35*(2), January.

Tung, V. W. S., & Ritchie, B. J. R. (2011). Exploring the essence of memorable tourism experiences. *Annals of Tourism Research*, *38*(4), 1367–1386.

Turner, L., & Ash, J. (1975). The golden hordes. *International tourism and the pleasure periphery*. Constable and Company Limited.

United Nations World Tourism Organization (UNWTO) (2021). Tourist numbers down 83% but confidence slowly rising, 2 June. Retrieved July25, 2021, from https://www.unwto.org/news/tourist-numbers-down-83-but-confidence-slowly-rising

Urry, J. (1995). *Consuming places*. Routledge.

Vega-Muñoz, A., Arjona-Fuentes, J., Ariza-Montes, A., Han, H., & Law, R. (2019). In search of 'a research front' in cruise tourism studies. *International Journal of Hospitality Management*. https://doi.org/10.1016/j.ijhm.2019.102353

Vogel, M. P., & Oschmann, C. (2013). Cruising through liquid modernity. *Tourist Studies*, *13*(1), 62–80.

Wang, N. (1999). Rethinking authenticity in tourism experience. *Annals of Tourism Research, 26*(2), 340–370.

Wang, Y. (2007). Customized authenticity begins at home. *Annals of Tourism Research, 34*(3), 789–804.

Weaver, A. (2005a). The McDonaldization thesis and cruise tourism. *Annals of Tourism Research, 32*(2), 346–366.

Weeden, C., Lester, J. A., & Thyne, M. (2011). Cruise tourism: Emerging issues and implications for a maturing industry. *Journal of Hospitality and Tourism Management, 18*, 26–29.

Williams, S., & Lew, A. A. (Eds.). (2015). *Tourism geography. Critical understandings of place, space and experience* (3rd ed.). Routledge.

Wu, M.-Y., Wall, G., & Pearce, L. (2014). Shopping experiences: International tourists in Bejings silk market. *Tourism Management, 41*, 96–106.

Yeoman, I. (2013). A futurist thought on consumer trends shaping future festivals and events. *International Journal of Events and Festival Management, 4*(3), 249–260.

# 2 Exploring concepts

In this chapter, I explore the main concepts that have arisen during my research, such as cruise tourism, authenticity, tourist bubble, time-space compression, overtourism, imaginaries and social capital. The research draws on a micro-sociological study and connects as well with the anthropology of tourism and the political economy of tourism.

The current dominating global capitalist system or "hypercapitalism" (Piketty, 2020) has resulted in increased forms of structural violence, the production of inequalities, waste and "spaces of exception" (Büscher & Fletcher, 2017) or "tourist bubbles" (Jaakson, 2004) while international travel became a routine for many (Piketty, 2020, p. 649). Tourism is a very dynamic phenomenon, impacting destinations and the entire tourism system in different time dimensions (Saarinen, 2021). Tourism scholars have highlighted the importance of more sustainable, just, ethical and a more people and environment-centred tourism development (Cheer et al., 2019; Galvani et al., 2020; Higgins-Desbiolles, 2021; Ioannides & Gyimóthy, 2020; Jamal & Higham, 2021; Lew et al., 2020; Renaud, 2020). My research aspires to create awareness about a more ethical development while analysing current issues underlying overtourism within the political economy and the sociology of tourism. I will first start exploring the concepts of mobility and increased time-space compression.

## Mobility and time-space compression

Mobilities are an essential part of modern consumerism and liquid life (Bauman, 2005, 2007), where society and life cannot stand still. Being 'on the go' has been linked with freedom, liberty and even as a prerequisite to power (Adey, 2017). Mobilities shape our everyday lives and even people's life chances. Mobilities have changed the way people use, experience and perform in places, within different cultures and natural environments (Milano & Koens, 2021).

In the past, mobility was part of the everyday lives of hunter and gatherer societies, or those that were forced to search in order to cover their basic needs for food, water, fuel and shelter. Mobility and migration were only used when necessary and regarded as primitive and unnecessary

DOI: 10.4324/9780429424946-2

movements. "Our kind has always minimized the cost and exertion of movement" while the home acted as attractors. The geographer Vidal de la Blache et al. (1965) described the movements and the way of life of nomads as being close to the natural and animal life moving like "herds of animals roaming over the steppes, or great flocks of birds swooping down upon stretches of water" reducing the movement to an animal-like barbarian who moved in hordes (Vidal de la Blache et al., 1965). Later on, regional and worldwide commerce, religion and just the pleasure of movement kept people *on the go*. To be on the move was seen as to be out of place and even "placeless" (Tuan, 1978).

As a consequence of fast mobilities, through increased time-space compression and globalization, our planet became a village. Nowadays, people are more connected leading to an increased interdependence between people and places across different continents (Mowforth & Munt, 2009). Since the 19th century, societies have accelerated "the turnover time of capital" (Harvey, 1989, p. 285) which has facilitated "the visualisation of culture, the collapse of stable identities and the transformation of time" (Urry, 1995, p. 219). The just-in-time production and improved information technologies have accelerated the speed of consumption, international financial services and financial exchange (Harvey, 1989). This has increased short, inexpensive travel within enclosed, isolated environments like cruise liners. Cruise liners and other modes of transportation have promoted a democratization of travel or a "cultural globalisation" (Mowforth & Munt, 2009). This was followed by an increased consumption of services (Harvey, 1989) and more flexible forms of tourism to less developed countries in the Global South (Mowforth & Munt, 2009) with sunny weather promoting images of *sea, sun and sand*.

Time is speeded up (Harvey, 1989; Urry, 1995), but at the same time, decreasing the importance and value of social capital. Time-space compression resulted in a "three-minute culture" (Urry, 1995) and a "cult of speed" in all spheres (Howard, 2012), which highlights the "instantaneity" of satisfactions and ephemerality, e.g. of culture, health services, business including fashion, entertainment, production techniques, labour processes, ideas, values and established practices etc. (Harvey, 1989, p. 285f.). Modern society is perceived as "a network of random connections and disconnections" (Harvey, 1989). Hence, time-space paths of individuals are desynchronized resulting in more consumer segmentation of travel products and a "compression of eternity" (Vogel & Oschmann, 2013).

Consumer products become "transient objects" that are meant to be consumed and to disappear in the process of their consumption, e.g. disposable lunch boxes, coffee cups or fast tourist experiences (Bauman, 2000, p. 125). People in general primarily focus on the present only, according to the motto "all that is solid melts into air" (p. 285). So, the temporariness of consumer products, values and personal relationships are the most important results (Urry, 1995). However, there is a counter-movement in many parts of the world where money-mindedness is being replaced by more mindfulness, time-mindedness and social needs (Krippendorf, 1987) including simplicity and slowness (Howard, 2012). Because of the continuous "bombardment of stimuli" creating problems of sensory overload in the everyday lives of people, there is a search for a shield against time-space compression through authenticity (Harvey, 1989) and nostalgia. People wish to escape from their everyday lives, searching for a deeper meaning beyond consuming and a more authentic life elsewhere. Such more authentic lifestyle they may find during their holidays.

## Authenticity

Authenticity is a process of social construction, depending on the amount of control the actor has over its cultural production. Authenticity is also a cultural value that refers to the representation or branding of a destination and performance within the environment (Bruner, 1991). Especially for tourists from the Global North, their search for authenticity has shifted the representation of *the Other* in the media to the tourist destination itself (Wels, 2004).

Tourist places are often socially constructed to reflect the tourists, rather than the communities in destinations visited (Williams & Lew, 2015). Often tourists are searching for authenticity and an 'exotic Other' from a different culture and an original state seen as more "pure and as yet not polluted by Western civilization" (Bruner, 1991, p. 240). The tourists' experiences are mediated by beliefs about the site visited, their own roles in these experiences, and their cognitive and emotional attachment to the destination, conceptualized as "geopiety" (Belhassen et al., 2008). Hence, a tourist's world view and the travel motivation provide a basis for understanding individual tourist experiences of authenticity (p. 686). Any space, tourist experience and perception can be perceived as being authentic, where the tourist community shares an organized, joint "experience of nothingness" (Minca, 2012). For many tourists, being on holidays inhabits a sense of freedom, joy, having a good time, being infinite and free from any time constraints (Ryan, 2002) realizing their own selves, an "existential authenticity". For some tourists travelling is rather about realizing an intra-personal authenticity, e.g. within the family, within a guided group or within a cruise community (Wang, 1999) and they are searching for "inauthenticity" but for things they already know (Ritzer & Liska, 1997; Wilkinson, 1999). While travelling with a cruise ship, the originality of a destination that tourists visit on shore and their experiences have been questioned (Klein, 2011; Wilkinson, 1999). Tourists wish their experiences to be controlled and standardized as much as their everyday lives at home (Ritzer & Liska, 1997, p. 99). Consequently, some destinations have been visually homogenized, remade as special objects for the tourist gaze, so that there is no "simple reality" (Urry, 1995). Services are staged to create more value for visitors (Pine & Gilmore, 2011). Such a "staged authenticity" may relieve pressure from tourist destinations while protecting the people, their cultures and their values from curious mass-tourists (Wang, 1999; Williams & Lew, 2015).

Authenticity is a pluralistic concept, depending on the type of tourist (Williams & Lew, 2015). Tourists perceive the world through a certain filter, according to their class, age, gender, ethnicity and the type of travel (Urry & Larsen, 2011). Authenticity is a projection or a label of the tourist's own beliefs, expectations and preferences of something familiar, a *customized authenticity* (Wang, 2007). Reflecting on that idea, Wang (2007) notes that tourists visiting homestays in a Chinese village were searching for a *home*, an "objective authenticity" of the host culture, in which tourists play an active role in the host-guest encounter, presenting a "customized authenticity" of their local culture (p. 801). Such a "customized authenticity" is influenced by a *"symbolic authenticity"* that is the projection of a certain view or stereotyped images circulated within the media and tourism marketing brochures (Jansson, 2002). Some tourists are willing to accept such an authentic reproduction (Wang, 2007). A church that is open for tourism is *objectively authentic*, being part of the local flow of life of the community, compared to a museum that showcases a *staged authenticity* for paying visitors only (Cohen, 2012). The concept of "theoplacity" in a pilgrim's experience highlights three characteristics: the toured place, the visitor's belief system and its meaning, as well as the self and the action within the space (Belhassen et al., 2008). These features together create a complex notion of *experienced authenticity* (p. 685), which includes the sensory interaction with the place, leading to emotional responses such as wonder and awe, empathy and immersion, calm versus excitement. Tourism can be seen as a way of engaging in a "self-transformation", away from everyday life and of practising tourism spaces (Bruner, 1991; Crouch, 1999).

## Tourist performances

When tourists visit destinations, their consumption patterns such as gazing, their sociality with others, their multi-sensuous encounters and their talking influence their on-site experiences (Crang, 1997). They are involving "metaphors of performance" such as practice, rehearsal, scripting and staging (Chaney, 2002). Often predetermined social definitions of the tourism setting, e.g. as a spectacle influence their on-site performances (Crang, 1997). Such an interplay between the body and space (Chronis, 2015) becomes more important through the involvement of cultural brokers like tour guides and their "communicative staging", their storytelling or through monuments, landscapes and other artefacts, the "material staging" (p. 137).

Tourist spaces have five dimensions: the physical environment, embodiment, sociality, memory and image (Bærenholdt et al., 2004, p. 32). There are three types of tourist performances (Edensor, 2000). The first is the "disciplined ritual", e.g. during a guided walk at a tourist site. Tourists are directed to the site. Their performances are restricted and often repetitive. The second type is an "improvised performance", which is more reflexive and directed by the tourists themselves, e.g. during a walk without guidance.

The third type is the "unbound performance" that appears in unfamiliar scenery, such as a souq or an open desert landscape visited by European tourist. Because the visual sense has been overemphasized in our everyday lives and in tourism research other bodily senses have been neglected (Crouch, 2002). Chronis (2015), Edensor (1998, 2000) and MacCannell (1999), argue that tourists are performing on different stages while Bærenholdt et al. (2004) noted that the tourist's consumption of places is more than stages for performances but a form of "networking material, social and cultural elements" (p. 31). In performances the body is used as a sign to communicate cultural and social knowledge, transforming the surrounding space into front-stages and back-stages (p. 52). The embodied encounter includes a subjective and inter-subjective performativity, including the social interaction with other visitors. It creates enjoyment and a feeling of belonging, being part of a community as well as spatial-temporal mobilities, which are often regulated encounters. Such encounters are directed, e.g. by cultural mediators, who dictate the speed and the direction of the movement (Park, 2014).

Cultural brokers interpret and mediate the tourist gaze (Salazar, 2010), constructing "imagined communities" (Bauman, 2000; Urry, 1995). They shape, reconstruct and control the interpretation of tourist places and local communities. (Jennings & Weiler, 2006). They direct, choreograph, educate, manage and monitor appropriate tourist performances and they ensure profits of the tourism businesses (Mordue, 2005).

## The local community

The concepts of *community* (Bauman, 2001) as well as "authenticity" or genuineness and nostalgia about the past (Harvey, 1989) are seen as emerging in contrast to globalization and time-space compression and as a way of romanticism. "Community stands for whatever has been left of the dreams of a better life shared with better neighbors all following better rules of cohabitation" (Bauman, 2000, p. 92). This search or longing for being an integral part of a community stands for a warm, cosy and comfortable place (Bauman, 2001) and as a source of "being-in-the-world" (Heidegger, 2010). An important indicator for the well-being of the local community (M. K. Smith & Diekmann, 2017) is the number of tourists visiting a destination. A large number of people visiting a destination within a short time as part of their tour package reflects a grazing behaviour (Vogel & Oschmann, 2013), creating social challenges for local communities.

For instance, large-scale cruise tourism has sociocultural impacts on culturally sensitive, emerging destinations worldwide. In various small, emerging destinations such as Antarctica In various small, emerging destinations such as Antarctica, cruise tourism is incompatible with the lifestyle, facilities and services of the local community and their fragile biodiversity (Klein, 2010). In Tonga (Polynesia) (Urbanowicz, 1989) and Dubrovnik (Croatia), the increase in tourist numbers has been ascribed to a visitor invasion caused by mass-cruise tourism (Ljubica & Dulcic, 2012; Milano et al., 2019).

Stressful interactions between hosts and tourists appear to increase proportionately to the larger numbers (V. L. Smith, 1989). A concept measuring the social, economic, environmental and physical sustainability of a place is the "carrying capacity", defined as "the maximum use of a place without causing negative effects on local resources – the community, the economy and its culture or reducing the visitor satisfaction" (Wahab & Pigram, 1997). Definitions of the physical carrying capacity include numbers of tourists that an area can absorb without negative impacts on the physical environment, its limited natural resources and the quality of the tourist experience (O'Reilly, 1986; Wall, 1997), in addition to the values of the community and their often changing perceptions (Saarinen, 2006). Getz (1987) analysed six different approaches regarding carrying capacity, one of them was the social carrying capacity by using attitudes and tolerance levels of the local community towards tourism development. With the increase in cruise tourism worldwide, analysing the tolerance level of local communities towards tourism development is essential. In the following, I will elaborate on the concept of cruise tourism.

## Cruise tourism

In line with globalization, its continuous "time-space compression" (Harvey, 1989) and an increased search for authenticity of the tourist experience and the destinations visited, is the rapid increase in large-scale, ocean cruise tourism in the past decades, reflecting globalization and neoliberalism – a spiral of endless growth, money supply and debt creation (Harvey, 2020). Mega-cruise tourism was introduced on a large-scale when social changes occurred in Western societies after World War II. Cruise liners promoted more liquid social structures in contrast to solid forms, patterns of acceptable behaviour, changing and melting faster within a short life-expectancy. As a consequence, the power that was there in the past to act locally has been transferred to a larger, global level, while politics and local decision-making are bound to the local level. The absence of any political control makes the newly emancipated powers of such cruise liners into a "source of profound uncertainty" and the concepts of community and inter-human bonds become more vague and temporary (Bauman, 2007).

Cruise tourism has become an important sector within mass tourism (Wood, 2000). The scale of cruise passengers arriving in each port of call has increased dramatically worldwide since the 1980s. In the Bahamas, e.g., cruise tourism began soon after World War II, where 241,000 cruise arrivals were recorded in 1964 compared to 1.6 million in 1996 (Wilkinson, 1999, p. 264). At that time, the Caribbean, Europe and the United States were the main cruise destinations. Tourist numbers increased from 1.4 million cruise tourists in 1980 to 15 million tourists in 2006, 21 million in 2013 and 30 million cruise travellers in 2019 (Cruise Lines International Association, 2021).

The fast consumption of products within "liquid life" (Bauman, 2000) has contributed to the emergence of compressed, one-week, circular itineraries in comparison with long-term, luxury cruising. In the past, the ship was seen as a relatively slow means of transportation, e.g. compared to air travel. Cruise tourism in Europe was part of an elite luxury travel, until the 1970s. This perception changed when mega-cruise liners carrying more than 2,000 passengers were introduced between the 1980s and early 2000 (Klein, 2005). Since that time, the average age and income of cruise travellers have fallen continuously (Wood, 2000), which has also resulted in a democratization of cruise travel. There has been increasing investment in the cruise industry followed by extensive marketing campaigns in the Global North. The popularity of social media posts and influencers including pop-stars visiting certain places as well as popular movies and TV series have played an important 'push-factor' in the promotion of mass tourism and in particular of cruise travels. A few examples are the movie *Titanic* (Wood, 2000) and the US-TV series *The Love Boat* (Weaver, 2005b). Influential TV series for German tourists has been the series *Das Traumschiff* (in English: the dreamship) that has been sailing to various destinations around the world for more than four decades, since the 1980s. The series has attracted generations of spectators to exotic far-away destinations including the Sultanate of Oman where the ship anchored in 2008.

In 2021 a total total of 270 cruises were operated worldwide including 20 new ships that started operations (Cruise Lines International Association, 2021). The number of ships has increased year by year whereas the travel time on board a ship decreased, the travel time on board a ship decreased. The majority of cruise tourists travel for seven days, followed by 4–6 days and 8–13 days (Cruise Lines International Association, 2018). To describe the scale of a ship, notions such as "mega-ships" (Klein, 2005), "mega-liners" (Weeden et al., 2011) or "floating hotels" have been used for ships, accommodating more than 2,000 passengers plus crew. Most of the mega ships operated by AIDA, MSC, Costa Cruises, Hapag Lloyd and others are built in large shipyards in the Global North, namely in Italy, Germany, Finland, France, Japan and South Korea, creating jobs in the Global North (Qubein, 2020).

Cruising has become a reflection of "liquid modernity" while developing into a multibillion-dollar business (Vogel & Oschmann, 2013). Nowadays, several destinations and even continents can be "packaged" and toured within the same trip and within a very short time frame, e.g. one week. For many cruise passengers, "the journey is the destination". Having new experiences is the purpose of the journey and the cruise ship is the vehicle that takes tourists from one "experiential grazing place" to the next one (Vogel & Oschmann, 2013). Rapid changes in taste and fashion have accelerated the turnover of tourist sites and tourist experiences. Moreover, there is an increased market segmentation and production of tourist products with shorter life spans (Klein, 2005), reflected in the increase in short and inexpensive travel within enclosed, isolated environments, conceptualized as "tourist bubbles" (Wood, 2000).

Mega-cruise liners carrying thousands of passengers and crew members from one destination to the next, enhance hybrid "forms of deterritorialization of financial capital, labor and tourist destinations" (Wood, 2000). Cruise ships disconnect social relations from the destination visited, the local culture and the people as well as imaginaries. These imaginaries are created from the circulation of collectively held imaginaries, which have been constructed and reconstructed over a very long time of cross-cultural encounter (Salazar & Grabun, 2014). In places for mass-consumption or "playscapes" (Junemo, 2004), like cruise liners, theme parks and shopping malls (Bauman, 2000; Urry, 1995) "the world's geography can be experienced as a simulacrum" (Harvey, 1989, p. 300). Such simulacrum enhances nostalgia and the feeling of being transported to a different world (Bauman, 2000). Cruise liners with their ample leisure facilities on board offer freedom and diverse experiences (Vogel & Oschmann, 2013). The main goal on board the cruise ship is to "encapsulate individuals" (Weaver, 2005a) in order to maximize containment and profits (Larsen et al., 2013; Weaver, 2005b; Weeden et al., 2011).

However, due to different moral and value systems and increased power relations (London & Lohmann, 2014), sociocultural impacts including culture shock situations in small, emerging cruise destinations are enhanced (Gutberlet, 2016b). To minimize the social contact between cruise tourists and port communities, there has been an increasing focus on the ship as the main destination, which is "secure, comfortable, and tightly controlled" (Jaakson, 2004), forming a "temporary, exclusive community" (Minca, 2012), or even an independent nation on its own (Vogel & Oschmann, 2013).

To address polluting fuels for host communities, cruise lines were impacted by new regulations affecting the marine environment in 2020. According to marine specialists, cruise ships burn as much fuel as entire towns. They also use more power than container ships. Cruise liners are accused of "emissions dodging" rather paying for more expensive and cleaner fuels. Even when they burn low Sulphur fuel, it is 100 times worse than diesel fuel. Mega-cruise lines should act fast to save their corporate legitimacy and address the reality of their negative environmental impacts (Higgins-Desbiolles, 2019).

Most cruise liner research has focused on the economic impact of cruise tourism in the Caribbean, North America, East Asia and Europe. There is very little research done in the Middle East and if so it is business-oriented and little people-oriented. Until beginning of 2020, the cruise travel trend shifted from North America and Europe towards Asia that developed as the fastest-growing continent in the cruise industry, creating "enclosed tourist bubbles". I will further explain these "exceptional spaces" or "tourist bubbles" in the following paragraphs.

## Tourist bubbles

A *tourist bubble* is a liminal space combining tourism and leisure so that tourists can forget everyday problems back home while being part of a temporary community of like-minded consumers (Yarnal & Kerstetter, 2005).

They are also conceptualized as "environmental bubbles" or "total institutions" (Ritzer & Liska, 1997). Cruise liners are "enclosed bubbles on sea" or "resort enclaves" (Freitag, 1994). They create "spaces of exception" and increased inequalities (Büscher & Fletcher, 2017), while disconnecting from local environments, social relations, cultures and the local people. Jansson (2002) conceptualized "tourist bubbles" as "socioscapes" that are places for social interactions. Such a confined space is similar to a "playscape" (Junemo, 2004) or a cocoon which has a closed environment and a temporary society on board.

Similar to hotel resorts and even fast-food chains, mega-cruise ships offer standardized, efficient, calculable and predictable holidays (Ritzer & Liska, 1997). Spontaneous contacts or experiences are avoided or staged within a tourist bubble or within the port area and in front of the ship, e.g. a music band plays for a welcome and locals sell souvenirs. Such a bubble can be open and shared with locals or 'enclosed' like a hotel resort (Jaakson, 2004). Augé (1994) conceptualized these enclosed environments as "non-places" in French *Non-Lieux*, similar to airports, shopping malls or coach stations. Non-places are placeless environments with their own inner world (Jaakson, 2004). There movements of tourists and employees are scripted, scheduled and controlled (Weaver, 2005b). Like hotel resorts, cruise ships are partially owned by large US-based hotel chains like Hyatt (Royal Caribbean), Ramada or Radisson Hotels that are offering so-called active and passive tourist activities (Yarnal & Kerstetter, 2005). Such on-board activities include cafes, restaurants, casinos, bars, spa and sports (Klein, 2005) as well as shopping malls, golf courses and even ice-skating rinks (Wood, 2000), climbing walls or Broadway productions. Moreover, luxury consumer brands like Hermes and various food brands are part of the cruise experience, customized to the tastes of the passengers, for all ages and from luxury to family-oriented (CLIA, 2015). Moreover, some cruises like AIDA have even introduced their own food brand. Hence, mega-cruise liners offer an increasingly standardized "McDonaldized tourism" for the masses (Ritzer & Liska, 1997). They are like towns or cities, offering efficient, calculable and predictable holidays, like sameness of McDonalds restaurants (Ritzer & Liska, 1997). On board a cruise ship, tourists are encouraged to spend their time and money, buying branded items for discounted prices, instead of consuming in the port (Klein, 2005; Larsen & Wolff, 2016; Weaver, 2005a). Holidays on board a mega-cruise ship can be seen as an escape from a hectic life, holding a promise for "reliability, predictability and a routine" while being surrounded by people who seem to be like-minded (Vogel & Oschmann, 2013). Such tourist experiences help to overcome the tourists' travel motivation, an inauthentic lifestyle at home (Vogel & Oschmann, 2013; Wang, 1999). Moreover, the pre-packaged travel arrangement allows metropolitan companies from the Global North to influence the tourist volume and to gain a competitive advantage over local tourism operations in destinations

(Britton 1982). At the same time, they are "bordering off" local communities (Saarinen, 2017), reinforcing a gap and dependency between the capital and the periphery, the Global North and the South as well as between the capital and the countryside (London & Lohmann, 2014). For example, cruise ships in Antarctica (Klein, 2010) or in Norway (Larsen et al., 2013) stay only a few hours in the port. Hence, the tourists consume little and spend little, compared to individual or group tourists who stay longer and spend more money. Those tourists who spend the least amount of time in a local market-place spend little on the local consumption. Cruise tourists were described as having a low spending behaviour, avoiding to purchase locally produced souvenirs (Gutberlet, 2016a; 2016b; Henthorpe, 2000; Higgins-Desbiolles, 2019; Wilkinson, 1999). Often cruise liners even offer similar shops as on land, with lower prices and discounted, duty-free offers (Weaver, 2005a). Hence, local ports are being transformed into fantasy environments similar to the ones on board the ship. These environments are reproducing tour-ist enclaves on shore (Wood, 2000). Researchers have been suggesting that cruise liners should find opportunities to create value for the society and not just on board their own ships (Font et al., 2016). In some destinations, e.g. in the Caribbean, cruise ships offer similar shops as on land, with lower prices and better offers (Renaud, 2017; Weaver, 2005b) and within a familiar space or tourist bubble. As such, the experience becomes rather inauthentic and commodified to satisfy the tourist's expectations (Williams & Lew, 2015). Such special islands have very similar features as mega-cruise ships. They are controlled spaces where tourists are shielded from negative situations. People on board are cut off from society for a certain time and controlled (Weaver, 2005a). Even on shore, tourist spaces are designed to take cruise passengers back to the genuine, authentic Caribbean – one that only existed in the 1970s (Wood, 2000). An artificially created island experience in the Caribbean becomes inauthentic and commodified to satisfy the tourist's expectations (Williams & Lew, 2015). Contact or experiences with the local community are avoided.

### The cruise communitas

Cruise tourists become members of "a community of consumers" (Urry, 1995) within a limited space and time. They form a 'communitas', provid-ing them with a sense of solidarity and belonging on board and off board (Yarnal & Kerstetter, 2005). This idea is conceptualized as 'a space of compensation' for the increased loss of community values and bonding in Western societies (Minca, 2012). The physical design of cruise liners pro-motes social interaction and a feeling of belonging. Often mega-cruise lin-ers are like theme parks, replicating historical sites from different countries or, from themed resort destinations like Disneyland, enhancing nostalgia. Carnival Cruises introduced the "Fun-Ship" in the 1970s (Wood, 2000). This highlights the visual consumption of places, global miniaturization and time-space compression (Urry, 1995), the "destinization" (Weaver, 2005a). The formation of enclavic, special spaces for cruise tourists and the dependency of the local community has developed in the Caribbean where cruise tourism modifies and defines territorial relations between different stakeholders (Renaud, 2017). This dependency empowered foreign interest groups and privileged certain social classes in the destination, instead of promoting local involvement from different stakeholders within the community (Britton 1982; London & Lohmann, 2014; Saarinen, 2017). Hence, positive outcomes for the destination fail when cruise tourism is developed without direct investment and local community involvement (MacNeill & Wozniak, 2008). There is a demand for more ethics and a greater, more responsible power and profit sharing between the cruise liner and local stakeholders (Da Cruz, 2018; Del Chiappa & Abbate, 2016; Font et al., 2016; Johnson, 2006; Klein, 2011; Logossah, 2011; London & Lohmann, 2014; Lopes & Dredge, 2018; MacNeill & Wozniak, 2008; Milano et al., 2019; Renaud, 2017). A more ethical approach has been confirmed in Norway (Larsen & Wolff, 2016), in Denmark (Lopes & Dredge, 2018), in Italy (Del Chiappa & Abbate, 2016), in Mexico (Jaakson, 2004) and in Oman (Gutberlet, 2016a, 2017, 2020, 2021, 2022a, 2022b). In this line of thoughts, Da Cruz (2018) and Renaud (2017) questioned the territorial expansion and power of cruise liners within a destination when only foreign investors and local elites gain from cruise tourism.

Tourism is one of capitalism's most creative and versatile manifestations, characterized by "the dynamic of a destructive creation" (Büscher & Fletcher, 2017). For tourists, it is about being in an exceptional environment, a "tourist bubble", away from home and not being there in the real environment, even though tourism products often depend on the sociocultural and historical context of the destination (p. 662). Font et al. (2016) say that community is being used by the cruise industry, instead of the local community using the cruise liner business. Tourist bubbles are the result of postmodernity, the effects of globalization (Bauman, 2007; Harvey, 1989) and capitalism; thus "tourism-as-capital" or "value in motion".

## Overtourism

"Venice is so delicate, we need a balance", said a local resident about overtourism in the city (Giuffrida, 2021), highlighting the sociocultural and environmental stress caused by the mega-ships and a large number of people passing through the narrow streets of the old city centre. Overtourism can deteriorate relationships between visitors and locals and it can erode the culture around that it grows and depends on (Kay, 2018). Overtourism is the result of too many people travelling worldwide within time and space enhanced through the fast development in technology, increased prosperity (Kay, 2018), less visa restrictions, population growth and the branding of destinations (Séraphin et al., 2019). In 1950, 25 million people travelled worldwide, while in 2019 a total of 1.4 billion tourists were travelling (Statista, 2021). In many places, this has caused a reduction in the quality of life of local communities and on-site tourist experiences, while the contribution of tourism to local businesses is limited (Séraphin et al., 2018). The fast pace of growth of mass tourism like mega-cruise tourism created various challenges to the sustainability of the tourism industry, to ports and to the well-being of local communities (Klein, 2011). Mass tourism often damages communities, their everyday lives and sociocultural values. It is therefore time to redefine and reorient tourism operations and planning, representing the interests of local stakeholders (Higgins-Desbiolles, 2020) instead of prioritizing foreign interests. Overtourism is associated with unsustainable tourism growth and concepts like visitor pressure, the level of acceptable change and the social and physical carrying capacity of space (Cheer et al., 2019; Koens et al., 2019; Milano & Koens, 2021). The phenomenon of a large number of people spending a limited time in a destination is also conceptualized as a "shock loading" effect (Wilkinson, 1999). The term describes the dramatic impact on local people when the number of tourists exceeds the capacity of the place, causing overcrowding (Klein, 2010). Tourism stakeholders in European cities like Barcelona, Venice, Berlin or Amsterdam have been struggling with handling too many tourists in one time and in one destination. For example, more than 15.7 million US tourists visited Europe in 2017, an increase by 16% compared to the previous year (Abend, 2018). Mediterranean cruise destinations have become less attractive for some tourists as they are often overcrowded during the tourist season (Schemmann, 2012).

Overtourism is linked to population growth worldwide, a growth of the middle class, especially in China and India, who now spend more money on leisure activities. In addition, flight tickets and packaged holidays are cheaper and online services like Airbnb, couchsurfing.com or booking.com are easily accessible (Fyall, 2019). The increase of low-cost transportation including airlines like easyJet, Ryanair, Vueling in Europe or SalamAir and Air Arabia in the Middle East has increased the number of tourists, especially in urban destinations. New airlines expanded their fleets offering competitive, affordable prices, especially for regional flights. Moreover, such affordable mass-market air travel has enabled cruise tourists to reach the port of embarkation cheap and easy via charter flights (Weaver, 2005b). Moreover, Airbnb was launched in 2008 and made accommodation more affordable (Abend, 2018). At the same time, the cruise industry increased rapidly in the 2000s, e.g. growing by 49% in Europe (CLIA, 2018). All these factors have caused a rapid increase in global mobilities leading to unregulated capital accumulation and overwhelmed communities that became tourism products. It is a "selling out" of urban spaces and communities like consumer products or commodities (Milano et al., 2019). Too many tourists can overwhelm a society. It can damage the city's infrastructure as well as natural and social environments (Koens et al., 2019; Milano et al.,

2019). Overtourism has been occurring in popular, urban destinations like Barcelona, Venice or Amsterdam, having negative, disruptive impacts on host communities and their everyday tolerance levels within their natural, physical, social and cultural environments. This tolerance level is related to the pollution of their environment (Giuffrida, 2021), overcrowding of public spaces, the increase in housing prices and the physical touristification of neighbourhoods where locals and their infrastructure, e.g. grocery shops and medical doctors have been pushed out of their residential areas.

According to V. L. Smith (1989), the critical point in the development of a tourist industry is achieved when tourist facilities are implemented, e.g. special parking for tourist buses, tourist hotels and tourist restaurants. As a result, a large numbers of tourists can be handled by industrial methods with standardization and mass production of different services (Krippendorf, 1987).

### Tourismphobia

"Welcoming tourists is not an absolute concept, similar to luxury" (Maroldt, 2017). The rise of mass tourism and a tourism monoculture have led to the rise of a local counter-movement, *tourismphobia* in European cities like Barcelona, Palma de Mallorca, Venice and Berlin. The term "tourismphobia" appeared for the first time in the Spanish daily *El País* in 2008. It has been linked to social discontent as well as to unbalanced planning and development strategies (Milano et al., 2019). Some cities have seen activities of tourismphobia and have even taken measures to stop tourists from visiting their countries (Séraphin et al., 2019). In the Island of Mallorca (Spain), demonstrators conducted "a summer of action", expressing their anger in July 2018, welcoming tourists with signs that said "Tourism kills Mallorca" (Abend, 2018, p. 28). In Venice (Italy) and in other European cities, tourism drives out locals, leaving space for restaurants and other shops that cater for tourists only. When local residents leave their districts and the tourists take over, "what is left behind can lose some of its charm" (p. 32). For example, Venetian residents complained that Venice is not a film-set or a Disneyland (Giuffrida, 2021; Poggioli, 2013). In Barcelona, it has become everyday reality, when four to five cruise liners are in the city during the high season in the spring and summer, residents and other tourists cannot walk anymore at the well-known Rambla Boulevard (Abend, 2018). Various impacts describe an increased local-foreign-divide: a loss of belonging, increased traffic congestion, the privatization of public spaces, the rise in real estate speculation (Milano et al., 2019). In the German capital Berlin citizens ask whether the promotion of the image as a city of individual freedom and tolerance (Maroldt, 2017) which has paved the way for more mindless tourist behaviours, needs to start setting up limitations on the current open door policy for tourists. Therefore, positive economic impacts of tourism such as job creation and consumption of local products have been increasingly overshadowed by negative impacts including the exclusion of members of the local community. Until spring 2020 and the stop of international tourism due to the corona pandemic, the Arabian Peninsula did not witness major outspoken resistance against mass tourism. In the following, I will introduce some regulatory measures to limit negative impacts in popular tourist destinations.

## Regulatory measures

To compensate for negative impacts caused to communities through mass-tourism development, a tourist tax or fees, environmental and economic accounting or auditing have been suggested (Fyall, 2019). Tourist-generating regions should get financially involved and "pay for some of the impacts of the vacations taken in someone else's backyard" (Jafari, 1987). Jafari argued that Europe owes much to countries in the Global South like Tunisia and Senegal as their preferred and recreative tourist destinations. Iceland is planning to introduce a tax for non-European visitors, and Greece has introduced a tourism tax in 2018. Iceland and Thailand have both closed popular nature destinations. For example, Maya Bay in Thailand was damaged by too many visitors (Fyall, 2019). Other places like the city of Barcelona have introduced regulatory measures such as a tourist quota system for cruise liners as well as a *tourist police*, observing, punishing and sanctioning misbehaviour of tourists. The city penalizes inappropriate tourist behaviour with fines, e.g. inappropriate dress behaviour, wearing of swimming suits while walking through the city or excessive alcohol consumption. In Venice, the city has introduced more than 20 stewards in #enjoyrespectvenezia who prevent tourists from misbehaviour such as sitting on monuments, jumping in the canal, or other misbehaviour. The city of Amsterdam has implemented a *fining system* for rowdy behaviour, including drunkenness, excessive noise, littering and public urination (Abend, 2018). In Venice (Italy), tourists are distributed to other areas outside the popular old city centre and the city's government introduced a fast lane for residents using public transportation. In Barcelona's popular main market, Boquería, large tourist groups are prohibited at certain times of the day. The city also considers introducing measures to restrict a *business monoculture* in order to protect their residents, so that they can still buy their groceries in the centre instead of snacks and tourist souvenirs. Cruise liners that want to stop-over in the Barcelona for one day, may have difficulties to get a docking license. Barcelona prioritizes those ships that start or end their journey in the city as a home-port (Abend, 2018). In Amsterdam, overcrowding, congestion and waste are putting pressure on the liveability of some neighbourhoods. For the locals, the monoculture of shops does not make the city an attractive place to live. A new balance is required, one which puts residents at its core and still welcomes visitors. Amsterdam is a city to live, work and do business in. It is secondly a tourist site, said the city council in an agreement named "Balance in the city" (cited in Hodes et al., 2018). The Amsterdam City Council ordered in 2018 the closure of the Cheese Company chain being set-up in the city centre since 2017, catering to tourists on overpriced Dutch cheeses, wrapped in touristy packages with tulips and van Gogh design. This increasing monoculture of shops like mini-supermarkets and game-shops has upset local residents. Finally, the State Consultative Council's Department of Justice decided that Amsterdam had the right to order the close-down, but added that the owner of the Cheese Company could keep a shop, since he already had the rental contract for many years (Niemantsverdriet, 2018). This shows the power struggle between different stakeholders in the government and private businesses. In the old city of Dubrovnik (Croatia), a number of cameras were installed to monitor continuously tourist movements and to help enforce a quota of 8,000 tourists per day limit (Abend, 2018). Other places have introduced tourist exit or *"Trexit"*-measures that stop marketing measures and incentives for tourists to visit the country (Séraphin et al., 2018).

### *Undertourism*

In light of the global COVID-19 pandemic, the development of overtourism in destinations has been overtaken by the other extreme of undertourism. Undertourism literally means little tourism or no tourism. Both extremes have impacted the lives of communities around the globe (Milano & Koens, 2021), especially in the Global South. Worldwide, the tourism sector has experienced a sharp decline of more than 80% in 2020 (OECD, 2020). Undertourism has impacted local communities with increased unemployment and the closure of tourism businesses, e.g. small- and medium-size businesses that did not receive any funding support, whereas large companies were more supported through their networks.

As for the post-COVID-19 recovery, there are opposing voices "to return to business as usual versus those that envision possibilities for greater sustainability, equity and justice" (Higgins-Desbiolles, 2021). The optimum would be an equilibrium and a pro-community vision for a sustainable recovery of destinations. However, within the current capitalist economic system, such balance will be difficult to realize. Capitalism has created various forms of "structural violence, the production of increased inequalities, waste and spaces of exception" (Büscher & Fletcher, 2017), which require a critical reflection about the future of tourism worldwide (Benjamin et al., 2020; Lew et al., 2020), including an analysis of the social capital in destinations.

## Social capital

Social capital and community cohesion have seen an increasing interest in research. Social capital is a concept to analyse the social ties that connect community stakeholders, linking stakeholder groups with each other to support tourism destinations promoting an inclusive, sustainable tourism. Social capital offers opportunities to evaluate perspectives of how groups are included within the community and whether they have the confidence to reach out to other groups and government entities (Park et al., 2015). Social capital, social identity and social networks in community-based tourism development provide important assets for business exchange, economic development and positive community attitudes while sometimes creating challenging power issues within communities, marginalization and even social exclusion of locals (Colic-Peisker & Robertson, 2015; Hall et al., 2008; Musavengane & Kloppers, 2020; Palmer et al., 2013; Park et al., 2015; Soulard et al., 2018; Telfer, 2003; Waldinger, 1995).

The economic term *capital* implies that local communities can protect, sell or consume their natural, physical and social assets to promote tourism development (Soulard et al., 2018). Non-materialistic components of an exchange relationship in tourism, such as tourism's contribution to the community's well-being, have a significant influence on the individual support for tourism development (Park et al., 2015). For example, responsible cruise tourism is seen as a challenge and difficult to implement, requiring increased bridging social capital and a participatory, collaborative policy-making approach among local authorities, government agencies, businesses and host communities, who should work, plan and regulate together for a community-centred development (Del Chiappa & Abbate, 2016). However, socio-economic fragmentation, the pursuit of individual success, high social mobility and ethnically diverse populations have been some of the main reasons behind decreasing social capital in communities (Colic-Peisker & Robertson, 2015). Hence, the business culture of the destination needs to be reconsidered, limiting the involvement of a wide range of stakeholders (Soulard et al., 2018). The social identity of locals impacts their continuous involvement and advocacy for the tourist destination, conceptualized in the sharing of knowledge and word-of-mouth promotion (Palmer et al., 2013). The control of tourism businesses by certain ethnic groups like elites, leads to the marginalization or even exclusion of others (Waldinger, 1995), creating an unsustainable development path.

Bonding social capital and bridging social capital are essential for promoting the well-being of communities. Bonding social capital explains the social ties between community members, e.g. an informal community support group. Bridging social capital refers to the ties between local stakeholder communities or networks, e.g. between regions, industries and government entities. For example, the national tourism board is invited to a meeting with an informal local community group. Hence, bridging social capital links community networks, organizations and governmental representation, through trust, reciprocity and cooperation.

Bonding social capital enhances local community ties through direct involvement or closer cooperation. It provides a tool to evaluate power struggles and a lack of trust within local communities. It strengthens relationships between government institutions and an informal web of networks, relationships and norms, creating a valuable link with tourism businesses, e.g. an informal tourism association or a community tourism support group that meets regularly to exchange information about local initiatives, enhancing the local bonding social capital (Soulard et al., 2018). A lack of consultation and communication decreases the bonding of social capital, creating feelings of exclusion, being left out of the development process (p. 197).

Collectivist societies in Asia or in Africa put more emphasis on group memberships and social relations compared to individualistic cultures in Europe, in North America or in Australia and New Zealand where people value social memberships, norms and values less (Park et al., 2015). Within collectivist societies, characteristics such as trust, social norms, and interpersonal networks are crucial to enhance a positive economic, social, cultural and political development (Putnam, 1993). Possible negative effects of social capital are that social networks and bonding create a demand for social conformity, where community members are expected to behave according to well-known established values and norms (Portes, 1998). Reciprocity is a sense of mutual and fair exchange, e.g. through the representation of cultural and ethnic minorities such as Aboriginal culture (Soulard et al., 2018). The bridging social capital increased when tourism stakeholders like hotels, attractions and destination management companies cooperate to make tourism politically, socially and economically recognized within the local community (p. 197). Finally, bonding and bridging social capital are essential for valuing heritage sites and conservation, for instance through skills training (Musavengane & Kloppers, 2020). In heritage tourism shared social memories and local experiences can be generated, conceptualized and reconceptualized, enhancing the formation of shared local identities, which are important assets for tourist experiences and imaginaries.

## Tourism imaginaries

Imaginative geographies and social discourses that distinguish the dichotomy between 'home' and 'away' are important concepts in tourism research (Crang, 1997). Di Giovine (2014) argued that there are ample imaginaries: as many as there are tourists. These imaginaries serve to frame a particular tourist site (p. 167). Imaginaries are produced through the body (Chronis, 2012), the senses (Crouch & Desforges, 2003; Rodaway, 2002), experiences and desires as well as through encounters between people and their expectations (Crouch, 1999). Hence, imaginaries and the reality of space should be considered as being interconnected (Chronis, 2012; Gao et al., 2011).

Prior to a travel, people develop fantasies or dreams. Millions of journeys are imagined in the tourists' fantasies, in the media and in marketing materials. "Every tour begins with a desire" (MacCannell, 2011, p. 64). Through linking a tourist site, a visitor and a marker, MacCannell (1999) was one of the first scholars who highlighted the importance of visual tourist images and imagined concepts.

Tourism can be seen as an important way of ordering societies and modernity, creating "ordering effects" (Franklin, 2004). In the relationship between the Global North and less developed or emerging tourism destinations, e.g. in the Middle East, imaginaries are based on a dependency between the core and the periphery and within a postcolonial discourse (Tucker & Akama, 2010). In Western imagination, especially remote places with a romantic flair such as the sand desert in Arabia or a long beach on a Pacific Island or the Caribbean are promoted with female attributes as being virgin or like a paradise, without considering the real everyday life of the community, which may differ from romantic tourist images (Cohen, 1978). Imaginaries often communicate historically inherited stereotypes, based on dreams (Salazar & Grabun, 2014). For example, a Kasbah (a fort in Morocco) or a souq (a marketplace in Arabic) are part of local neighbourhoods in the Middle East and in North Africa, representing a "materiality of colonial imaginings" (Wagner & Minca, 2015). They offer special tourist experiences (Wu et al., 2014), while being part of the local flow of everyday life. The tourist's fantasies created through guidebooks or social media photos about the exotic *Other* is embedded in a continuous search for other places different from everyday life, a search for authenticity and a more genuine way of life (MacCannell, 1999). In order to increase the consumption and profits the tourism industry tries to increase the tourists' interests, dreams, hopes and desires through imagination and "phantasmagoria" (Jansson, 2002). The mediatization of images generates a regime of "imaginative hedonism" through which viewers are inspired to experience tourism destinations in reality (Jansson, 2002).

Visiting and encountering differences through race, gender and nature, the exotic can be identified with another cultural lens of superiority of the Global North over the Orient. Often the predominant white, male and racial logic of modern tourism is saturated onto the landscape, nature tourism and its moral undertones and understandings. "Whiteness of tourism is affirmed through the bodies of tourists and their hosts, but also by meanings given to the landscape visited" (Erickson, 2018, p. 44). Tourism clichés are what people expect and clichés they will buy (Krippendorf, 1987). A well-known example of a tourist cliché is the encounter with a yodelling, flag-waving, alphorn-blowing and cheese-carrying Swiss or Bavarian male herdsman dressed in a colourful shirt and a knee-length leather trouser (p. 34). In the context of tourism to developing countries, tourist representations reflect images of Western ideas about how the *Other* is imagined to be (Salazar, 2010). These images are often binary, such as "unchanged, unrestrained and uncivilized" (Echtner & Prasad, 2003), reflecting power relations of superiority and inferiority between the Occident and the Orient (Said, 2003). Tourists come to observe them, *the Other*, often seen in opposition as being powerless, backward or primitive and prehistoric (Bruner, 1991). Imaginaries socially create a place (Chronis, 2012), "labelling" a place (Palmer, 1994). Such imaginaries are taken from the media, literature, film or fine arts (Urbain, 1993), reflecting power relations of colonialism and imperialism (Said, 1993) as well as gendered relations between hosts and guests. While travelling to a destination, tourists find moments of difference, e.g. in food, rituals, in comfort levels and in privileges, and position. These differences act as a drive to self-actualization and being part of a global culture (Erickson, 2018). Imaginaries are attached to a certain place that can have multiple imaginaries (Chronis, 2012), therefore highlighting its character through material markers, "commercial staging" and place narratives (p. 1811). Imaginaries are authentic (Di Giovine, 2014), because they are genuine or real. They try to construct authentic feelings and knowledge (Di Giovine 2014; Swain (2014)

Imaginaries are constantly reformed (Di Giovine, 2014, p. 151). This means that people and places are continuously reinvented as tourism creates powerful sociocultural representations about them (Salazar, 2006). Initially, in the pre-travel stage, tourists have a mental image of what the destination will look like. While travelling in the destination, tour operators organize trips accordingly with idealistic visual and narrative representations. Moreover, cultural mediators like tour guides and drivers have to ensure that tourists experience what they expect and what they booked prior to the trip (Salazar, 2010, p. 79).

While on tour, cultural brokers assist in the tourist's (re)constructions of his or her experience as well as the representation of that experience (Jennings & Weiler, 2006, p. 58). Imaginaries are formed through such continuous experiences. In the first phase of their travel, imaginaries are created; in the second phase, they are contested and negotiated while visiting the tourist site. Imaginaries are not neutral representations. Power issues and ideologies are constantly involved, representing something special to a particular tourist (Saarinen, 2004). Tourist places often reflect an artificial, "staged authenticity" (MacCannell, 1999) engaging the imagination, in "imaginariums" (Swain, 2014). Imaginaries adapt to different markets, politics and local identities, combining cultural and political capital into many different imaginaries (Swain, 2014). This power of mass-mediated imaginaries to market certain tourist expectations has been utilized by destination marketing and promotion (Beeton et al., 2006). Mass-media influences worldviews, directing tourists to specific destinations (Salazar & Grabun, 2014), constructing the social reality through standardized symbols, e.g. local communities dressed in traditional costumes and storytelling (Chronis, 2012). The tourists perceive the destination in terms of this image. Hence, the tourist experience has become mediated by the media (Jansson, 2002), enabling people to be a virtual tourist without being physically present, conceptualized as "mediatized mediascapes" (Månsson, 2011). The tourist gaze has become interwoven with the consumption of mediatised images (Jansson, 2002). Mediated images are often becoming the originals against that experiences of simulated landscapes and socioscapes are measured, a "symbolic authenticity" (Wang, 1999).

A number of researchers have studied visual or mental imaginaries, in particular in the Global North and some including their links to the Global South (Chronis, 2005, 2012, 2015; D'Hauteserre, 2011; Di Giovine, 2014; Gao et al., 2011; Jovicic, 2000; Pink, 2008; Salazar, 2006; Salazar & Grabun, 2014; Urry, 1995). Cauvin Verner (2007) analysed the French tourists and local guide interactions in the Sahara, a place that is mediated by French post-colonial imaginaries. Edensor (1998) researched European tourist-local imaginaries and performances at the Taj Mahal, a site with colonial imaginaries. Chronis (2005, 2015) conducted research at a US memorial site, where social values, patriotism and unity were highlighted through guided tours. He argued that a guided tour around the memorial site is symbolic, unreal, imaginative and reconstructed from history. The place narratives and its material staging are often sold to tourists and not the physical place of a destination (Chronis, 2012). Imaginaries often inhabit an ideological role. During the process of "refiguration" tourists shape their imaginaries through "emplacement", the bodily presence while being at a destination (Chronis, 2012), the "individual narrative disposition" of each tourist, their "emotional connection" with the tourist site and their "moral valuation", which leads to an "ideological reinforcement", shaping individual as well as group identities.

In my research in Oman, European tourist experiences in the souq in Muttrah and in the sand desert are framed by imaginaries, geopolitically and socially transmitted representations and narratives. These are embodied and used as means to make sense of the world (Mostafanezhad & Norum, 2016; Santos, 2014).

## Oriental imaginaries

The Global North has compared "the Orient" with an imaginary, exotic, female space *Eden* or a *paradise* and as an "Old World to which one returned" (Said, 1989, p. 58), similar to the Caribbean (Sheller, 2003). In Asian and Africa, discourses of post-Orientalism, colonialism and imperialism seem to form the basis for tourism dreams (Salazar & Grabun, 2014; Sönmez, 2001). Said (2003) described in "Orientalism" how postcolonial discourses and visual representations created by the Occident defined the constructed Orient. He argued that both the Orient and the Occident "are man-made" (Said, 2003) exercising power over the Orient and producing the Orient as "a (material, embodied) reality" (Haldrup & Larsen, 2010). Often those imaginaries have little to do with reality but are linked with the country's colonial past, creating "stereotyped ethnic and cultural images" (Palmer, 1994, p. 805) that impact the tourist-host encounter. Hence, host communities can find themselves trapped in post-colonial settings (Hall & Tucker, 2004), being "frozen in their archaism" (Cauvin Verner, 2007) and Global North–South power relations. In the Orient, tourists want to discover "legendary lands" (Echtner & Prasad, 2003). Since the 19th century, Oriental images like harems, minarets, souqs and mint tea have been seen as exotic representations (De Botton, 2003). Geopolitical imaginaries create connections between the tourist's images, the place, the on-site experiences, the identity and the value of the place visited. A geopolitical, Oriental imaginary can evoke feelings of being safe, having an important impact on "the framing of space as prototypical, comprehensible forms" (Mostafanezhad & Norum, 2016, p. 227).

Social realities may create barriers preventing communication, raising false expectations and "dangerous assumptions" (Beeton et al., 2006). The impact of a time-space compression applied in marketing material about Cambodia is a substantial feature of the experience. The geographical distance between the destination and the tourists' country of origin evokes a need for an "exotic experience" (Ferraris, 2014).

Princess Sayyida Salme, the daughter of Sayyid Said ibn Sultan Al Busaidi, who ruled the Sultanate of Oman from Zanzibar in the 19th century, created Oriental imaginaries about her everyday life in an "Oriental family palace". In her autobiography "Memories of an Arabian Princess from Zanzibar" (Ruete, 2004) she explores its harem from her native Zanzibar perspective. The princess married a German businessman and took the name Emily. Her imaginaries were conceptualized as "counter-imaginaries" (Leite, 2014). Zanzibar and other parts of East Africa were colonized by Germany between 1897 and 1916, when German East Africa was a colony (Tanzanian Government, 2016). A common characteristic of Western Orientalism was to legitimate a kind of arrogance, intellectual superiority and even *authority* over the Orient (Said, 2003) while producing and privileging the Global North and *whiteness* (Erickson, 2018). Locals were described as "childlike", "innocent", and as "being backward" (Palmer, 1994). Consequently, a quasi-parental power can be exercised by Western tourists (Morgan & Pritchard, 1998). Comparing British and French Orientalism, which was "real and experienced" due to their colonial histories, German Orientalism was shorter and scholarly, referring to a German "classical Orient" that was made the subject of lyrics, fantasies and even novels (Said, 2003, p. 19). Travelling to destinations in the Middle East, a Western tourist expects to go "back in time and space to a world of ancient civilizations" (Echtner & Prasad, 2003), to discover "the unchanged", "the uncivilized", "legendary lands" having "mystical secrets" "exotic people" (Echtner & Prasad, 2003), and to experience the "Eastern mystery versus Western rationality" (Edensor, 1998). Back in the mid-19th century, when few rich people were travelling, European travellers and writers like Gustave Flaubert were seen as observers who were not involved but detached from the places and cultures visited (Said, 2003). One of the most famous classic German works of literature about the Orient is Goethe's poetry entitled "West-East Divan" (Goethe, 2003). However, Goethe never travelled; his poems developed in his mind, while travelling through Germany, at the beginning of the 19th century. The aim of German Oriental scholarship was "to refine and elaborate techniques whose application was to texts, myths,

ideas, and languages almost literally gathered from the Orient by impe-
rial Britain or France" (Said, 2003). Writers like Gustave Flaubert, Guy
de Maupassant and the female traveller Isabelle Eberhard experienced the
Orient as being "mystical, erotic and savage" (Jovicic, 2000).

### The souq and the desert

Geopolitical imaginaries of a place and its local people are formed by
romanticized, dominant narratives that are often projections from Western
consciousness (Bruner, 1991). The Orient has been encountered through
the journey, the history, the fable, the stereotype and a polemic confrontation (Said, 1989) influencing the perception of the Orient and the encounter between Orient and Occident. Western-influenced Oriental images of
camels, Bedouins, deserts, oases and the Arabian Nights are "fragments
and materials for staging improvised play and often ironic performances
and representations" (Haldrup & Larsen, 2010). These imaginaries are
materialized in advertisements, marketing brochures as well as in popular
discourses and cultures such as Hollywood movies featuring tourist experiences like *The English Patient* or *The Sheltering Sky*, and German TV-series
such as *The Dream Ship* (in German: Das Traumschiff) featuring stories of
German tourists and staff on and off board a luxury cruise-liner, as well as
German TV-series *Adventure in Arabia* (in German: Abenteuer in Arabia).
These films mediated imaginaries about the Sultanate of Oman being an
exotic, dry desert country with camels, the *Oriental Other* and colourful
souqs.

Throughout history, Oriental markets (in Arabic: souqs) were appreciated
by the community for their opportunities they offered for exchange, trade and
networking symbolizing an exchange of commodities and cultures (Pourjafar
et al., 2014). Once inside a souq, a labyrinth of small alleys provides different
opportunities for encounters, gazing and walking performances (Edensor,
2000). As such, a souq has been conceptualized as a "socioscape" (Jansson,
2002) or as a "heterogeneous space" (Edensor, 2000), where facilities coexist
with small businesses, shops, street vendors and housing for local residents.
Tourists are often attracted to such a lively, "glocal(ized)" neighbourhood
with Western amenities and local everyday life (Salazar, 2005).

Similar to everyday life in a souq, there is nostalgia about life in the desert
being more authentic, spiritually and socially richer than that led by the people
of the civilized, urban society (Graulund, 2009). The desert has been valued as
a natural and culturally imprinted space influenced by postcolonial discourses
and discoveries (Wagner & Minca, 2015) as well as an important part of religious texts. The Bible and the Quran highlight the desert as a unique, spiritual
space (Cauvin Verner, 2007). Other religions like Hinduism, Buddhism and
Chinese Daoist tradition connect humans and nature (Holden, 2008). Up to the
present, there are still unexplored desert areas, having had few human visitors
(Martin, 2004). Back in history, in particular, male explorers like Marco Polo

created awareness in Europe about the deserts in Asia. In the 13th century, he travelled through Persia and along the Silk Road. British explorers, Getrude Bell and T.E. Laurence, named Laurence of Arabia, travelled through different countries in the late 19th and early 20th century. They both belonged to a social elite. Moreover, the British Bertram Thomas (1892–1950) crossed the Rub al-Khali desert on the Arabian Peninsula, which is the largest desert on Earth. However, a complete crossing was only achieved by Wilfred Thesiger in 1946 and 1948 (Martin, 2004). Thesiger endured a simple life with physical hardship in the desert:

> *I was tired; for days I had ridden long hours on a rough camel, my body racked by its uneven gait. I suppose I was weak from hunger.*
>
> (Thesiger, 2007, p. 12)

Thesiger's narratives highlighted the harsh features of the desert environment on the Arabian Peninsula. The physical and psychological hardship he endured created a myth and a nostalgia about the Desert Noble Savage reflecting a superiority to the non-desert people. Bedouins in the desert were characterized as being physically and mentally fit, isolated from civilization, tradition and comradeship (Graulund, 2009).

In this chapter, I have elaborated various concepts used in my research, linked with global mobilities and increased connectedness through time-space compression. This has impacted tourist experiences, the people and locations visited as well as the formation of *enclosed tourist bubbles* and Oriental imaginaries about the places and hosts visited. In the next chapter, I will outline the research setting including the rapid tourism development in the Sultanate of Oman. This is followed by the history of Souq Muttrah and Sharqiyah Sands as well as an in-depth analysis of my research results on the Arabian Peninsula.

## References

Abend, L. (2018, August 6–13). The tourism trap. As vacationers threaten to turn Europe into a theme park, the continent is pushing back. *Time Magazine*, 26–32. Time Magazine Europe.

Adey, P. (2017). *Mobility* (2nd ed.). Routledge.

Bærenholdt, J. O., Haldrup, M., Larsen, J., & Urry, J. (2004). *Performing tourist places*. Ashgate Publishing.

Bauman, Z. (2000). *Liquid modernity*. Polity Press.

Bauman, Z. (2001). *Community. Seeking safety in an insecure world*. Ebook for PC. Polity.

Bauman, Z. (2005). *Liquid life*. Ebook for PC. Polity Press.

Bauman, Z. (2007). *Liquid times. Living in an age of uncertainty*. Ebook for PC. Polity Press.

Beeton, S., Bowen, H. E., & Santos, C. A. (2006). State of knowledge: Mass media and its relationship to perceptions of quality. In G. Jennings & N. Polovitz-Nickerson (Eds.), *Quality tourism experiences* (pp. 25–37). Elsevier Butterworth-Heinemann.

Belhassen, Y., Caton, K., & Stewart, W. P. (2008). The search for authenticity in the pilgrim experience. *Annals of Tourism Research*, *35*(3), 668–689.

Benjamin, S., Dillette, A., & Alderman, D. H. (2020). "We can't return to normal": Committing to tourism equity in the post-pandemic age. *Tourism Geographies*, *22*(3), 476–483. https://doi.org/10.1080/14616688.2020.1759130

Britton, S. G. (1982). The political economy of tourism in the Third World. *Annals of Tourism Research*, *9*(3), 331–358.

Bruner, E. (1991). Transformation of self in tourism. *Annals of Tourism Research*, *18*, 238–250.

Büscher, B., & Fletcher, R. (2017). Destructive creation: Capital accumulation and the structural violence of tourism. *Journal of Sustainable Tourism*, *25*(5), 651–667.

Cauvin Verner, C. (2007). *Au désert. une anthropologie du tourisme dans le sud marocain*. L'Harmattan.

Chaney, D. (2002). The power of metaphors in tourism theory. In M. Crang & S. Coleman (Eds.), *Tourism between place and performance* (pp. 3867–4140). Kindle Ebook for PC. Berghahn Books.

Cheer, J, Milano, C., & Novelli, M. (2019) (Eds.) Afterword: Over overtourism or just the beginning? In *Overtourism: Excesses, discontent and measures in travel and tourism* (pp. 227–232). CABI.

Chronis, A. (2005). Coconstructing heritage at the Gettysburg storyscape. *Annals of Tourism Research*, *32*(2), 386–406.

Chronis, A. (2012). Between place and story: Gettysburg as tourism imaginary. *Annals of Tourism Research*, *39*(4), 1797–1816.

Chronis, A. (2015). Moving bodies and the staging of the tourist experience. *Annals of Tourism Research*, *55*(1), 124–140.

Cohen, E. (1978). The impact of tourism on the physical environment. *Annals of Tourism Research*, *5*(2), 215–237.

Cohen, E. (2012). 'Authenticity' in tourism studies: Après la lutte. In T. V. Singh (Ed.), *Critical debates in tourism* (pp. 256–261). Kindle Ebook for PC. Channel View Publications.

Colic-Peisker, V., & Robertson, S. (2015). Social change and community cohesion: An ethnographic study of two Melbourne suburbs. *Ethnic and Racial Studies*, *38*(1), 75–91.

Crang, P. (1997). Performing the tourist product. In C. Rojek & J. Urry (Eds.), *Touring cultures* (pp. 137–114, Transformations of Travel and Theory). Routledge.

Crouch, D. (1999). Introduction, encounters in leisure/tourism. In D. Crouch (Ed.), *Leisure/Tourism geographies. Practices and geographical knowledge* (pp. 1–16). Routledge.

Crouch, D. (2002). Surrounded by place. Embodied encounters. In M. Crang & S. Coleman (Eds.), *Tourism between place and performance* (pp. 4153–5372). Kindle Ebook for PC. Berghahn Books.

Crouch, D., & Desforges, L. (2003). The sensuous in the tourist encounter. Introduction: The power of the body in tourist studies. *Tourist Studies*, *3*(1), 5–22.

Cruise Lines International Association CLIA (2015). *State of the Cruise Industry Outlook: Continued Evolution of Cruise Travel Drives Industry Growth*.

Cruise Lines International Association (2018). *CLIA one reSource Q1 2016, 2017 and 2018 Quarterly Global Report as of August 2018*. Retrieved August 22, 2018, from https://cruising.org/docs/default-source/market-research/2017-clia-global-quarterly-report-q1-2018.pdf?sfvrsn=0

Cruise Lines International Association (2021). *State of the Cruise Industry Outlook.* Retrieved June 17, from https://cruising.org

Da Cruz, R. (2018). Maritime cruises: Oligopoly, centralization of capital and corporate use of Brazilian territory. In D. Müller & M. Wieckowski (Eds.), *Tourism in transitions. Recovering decline, managing change.* Springer International Publishing.

De Botton, A. (2003). *Die Kunst des Reisens.* S. Fischer Verlag GmbH.

Del Chiappa, G., & Abbate, T. (2016). Island cruise tourism development: A resident's perspective in the context of Italy. *Current Issues in Tourism, 19*(13), 1372–1385.

D'Hauteserre, A. (2011). Politics of imaging New Caledonia. *Annals of Tourism Research, 38*(2), 380–402.

Di Giovine, M. A. (2014). The imaginarie dialectic and the refashioning of Pietrelcina. In N. B. Salazar & N. H. Grabun (Eds.), *Tourism imaginaries anthropological approaches* (pp. 147–172). Berghahn Books.

Echtner, C. M., & Prasad, P. (2003). The context of third world tourism marketing. *Annals of Tourism Research, 30*(3), 660–682.

Edensor, T. (Ed.). (1998). Tourists at the Taj, *Performance and meaning at a symbolic site.* Routledge.

Edensor, T. (2000). Staging tourism – Tourists as performers. *Annals of Tourism Research, 27*(2), 322–344.

Erickson, B. (2018). Anachronistic others and embedded dangers. Race and the logic of whiteness in nature tourism. In B.S.R. Grimwood, K. Caton, and L. Cooke (Eds.), *New moral natures in tourism* (pp. 43–56). Routlege Ethics in Tourism.

Font, X., Guix, M., & Bonilla-Priego, M. J. (2016). Corporate social responsibility in cruising: Using materiality analysis to create shared value. *Tourism Management, 53*, 175–186.

Franklin, A. (2004). Tourism as an ordering. Towards a new ontology of tourism. *Tourist Studies, 4*(3), 277–301.

Freitag, T. G. (1994). Enclave tourism development – For whom the benefits role? *Annals of Tourism Research, 21*(3), 538–554.

Fyall, A. (2019). *Too many tourists? The problem of Overtourism – and how to solve it, Summer 2019, Pegasus.* The Magazine of the University of Central Florida. Retrieved November 13, from https://www.ucf.edu/pegasus/too-many-tourists/

Galvani, A., Lew, A. A., & Sotelo Perez, M. (2020). COVID-19 is expanding global consciousness and the sustainability of travel and tourism. *Tourism Geographies, 22*(3), 567–576. https://doi.org/10.1080/14616688.2020.1760924

Gao, B. W., Zhang, H., & Decosta, P. L. (2011). Phantasmal destination: A post-modernist perspective. *Annals of Tourism Research, 39*(1), 197–220.

Getz, D. (1987). Capacity to absorb tourism – Concepts and implications for strategic planning. *Annals of Tourism Research, 10*(2), 239–261.

Giuffrida, A. (2021). Monsters or a must? Venice tussles with return of cruise shops. The Guardian. Retrieved June 14, from https://www.theguardian.com/world/2021/jun/14/monsters-or-a-must-venice-tussles-with-return-of-cruise-ships

Goethe, J. W. (2003). *West-Östlicher divan. insel taschenbuch.* Surkamp Verlag.

Graulund, R. (2009). From (b)edouin to (A)borigine: The myth of the desert noble savage. *History of the Human Sciences, 2*(1), 79–104.

Gutberlet, M. (2016a). Socio-cultural impacts of large-scale cruise tourism in Souq Muttrah. *Fennia, 194*(1), 46–63.

Gutberlet, M. (2016b). Cruise tourist dress behaviors and local-guest reactions in a Muslim country. *Tourism Culture & Communication*, *16*, 15–32.

Gutberlet, M. (2017). Staging the Oriental Other: Imaginaries and performances of German-speaking cruise tourists. Published online first and in 2019, *Tourist Studies*, *19*(1), 110–137.

Gutberlet, M. (2020). "They just buy a karak and leave" – Overtourism in Souq Muttrah, The Sultanate of Oman, *Zeitschrift für Tourismuswissenschaften*, De Gruyter Oldenburg, 13 October. https://doi.org/10.1515/tw-2020-0004

Gutberlet, M. (2021). Valuing social capital and a legacy: "The old shops are the beauty of the place. In J. Saarinen & J. Richardson (Eds.), *Change in tourism/ tourism in change* (pp. 135–150). Routledge Publishing House.

Gutberlet, M. (2022a). Geopolitical imaginaries and cultural ecosystem services (CES) in the desert. *Tourism Geographies*, *24*, 4–5.

Gutberlet, M. (2022b). *Insight 288: Tourist bubbles and climate change in the GCC*. COP 27 and Climate Action in the Middle East, Middle East Institute, National University of Singapore, October 24.

Haldrup, M., & Larsen, J. (2010). *Tourism, performance and the everyday: Consuming the orient*. Routledge.

Hall, C. M., & Tucker, H. (2004). Tourism and postcolonialism. An introduction. In C. Hall & M. Tucker (Eds.) (pp. 1–23), Kindle Ebook for PC. *Tourism and postcolonialism*. Routledge.

Hall, C., Prayag, G., & Amore, A. (2008). *Tourism and resilience: Individual, organisational and destination perspectives*. Channel View Publications.

Harvey, D. (1989). *The condition of postmodernity*. Blackwell.

Harvey, D. (2020). *Anti-Capitalist politics in the time of COVID-19*. Retrieved November 30, 2020, from www.davidharvey.com

Heidegger, M. (2010). *Being and time*. Translated by Joan Stambaugh. State University of New York Press.

Henthorpe, T. (2000). An analysis of expenditures by cruise ship passengers in Jamaica. *Journal of Travel Research* (38)3, 246–250.

Higgins-Desbiolles, F. (2019). The dark side of the 'mega' cruise ships that have revolutionised travel. Retrieved June 5, from https://www.abc.net.au/news/2019-06-05/the-problem-with-cruise-ships/11174110

Higgins-Desbiolles, F. (2021). The "war over tourism": Challenges to sustainable tourism in the tourism academy after COVID-19, *Journal of Sustainable Tourism*, *29*(4), 551–569.

Hodes, S.;,Boisen, M., Hoffschulte, C., Mosk, I., & Arts, J. (2018). Spread and overtourism. In *Amsterdam in progress* (AiP) (12 issue). Amsterdam in Progress. Retrieved September 2018, from www.amsterdaminprogress.com

Holden, A. (2008). *Environment and tourism*. Routledge Introductions in Environment Series, 2nd ed. Routledge.

Howard, C. (2012). Speeding up and slowing down: Pilgrimage and slow travel through time. In S. Fullagar, K. Markwell, & E. Wilson (Eds.), *Slow tourism. Experiences and mobilities*. Channel View Publications.

Ioannides, I., & Gyimóthy, S. (2020). The COVID-19 crisis as an opportunity for escaping the unsustainable global tourism path. *Tourism Geographies*, *22*(3), 624–632. https://doi.org/10.1080/14616688.2020.1763445

Jaakson, R. (2004). Beyond the tourist bubble? Cruise ship passengers in port. *Annals of Tourism Research*, *31*(1), 44–60.

Jafari, J. (1987). Tourism models: the sociocultural aspects. *Tourism Management* 8(2), 151–159.

Jamal, T., & Higham, J. (2021). Justice and ethics: Towards a new platform for tourism and sustainability. *Journal of Sustainable Tourism, 29*(2–3), 143–157.

Jansson, A. (2002). Spatial phantasmagoria: The mediatisation of tourism experience. *European Journal of Communication, 17*(4), 429–433.

Jennings, G., & Weiler, B. (2006). Mediating meaning: Perspectives on brokering quality tourist experiences. In G. Jennings & N. Polovitz Nickerson (Eds.), *Quality tourism experiences* (pp. 57–78). Elsevier Butterworth-Heinemann.

Johnson, D. (2006). Providing ecotourism excursions for cruise passengers. *Journal of Sustainable Tourism, 14*(1), 43–54.

Jovicic, J. (2000). L'Habitus touristique: Le cas des Lettres d'Orient (1800–1900). *French Cultural Studies, 11*, 101–116.

Junemo, M (2004). Let's build a palm island! Playfulness in complex times. In M. Sheller and J. Urry (Eds.), *Tourism mobilities, places to play, places in play.* Routledge.

Kay, J. (2018). Wonderings? Has tourism become toxic in 2018? *Lonely Planet Blog.* Retrieved January 13, 2019, from https://www.lonelyplanet.com/blog/2018/11/23/wonderings-has-tourism-become-toxic-in-2018

Klein, R. A. (2011). Responsible cruise tourism: Issues of cruise tourism and sustainability. *Journal of Hospitality and Tourism Management, 18*, 107–116.

Koens, K., Postma, A., & Papp, B. (2019). Management strategies for overtourism – From adaptation to system change. In H. Pechlaner, E. Innerhofer, & G. Erschbamer (Eds.), *Overtourism, tourism management and solutions.* Routledge.

Krippendorf, J. (1987). *The holiday makers.* Butterworth-Heinemann.

Larsen, S., & Wolff, K. (2016). Exploring assumptions about cruise tourists' visits to ports. *Tourism Management Perspectives, 17*, 44–49.

Larsen, S., Wolff, K., Marnburg, E., & Ogaard, T. (2013). Belly full purse closed. *Tourism Management Perspectives, 6*, 142–148.

Leite, N. (2014). Afterword. Locating imaginaries in the anthropology of tourism. In N. Salazar & N. Grabun (Eds.), *Tourism imaginaries. Anthropological approaches* (pp. 260–278). Berghahn Books.

Lew, A., Cheer, J. M., Haywood, M., Brouder, P., & Salazar, N. B. (2020). Visions of travel and tourism after the global COVID-19 transformation of 2020. *Tourism Geographies, 22*(3), 455–466. https://doi.org/10.1080/14616688.2020.1770326

Ljubica, J., & Dulcic, Z. (2012). Megaships and developing cultural tourism in Dubrovnik. In A. Papathanassis, T. Lukovic, & M. Vogel (Eds.), *Cruise tourism and society* (pp. 17–28). Springer Verlag.

Logossah, R. (2011). L'industrie de croisière dans la Caraibe: Facteur de développement ou pale reflet de la mondialisation? In R. Kiminou (Ed.), *Economie et droit des affaires de la caraibe et de la Guyane* (pp. 17–34). Editions Publibook.

London, W. R., & Lohmann, G. (2014). Power in the context of cruise destination stakeholders' interrelationships. *Research in Transportation Business & Management, 13*, 24–35.

Lopes, J. M., & Dredge, D. (2018). Cruise tourism shore excursions: Value for destinations? *Journal of Tourism Planning and Development, 16*(6), 633–652.

MacCannell, D. (1999). *The tourist – A new theory of the leisure class.* University of California Press.

MacCannell, D. (2011). *The ethics of sightseeing.* University of California Press.

MacNeill, T., & Wozniak, D. (2008). The economic, social and environmental impacts of cruise tourism. *Tourism Management, 66,* 387–404.

Månsson, M. (2011). Mediatized tourism. *Annals of Tourism Research, 38*(4), 1634–1652.

Maroldt, L. (2017, August 10). Auch Gästen muss man Grenzen setzen. *Der Tagesspiegel.* Retrieved January 25, 2019, from https://www.tagesspiegel.de/politik/tourismusboom-in-berlin-auch-gaesten-muss-man-grenzen-setzen/20175536.html

Martin, M. (2004). *Deserts of the earth – Extraordinary images of extreme environments.* Thames & Hudson.

Milano, C., & Koens, K. (2021). The paradox of tourism extremes. Excesses and restraints in times of COVID-19. *Current Issues in Tourism.* https://doi.org/10.1080/13683500.2021.1908967

Milano, C., Novelli, M., & Cheer, J. M. (2019). Overtourism and degrowth: A social movements perspective. *Journal of Sustainable Tourism.* https://doi.org/10.1080/09669582.2019.1650054

Minca, C. (2012). No country for old men. In C. Minca & T. Oakes (Eds.), *Real tourism: Practice, care and politics in contemporary travel culture, contemporary geographies of leisure* (pp. 478–1045). Tourism and Mobility.

Mordue, T. (2005). Tourism, performance and social exclusion in "Olde York". *Annals of Tourism Research, 32*(1), 179–198.

Morgan, N., & Pritchard, A. (1998). Tourism promotion and power. *Creating images, creating identities.* John Wiley and Sons.

Mostafanezhad, M., & Norum, R. (2016). Towards a geopolitics of tourism. *Annals of Tourism Research, 61*(C), 226–228.

Mowforth, M., & Munt, I. (Eds.). (2009). *Tourism and sustainability. Development, globalisation and new tourism in the third world.* Routledge.

Musavengane, R., & Kloppers, R. (2020). Social capital: An investment towards community resilience in the collaborative natural resources management of community-based tourism schemes. *Tourism Management Perspectives, 34,* 100654.

Niemantsverdriet, T. (2018). *Amsterdam mag doorgaan met weren van toeristenwinkels.* https://www.nrc.nl/nieuws/2018/12/19/amsterdam-mag-doorgaan-met-weren-van-toeristenwinkels-a3126410.

OECD (2020, December 1). *OECD economic outlook* (Vol. 2020, Issue 2: Preliminary version). OECD Publishing. https://doi.org/10.1787/39a88ab1-en.

O'Reilly, A. M. (1986). Tourism carrying capacity: Concepts and issues. *Tourism Management, 7*(4), 254–258.

Palmer, A., König-Lewis, N., & Jones, L. E. M. (2013). The effects of residents' social identity and involvement on their advocacy of incoming tourism. *Tourism Management, 38,* 142–151.

Palmer, C. (1994). Tourism and colonialism. The experience of the Bahamas. *Annals of Tourism Research, 21*(4), 792–811.

Park, H. (2014). *Heritage tourism.* Routledge.

Piketty, T. (2020). *Capital and ideology* (Kindle ed.). Harvard University Press.

Pine, B. J. II, & Gilmore, J. H. (2011). *The experience economy* (Updated ed.), Kindle Ebook for PC. Harvard Business Review Press.

Pink, S. (2008). An urban tour. The sensory sociality of ethnography place-making. *Ethnography, 9*(2), 175–196.

Poggioli, S. (2013). In Venice, huge cruise ships bring tourists and complaints. Retrieved July 13, 2014, from http://ww.npr.org/blogs/parallels/2013/07/15/202347080/In-Venice-Huge-Cruise-Ships-Bring-Tourists-And-Complaints

Portes, A. (1998). Social capital: Its origins and applications in modern sociology. *Annual Review of Sociology, 24*, 1–24.

Pourjafar, M., Amini, M., Varzaneh, E. H., & Mahdavinejad, M. (2014). Role of bazaars as a unifying factor in traditional cities of Iran: The Isfahan bazaar. *Frontiers of Architectural Research, 3*, 10–19.

Putnam, R. (1993). *Making democracy work: Civic traditions in modern Italy*. Princeton University Press.

Qubein, N. (2020). Where are cruise ships built? *The Cruise Critic*. Retrieved June 17, 2021, from https://www.cruisecritic.com/articles.cfm?ID=3929

Renaud, L. (2017). Résister au débarquement: Tourisme de croisière et dynamiques territoriales au Québec et dans la Caraïbe. *RITA* [online], N°10. Retrieved July, from http://revue-rita.com/thema/resister-au-debarquement-tourisme-de-croisiere-et-dynamiques-territoriales-quebec-caraibe.html

Renaud, L. (2020). Reconsidering global mobility—Distancing from mass cruise tourism in the aftermath of COVID-19. *Tourism Geographies, 22*(3), 679–689.

Ritzer, G., & Liska, A. (1997). 'McDisneyzation' and 'Post-Tourism'–Complementary perspectives on contemporary tourism. In C. Royek & J. Urry (Eds.), *Touring cultures. Transformation of travel and theory* (pp. 98–109). Routledge.

Rodaway, P. (2002). Sensuous geographies: Body. *Sense and place*, Kindle Ebook for PC. Taylor and Francis e-Library.

Ruete, E. (2004). *Memoiren einer arabischen Prinzessin*. Gallery Publications.

Ryan, C. (2002). The time of our lives' or time for our lives: An examination of time in holidaying. In C. Ryan (Ed.), *The tourist experience* (pp. 201–220). Thomson Learning.

Saarinen, J. (2006). Traditions of sustainability in tourism studies. *Annals of Tourism Research, 33*(4), 1121–1140.

Saarinen, J. (2017). Enclavic tourism spaces: Territorialization and bordering in tourism destination development and planning. *Tourism Geographies, 19*(3), 425–437.

Saarinen, J. (2021). Tourism for change. Change management towards sustainable tourism development. In J. Saarinen & J. Richardson (Eds.), *Change in tourism/tourism in change* (pp. 135–150). Routledge Publishing House.

Said, A. A. (1989). The paradox of development in the Middle East. *Futures*, 619–627.

Said, E. (2003). *Orientalism*. Modern Classics Penguin Books.

Salazar, N. B. (2005). Tourism and glocalisation "local" tour guiding. *Annals of Tourism Research, 32*(3), 628–646.

Salazar, N. B. (2006). Touristifying Tanzania. Local guides, global discourse. *Annals of Tourism Research, 33*(3), 833–852.

Salazar, N. B. (2010). *Envisioning Eden: Mobilizing imaginaries in tourism and beyond*. Berghahn Books.

Salazar, N. B., & Grabun, N. H. H. (Eds.). (2014). Introduction. Toward an anthropology of tourism imaginaries. *Tourism imaginaries anthropological approaches* (pp. 1–28). Berghahn Books.

Santos, P. A. (2014). The imagine nation: The mystery of the endurance of the colonial imaginary in postcolonial times. In N. B. Salazar & N. H. H. Grabun (Eds.), *Toward an anthropology of imaginaries. Tourism imaginaries, anthropological approaches* (pp. 194–219). Berghahn Books.

Saveriades, A. (2000). Establishing the social tourism carrying capacity for the tourist resorts of the east coast of the Republic of Cyprus. *Tourism Management, 21*(2), 147–156.

Schemmann, B. (2012). User-driven innovation concepts and the cruise industry. In A. Papathanassis, T. Lukovic, & M. Vogel (Eds.), *Cruise tourism and society* (pp. 153–172). Springer Verlag.

Séraphin, H., Sheeran, P., & Pilato, M. (2018). Over-tourism and the fall of Venice as a destination. *Journal of Destination Marketing & Management, 9*, 374–376.

Séraphin, H., Zaman, M., Olver, S., Bourliataux-Lajoinie, & Dosquet, F. (2019). Destination branding and overtourism. *Journal of Hospitality and Tourism Management, 38*, 1–4.

Sheller, M. (2003). Consuming the Caribbean. *From Arawaks to Zombies*. Routledge.

Smith, M. K., & Diekmann, A. (2017). Tourism and wellbeing. *Annals of Tourism Research, 66*, 1–13.

Smith, V. L. (1989). Introduction. In V. Smith (Ed.), *Hosts and guests* (pp. 1–14). University of Pennsylvania Press.

Sönmez, S. (2001). Tourism behind the veil of Islam: Women and development in the Middle East. In Y. Apostolopoulos, S. Sönmez, & D. J. Timothy (Eds.), *Women as producers and consumers of tourism in developing regions* (pp. 113–142). Praeger.

Soulard, J., Knollenberg, W., Boley, B. B., & Perdue, R. R. (2018). Social capital and destination strategic planning. *Tourism Management, 69*, 189–200.

Statista (2021). Number of international tourist arrivals worldwide from 1950 to 2020, released in October 2012. Retrieved November 13, from https://www.statista.com/statistics/209334/total-number-of-international-tourist-arrivals/

Swain, M. B. (2014). Myth management in Tourism's imaginariums: Tales from southwest China and beyond. In N. B. Salazar & N. H. H. Grabun (Eds.), *Tourism imaginaries: Anthropological approaches* (pp. 103–125). Berghahn Books.

Tanzanian Government Portal. (2016). *History*. Retrieved December 18, 2016, from http://www.tanzania.go.tz/home/pages/72

Telfer, D. J. (2003). Development issues in destination communities. In S. Sing, D. J. Timothy, & R. K. Dowling (Eds.), *Tourism in destination communities* (pp. 155–180). CABI Publishing.

Thesiger, W. (2007). *Across the empty quarter, the Arabian desert, 1947*. Penguin Great Journeys No. 19. Penguin Books.

Tuan, Y. F. (1978). Space, time, place: A humanistic perspective. In T. Carlstein, D. Prakes, & N.Thrift (Eds.), *Timing space and spacing time* (Vol. 1). Arnold.

Tucker, H., & Akama, J. (2010). Tourism as postcolonialism. In T. Jamal & M. Robinson (Eds.), *The handbook of tourism studies* (pp. 504–520). Sage Publications.

Urbain (1993). L'Idiot du voyage. Histoires de touristes. Paris: Editions Payot et Rivages Urry, J. (1995). *Consuming places*. Routledge.

Urbanowicz, C. (1989). Tourism in Tonga revisited: Continued troubled times? In V. Smith (Ed.), *Hosts and guests* (pp. 105–117). University of Pennsylvania Press.

Urry, J. (1995). *Consuming places*. Routledge.

Urry, J., & Larsen, J. (Eds.). (2011). *The tourist gaze 3.0*. Sage Publications.

Vidal de la Blache, P., Martonne, E. D., & Bingham, M. T. (1965). Principles of Human Geography, Constable S.I.

Vogel, M. P., & Oschmann, C. (2013). Cruising through liquid modernity. *Tourist Studies, 13*(1), 62–80.

Wagner, L., & Minca, C. (2015). Topographies of the Kasbah route: Hardening of a heritage trail. *Tourist Studies*, 17, 1–27.

Wahab, S., & Pigram, J. J. (1997). Tourism and sustainability – Policy considerations. In S. Wahab, & J. Pigram (Eds.), *Tourism and sustainability in tourism, sustainability and growth* (pp. 277–290). Routledge.

Waldinger, R. (1995). The 'other side' of embeddedness: A case-study of the interplay of economy and ethnicity. *Ethnic and Racial Studies*, *18(3)*, 555–580.

Wall, G. (1997). Sustainable tourism – Unsustainable development. In S. Wahab & J. J. Pigram (Eds.), *Tourism and sustainability in tourism, sustainability and growth* (pp. 33–49). Routledge.

Wang, N. (1999). Rethinking authenticity in tourism experience. *Annals of Tourism Research*, *26*(2), 340–370.

Wang, Y. (2007). Customized authenticity begins at home. *Annals of Tourism Research*, *34*(3), 789–804.

Weaver, A. (2005a). The McDonaldization thesis and cruise tourism. *Annals of Tourism Research*, *32*(2), 346–366.

Weaver, A. (2005b). Spaces of containment and revenue capture: 'Super-Sized' cruise ships as mobile tourism enclaves. *Tourism Geographies: An International Journal of Tourism Space, Place and Environment*, *7*(2), 165–184.

Weeden, C., Lester, J. A., & Thyne, M. (2011). Cruise tourism: Emerging issues and implications for a maturing industry. *Journal of Hospitality and Tourism Management*, *18*, 26–29.

Wels, H. (2004). About romance and reality. Popular European imagery in postcolonial tourism in Southern Africa. In C. M. Hall & H. Tucker (Eds.), *Tourism and postcolonialism* (pp. 76–193), Kindle Ebook for PC. Routledge ELibrary.

Wilkinson, P. F. (1999). Caribbean cruise tourism: Delusion? Illusion? *Tourism Geographies: An International Journal of Tourism Space, Place and Environment*, *1*(3), 261–282.

Williams, S., & Lew, A. A. (Eds.). (2015). *Tourism geography. Critical understandings of place, space and experience* (3rd ed.). Routledge.

Wood, R. (2000). Caribbean cruise tourism: Globalization at sea. *Annals of Tourism Research*, *27*(2), 345–370.

Wu, M.-Y., Wall, G., & Pearce, L. (2014). Shopping experiences: International tourists in Bejings Silk Market. *Tourism Management*, *41*, 96–106.

Yarnal, C. M., & Kerstetter, D. (2005). Casting off—An exploration of cruise ship space, group behavior and social interaction. *Journal of Travel Research*, *43*, 268–379.

# 3  The research setting

To accommodate an increasing demand by mega-cruise companies for port services, governments on the Arabian Peninsula have been expanding rapidly their ports in the past decade. This chapter seeks to link my study on overtourism and mega-cruise tourism with its setting on the Arabian Peninsula. I will introduce the geographic, historic, economic and sociocultural environment of my research.

The first sections look at general information about the Sultanate of Oman and its modern history, developing from a remote underdeveloped country to a modern economy based on oil and gas exports and its recent diversification efforts including tourism development. Tourism promises to create jobs for the young population. I will highlight the fast development of mega-cruise tourism. This is followed by an introduction to my case study locations that are visited during popular day-tours offered by mega-cruise ships. These are an urban destination Souq Muttrah, an ancient market, the main trading place until the 1970s, located just opposite the cruise terminal in the bay of Muttrah in Muscat and a peripheral destination, an oasis settlement and the Sharqiyah Sands desert located in the Interior, around 200 kilometres from the capital Muscat.

## The Sultanate of Oman – The Jewel of Arabia

The Sultanate of Oman has a long history as a seafaring country. Trade and exchange have been a major part of the economy. Because of its diverse landscape, the Sultanate has been called the *Jewel of Arabia* and the *Arabian Switzerland*, because of its neutrality and mediation in numerous peace talks in the Middle East, e.g. in the war in Yemen, the 3.5-year economic blockade in Qatar (Ramani, 2021) and the secret nuclear talks with Iran leading to the Iran nuclear deal in 2015 (Al Jazeera, 2020).

The Omani people have been used to interacting with different cultures from different continents. Located on the North-eastern tip of the Arabian Peninsula, neighbouring the United Arab Emirates, Saudi Arabia and Yemen. From the sea, the Sultanate of Oman is surrounded by the Strait of Hormuz, the Arabian Gulf, the Sea of Oman and the Indian Ocean.

DOI: 10.4324/9780429424946-3

Since the 1970s and the exploration of oil and gas, Oman has experienced fast economic development under the late H.M. Sultan Qaboos bin Said Al Said. This was the start of the so-called *Renaissance*. Under the late Sultan Qaboos' rule, the country developed into the modern state that it is today (Oxford Business Group, 2019). He has symbolized a caring father of a young nation, a strong, wise political leader and the head of a country within a prospering but geopolitically volatile Arabian Gulf region. Late H. M. Sultan Qaboos died, aged 79, on 11 January 2020. He was an absolute monarch and the longest serving ruler in the Arab world (BBC, 2020). For the Omani people, he represented not only a strong leader but a father who listened attentively to the people, especially during his legendary annual *meet the people tours* around the Sultanate. Since January 2020, H. M. Sultan Haitham bin Tarik Al Said, one of his cousins, the former Minister of Heritage and Culture was sworn in before the ruling family council. He has been ruling the country since then (Al Jazeera, 2020).

In 1970, when late H. M. Sultan Qaboos took over the power from his father, the population of Oman was only around 724,000 people, with an average age of 17 years, compared to 5.2 million inhabitants and the median age of Omanis was 30.6 years in 2021. Nowadays, 87% of the Omani population lives in cities (Worldometer, 2021), whereas in the past the majority lived in rural areas. Around 80% of them derived their livelihoods from agriculture, animal husbandry and fishing (Merschen, 2007). Until the 1970s, Oman was isolated internationally and the country was sparsely populated. Until that time, the Sultanate was lacking in basic infrastructure, having only a few kilometres of paved roads between Muttrah and Old Muscat, in addition to a small airport that was located in the present main business district of Ruwi. Traders arrived by boat or by camel at Souq Muttrah, which was the main marketplace in Oman. Roads were built from the 1970s onwards. That was the time when cars were introduced as part of the social and economic development of the Sultanate. Prior to this, boats, camels and donkeys were the main means of transportation. A journey from the interior to the coastal city of Muscat took many days. Nowadays, fast and luxury cars including SUVs are a symbol of modernization and social status. Slower modes of transportation like buses and bicycles are seen as a symbol of backwardness, linked with slowness, race and social status. Bicycles are used as a means of transportation by low-income male expatriates from Asia who cannot afford a car. On weekends, some male Omanis use bicycles for leisure purpose, but not as a mode of transportation as, for example in Europe or Southeast Asia. In adventure tourism, camels and donkeys are occasionally used as modes of transportation for luggage in some remote areas that are not accessible by cars, e.g. along hiking paths. This contrast between the rural and the urban tourism development within "liquid modernity" (Bauman, 2000) has been part of my research in two locations.

In 2019, the year when international tourism came to a sudden standstill, the total population had reached 4.675 million, comprising 57.40% Omanis and 42.60% expatriates (NCSI, 2019). The Governorate of Muscat has the highest expatriate population share. As a consequence of the economic downturn and Omanisation measures, prioritizing the creation of jobs for the Omani youth, between March 2020 and March 2021, a total of 218,000 expatriates had left their jobs (Times News Service, 2021a). Most of them returned to their home countries due to unemployment, accelerated by falling oil prices, an uncertain economic future and a high unemployment rate among the youth. In the following, I will elaborate on the two research locations.

## Souq Muttrah

Souq Muttrah is the oldest central market in the Sultanate of Oman. It is located in the bay of Muttrah in Muscat (see Figure 3.1). The souq has been the heart of the city's seafaring trade. The Muttrah district has been the central commercial hub of Oman since the Portuguese occupation in the 16th century (Gaube, 2012). Muscat harbour was colonized by the Portuguese, Persian and Ottoman empires (Causevic & Neal, 2019). Along with the coastal city of Sur, both places were key hubs for a hidden, dark side of the Omani history. The slave trade from Africa, a very sensitive taboo subject in Oman, where social divisions and inequalities are not discussed publicly (Causevic & Neal, 2019, p. 512). Traditionally, Souq Muttrah was called the *dark souq* since there was no electricity and the souq closed during sunset. It has been divided into two areas: one for retail and one for wholesale where food, household items, textiles and traditional Omani clothes are sold.

Until the 1970s, Souq Muttrah was the central trading hub in the Sultanate, linking farmers, traders and craftsmen from outside Oman with their counterparts in the interior of the country. Traders arrived by boat or by camel at the souq. The souq was already mentioned as being a meeting place for the multi-ethnic community from India and Pakistan (Richardson & Dörr, 2003; Scholz, 1990). It was a meeting place where the male communities gathered to exchange news, to work and to trade. At that time, women were not seen in the souq. Males went to the souq: Arab and Gulf traders, merchants and labourers from India and Baluchistan, crews and passengers from ships seeking anchorage and supplies in Muttrah. Also converging at the souq were Omani villagers, including Bedouin tribesmen from the interior and urban residents alike came to the souq to buy, sell and barter (Richardson & Dörr, 2003, p. 214). Because of these commercial activities, Muttrah had a lively, multi-ethnic community consisting of Arabs, Africans from East Africa and Zanzibar, Baluchis from Baluchistan (a province in Pakistan) as well as Persians and Indians. Because most of its inhabitants migrated to Oman in the past, especially the multi-ethnic population of Muttrah has been very welcoming and open to trade and international tourism (Gutberlet, 2021).

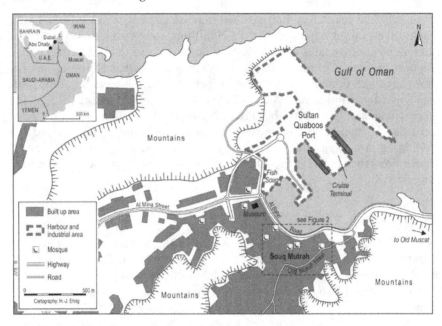

*Figure 3.1* Map of the district of Muttrah, including Souq Muttrah and Port Sultan
        Qaboos

Source: Map by Ehrig, RWTH Aachen University.

Since the 1970s and the reign of the Late Sultan Qaboos bin Said Al Said,
the rapid economic development was followed by the introduction of large
supermarkets. Ultimately, Muttrah lost its importance as a major commercial hub. Vendors lost their customers and some businesses moved to other
newly built districts. Scholz (1990) observed structural changes occurring
in Souq Muttrah during the late 1970s and 1980s when the souq developed
from a traditional market predominantly providing textiles, food and household items for locals to a souq that catered more and more to the increasing
Asian, Arab and European expatriate communities.

Up to today, Muttrah has one of the largest number of expatriates living
within a densely populated area. In 2018, there were 218,027 Asian expatriates
living in Muttrah, accounting for the majority of the local population. Omanis
numbered 64,089 (Nair, 2019). Nowadays, the large majority of the expatriate vendors in Muttrah do not belong to the well-established Banyan trading
families, but they are newly arrived vendors from Asia, especially from India,
Pakistan and Bangladesh. Most of them live and work within walking distance. Up to today, many Omanis and expatriates living in Muttrah buy their
groceries, household items and textiles in the souq. Due to cheaper prices,
Omanis from the interior of the country come to buy household items, local
perfumes, textiles and readymade clothes. According to the Wali (governor)

of Muttrah, around 800 shops were located in Muttrah in 2012. All the shops were licensed by Muscat Municipality (Gutberlet, 2016a, 2020, 2021). There were no regulations regarding the cultural heritage management in place, e.g. building regulations and the type of products on sale in Souq Muttrah. In the following, I will elaborate on the geography and the sociocultural and economic setting of the oasis and the Sharqiyah Sands desert.

## The oasis and the Sharqiyah Sands desert

The Sharqiyah region (see Figure 3.2) is the third most densely populated region in the Sultanate of Oman, having a total population of around half a million inhabitants, located in the North-east of the country (NCSI, 2019).

*Figure 3.2* Map of the Sultanate of Oman including Sharqiyah Sands desert

Source: Schneider, Bonn University, 2018.

Since the introduction of tourism in Oman, old oasis settlements, forts, castles, museums and archaeological sites have been promoted as heritage sites and connected with the capital Muscat by road. The distance from Muscat to the desert is approximately 250 kilometres. Between 2013 and 2019, a large highway connecting Muscat and the Sharqiyah region was constructed. The highway facilitates access to the oasis settlements and the Sharqiyah Sands desert.

Agriculture has been "the cultural and economic backbone" in Northern Oman, where a total of 2,663 oases are located (Lűdeling & Bűrkert, 2010, p. 28). Following the discovery of oil and the resulting socio-economic changes in the 1970s, the importance of oasis settlements has reduced extensively (Gangler & Gaube, 2012; Merschen, 2001). The capital of the Sharqiyah region is Sur, an ancient port and seafaring town. Sur was a leading trading hub for products and people between Oman, East Africa (in particular Tanzania and Zanzibar) and India. The transportation of local products like fish and dates was conducted by Bedouin tribes who organized camel caravans for local traders until the late 1960s. With the modernization of the country and the construction of roads from the 1970s onwards, the organization of trade changed significantly. As a result, Bedouins were no longer needed for transporting local products and the importance of local trade declined (Hoek, 1998, p. 172), which resulted in reduced job opportunities. In the past 20 years, the Sharqiyah region developed as a transit region. Many Omani families moved to the capital Muscat where there are more job opportunities. They only return to their family homes in the interior on weekends. Its desert, the Sharqiyah Sands, and its surrounding oases have developed as a "transit destination", where tourists pass through for a few hours or overnight. Some stay in a desert camp, doing wild camping or they stay overnight in small hotels in Sur. The ancient trading oasis of Al Mudairib is a relatively new tourist destination on the edge of the desert; about 2.5 hours' drive from Muscat.

The old centre of the oasis has a falaj system (ancient irrigation system) that runs through the fields, a privately owned heritage museum, an old souq (market), built of traditional sarooj building material, which however erodes slowly, with each rainfall (see Figure 3.3). The area is not functional (Gutberlet, 2019). These old buildings and the marketplace are public spaces shared by locals and tourists alike. The place is surrounded by lush green oasis farms (Figure 3.4).

Tourists usually come to the marketplace in the morning hours, while local males meet there during the cooler afternoons and in the evenings.

In recent years, the Sharqiyah Sands desert has become a nature and adventure destination (Gutberlet, 2019, 2022a). The desert tourism that has developed in Sharqiyah Sands can be compared with desert tourism development in Morocco (Wagner & Minca, 2016). However, nowadays the desert tribes live in recently built cement houses located on the edge of

*Figure 3.3* The old souq area in Mudhairib

Source: Gutberlet (2013).

*Figure 3.4* Lush greenery in the oasis in Al Mudhairib

Source: Gutberlet (2013).

the desert. Some Bedouins still own desert huts, where they welcome tourists during the cooler winter months. Local residents from the oasis towns nearby started rather unplanned and unmonitored, small-scale tourism in Sharqiyah Sands with the first guesthouse built beside the main street, the Al Qabil Resthouse. The first tourist camp was set-up in 1990. By 2002, there were six desert camps in Sharqiyah Sands. These were mainly palm frond huts in the style of traditional Bedouin accommodation (Merschen, 2007). Between 2002 and 2013, the number of camps doubled, according to Omani camp owners. In 2013, a total of 12 desert camps existed, most of them luxury, concrete-built camps with up to 200 beds, having water and electricity (Gutberlet, 2019).

Day-visitors like weekend tourists from the capital Muscat and mega-cruise tourists drive often in large convoys of more than 10 cars to the desert, where they stay for two to three hours and then drive back to Muscat (Gutberlet, 2019). Until 2021, there were no existing regulations, limiting the number of cars driving into the desert sands, although I was told by the Ministry of Tourism in 2018 that restrictions would be implemented soon. In the previous paragraphs, I have briefly outlined the research locations. In the following sections, I will elaborate on the fast growth of tourism development and the economy in Oman.

## Tourism development

Initially, tourism was limited to the wealthy elite from the West including business travellers like traders, consuls, advisers and representatives of oil companies. In the 1980s, the country opened up slowly to international tourism along with its neighbouring countries. At around the same time, the first road connecting Muscat with its main airport with the interior regions was built (Gutberlet, 2019). Tourism was seen as a small-scale activity, focusing on business and luxury tourism with the setting up of a modern infrastructure with hotels, roads and airports (Gutberlet, 2017).

Similar to other emerging small destinations around the world, tourism in Oman has been a tool to boost and diversify the local economy, create employment for a booming, young population as well as a tool to serve as an alternative to oil and gas exports, of which have been on the decline (Gutberlet, 2020, 2022a). The Oman Five-Year Development Plan 1996–2020, coupled with the so-called Oman Vision 2020, aimed at achieving "sustainable development through the diversification of the economy, without relying solely on oil as the major source of income" (Ministry of Environment and Climate Affairs, 2012, p. 10). The Vision 2020 development strategy focused on a transition from an oil-based economy to a knowledge-based economy through ongoing human development programmes in different sectors, including tourism and an increased support for small and medium-sized companies and "Omanisation", a policy with a quota system that prioritizes Omanis against expatriates in the workplace (Gutberlet, 2021). The strategic tourism plan, the National Tourism Strategy 2040 (NTS), was launched in 2016 with its main goal to increase the number of international tourist arrivals to reach 11.7 million by 2040 and to increase the sector's share of the GDP to more than 6% (Oxford Business Group, 2019). The mission of the Oman Tourism Strategy 2040 is to diversify the economy and to create jobs through exceptional tourism experiences and with Omani personalities, strengthening local pride and identity, developing tourism SMEs, cultivating the Omani culture, heritage and local traditions (Innovative Tourism Advisors, 2016).

Tourism infrastructure has been developed predominantly in the Northern regions of Oman, in the capital area of Muscat, in Al Dakhiliyah and in Al Batinah region. Muscat has the major tourism infrastructure including Muscat International Airport. A Gulf Cooperation Council (GCC) railway project, connecting the main cities along the coastline of the peninsula has been planned but not realized yet. International tourism in Oman is seasonal, between October and March. In winter, cruise ships anchor in Muscat, Salalah in the South and in Khasab, located in the far Northern region of Oman, Musandam. In summer, temperatures can reach up to over 50 degrees; however, they are 10 degrees lower in the South of Oman, in the Dhofar region, compared to the rest of the peninsula. During the monsoon rainy season, the Dhofar region turns into a popular destination for visitors from the GCC region.

In mid-2019, the Middle East recorded USD73 billion in tourism receipts in the region witnessing high investments in tourism development (UNWTO, 2019). Countries from the GCC were boosting their infrastructures to accommodate tourists from abroad: From October 2021 to March 2022, the Expo 2020 was held in Dubai with 159 pavilions, showcasing their cultures and innovative technologies, while Qatar has been preparing for the FIFA World Cup 2022. Both events may have a spill-over effect for Oman, when COVID-19 entry restrictions are eased and new highly contagious COVID-19 variants do not appear.

Until 2020, the outbreak of the COVID-19 pandemic and the worldwide lockdown, the Middle East and Asia were seen as the world's fastest emerging tourism markets. With 3.5 million international visitors in 2019, compared to 1.4 million in 2010, the Sultanate was focusing on a continuous tourism development strategy (Table 3.1). In the same year, tourism's contribution to the GDP was 2.5%. This was in line with the vision of the government, focusing more on niche tourism like adventure and nature-based tourism such as hiking, climbing or diving and cultural tourism (Kothaneth, 2017), thus attracting tourists beyond the 'sea, sun and sand' tourism.

A large number of new jobs were created in the tourism sector in the past two decades. A total of 106,731 employees worked in the tourism sector in 2013, most of them in restaurants and coffee shops. The Omanisation rate was 11.2% (Ministry of Tourism, 2015b). Many Omanis were not fully employed and worked as freelancers, e.g. as tour guides. In 2020, 142,247

*Table 3.1* Inbound tourists in Oman

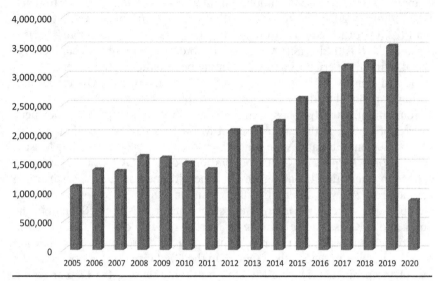

Source: Ministry of Heritage and Tourism (2021).

people worked in the tourism sector; however, the Omanisation rate was low, at 10.9% only (Times News Service, 2021c). The former Minister of Tourism, H.E. Ahmed bin Nasser Al Mahrzi, who was in office until summer 2020, highlighted the need to promote the local workforce in tourism "to involve Omanis as a principal pillar in tourism while promoting luxury tourism". "We want quality tourism and not tourism of numbers", he said on several occasions and the last time when I interviewed him, before the start of the coronavirus pandemic in spring 2020. He stressed that low-cost tourism is not promoted in Oman. He expressed his wish to protect the local identity, its rich history and culture, e.g. in Souq Muttrah, and to offer a unique tourist experience to the world (interviews in July 2012 and in February 2020). To boost more high-end tourist arrivals from Europe, the Sultanate of Oman was chosen as the main sponsoring country of the International Tourism Fair in Berlin (ITB) in March 2020. However, following the sudden outbreak of the coronavirus pandemic worldwide, the ITB was cancelled and international efforts and marketing measures were stopped. In the following months, European representation offices closed, e.g. in Germany and Italy, only the Paris representation office remained open. Moreover, a number of local tour operators in Oman based in Muscat closed down their offices completely or they continued to work remotely from their home countries. To support businesses in the recovery stage after the socially, economically devastating pandemic, the Dean of the College of Business and Political Sciences, Sultan Qaboos University, Al-Mukhtar Al-Abri, suggested: "Businesses and commercial companies should modify their business model after the pandemic by making their structures leaner and more responsive to shocks …. The coronavirus pandemic will lead to restructuring supply chains in many countries and make them more stable and less vulnerable to disruption during crises" (Sultan Qaboos University, 2020). This could lead to more outsourcing in the tourism sector. Already during my field-research in Muscat and in the interior of Oman, the majority of employees who worked especially outdoors in tourism operations, e.g. at luxury hotel swimming pools were outsourced and not part of the regular in-house employees. They had low salaries, little or no social security as well as more work days, compared to full-time employees. A total of 30,000 visitors arrived in Oman in 2020, compared to around 3.5 million in 2019. The tourism sector was one of the most affected sectors of the Omani economy in 2021. According to the new Minister of Heritage and Tourism, H.E. Salim Al Mahrouqi, who was appointed in summer 2020, revenues decreased by 60%. The number of visitors declined by 75% in 2020 and the number of hotel guests dropped by 52%. To counteract these economic impacts, a recovery plan was developed to boost local and regional tourism. The government aims to attract investments totalling around 2 billion OMR by 2024 (Times News Service, 2021b).

## Economic development

With its oil and gas reserves, the Arabian Peninsula is one of the richest regions worldwide. However, the COVID-19 pandemic has severely shocked and slowed down the entire economy in the region and in particular in Oman (Al Shaibany, 2021). In 2020, oil-exporting countries in the Middle East were hit by a double crisis, due to a number of full or half lockdowns, where public life came to a standstill and the sudden fall of oil prices worldwide. Oil and gas exports account for 75% of the Omani government's revenue, compared to 45% of the GDP in Saudi Arabia (Oxford Business Group, 2021). In 2019, the Omani economy was already weak, with the GDP contracting by 0.8% due to different factors: a bloated public workforce (administration), extensive public debts and deficits as well as low international oil prices (Al-Monitor, 2021b). In 2020, the economy contracted by 6.4% (Al-Monitor, 2021b) while the GDP fell by 20% (at current prices) compared to 2019 (Times News Service, 2021a) leading to increased unemployment.

The key factors for economic recovery and a recovery of the people, were a high vaccination rate and innovation within local community's bonding and bridging capital. The vaccination campaign against the COVID-19 virus was slow and the risk of new waves of infection remained high in 2021 (Moody's Analytics, 2021). By July 2021, only 6.7% of the population of 5 million were vaccinated in Oman, compared to 70% in the neighbouring United Arab Emirates (Al-Monitor 2021b). However, a few months later, by

October 2021, more than 70% of the population were vaccinated, according to the Omani government.

Small and medium-sized companies including in the tourism sector were the most affected by the pandemic. A number of tour operators had to close down their operations, freeze salaries, send back their employees to their home countries, e.g. India or the Philippines or they shifted to remote office work. Consequently, part-time work and unemployment increased. To reduce unemployment rates among the youth, a forced retirement scheme was introduced for those Omanis who had completed more than 30 years in the civil service. Moreover, another initiative was the introduction of the value-added tax (VAT) in May 2021. H.M. Sultan Haitham Bin Tarik had already introduced before the outbreak of the pandemic in Oman an economic reform programme with the key goal of having a "leaner, younger and more technocratic government" (Castelier, 2021). Consequently, a large number of government employees in their 50s and 60s had to retire. They were replaced by young Omanis in their 20s and 30s. In May 2021, Sultan Haitham promised to employ 32,000 Omanis in full-time and part-time jobs, after street protests of hundreds of young Omani males broke out in the main cities like Sohar, the industrial hub in the North of the country, and in Salalah, the second largest city in the South of the Sultanate. These protests lasted for several days. They were demanding jobs and more transparency (Castelier, 2021). As a result, one third of the young Omani job-seekers were promised employment in the military, in the civil service and the private sector.

As an incentive, H.M. Sultan Haitham ordered a grant of 200 OMR ($500) per month to private sector companies who employ Omanis. Those who lost their jobs during the pandemic were promised a stipend of 200 OMR ($500) for six months. Around 65,400 people were jobseekers in 2021, with a high-unemployment rate among females who are often highly qualified. About 24,500 jobseekers were male, while 40,900 were female. However, social and culturally defined primary roles at home, as mothers and wives, often prevent women from being fully absorbed in public and as employees in the job sector. A female protestor mentioned during the protests that she hoped that women will be considered equally with men and employed in newly created jobs (Al Shaibany, 2021). It was not clear whether the economic reforms are a quick-fix, short-term solution for the weak economy, to calm down the unrest and to strengthen the safety nets that have been strained by COVID-19 and whether Oman can really stick to a demanding long-term austerity and diversification programme (Castelier, 2021). To counteract the economic downturn created by the COVID-19 pandemic, regional trade cooperation between the six countries of the GCC has been enhanced, e.g. through the creation of a joint food supply network (Oxford Business Group, 2020). There are high hopes for the future, as with rising oil prices and a strict economic reform. According to the IMF, the economy in Oman will recover in 2022 with a growth of 7.4%, the highest rate of growth projection in the region (Al-Monitor 2021b).

## Mega-projects: Airports, ports and a waterfront

The GCC has been expanding its aviation and ports in the past decade. There is a need to increase foreign direct investments in Oman, said Sheikh Aimen bin Ahmed Al Hosni, CEO of Oman Airports, during a public speech on the aviation industry in the region ("A story of growth" at the Kempinski Muscat, 1 May 2019).

Muscat International Airport, the largest tourism project of recent years, was inaugurated in March 2018 (Oxford Business Group, 2019). The airport has a current maximum capacity of 12 million passengers. Future upgrades of the airport are planned to increase this capacity to 24 million, 36 million and 48 million passengers in subsequent phases (Oxford Business Group, 2019). The extension of the tourism infrastructure stopped in 2020. According to an official in the aviation sector, the number of passengers dropped dramatically during the coronavirus pandemic, falling at times to only 3,000–4,000 passengers per day at Muscat International Airport in 2020. As a consequence, the national airline Oman Air had to reduce its workforce. A large number of pilots, flight attendants and airport personnel had to leave their jobs. During the coronavirus pandemic, a large number of expatriates from different continents had to leave the Sultanate (Times News Service, 2021a). Aside from the aviation sector,

*Figure 3.5* A mega-cruise liner in the port of Muscat

Source: Gutberlet (2013).

the government with its tourism development and investment company (Omran) in cooperation with UAE-based company Damac was planning to implement the second biggest tourism development – a new $2 billion Waterfront Development project in Muttrah before the end of 2019 (Muscat Daily, 2019). Due to the rapid increase of large-scale cruise tourism, the Omani government had planned to transform the port in Muscat into a home port for cruise liners, similar to Dubai (Muscat Daily, 2016). It was planned to transform Port Sultan Qaboos into an "enclosed tourist bubble" for cruise tourism, with a large cruise liner terminal and a newly designed waterfront area, a large hotel, a shopping mall and other facilities. Once fully developed, the waterfront area should be able to accommodate a maximum of 33,000 cruise passengers at one time, creating a new identity for the waterfront (Oman Daily Observer, 2013). It was planned to welcome up to 1.6 million cruise tourists by 2020 (Oman Daily Observer, 2015). An official of the Ministry of Transportation who wished to remain anonymous said that the main idea for the Muttrah waterfront and port development is a luxury, marine tourism project:

> … *Muttrah will become a nice and safe place to be,* he explained.
>
> (Gutberlet, 2016a)

He therefore implied a small-scale luxury city port, having a "staged authenticity" without mega-cruise ships. The waterfront project was planned to be located next to Souq Muttrah. In the first phase of the development project, a new fish market was realized within a huge 4,000 m² building with an impressive canopy roof. Designed by the architecture company Sonhetta from Norway, the building merges within the bay area in Muttrah, creating a tourist attraction of its own. The construction of the fish market took eight years. It was inaugurated in September 2017 (Oman Architecture News, 2018). The large majority of cargo activities for commodities, with the exception of food grains such as wheat, were shifted to the port in Sohar by 2014, one year later as planned (Oman Daily Observer, 2013). The waterfront project in Muttrah has been benchmarked with international projects such as the Waterfront in Cape Town, South Africa. In 2020, the project development shifted back to the government and had not been realized until 2021.

Neighbouring Dubai, the home-port for many mega-cruise ships arriving in Oman, has built a new Dubai Harbour including a cruise terminal that can accommodate up to three mega-ships at the same time (Saudi Gazette, 2018). The new cruise port is operated by Meeras and the cruise company Carnival Corporation (Gulf News, 2018). A few months later, in December 2018, Dubai welcomed a total of five cruise liners in a single day, carrying 25,000 European passengers on board. Hence, affirming its dominant position as a cruise hub of the Gulf region (Trade Arabia News Service, 2018). More than half a million people (600,000 passengers) arrived in Dubai in winter 2016/2017.

Neighbouring Bahrain received its first cruise liner only in November 2018 (Bahrain News Agency, 2018), while Qatar received 43 cruise ships carrying 140,000 visitors during the cruise season 2018/2019 (Bukhari, 2018). Qatar is also planning to extend its cruise infrastructure and construct a special cruise port, located close to the city centre. Qatar and Bahrain faced political instability in recent years. Qatar faced an economic blockade in July 2017 that was lifted in January 2021, while Bahrain faced political instability during 2011 and 2014, which had negative impacts on the arrival of international tourists including cruise tourists.

## Mega-cruise tourism

The mega-cruise liners of my research called in Muscat, as the sole destination in Oman. In the wake of the introduction of direct flights to Europe especially between Muscat and Germany in 2008, cruise tourism increased in scale. The direct flight time between Muscat and Germany with its airports Munich and Frankfort is roughly seven hours.

Together with Qatar, UAE and Bahrain within a joint *Cruise Arabia Alliance*, the former Ministry of Tourism had promoted an aggressive increase in large-scale cruise tourism until the COVID-19 pandemic erupted. Through cooperation with the other GCC countries, it was initially planned to attract 1.6 million cruise tourists yearly by 2020 and 2.1 million by 2030 (Oman Tribune, 2015). Large-scale cruise tourism started in Muscat in 2004 when the first AIDA mega-cruise liner arrived. The cruise ship was followed by Costa Cruises and others in the next years. Until the outbreak of the coronavirus pandemic that stopped all tourism activities in March 2020, it was common to see two or three mega-cruise ships in the port in Muscat at one time. There are three cruise ports in Oman: Muscat, the capital, is the main port, in addition to Khasab in the North, and Salalah in the South of the Sultanate. In future, it is planned to open more Omani ports for cruise liners at Suwaiq, Duqm, Sur and Sohar (Muscat Daily, 2018).

Between 2005 and 2012, the number of cruise liners arriving in Muscat increased more than 80-fold. The number of cruise tourist arrivals in Oman has increased continuously in scale from 25 ships and 7,783 tourist arrivals in 2005 to 135 ships carrying 257,000 tourists in 2013 (Ministry of Tourism, 2015a). In Muttrah, the location of the port area, the number of inhabitants totalled 189,785 in 2011 with only 25.39% of them being Omani. In 2014, the number of cruise tourists dropped to 125,375 while in 2015 the number of passengers rose again to 146,509 (Ministry of Tourism, 2016). In 2017, a total of 221,800 cruise tourists arrived in Oman (Muscat Daily, 2018). This was already more than the total population in the district of Muttrah, where the port is located.

Until 2019, cruise tourism represented around 10% of the overall tourist arrivals in Oman. A total of 283,488 cruise tourists arrived on board 159 ships in the Sultanate in 2019, compared to 193,467 tourists the year before (Table 3.2). During the tourist season October 2019 to April 2020, a total of 275 cruise ships arrived in Oman, which was 20% more than the

*Table 3.2* Ocean cruise tourist arrivals in Oman (2009–2020)

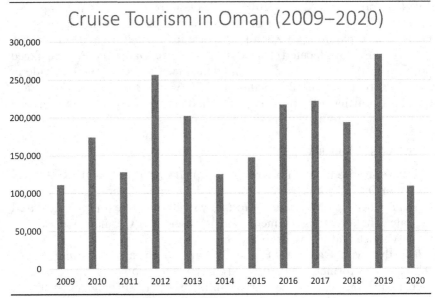

Source: Ministry of Heritage and Tourism (2021).

previous tourist season (Ministry of Heritage and Tourism, 2021). In comparison with the number of locals living in the district of Muttrah, the number of cruise tourists was higher. In 2020, a total of 230,881 people lived in Muttrah, which was the most densely populated district in Oman (City Population, 2020). In 2020, the number of cruise tourists dropped to 109,068 people arriving in Oman due to the global COVID-19 restrictions and border closures worldwide (Ministry of Heritage and Tourism, 2021).

In Muscat, the ships call at Sultan Qaboos Port in Muttrah while some also dock at Port Khasab, on their way to Muscat and Salalah, en route to Egypt and the Mediterranean. The majority of the mega-liners that carry European tourists such as AIDA, Mein Schiff or Costa Cruises were on a seven-day trip around the Arabian Peninsula. They arrive from Dubai and carry between 2,500 (AIDAblu and AIDAdiva) and 3,780 (Costa Favolosa) passengers plus 600–1,000 crew members every week in winter. The ship usually stays in Muscat for around nine hours and then continues the journey via Bahrain, Abu Dhabi and then back to Dubai. German-speaking tourists are the second largest group, visiting Oman on-board cruise liners, after British and Italian tourists.

Different stakeholders such as Muscat Municipality, the Ministry of Environment and Climate Affairs, Ministry of Culture, Omran and foreign tourism developers like Majid Al Futtaim (UAE) had been involved in the decision-making and execution of large-scale tourism development in Oman. Throughout my research, I realized that the decision-making process is not clear. There has been a lack of a common, joint Omani vision for tourism and in particular a cruise tourism strategy (Gutberlet, 2020, 2021,

2022a). The impact of cruise tourism on the social carrying capacity of the community has been high due to the limited geographical space in Muttrah. The area is surrounded by a mountain range, and there is a relatively small number of inhabitants in the coastal district where mega-cruise liners arrive and pass through (Gutberlet, 2016a, 2019, 2020, 2021).

In 2021, following a global standstill in cruise operations, cruise travel resumed slowly in parts of Europe, e.g. in the Mediterranean, Asia and the South Pacific (Cruise Lines International Association, 2021). The majority of the cruise passengers are from North America, Europe and Asia. The most popular destinations in 2019 were by far the Caribbean followed by Asia and China as well as the Mediterranean. The biggest fixed cost for cruise lines is fuel. As a result of the oil collapse during this economic downturn in 2020, cruise lines may benefit from these lower costs. In an effort to gain customer support after travel restrictions are lifted, companies launched strong advertising campaigns, reducing their prices in order to compete and draw demand back to the industry. Cruise liners like AIDA started to advertise large discounts on the cruise packages in their websites. Additionally, the industry had to commit to safety protocols on board that reduce the risk of diseases (Giese, 2021).

In this chapter, I have briefly outlined the research setting within a growth-oriented, boosterism local and regional tourism development strategy. Oman and its partners in the GCC region have been expanding their maritime and aviation infrastructure in a fast pace while competing with each other. Oman's mega-cruise tourism ambitions were spurred by the growth of mega-cruise tourism in neighbouring Emirate of Dubai. In the following chapters, I will elaborate on my research results, the sociocultural impacts of mega-cruise tourism within time-space compression in both research locations, creating "enclosed tourist bubbles" and staged tourist experiences.

## References

Al Jazeera (2020, January 11). Haitham bin Tariq sworn in as Oman's new sultan. *Al Jazeera*. Retrieved November 8, from https://www.aljazeera.com/news/2020/1/11/haitham-bin-tariq-sworn-in-as-omans-new-sultan

Al-Monitor (2021a, June 11). The reform challenge: What Oman and others might learn from Egypt. *Al-Monitor*. Retrieved June 16, from https://www.al-monitor.com/originals/2021/06/reform-challenge-what-oman-and-others-might-learn-egypt

Al-Monitor (2021b, July 30). Middle East economic outlook hinges vaccinations. *Al-Monitor*. Retrieved August 1, from https://www.al-monitor.com/originals/2021/07/middle-east-economic-outlook-hinges-vaccinations

Al Shaibany, S. (2021, May 26). Oman: Government promises 32,000 jobs and a stipend after days of protest. *The National*. Retrieved June 16, from https://www.thenationalnews.com/gulf-news/oman-government-promises-32-000-jobs-and-a-stipend-after-days-of-protest-1.1230443

Bahrain News Agency (2018, November 5). Bahrain welcomes the first cruise ship. Retrieved January 15, 2019, from http://www.bizbahrain.com/bahrain-welcomes-the-first-cruise-ship/

Bauman, Z. (2000). *Liquid modernity*. Polity Press.

BBC News (2020, January 11). Sultan Qaboos of Oman, Arab world's longest-serving ruler, dies aged 79. *BBC News*. Retrieved November 8, 2020, from https://www.bbc.com/news/world-middle-east-50902476

Bukhari, I. (2018, December 22). Boost in cruise tourism as many ships dock at Doha Port. Retrieved January 15, 2019, from https://thepeninsulaqatar.com/article/22/12/2018/Boost-in-cruise-tourism-as-many-ships-dock-at-Doha-Port-since-October

Castelier, S. (2021, June 9). Omanis demand benefits from economic reforms. *Al-Monitor*. Retrieved June 17, from https://www.al-monitor.com/originals/2021/06/omanis-demand-benefits-economic-reforms

Causevic, S., & Neal, M. (2019). The exotic veil: Managing tourist perceptions of national history and statehood in Oman. *Tourism Management, 71*, 504–517.

City Population (2020). City population, Oman: Administrative division. Retrieved November 20, from https://www.citypopulation.de/en/oman/admin/

Cruise Lines International Association (2021). State of the Cruise Industry Outlook. CLIA Cruise Line International Association. Retrieved July 12, from http://www.cruising.org/about-the-industry/press-room/press-releases/pr/state-of-the-cruise-industry-outlook

Gangler, A., & Gaube, H. (Eds.). (2012). *Transformation processes in oasis settlements of Oman*. Al Roya Press and Publishing House.

Gaube, H. (2012). *Muttrah redevelopment master plan. Cultural heritage stage 2. Conclusions and recommendations*. Working paper 20. Norplan AS.

Giese, M. (2021). COVID-19 impacts on the global cruise industry. KPMG Blog. Retrieved June 17, from https://home.kpmg/xx/en/blogs/home/posts/2020/07/covid-19-impacts-on-global-cruise-industry.html

Gulf News (2018, May 14). Meeras and Carnival sign deal to transform Dubai into a major tourism hub. Retrieved January 15, 2019, from https://gulfnews.com/business/tourism/meraas-and-carnival-sign-deal-to-transform-dubai-into-a-major-maritime-tourism-hub-1.2221410

Gutberlet, M. (2016a). Socio-cultural impacts of large-scale cruise tourism in Souq Muttrah. *Fennia, 194*(1), 46–63.

Gutberlet, M. (2017). Staging the Oriental Other: Imaginaries and performances of German-speaking cruise tourists. Published online first and in 2019, *Tourist Studies, 19*(1), 110–137.

Gutberlet, M. (2019). In a rush: Time-space compression and its impacts on cruise excursions, *Tourist Studies, 19*(4), 1–29. Published online first, April.

Gutberlet, M. (2020). "They just buy a karak and leave" – Overtourism in Souq Muttrah, The Sultanate of Oman, *Zeitschrift für Tourismuswissenschaften, De Gruyter Oldenburg,* 13 October. https://doi.org/10.1515/tw-2020-0004

Gutberlet, M. (2021). Valuing social capital and a legacy: "The old shops are the beauty of the place. In J. Saarinen & J. Richardson (Eds.), *Change in tourism/tourism in change* (pp. 135–150). Routledge Publishing House.

Gutberlet, M. (2022a). Geopolitical imaginaries and cultural ecosystem services (CES) in the desert. *Tourism Geographies 24*, 4–5.

Gutberlet, M. (2022b). Insight 288: Tourist bubbles and climate change in the GCC. COP 27 and Climate Action in the Middle East, Middle East Institute, National University of Singapore, October 24.

Hoek, C. W. (1998). *Shifting sands. Social-economic development in al-Sharqiyah region, Oman*. Nijmegen University Press.

Innovative Tourism Advisors (2016, July 8). *Oman Tourism Strategy,* Executive Summary for the Ministry of Tourism of the Sultanate of Oman, Doc. 309, extended version.

Kothaneth, L. (2017, May 7). Sultanate targets special interest tourists. *Oman Daily Observer.*

Lůdeling, E. & Bůrkert, A. (Eds.). (2010). Typology of oases in Northern Oman. In A. Bůrkert & E. Schlecht (Eds.), *Oases of Oman. Livelihood systems at the cross-roads* (pp. 34–37). Al Roya Press and Publishing House.

Merschen, B. (2007). Development of community-based tourism in Oman: Challenges and opportunities. In R. F. Daher (Ed.), *Tourism in the Middle East. Continuity Change and Transformation* (pp. 188–214). Channel View Publications.

Minca, C., & Wagner, L. (2016). *Moroccan Dreams – Oriental myth, colonial legacy.* I.B. Tauris.

Ministry of Environment and Climate Affairs (2012). The National Report on Sustainable Development Rio-Brazil. Committee for Sustainable Development chaired by the Undersecretary of the Ministry of Environment. Muscat.

Ministry of Heritage and Tourism (2021). Department of Planning, Follow-up and Information, Muscat, April 2021.

Ministry of Tourism (2015a). *Number of cruise tourists arriving in Muscat 2013-2015.* Statistics from the Directorate General of Planning, Follow-up and Information, Ministry of Tourism, Muscat.

Ministry of Tourism (2015b). *The local workforce in tourism.* Statistics from the Directorate General of Planning, Follow-up and Information, Ministry of Tourism, Muscat.

Ministry of Tourism (2016). *Number of cruise visitors.* Statistics from the Directorate General of Planning, Follow-up and Information, Ministry of Tourism, Muscat.

Moody's Analytics (2021). Middle East and North Africa Outlook: Slow recovery for oil exporters. Oman – Economic Indicators. Retrieved June 15, from https://www.economy.com/oman/indicators

Muscat Daily (2016). PSQ development projects to cost RO500mn, expected to generate about 12,000 jobs. *Apex Press and Publishing,* January, 5.

Muscat Daily (2018). Ministry of Tourism plans to extend cruise tourism to ports in Sohar, Sur, Duqm and Suwaiq. *Apex Press and Publishing,* September, 4.

Muscat Daily (2019). Work on $2 bn Mina al Sultan Qaboos project to begin in Nov., Muscat Daily, Muscat: *Apex Media Publication.*

Nair, V. (2019, August 5). Muscat Governorate home to highest expat numbers, *Oman Daily Observer.*

National Centre for Statistics and Information (NCSI) (2019). Population in Oman. Retrieved November 14, from https://www.ncsi.gov.om/Elibrary/Library ContentDoc/bar_Statistical%20Year%20Book%202019-1 54dd829c-6857-4200-b720-60e638979a4e.pdf

Oman Architecture News (2018, October 9). Oman's new fish market in Muscat: A perfect blend of traditions with modern architecture. Retrieved June 17, 2021, from https://worldarchitecture.org/architecture-news/ephnm/omans-new-fish-market-in-muscat-a-perfect-blend-of-traditions-with-modern-architecture.html

Oman Daily Observer (2013, October 7). *Deadline set for cargo vessels at port.* Oman Establishment for Press, Publication and Advertising.

Oman Daily Observer (2015, February 18). *Oman to welcome 1.6 m cruise tourists by 2020.* Oman Establishment for Press, Publication and Advertising.

Oman Tribune (2015, February 18). Number of cruise tourists rising, to hit 1.6 m in 2020.

Oxford Business Group (2019). The Report Oman 2019.

Oxford Business Group (2020, November 18). How will COVID-19 affect Gulf diversification efforts? Retrieved June 17, 2021, from https://oxfordbusinessgroup.com/news/how-will-covid-19-affect-gulf-diversification-efforts

Oxford Business Group (2021). *The Report Oman 2021.*

Ramani, S. (2021). The Qatar blockade is over, but the Gulf crisis lives on, foreign policy. Retrieved January 27, from

Richardson, N., & Dörr, M. (2003). Crossroads of culture. In H. H. Seyyid Shihab bin Tariq Al Said (Ed.), *The craft heritage of Oman* (Vol. 1). Motivate Publishing.

Saudi Gazette (2018, May 25). Dubai Cruise Terminal to be main hub for cruise tourism. Retrieved June 20, from http://saudigazette.com.sa/article/535571

Scholz, F. (1990). Muscat. Sultanat Oman. Geographische Skizze einer einmaligen arabischen Stadt. Das Arabische Buch.

Sultan Qaboos University (2020, October 20). Impact of COVID-19 on Development in Oman. Research Highlights. Retrieved June 15, 2021, from https://www.squ.edu.om/research/Research-Output/Latest-Research-Highlights/ArticleID/865/Impact-of-COVID-19-on-development-in-Oman

Times News Service (2021a). Oman's tourism sector highly affected by COVID-19 pandemic. *Times of Oman*. Retrieved June 15, from https://timesofoman.com/article/101582-omans-tourism-sector-highly-affected-by-covid-19-pandemic

Times News Service (2021b). Omanisation, replacement policy behind expatriate worker decline. *Times of Oman*. Retrieved June 15, from https://timesofoman.com/article/101619-omanisation-replacement-policy-behind-expatriate-worker-decline

Times News Service (2021c). 10.9 per cent Omanisation in tourism: Ministry. *Times of Oman*. Retrieved November 20, from https://timesofoman.com/article/101587-109-per-cent-omanisation-in-tourism-sector-ministry

Trade Arabia News Service (2018, December 8). Dubai welcomes 25,000 tourists on a single day. Retrieved January 15, 2019, from http://www.tradearabia.com/news/TTN_348480.html

United Nations World Tourism Organization, UNWTO (2019, March). *Tourism in the MENA region*. UNWTO.

Worldometer (2021). Oman Population Live, *worldometer.com*. Retrieved June 17, from https://www.worldometers.info/world-population/oman-population/

# 4 Methods

In this chapter, I outline in detail the mixed methods used throughout my long-term micro-sociological research presented. I explain my approach, the research process in both locations and the male gaze. I will introduce my female experiences as a researcher in the field, conducting social research in male-dominated public spaces. Moreover, I refer to the male gaze and gendered spaces that have shaped my research throughout time and space.

For my research presented here, I have applied qualitative and quantitative methods including content analysis of promotional material, two large-scale questionnaire surveys, participant observation, travel ethnography, counting, photography, in-depth interviews and walking interviews as well as informal conversations with local stakeholders. In-depth interviews with German-speaking mega-cruise tourists, group tourists and individual tourists of different age groups and with local stakeholders were held in various stages – between 2012 and 2021.

My results presented later on in this book focus primarily on qualitative research results, which offer a deeper understanding of the people and their cultural, political and social connections in tourism (Wilson & Hollinshead, 2015). Moreover, I will introduce my female experiences as a researcher in the field, conducting social research in male-dominated public spaces. I refer to the "male gaze" and "gendered spaces" that have shaped my research throughout time and space.

## My approach

Methodologically, my book is a conceptual and theoretical reflection of my long-term, slow, "empathetic research" (Larsen et al., 2021) and an "action research" that aims at promoting awareness and a discussion about the phenomenon of overtourism in emerging cruise destinations in the Middle East. The research presented draws on a micro-sociological study but connects as well with the anthropology of tourism and the political economy of tourism. My findings are part of extensive field-studies in emerging tourist destinations, one urban destination and one rural destination in the periphery. Due to my work experiences in tourism, I observed a dramatic increase in tourists

DOI: 10.4324/9780429424946-4

from 2005 onwards in the Corniche area in Muscat. The initial research idea was to analyse the tourist-host interaction and the tourist experience in-situ of an "Oriental" destination. Both destinations chosen – the desert, an oasis and the souq are very different from a home context in Europe. I have examined imaginaries, the construction of space, tourist experiences and the overall sociocultural impacts of mass-cruise tourism on the multi-ethnic communities, their attitudes towards tourism development, their well-being, the ethics in tourism and human-nature interaction (Gutberlet, 2016a, 2016b, 2017, 2019b, 2020, 2021, 2022a, 2022b).

My qualitative research methods are entirely inductive, which assumed my involvement in the research setting to collect the data (Farkić et al., 2020) and analysing the concepts developed. I have been using a "critical pedagogical approach", generating knowledge, giving an educational impulse to the society, from an endemic, community angle, cultivating values or identifying social identities from a certain community angle (Wilson & Hollinshead, 2015). My qualitative research is positioned within a social constructivist approach, exploring the world as it is constructed through a person's experiences and practices in space (Crouch, 2005). Within that approach, knowledge is gained through the interview.

It is necessary to mention my own positionality as a researcher, as it influenced the framing of my entire research. I recognize that my gender, my Western European/German nationality, my Whiteness, my prior work experiences and my multi-language skills have often privileged and facilitated but at times also challenged my fieldwork. In 2006, with the arrival of the first mega-cruise liner in Muscat, I was guiding German-speaking tourists and especially cruise tourists. At that time, I observed the first social changes occurring in space. Hence, my main focus was on contributing to the understanding of the changes that occurred in Souq Muttrah, in Sharqiyah Sands and the oasis, encompassing a rather holistic, inductive research process. My life and work experiences in tourism operations, journalism and public relations since 2004 on the Arabian Peninsula along with my Arabic language skills facilitated the access to different local stakeholders. I have studied Arabic in Germany and in North Africa. I have been living in The Sultanate of Oman since 2004 where I worked as a tour guide and representative for German and French-speaking tourist groups in Oman and United Arab Emirates, as well as a staff journalist for a local English and Arabic newspaper, as a freelancer for German media and as public relations manager at the German University of Technology in Oman (GUtech). My research is influenced by my lived experiences in the region, it is experience-based. Hence, some well-established shopkeepers, business owners, tour guides and tour operators knew me from my previous work. As a journalist, I wrote about the society and culture including tourism development in Oman and as a tour guide I conducted a large number of day-excursions with cruise tourists and group tourists between 2004 and 2013. All these perspectives helped to analyse and interpret different opinions and to observe the changes that have occurred within time, space and the culture throughout the years, from a resident and a rather "insider" perspective (Gutberlet, 2016a). Despite all my life and work experiences and my language skills, I strongly recognized that being an expatriate it is difficult to be fully integrated and regarded as an insider by the local society. However, my prolonged involvement, my diverse language skills and insights in tourism in Oman enabled me to be accepted "as one of them" among local guides and drivers, but also among the German tourists. During the field research and while on tour with tourists, I was not only observing but participating, acting often as an additional cultural mediator, answering questions about the place while interviewing and observing tourists and actions of others in space, e.g. vendors, residents and tourists.

Within this research approach, remaining objective or "semi-objective" means being positioned as a semi-detached observer and "in between" with regard to the interviewee practices and experiences. This was at times difficult given my work expertise and my long-time immersion in the local culture, especially in Souq Muttrah, which is a place I visited so many times throughout the years and that became one of my favourite places in Oman.

## The research process in Souq Muttrah

I conducted the research in different stages with tourists and the local community in Oman throughout the past decade (Gutberlet, 2016a, 2017, 2019b, 2020, 2021, 2022a, 2022b). In addition, my research draws on empirical examples from recent events of the COVID-19 pandemic in 2020/2021. Due to a lack of time, financial budget and long-term commitment to a research topic and a location, longitudinal research have received little attention in the academic literature on destination management and tourism development. Nevertheless, tourism practitioners and destination managers are often concerned about the developments of a place throughout time. Hence, longitudinal research can provide in-depth insights into tourism development and a legacy (Ritchie, 2005, p. 138).

In a first step, during my initial desk research, I reviewed the scientific literature on cruise tourism worldwide. Moreover, I conducted content analysis of local media articles, tourism articles on the Internet as well as blogs and official statistics from the government and from other online sources were used to explore the field. Promotional brochures and websites of mega-ships that stop-over in Oman carrying predominantly German-speaking cruise tourists such as AIDAblu, Costa Cruises, Mein Schiff, Royal Caribbean, MSC and Brilliance of the Sea were studied prior to the design of the questionnaire and throughout the field research. In addition, media articles in the local media and in the German print media, guidebooks, cruise guidebooks and newsletters from the cruise liner as well as online travel blogs were studied. I had sometimes requested information from tourists and on-board staff that were interviewed. Most of the materials originated from Germany or were distributed, e.g. by the Ministry of Tourism. As a consequence, a mix of rather stereotypical Oriental images and modern images such as skyscrapers, the desert and migrants were identified. I analysed the "framing" of the tourist's imaginaries through cultural mediators, the media and marketing material (Gutberlet, 2019). Such "framing" helps to investigate mass-mediated messages and to identify the links between the media, the tourist practices and the sociocultural forces that create the Other (Santos, 2005). The results were moulded into the analysis and supported my qualitative research results. The credibility of the research results was validated through the application of research procedures (Yarnal & Kerstetter, 2005), qualitative methods were supported by demographic data and the analysis of official statistics, news articles and marketing material as well as regular interaction with local gatekeepers in both locations; thus an immersion in the research setting was optimized.

In a second step, and to capture the impacts of cruise tourism in space I used photography and counting of tourists and locals in Souq Muttrah. I positioned myself in front of one of the Omani frankincense shops in the souq and counted in the mornings (between 10 and 12 noon) and in the afternoon hours, before the departure of the ships (Figure 4.1). I always counted with two hand-tally counters in each hand: one counter for the tourists and the other one for the locals entering during a time-span of 15 minutes per hour. The counting and the survey were followed by walking in-depth interviews, participant observation, travel ethnography, including long-term immersion and photography of the tourist and guide performances in the place. I used photography to record the moment in space (Pan et al., 2014),

*Figure 4.1* During my fieldwork in Souq Muttrah

Source: Anonymous tourist, 2012.

as well as the tourist and guide performances. I took photos along the main street and from inside the small elevated frankincense shop. At times, while I was sitting in the small shop, I was seen as a tourist attraction and part of a tourist photograph.

In a third step, I conducted a questionnaire survey among German-speaking cruise tourists. I started my field-research in Souq Muttrah with an initial sample questionnaire that I distributed to 20 German-speaking cruise tourists in winter 2011. According to their feedback, I designed the final two pages questionnaire. To understand tourist imaginaries, narratives and performances that frame the qualitative interview questions and the demographics of cruise passengers, the questionnaire was then distributed among tourists of a mega-cruise liner. Similar to Milano et al. (2019), I had a set of predetermined interview questions that served as a guideline. Prior to the departure of the buses, the tour guides were briefed about the survey and its distribution. Then the questionnaires along with pens for each survey were handed to all German-speaking tour guides of each half-day Muscat coach tour (Figure 4.2). From my experience, it took around five minutes to fill in the questionnaire survey inside the bus on their way back to the port and after their visit to the souq. My questionnaire was designed to analyse the tourist imaginaries and experiences including ideas about their pre-travel imaginaries, the on-site experiences and their

*Figure 4.2* Guiding mega-cruise tourists through Muscat by bus. German-speaking tour guides Alice, Daniela and myself at the cruise port

Source: Gutberlet (2012).

overall satisfaction. The questionnaire offered further questions regarding the tourist's pre-travel preparation, the multi-sensuous experiences, such as the smells, crowding and the demographic data. A question regarding the pre-arrival imaginaries offered a set of 13 different images along with the statement: In your view, which images did you have prior to travelling to Oman with the cruise liner? The following statements were given.

> *Oman is a country of: The Arabian Nights, with a sultan, with colorful markets, migrants from Asia, with an oasis, with frankincense, with camels, with sand desert, with skyscrapers, with veiled women, with Bedouins, with petrol and with minarets.*

My research sample was limited to German-speaking tourists from Germany, Switzerland, Austria and Luxembourg. At the time of my field research, German-speaking tourists represented the majority of cruise tourists visiting Oman. When I started my fieldwork, Germans were leaders in travelling internationally for years. According to the UNWTO (2013), Germany ranked second in international tourism expenditure in 2012 and first in 2011. According to one of the main tour operators in Muscat that organized most of the cruise excursions, both locations of my field research, the souq, the desert and the oasis, have been the main tourist attractions.

The first AIDA mega-cruise liner arrived in Muscat in November 2004 and others followed. For instance, Costa Cruises followed two years later. According to one of the major shipping agencies in Muscat, at that time AIDA Cruises had been transporting around 2,500 passengers every week to the Sultanate of Oman, during winter and spring, between November and April. The cruise liner is a "contemporary" mega-cruise liner with an all-inclusive club atmosphere on board.

Ninety-nine percent of the tourists surveyed were German, representing a couple or a family of different age groups and having an average income. During the tourist season 2012/2013 AIDAblu docked 15 times in Muscat carrying between 1,800 and 1,900 tourists plus crew (Ministry of Tourism, 2013). A total of 830 cruise tourists filled out the first survey about Souq Muttrah, out of some 1,040 approached. This represented around 80% of the surveyed cruise tourist sample. A large majority (88%) of the cruise tourists surveyed in the questionnaire survey were travelling with a partner, representing different age groups.

Moreover, between 2012 and 2014, I continued my fieldwork using qualitative methods in both places, in Souq Muttrah and in Sharqiyah Sands. To record the changes in the development of cruise tourism, I conducted follow-up research from 2015 to 2019 and between 2020 and 2021. Such long-term research increases the credibility, trustworthiness and robustness of my results and the concepts used (Baxter, 2010). Initially, I conducted in-depth interviews with tourists on 15 Sundays during the winter season, between February and May 2012. Those tourists interviewed were not part of my questionnaire survey. I interviewed the following number of tourists in Souq Muttrah in 2012–2013: Individual traveller ($N = 7$ couples), group traveller ($N = 5$ couples), cruise tourist from a luxury cruise ($N = 1$ couple), cruise tourist from mega-cruise liners AIDA, Costa or Brilliance of the Seas ($N = 8$ couples); on-board tour guides from mega-cruise ships ($N = 5$ individuals), on-board lecturers from two mega-cruises ($N = 2$ individuals), local tour guides of different nationalities (Omani, Indian, Sri Lankan, German, Austrian) ($N = 11$ individuals). They stopped at the small frankincense shop close to the main entrance of Souq Muttrah. The tourists were approached during the peak tourist timings, between 10.00 a.m. and 1.00 p.m. During in-depth walking interviews, the concepts of my survey were further explored. I always saw myself as an active participant, "travelling along with interviewees" (Legard et al., 2003), co-creating the experience. We both actively collaborated with each other. The interviewer plays an important part in the interview experience while narratives of the tourists, tour guides and the local community reveal the significance of a place (Rickly-Boyd, 2010).

I used in-depth interviews to give a voice to the different views while adding more depth and understanding to the research (Jennings, 2005). During a standard interview about a place and the experience respondents usually recall memories and images of places without direct visual, audible, olfactory or tactile stimuli. A "walking in-depth interview" meant performing, interviewing and observing tourists while participating in their on-site experiences (Haldrup & Larsen, 2010). The walk facilitated interaction between the tourists and the place and between the researcher and the tourists (Trell & Van Hoven, 2010). Moreover, it was easier to understand the meanings and the emotions during the embodied on-site tourist experiences (Andereck et al., 2006). The physical movement through the place can show new aspects of the experience. During a walk, the encountered objects or situations may enhance thoughts about more abstract aspects of the place and the people. Often, it is important to see, hear, smell or feel a tourist site in order to make sense of it and to communicate it to outsiders (Trell & Van Hoven, 2010). While walking, a natural conversation was held with the tourists. I was socializing, performing and observing along with the tourists, participating in their on-site experiences. The walk along with the tourists offered a process of learning through shared experiences, creating a kind of intimacy with the research interviewees' experiences of the place and the people (Pink, 2009) while consuming smells, sounds and visual displays (Gutberlet, 2017). The walk followed similar ethnographic research conducted by Pink (2008) during a walk through an urban garden. For these walking interviews, I sometimes used a camera. The interviews included a continuous comparison of the present results and the on-site, multi-sensory experiences, creating a sense of place and an imaginary tourist space in the tourist's minds. The tourists wished to enjoy themselves and the atmosphere and it was important that the interview was not disturbing their experiences, thus too disruptive (Crouch, 2005). Sharing the same cultural background with German-speaking tourists was helpful in understanding the tourists' narratives.

The duration of the interviews varied between 20 and 90 minutes, depending on the tourists' available time in the souq and the 'saturation effect'. Due to limited manpower and time, I applied an accidental sampling method (Gutberlet, 2016a, 2016b, 2017, 2019, 2020, 2022a). The sample population for the tourist interviews was generated through a flow population (Ritchie et al., 2003a). I approached those German-speaking tourist couples (usually male/female or two females, two males) who were standing at the frank-incense shop at the peak tourist arrivals. I conducted the interviews with tourists in German. The anonymity of my interviewees was assured. Their replies were immediately noted down in a notebook or recorded with a voice recorder while walking with the tourists through the souq. Then they were translated into English shortly thereafter (Gutberlet, 2017). Participant observation and photography were applied in Souq Muttrah on Sundays.

To overcome limitations of the verbal discourse and to access embodied experiences of tourists' encounters, I used ethnography. To better understand the social context of mega-cruise tourism, I conducted participatory observation. Hence, the inside of the frankincense shop was chosen as the ideal location for my observation (Reuber & Pfaffenbach, 2005), which was close to the main entrance. I was standing or sitting on a small chair, being part of the elevated shop, overlooking the street, as well as along the main ally of the souq. There most cruise tourists were walking along the street, as a "flaneur or flaneuse" observing the scenery (Wearing & Foley, 2017). Moreover, the frankincense shop is the first traditional Omani shop, having Omani products and one of the first attractions.

## The local community in Muttrah

I started conducting in-depth interviews with different stakeholders of the local, multi-ethnic community working in tourism in Souq Muttrah in Muscat in 2012 and 2013 (Gutberlet, 2016a, 2016b, 2017, 2020, 2021). I use the term *local community* to refer to a diverse community within the space: multi-ethnic shop vendors, business owners, Omani and expatriate customers visiting the souq, Omani and expatriate tour guides, tour-operators, residents of the area next to the souq and government officials including the Minister of Tourism, the Minister of Environment, another high-ranking government official, the Assistant Grand Mufti of Oman and the Wali (governor) of the district of Muttrah. To gain deeper insights into such local views on cruise tourism, the Minister of Tourism and representatives of major tour operators as well as a shipping company were interviewed in their offices in Muscat (Gutberlet, 2016a, 2019, 2021, 2022a). Through my social constructivist approach, the priority was to enable the local interviewees to provide insights into their on-site experiences and everyday lives as well as their memories about both locations.

The interviews were conducted in Arabic or English and followed a semi-structural guideline. In Muttrah, I visited the residential district beside the souq on several days when one or two cruise liners were in the port. Since the access for non-residents is highly restricted, even for Omanis, it was extremely difficult to conduct any interview within the walled residential area, the Sur al Lawati in Muttrah. I then conducted a few interviews at the entrance gate to the residential district. Due to the close social structure of the multi-ethnic community in Souq Muttrah and to allow critical views, the interviews with the local community were taken anonymously and noted down immediately. To immerse myself in space and time, I participated in the *local flow of life*, especially during the peak tourist timings in winter, which is during mid-day, while locals who worked in both places were interviewed in summer or at the end of the tourist season, from April onwards when there were less tourists there and they had more time to talk. Follow-up interviews and observations at the main tourist entrance of Souq Muttrah were conducted, when two contemporary mega-cruise liners were in the port.

As for the interviews with the shop vendors and owners, I revisited the same shops continuously, especially during the cruise seasons (Gutberlet, 2016a, 2016b, 2017, 2020). For the interviews with the male vendor community, I used snowball sampling, in particular with the Indian "diaspora communities". Each interview took between 10 and 60 minutes. To preserve their anonymity, the interviewees were given fictional names according to their nationality, e.g. Sujith or Abdul for Indian vendors. There was no recording made, but the entire interaction was documented in writing and coded manually afterwards on paper. The interviews were deliberately not recorded because it helped the interviewees to be open and engaged. The shops were located along the Corniche road and along the main tourist street leading from the Corniche road (Al Bahri Street) into the souq. I chose these shops according to my prior in-depth interviews with tourists. Those shops that were visited along with the tourists were chosen for my interviews. These shops covered the wholesale and retail sector as well as the main streets of the souq – the Corniche road and the small inside alleys of the souq.

The shops were selling different products: local perfumes like frankincense and bokhur, halwa (local sweets), handicraft, pharmacy products, spices, groceries, kummas (traditional hats for men), pashmina scarves, foodstuffs and household items. I also interviewed the owner of a local coffee shop and the manager of a restaurant beside the main entrance of the souq. Overall, a total of 45 shops were covered. The shops were newly established or very well established and up to 250 years old. Interviews were conducted with the shop vendors and owners of different age groups (25–75 years), they were all male and of different nationalities: 16 Omani, 25 Indian, two Bangladeshi, one Pakistani and one Syrian.

Moreover, I interviewed Omani residents, an expatriate heritage expert, local Omani and expatriate decision-makers and Omani male and female customers ($N = 8$) from other districts in Muscat between 2012 and 2013. I also interviewed Omani and expatriate (predominantly male) tour guides ($N = 11$) of German-speaking tourists and Omani male and female members ($N = 7$) of the resident community living next to the souq. They were interviewed in English or Arabic about cruise tourism development in Muttrah.

The interviews were conducted individually, with business owners as well as with new and well-established shop vendors of different nationalities. All interviews were conducted anonymously and not recorded. I took notes and transcribed the interview shortly afterwards. Most of the shopkeepers interviewed were originally from the well-established Banyan diaspora community, who have their origins in Pakistan and India. They were living and working in Oman for several decades but were not yet granted the Omani nationality. Most of these interviewees were chosen by the snowball sampling method. Being introduced to them helped me as a female researcher to get trust and consequently access to the well-established male-dominated community. The semi-structured interviews were conducted individually, with business owners and with both well-established and new shop vendors of various ethnicities. My interview questions asked about: the history of the shop, the product range, the type of customers, the current situation of the shop, the selling approach, the cruise tourism development in Souq Muttrah and the future of the shop.

My main aim was to enable the interviewees to provide insights into their family history, the legacy of their shops, their experiences with customers, their current everyday lives as well as other memories of Souq Muttrah and a future outlook for the souq. I revisited these shops continuously during the cruise seasons. I observed the setting along the main streets, took photographs and conducted informal conversations and formal follow-up interviews with the remaining well-established local and expatriate vendors along the main streets of the souq. These interviews were conducted between 2017 and 2019 and again during the COVID-19 recovery stage of the pandemic in spring and summer 2021. I observed the scene along the main streets of the souq. I took photographs and conducted informal conversations and formal follow-up in-depth interviews in both English and Arabic with the remaining, well-established vendors along the main streets of the souq.

## The research process in the desert and the oasis

In my second case study, I participated in nine standardized day-excursions being part of a group of German-speaking day tourists. The 4 × 4 excursion to the oasis and the desert was chosen as one of the most popular cruise day excursions, representing an adventure, and heritage experience greatly different to that of everyday life in Germany. During my research in the Sharqiyah region, the mega-cruise liner was unnamed by request (Gutberlet,

2019a, 2019b). There are several mega-ships that offer the same itinerary arriving in Muscat. Hence, it is difficult to identify the exact cruise ship and its brand. Initially, the mega-ship travelled around the Canary Islands in spring/summer 2012. It arrived for the first time on the Arabian Peninsula in October 2012, where it spent the next five months. During an eight-day trip with five destinations (Dubai, Muscat, Manama, Abu Dhabi and then again Dubai), the cruise ship departs from Dubai on the first day and it docks the next morning in Muscat, where it stayed for around 11 hours.

A local tour agency offered eight packaged culture, seascape and nature excursions by bus, 4 × 4 or boat, among which are a full-day tour to an oasis and to the Sharqiyah Sands desert entitled *A Unique Desert Experience by Jeep* (cruise excursion brochure, November 2012/March 2013). For around 100 Euros per person that excursion was one of the most popular and most expensive ones, similar to a day-trip to the mountains in Oman.

For most cruise tourists, it was their first time ever to travel to a desert and an oasis (Gutberlet, 2019a, 2022a). The excursion had several stops, including in an oasis and the Sharqiyah Sands desert. The tour started in the morning around 8.30 a.m. from the port. The ship had arrived around two hours earlier at the port. The excursion included a stop along the way, in a motel where some initial explanations about the destination were given. The second stop was the centre of an oasis. Then the tourist convoy proceeded to a car workshop where the tires were deflated before heading to the sand desert. There dune driving and a lunch break in a luxury desert camp were on the programme before heading back to the port in Muscat. The total driving time was around five hours.

Prior to my qualitative methods applied and in order to review the overall perception of the cultural ecosystem services, the tourists' on-site experiences and their pre-travel imaginaries, a questionnaire survey in German was conducted between January and March 2013. The two-page survey was distributed during nine full-day tours with 4 × 4 cars. The questionnaires were distributed by myself and an Omani tour guide towards the end of the tour in the desert, prior to the return to the port, where the survey was collected immediately. The time of distribution may have influenced the tourists' choices in their responses regarding the strength of their pre-travel imaginaries, since imaginaries are changing and are processed throughout the entire travel (Di Giovine, 2014).

The response rate of the questionnaire was high. Out of 390 questionnaires distributed, a total of 235 tourists replied to the survey, achieving a response rate of 61%. A total of 99% of the respondents were Germans, half of them were males and half of them were females. Around 94% were visiting Oman for the first time ($N = 235$). Most of them travelled with a partner (78%) while 19% travelled within a group of 3, 4 or 5 people. About 74% were above the age of 40 years ($N = 234$). Regarding the tourists' education, 46% had a middle or basic school education, which is equivalent to ten years of schooling in Germany, 23% had a high school degree and 29% had a university or college degree, 1% had a PhD degree ($N = 216$).

Similar to my approach in Souq Muttrah, through travel ethnography and participant observation, I explored the group behaviour between the tourists and between the tourists and their cultural brokers (Rantala, 2010; Weaver, 2005). Following Schmid (2008) and Pink's approaches (2007, 2008, 2009), mega-cruise tourists, tour guides, drivers and an Omani coffee man were observed and interviewed. This was done while on the road or during one of the stops while socializing with them, walking, eating lunch together or contemplating the desert scenery. Similar to Pink (2008), I familiarized myself with their practices, their bodies, rhythms, tastes as well as their ways of seeing the destination (Pink, 2008). This supported my understanding of how tourists and cultural brokers imagine and make sense of their social, cultural and natural environments. While on tour with the tourists, I was often presented by the Omani tour guide as a social researcher conducting field research. Sometimes, I even served as an additional but unofficial tour guide, a translator or a cultural mediator. However, these roles helped me to have closer contact and more trust with the cruise tourists and the on-board tour guides. One of the primary methods through which my qualitative data was documented were field notes, applying a "social interactionist" approach, which acknowledges the social and physical environment (Yarnal & Kerstetter, 2005).

During the cruise excursions, most tourists were interviewed individually, six tourists were interviewed as couples. The majority of the tourists travelled as couples. In addition, five on-board cruise guides, an on-board photographer and an on-board lecturer were interviewed. A total of 22 cruise and group tourist couples, aged between 25 and 82 years, five on-board cruise guides, four drivers and guides, and one on-board lecturer were interviewed. These mobile or walking interviews with tourists and cruise employees were conducted until a "saturation effect" was achieved.

In addition to these interviews with tourists from a mega-cruise ship, I participated in two German-speaking group tours with more than 40 German tourists. They stayed overnight in two different desert camps as part of their one-week travel around the North of the Sultanate of Oman, similar to tourists travelling through the Moroccain desert (Bensa, 2007; Cauvin Verner, 2007). Overall, I was seen as having an insider role (Cauvin Verner 2007; Jennings, 2005). I was accepted by the tourists as "one of the Germans" through my language and nationality and by the tour guides who knew me as a colleague and the male Omani drivers who seemed to respect me as a member of the groups of tour guides. I conducted in-depth interviews with tourist couples and on-board employees during the tour, while in the desert, having lunch with them or towards the end of the lunchtime in the desert camp. Their answers were noted down immediately and not recorded. During these semi-structured interviews, the tourists were asked about their pre-travel preparation, their pre-travel imaginaries, their motivation to go on excursion, their on-site experiences, their level of satisfaction and whether they wished to return to the destination Oman. The interviews were taken in the late afternoon or in the morning during breakfast at the desert camp. Similar to Hays (2012) mobile ethnography, the natural environment was socially constructed, constantly reworked and contested. To understand how they perceive the space, I adjusted myself again to the participants of the tours. I observed their behaviours and interviewed them while on tour, walking through the desert, standing on one of the sand dunes or sitting along with them in the desert camp. I refer to Pink's (2007, 2008, 2009) ethnographic fieldwork within a "Cittaslow" urban space.

Moreover, I interviewed local stakeholders in the oasis and in the desert including a sheikh, who was the head of an extended family in the oasis, the owner of a small heritage museum in the old centre of the oasis, desert camp owners and desert camp managers as well as a few residents living just next to the old centre of the town with its falaj system. The sheikh, even invited me for lunch at his home, where I ate together with the female family members in a separate area. Overall, it was extremely difficult for me to connect with the male and female residents and to convince them about an interview for my research on tourism in the oasis. Therefore, I decided to ask an Omani tour guide from Muscat for support in mediating with the community in the oasis. The majority of the locals approached were males except one female resident who I met beside the old falaj. She invited me to have coffee with her at her home located next to the falaj system. This was as well the main meeting place for tourists. Interviews with local tour guides and drivers were conducted while working, thus driving to or from the Sharqiyah Sands desert back to Muscat. A few interviews were also conducted at a coffee shop at the Corniche road and on one occasion in the reception area or official living room of a private house, the majlis area. Due to time constraints during the tour and to get more detailed insights, I decided to interview the Omani coffee man at his home in Ibra, located close to the oasis. At that time, the male Omani lead tour guide was accompanying me. Within my social constructivist approach, the tour guides, drivers and cultural brokers from the ship were asked about their work experiences and exchange with German-speaking cruise tourists. Moreover, two environmental experts, one Omani from the Ministry of Environment and a German UNESCO advisor based in Bahrain, who was on a visit to Muscat, were interviewed in their offices about tourism development as well as nature conservation. In addition, I interviewed five Omani and expatriate managers and owners of desert camps in Sharqiyah Sands. They were interviewed while visiting the desert camps and one camp owner was interviewed at a coffee shop in Muscat.

All my interviews were conducted anonymously in German, English or Arabic. Their responses and some notes about my observations were noted down in a notebook immediately. Some interviews were recorded and transcribed later on when I was back in Muscat. To complement the interviews and my observations and to capture more details of the experience during the encounters, I applied photography (Scarles, 2010). The sampling method was purposive. Sometimes a snowball sampling occurred when tourists, tour guides or drivers were interviewed, which was similar to my research process in Souq Muttrah.

## Data analysis

My field notes, observations and in-depth interviews were transcribed shortly after the tour and engaged me in more reflexivity. To increase the validity of my data sets collected, I have used triangulation throughout the research process. Shortly after the interviews, I typed the notes of the interviews or the recorded interview into word documents. Then, I ana-lysed them manually within a table, without the use of software for qualita-tive data analysis. The key concepts were found through content analysis, by reading repeatedly, highlighting the concepts used. The key concepts developed through such a comparative analysis were, e.g. 'authenticity', 'self-transformation' and 'host-guest interactions'. Categories that emerged while reading the text repeatedly were highlighted. The data was then gath-ered in separate files within thematic charts with concepts like the *tourist experience, travel motivation, tourist behaviour, imaginaries, overtourism, time-space compression* etc. Each respondent had a different name within a vertical row in the matrix a vertical row in the matrix and each concept had a horizontal row. I compared them with each other and a central chart was constructed in order to understand the emerging concepts of each case in the data set. Hence, to organize and analyse the data-set, I applied cross-sectional codes and retrieve methods, using codes and labels, similar to Spencer et al. (2003). The questionnaires were analysed mainly descrip-tively using SPSS19 software. Participant observations and continuous field notes in both locations were supported by photography. As for the analysis of the content of images, it requires a "certain reading", where images need to be regarded as objects.

Photography reflects the photographer's inner state of mind (Banks & Zeitlyn, 2015, p. 60). While taking photos, I always tried to reflect the con-text of the tourist performance. For instance, I positioned myself in the inside of the frankincense shop, maintaining a local, semi-detached posi-tion and view. Moreover, the photos were taken from different angles, from a high angle (inside the shop) overlooking the scenery and from an eye-level. I also considered ethical issues when taking photographs. When the tourists were in front of the frankincense shop, some took a photo of the shop with the tour guide and the shop vendor. At the same time to represent the overall social context in the souq, I took a photo of the tourist group and the tour guide, like a "reverse gaze", from the opposite direction. A wide-angle per-spective (Banks, 2002) was taken from far away to get a view of the context of the guiding practices along the main streets of the souq.

The tourists, who were part of a small group, were asked if they could be photographed. I was standing just beside a tourist group, on the same level, hence, the photo was a "collaborative and directed image" (Banks, 2002), framed according to my visual aesthetics and at the same time a concretization of social facts. This was realized through the agency of the male Indian shop vendor, who explained to the tourists how to tie an Omani turban that is part of the Omani identity and not Indian. Such a scene involving the tourists and the vendors was not often observed in the souq, compared to scenes of male tour guides explaining the various products including types of incense available in the souq.

## Gendered spaces and the macho gaze

Being a young female, white and obviously European or Caucasian-looking researcher in the field in the Sultanate of Oman represented various, hidden challenges. I worked in both research locations within a male-dominated, patriarchal Arab/Asian space that resulted in various obstacles such as the male "macho gaze", the social obligation to wear a veil in the oasis and in the souq district as well as the indirect Asian and Arab communication style. The majority of the local community members interviewed were male, which reflected the patriarchal structure of the Omani society, where 65% of the population are male (NCSI, 2015) and where women are underrepresented in public places, in particular in the in rural areas. Traditional social values and norms restrict women's individual movements in public spaces up to today. One male Omani resident said about the souq in Muttrah: "This is a men's world". Until 1970, only men went shopping to the souq, women remained at home. Elder shop owners who lived in the souq area said that I could not enter the residential district without wearing a scarf and an abaya (local black cloak). However, this is not an obligation for female non-Muslims in public places in Oman. Not wearing an abaya and a lihaf scarf, I was "standing out" in both places. I sometimes felt like being a European tourist. Especially, Asian vendors were often gazing at me when I was walking along the streets in Souq Muttrah and conducting interviews on my own. I felt a curious, but sometimes rather intrusive gaze, while feeling safe within space at all times.

During the interviews in Souq Muttrah, I was on my own all the time. I sometimes faced "gender issues" and stigma against women. In particular, I encountered negative feelings while conducting interviews with the young, male South Asian community in Souq Muttrah. I experienced suspiciousness and even fear caused by the sometimes rather intrusive male, 'macho gaze' (Wilson & Little, 2011). Young Asian vendors seemed being rather suspicious about my research and my questions. I felt being too intrusive or curious like a policewoman and that they did not want to reveal their social realities to a female researcher. As a consequence, several new Asian shopkeepers that I approached in English did not want to be interviewed. I assume this was due to a lack of communication or fear of being critical. At times, I felt there was an air of formality as if I was regarded as a policewoman. I was not offered to sit down but had to stand during the interviews. In some shops, I felt obliged to buy something, e.g. a pashmina scarf in return for the interview and the information given. Whereas in other shops were Omanis where salespeople, there was no such unspoken obligation to buy something in exchange for an interview and information. I was even sometimes offered a small gift in return for my interview or an informal chat. For example, in the halwa shop located on the main street of the souq, I received a pot of fresh, warm halwa or the frankincense shop very often offered me some frankincense and other local perfumes as a gift. While conducting interviews with Omanis, they were extremely polite but curious about my research and my life in Muscat. They were open to speak to me in English or in Arabic. During the interviews with the local community in both locations, my Arabic knowledge helped to get access to them. Those community members who had been working in the souq for over ten years, or through several generations, were very hospitable and they recognized me from previous visits. We usually had a chat and I was often invited to sit down and offered sweet Indian milk tea (*karak tea*) and some sweets. At times, I had the impression being female and European was positive and there were more chances for interviews. An Omani interviewee said clearly: "I tell you this because you are one of us". Being familiar with the terrain, also meant that there were expectations, such as facilitating the sale of products to tourists, facilitating governmental support, realizing a tourism project, promoting the area to tourists and even an enquiry for getting involved in sales operations of a desert camp. However, it was not possible to meet these requests during my research.

At the time of my research tour guiding, being outside and visible in the public space was a highly male-dominated profession. In addition, conducting and conducting research in social sciences, within a discipline that is little known and recognized in the Arab world compared to natural sciences, engineering or medicine, was another challenge. I felt I needed to explain a lot and often. Sometimes I asked for male Omani support and mediation in order to be empowered and protected from intrusive views, the "macho gaze" or comments. This was the case in particular during interviews in the oasis. My research within the local male-dominated community, the gender segregation by culture and the cross-cultural interviews with the local communities added various "layers of complexity to the already-complex interactions of an interview" (Patton, 2002, p. 391). Interviewing the multi-ethnic, male-dominated, local community was much more challenging at times. Within the context of my research presented in this book, I consider myself both as an *outsider* conducting research, mainly unaccompanied – on my own, within a traditional, male-dominated souq and oasis/desert environment. Moreover, I was seen as a female *local* and as an *insider* within the tourism context. I speak Standard Arabic and English, the main languages used in Oman and in the other countries on the Arabian Peninsula. I have been living and working in Oman for many years including many visits to the souq and the desert as part of my work and leisure time. Thus, prior to my research, I had participated in the local flow of life for more than a decade (Gutberlet, 2021), which is similar to Amoamo (2011). At times, I felt that this gave me more local respect and opened doors of curiosity, especially in my research at Souq Muttrah. My attachment to the local space literally opened doors faster and continuously within the community. Doors that may have remained closed otherwise for a short fieldwork as a fly-in researcher.

Women interviewing men and men interviewing women will gain different insights from a person interviewing a person of the same gender (Jennings, 2005). However, especially in traditional patriarchal cultures, it can be seen as *a breach of etiquette* for an unknown individual to request for an interview with the opposite sex (Patton, 2002, p. 393). Therefore, a male Omani tour guide from Muscat helped sometimes in mediating with male community members in the oasis.

Interviewing German-speaking tourists, especially tourist couples and female tourists of all age groups, was not an obstacle at all. The tourists often regarded me as one of them. I was someone who shared the same language and an understanding for the European culture and values. Sometimes, I was even seen as a welcome facilitator or mediator between the German on-board guide and the local place. At other times, I felt like a *tourist attraction* and people wanted to take a photo with me. Some people were curious to know more about my life and work in the Sultanate. I was asked very often about the reasons for being in a place where others usually spend their holidays. They asked: What made you live in Oman? How is life in Oman for women?

In this chapter, I have outlined my research methods including my approach, the research process and my data analysis. In the next chapter, my research results will be analysed. This will be done according to the travel phases, the pre-travel preparation on land and the on-site experiences in both research locations. I analyse European tourist experiences while on tour. As such the text is structured as a flow of the tourist's activities and experiences, from the beginning of the tour until the end of the tour, alongside the views of the local community within these tourist experiences, tracing their views and paths throughout the excursion. I will also analyse in detail community perceptions about tourism development and tourist behaviours as well as social capital and the ethics of tourism (Gutberlet, 2020, 2021, 2022a), the tourists' imaginaries and experiences (Gutberlet, 2017), the main features that create the spiritual and aesthetic value of the desert, influencing the tourist's identity creation (Gutberlet, 2019, 2022a).

# References

Amoamo, M. (2011). Tourism and hybridity: Revisiting Bhabha's third space. *Annals of Tourism Research*, *38*(4), 1254–1273.

Andereck, K., Bricker, K. S., Kerstetter, D., & Nickerson Polovitz, N. (2006). In G. Jennings & N. Polovitz Nickerson (Eds.), *Quality tourism experiences* (pp. 81–98). Elsevier Butterworth-Heinemann.

Augé, M. (2010). *Nicht-Orte*. Verlag C.H. Beck.

Banks, M. (2002). Visual research methods. *Indian Folklore*, *1*(4), 8–10.

Banks, M., & Zeitlyn, D. (2015). *Visual methods in social research* (2nd ed.). Sage Publications.

Baxter, J. (2010). Case studies in qualitative research. In I. Hays (Ed.), *Qualitative methods in human geography* (3rd ed.). Oxford University Press.

Bensa, A. (2007). Préface—le tourisme, une économie du spectacle. In C. Cauvin Verner (Ed.), *Au désert. une anthropolgie du tourisme dans le sud marocain* (pp. 7–16). L'Harmattan.

Cauvin Verner, C. (2007). *Au Désert. Une Anthropologie du tourisme dans le Sud marocain*. L'Harmattan.

Crouch, D. (2005). Tourism research practices and tourist geographies. In B. W. Ritchie, P. Burns, & C. Palmer (Eds.), *Tourism research methods. Integrating theory with practice* (pp. 73–84). CABI Publishing.

Di Giovine, M. A. (2014). The imaginary dialectic and the refashioning of pietrelcina. In N. B. Salazar & N. H. Grabun (Eds.), *Tourism imaginaries anthropological approaches* (pp. 147–172). Berghahn Books.

Farkić, J., Filep, S., & an Taylor, S. (2020). Shaping tourists' wellbeing through guided slow adventure. *Journal of Sustainable Tourism*, 28(12), 2064–2080.

Gutberlet, M. (2016a). Socio-cultural impacts of large-scale cruise tourism in Souq Muttrah. *Fennia*, *194*(1), 46–63.

Gutberlet, M. (2016b). Cruise tourist dress behaviors and local-guest reactions in a Muslim country. *Tourism Culture & Communication*, *16*, 15–32.

Gutberlet, M. (2017). Staging the Oriental Other: Imaginaries and performances of German-speaking cruise tourists. Published online first and in 2019 *in. Tourist Studies*, *19*(1), 110–137.

Gutberlet, M. (2019). In a rush: Time-space compression and its impacts on cruise excursions, *Tourist Studies*, *19*(4), 1–29. Published online first, April.

Gutberlet, M. (2020). "They just buy a karak and leave" – Overtourism in Souq Muttrah, The Sultanate of Oman, *Zeitschrift für Tourismuswissenschaften*, De Gruyter Oldenburg, 13 October. https://doi.org/10.1515/tw-2020-0004

Gutberlet, M. (2021). Valuing social capital and a legacy: "The old shops are the beauty of the place. In J. Saarinen & J. Richardson (Eds.), *Change in tourism/ tourism in change* (pp. 135–150). Routledge Publishing House.

Gutberlet, M. (2022a). Geopolitical imaginaries and cultural ecosystem services (CES) in the desert. *Tourism Geographies*, *24*, 4–5.

Gutberlet, M. (2022b). Insight 288: Tourist bubbles and climate change in the GCC. COP 27 and Climate Action in the Middle East, Middle East Institute, National University of Singapore, October 24.

Haldrup, M., & Larsen, J. (2010). *Tourism, performance and the everyday: Consuming the orient*. Routledge.

Hays, C. M. (2012). Placing nature(s) on safari. *Tourist Studies*, *12*(3), 250–267.

Jennings, G. R. (2005). Interviewing: A focus on qualitative techniques. In B. Ritchie, P. Burns, & C. Palmer (Eds.), *Tourism research methods, integrating theory with practice* (pp. 99–117). Cabi International.

Larsen, J., Gomes Bastos, M., Skovslund Hansen, L. I., Hevink, L. M., Jostova, K., & Smagurauskaite, D. (2021). Bubble-wrapped sightseeing mobilities: Hop on-off bus experiences in Copenhagen, *Tourist Studies*, *21*(3), 1–17.

Legard, R., Keegan, J., & Ward, K. (2003). In-depth interviews. In J. Ritchie & J. Lewis (Eds.), *Qualitative research practice. A guide for social science students and researchers* (pp. 138–169). Sage Publications.

Lewis, J. (2003). Design issues. In J. Ritchie & J. Lewis (Eds.), *Qualitative research practice. A guide for social science students and researchers* (pp. 47–77). Sage Publications.

Milano, C., Novelli, M., & Cheer, J. M. (2019). Overtourism and degrowth: A social movements perspective. *Journal of Sustainable Tourism.* https://doi.org/10.1080/09669582.2019.1650054

Ministry of Tourism (2013). Cruise vessels schedule, winter 2012/13. In *Statistics from the directorate general for planning, follow-up and information.*

National Centre for Statistics and Information (NCSI) (2015). *Population statistics bulletin,* Issue 5.

Pan, S., Lee, J., & Tsai, H. (2014). Travel photos: Motivations, image dimensions, and affective qualities of places. *Tourism Management, 40,* 59–69.

Patton, M. Q. (2002). *Qualitative evaluation and research methods* (3rd ed.). Sage Publications.

Pink, S. (2007). Walking with video. *Visual Studies, 22*(3), 240–252.

Pink, S. (2008). An urban tour. The sensory sociality of ethnography place-making. *Ethnography, 9*(2), 175–196.

Pink, S. (2009). *Doing sensory ethnography.* Sage Publications.

Rantala, O. (2010). Tourist practices in the forest. *Annals of Tourism Research, 37*(1), 249–264.

Reuber, P., & Pfaffenbach, C. (2005). *Methoden der empirischen humangeographie. beobachtung und befragung* Das Geographische Seminar. Westermann Schroedel Diesterweg.

Rickly-Boyd, J. M. (2010). The tourist narrative. *Tourist Studies, 9*(3), 259–280.

Ritchie, B. W. (2005). Longitudinal research methods. In B. W. Ritchie, P. Burns, & C. Palmer (Eds.), *Tourism research methods: Integrating theory with practice* (pp. 131–141). CABI Publishing.

Ritchie, J., Lewis, J., & Elam, G. (2003a). Designing and selecting samples. In J. Ritchie & J. Lewis (Eds.), *Qualitative research practice. A guide for social science students and researchers* (pp. 77–108). Sage Publications.

Santos, C. A. (2005). Framing analysis: Examining mass mediated tourism narratives. In B. W. Ritchie, P. Burns, & C. Palmer (Eds.), *Tourism research methods, integrating theory with practice* (pp. 149–161). Cabi Publishing.

Scarles, C. (2010). Where words fail, visuals ignite opportunities for visual autoethnography in tourism research. *Annals of Tourism Research, 37,* 905–926.

Schmid, K. A. (2008). Doing ethnography of tourist enclaves. Boundaries, ironies and insights. *Tourist Studies, 8*(1), 105–121.

Spencer, L., Ritchie, J., & O'Connor, W. (2003). Analysis: Practices, principles and processes. In J. Ritchie & J. Lewis (Eds.), *Qualitative research practice* (pp. 199–218). Sage Publications.

Trell, E.-M., & Van Hoven, B. (2010). Making sense of place: Exploring creative and (inter)active research methods with young people. *Fennia, 188*(1), 91–104.

United Nations World Tourism Organization (UNWTO) (2013). *World tourism barometer.* Volume 11, Statistical Annex. UNWTO.

Wearing, S. L., & Foley, C. (2017). Understanding the tourist experience of cities. *Annals of Tourism Research, 65,* 97–107.

Weaver, A. (2005). Interactive service work and performative metaphors. The case of the cruise industry. *Tourist Studies, 5*(1), 5–27.

Wilson, E., & Hollinshead, K. (2015). Qualitative tourism research: Opportunities in the emergent soft sciences. *Annals of Tourism Research, 54*, 30–47.

Wilson, E., & Little, D. E. (2011). The solo female travel experience: Exploring the geography of women's fear. *Current Issues in Tourism, 11*(2), 167–186.

Yarnal, C. M., & Kerstetter, D. (2005). Casting off – An exploration of cruise ship space, group behavior and social interaction. *Journal of Travel Research, 43*, 268–379.

# 5 Results

## Oriental imaginaries, tourist experiences and the local quality of life

The following three chapters (Chapters 5, 6 and 7) are interconnected. I trace the tourists' views and their paths throughout a visit of Souq Muttrah, an urban destination and a rural destination, Sharqiyah Sands desert and an oasis. Tourists visit cities to experience their distinctive human difference, their neighbourhoods, the architectural design and cultural institutions. People are attracted to rural spaces for their character, the authentic cultural and natural landscape, the villages and traditional ways and norms of life that are different to urban life (MacCannell, 2011). The tourists' Oriental imaginaries in Souq Muttrah and in Sharqiyah Sands desert are realized in different stages of their journey, which is an under-researched area in tourism research (Chronis, 2015; Rakić & Chambers, 2012). My research aims to fill a gap in the discussion on mega-cruise tourism leading to an *overconsumption* of our resources. This is linked with Western, postcolonial imaginaries, on-site experiences and performances in a little-explored geographical location on the Arabian Peninsula.

### Discover, collect and consume

> *Enjoy the feeling of being at home everywhere around the globe*
> (CEO of a mega-cruise liner, brochure 2015/2016)

As a result of globalization, time and space are compressed during a cruise travel around the Arabian Peninsula. In the beginning of their one-week trip to four destination on the Arabian Peninsula, the German-speaking mega-cruise tourists arrive in Dubai by plane, where they embark on board a mega-cruise ship that displays a dominant German-speaking culture. The ship represents a temporary home for one week (Figure 5.1), being surrounded by like-minded people, who speak the same language and with similar values. They engage in similar activities and they share the same food like at home, creating a collective identity and a community.

DOI: 10.4324/9780429424946-5

*Figure 5.1* AIDABlu in Muscat

Source: Gutberlet (2013).

A feeling of "belonging" originates from being in the right place or having the right to be in a physical space of a "small nation at sea" where they are provided with a sense of security and being cared for. This is similar to British tourists in a hotel resort in Mallorca (Andrews, 2011). As a consequence of globalization, the need for a feeling of belonging is a necessary feature of a world that is facing increased insecurity and increasing loss of national identity (Andrews, 2011; Bauman, 2004). The tourists form an "imagined community", where "in the minds of each lives the image of their communion" (Anderson, 2016, p. 6). The feeling of a shared national communion, a longing for "wholeness and belonging to a kinship group" similar to a club membership (Anderson, 2016, p. 233). While on holidays with a cruise liner, the national identity is reinforced by homogeneity on board and socialization through group pressure. The tourists are searching for a better life based in their "home world", a home in which their fantasies of what is German can be lived out and constructed in a certain way (Andrews, 2011). On board the ship German is the main language of communication and even German food like dark, brown bread is baked freshly in the kitchen on board. Different popular sports activities, food, books, movies are shared and consumed that have no reference to the local culture in destinations; however, creating a sense of security (ibid., p. 118) and a pre-ordered world.

Along their circular journey, the tourists visit four Oriental countries: Dubai, The Sultanate of Oman, Bahrain, Abu Dhabi and then again Dubai. According to German on-board guides, an on-board lecturer and tourists interviewed, the "time-space compression" (Harvey, 1989) while travelling with a floating hotel that offers them a comfort zone like at home and even more along with the opportunity to consume or graze briefly on different destinations (Vogel & Oschmann, 2013) are the two main travel motivations. The tourists save money and time, compared to a land-based travel (Gutberlet, 2019b). If the tourists travel to Oman by plane, they will visit only one destination, which is as expensive as two cruise travels, said a German on-board guide in his 20s. The cruise tourists wished to consume as many destinations as possible for a discounted price like a consumer commodity, similar to an advertisement 'buy 3 for 1'.

During one of the excursions, an on-board guide told me that he was collecting the soils of the countries visited, even if it was briefly, for a few hours. He referred to an increased pleasure through time-space compression, accumulating travel knowledge and a "habitus", consuming as many places as possible like everyday commodities within "liquid life" (Bauman, 2000). While travelling with the mega-cruise ship, the tourists enhanced their own selves or their "social habitus" (Bourdieu, 1984), referring to the social structure and practices in space. Asked about the motivation for travelling with a cruise ship, a young male tourist in his 20s said, that in his view, it is too boring to travel to one destination only, linking the speed of the journey with an increased excitement while "grazing destinations". Similarly, a young female cruise tourist expressed her curiosity and extensive freedom when travelling on board a cruise liner, from one place to the next. *"The world is beautiful. There are endless destinations to be discovered"*, she said. This motivation was confirmed by a German tour operator who said: *"Most of the tourists are on a cruise trip to maximize their experiences"*, confirming time-space compression (Harvey, 1989) and the miniaturization of space (Urry, 1995).

Approximately two-thirds of the cruise tourists are travelling with the cruise ship because of its unique travel route, within a very different environment compared to the home environment (Gutberlet, 2019b).

> *"The tourists on board our cruise ship expect to have exciting holidays. They want to experience something different from home ... I think some tourists even do not care about the ports of call. If the destination is beautiful it's even better,"*

said an on-board guide expressing a sense of superiority towards the cruise tourists, highlighting the importance of being "sheltered" on board the ship, a safe place while being away. The on-board guide further explained they often realize during the travel that cruise tourists are little prepared for their travel and that they are more afraid, of finding themselves immersed in a very different culture.

The tourists want to experience some novelty within their cultural boundaries. They feel more comfortable when they book a common panorama tour, referring to the standardized nature of the coach sightseeing tour within an enclosed 'coach bubble', that stops at the major urban attractions. The similarity in the destination experiences such as a city tour by bus, a boat tour or a desert tour by 4 × 4 controls the tourists' experiences, contradicting the notion of freedom while on holidays (Andrews, 2011).

### "We are in Dubai"

As a result of time-space compression and global miniaturization, some mega-cruise tourists were disoriented. They felt being "out of place" and uncomfortable. According to German on-board guides I interviewed, some cruise tourists do not know the names of the different destinations along the ship itinerary, except Dubai, the home port of the cruise ship (Gutberlet, 2019b). Moreover, they thought the landscape in Oman would be similar to Dubai, the port of embarkation the previous day. In Dubai, the sandy desert is close to the cruise port (Gutberlet, 2019b). "We are in Dubai", said a male tourist in his 60s, standing in the Omani sand desert, fixing his geographical location as a way of fixing the self in the place (Andrews, 2011, p. 117). This indicates a lack of travel experience, pre-travel preparation as well as geographical orientation and knowledge, hence a lack of "aesthetic cosmopolitanism" (Urry, 1995). It also emphasizes a lack of interest in the destinations visited and the importance of the cruise ship as a tourist destination in its own right (Weaver, 2005b).

However, several German-speaking cruise tourists interviewed mentioned that their main travel motivation was to visit Dubai, the main port of call and the primary, trendy urban destination compared to the other little-known Oriental destinations including the Sultanate of Oman. The trip was seen as an opportunity to enjoy a sunny weather and a blue sky, getting a sun tan being a popular leisure activity enhancing the creation of a different physical appearance and identity. In the West, a sun tan is associated with well-being and with increased attractiveness.

Travel encourages a continuous process of "disembedment" in the countries visited (Gössling, 2002; Urry, 1995) or "decapsulation" (Jansson, 2002). Hence, due to the limited time spent in the destination and within the enclosed tourist bubble, mass-cruise tourists who travel on shorter cruises may not reflect on, appreciate and respect the uniqueness and culture of the destination (Hirtz & Cecil, 2008). Locals often serve as a visual backdrop or are observed through a "frame" (Urry, 1995). This disembedment or "lifting out" (Urry, 1995, p. 143) of the local, sociocultural context also depends on trust in the means of transportation used, which leads them comfortably through time and space. Hence, a cruise marketing brochure promised a carefree travel experience.

*You will be taken safely and directly to your destination – and you will be back on board the ship in good time.*
  (translated from German, cruise excursion brochure 2011/2012)

It is a promise of a safe travel through a standardized, packaged day-excursion offering little novelty. Similar to the ship itself, the car or coach constructs a safe, secure shell with comfortable seats, air conditioning and a water bottle, shielding the tourists from the soaring heat outside. Moreover, the tourists are guided by German-speaking tour guides providing them with a sense of security, belonging and familiarity, creating a feeling of "being at home and safe", which is similar to sitting in front of the TV screen (Gutberlet, 2019b). German is the main language of communication on board, creating a secure environment and a "customized authenticity" (Wang, 2007). A frequent cruise traveller, in his 80s, a retired accountant from Germany said that it was difficult for him and his wife to communicate in English expressing his lack of English language skills (Gutberlet, 2019b).

The walled environment of a 4 × 4 car or a bus symbolizes a mobile "tourist bubble" (Jaakson, 2004; 2004a; Weaver, 2005b) that can be seen as an extension or a periphery of the tourists' main destination, the "cruise ship bubble". The enclosed nature of the cruise ship controls and mediates the tourists' experiences, thereby contradicting notions of individual liberty, promoted by marketing slogans. In addition, the cruise liner aims to maximize its financial profits throughout the journey (Weaver, 2005a). The tourists are held in place or "strapped in" like in a hotel resort (Andrews, 2011, p. 119). The social environment on board the ship creates a shell, an artificial "simulacrum home" and a temporary "community" (Bauman, 2001, 2004) among an artificial nation of German-speakers.

## Oriental imaginaries

To create a place myth through postcolonial discourse of exploration and discovery of the unknown, the itineraries of the mega-cruise liners' of my research are called "Dubai & the Orient", promoting narratives and images of a modern, hybrid Emirate Dubai and "the rest" the mysterious, fairy-tale Orient (Gutberlet, 2017). In Oman, the Ministry of Tourism has promoted the country with the slogan "Beauty has an address".

The large majority of the cruise tourists, 92% ($N$ = 766), were first-time visitors to Oman (Gutberlet, 2017). Prior to their arrival, the tourists' imaginaries were mediated by postcolonial narratives, e.g. on websites, newsletters and in cruise brochures. With the slogan of *The Arabian Nights*, the cruise liner AIDA labels the destination (Palmer, 1994) Oman as a fairy-tale country, relying on fictional stories from the literature, film and arts to give authenticity to the destination visited (Salazar, 2012). A cruise brochure promises that the most beautiful dreams of The Arabian Nights will be realized in the Orient (AIDA, 2011, 2014/2012). It is therefore not surprising that

67% (*N* = 735) of the cruise tourists surveyed strongly agreed or agreed with the statement that Oman represents a country of "The Arabian Nights".

To contextualize the sample population of tourists who travelled with a mega-ship to Muscat, I outline briefly the demographic results (*N* = 797) of my tourist questionnaire conducted in Souq Muttrah. About 56% were female (*N* = 797) and most of the tourists were over 50 years of age: 27% (50–59 years), 29% (60–69 years) and 15% (over 70). This correlates with the literature on cruise tourism, e.g. in the study of Larsen et al. (2013) the cruise tourists' mean age was 50 years. In my research, 94% (*N* = 811) of the tourists surveyed were German, 4% Austrian and 2% were from other European countries, e.g. Luxemburg and Switzerland (Gutberlet, 2017). Prior to their arrival in Muscat, 61% (*N* = 785) had consulted tourist guidebooks and travel brochures (Gutberlet, 2016b). My in-depth interviews confirmed that individual tourists had similar imaginaries as cruise tourists in their minds. A tourist couple interviewed in Souq Muttrah stayed in one of the five-star hotels in Muscat. They mentioned that Oman was recommended to them as a country of "1001 Nights". Similar to cruise tourists, they expected to explore "legendary lands" (Echtner & Prasad, 2003), referring to the adventures of "Sindbad the seafarer" (Mein Schiff, 2012/2013a). From Oman, legendary Sindbad embarked on his travels. *"Cruise travel serves a certain cliché about the Orient, confirmed"* a male German on-board guide.

Different from what tourists see in the other ports of call in the Arabian Gulf region like Dubai, Abu Dhabi and Bahrain, the urban landscape around the old marketplace Souq Muttrah (Figure 5.2) confirmed a place

*Figure 5.2* The Corniche Road with Souq Muttrah, the residential area Sur Al-Lawatia and its mosque

Source: Gutberlet (December 2018).

myth, creating a sense of nostalgia for an untouched, postcard-like image of Arabia (Gutberlet, 2016a), which is however different in reality. Old towns and neighbourhoods that remain unchanged by modernity suddenly become economic assets (Cohen, 1978). Europeans who travel to Africa wish to experience the landscape and the people just as they read about it in fairy tales and as it was back in history (Salazar, 2006; Wels, 2004), during colonial times (Leite, 2014), creating place myths.

Oman represents a "mysterious place", remarked a male tourist during one of the tours. The inside front page of a German cruise guidebook pictures an Omani boy in dishdasha and kumma (cap for Omani males). The photo was entitled *"the successors of Sindbad the seafarer"*, labelling Omani children as inheriting legacies, reconstructing the "embodied Oriental Other" as a child, inferior to an adult tourist, so that a quasi-parental power can be exercised (Morgan & Pritchard, 1998). The embodied tourist experience becomes especially powerful within parental, gendered and racialized imaginary (MacCannell, 2011). Symbols and representations in excursion videos, events, lectures and conversations with on-board employees like tour guides and on-board lecturers, reinforced typical postcolonial, Oriental narratives. On two mega-liners, on-board lecturers and other staff members were reading *The Arabian Nights* in German. For children, stories like *Aladdin* were read in the on-board Kids Club. A male on-board lecturer in his 50s told me during an interview that he recounted some erotic stories from *The Arabian Nights* while explaining the history of belly dancing (Gutberlet, 2017). This was done as an introduction to an actual live performance by a female dancer on board.

> *He said that around forty people participated in his Arabian Nights lecture and they met inside a small room.*

He had a biased sexualized under-tone, eroticizing the "Oriental female", raising misleading, dangerous assumptions (Beeton et al., 2006) about the Omani culture and the people. Belly dancing is not an Omani dance and female dances are not part of the Omani culture. Women dance only among other females, e.g. during weddings and in separate places than men. Men dance folkloric dances during National Day celebrations or other festivals in public.

Another lecturer from AIDAblu mentioned that she read parts of the autobiography of Princess Salme from Zanzibar (Rüte, 2004) prior to the arrival of the ship in the port in Muscat. Princess Salme married a German businessman from Hamburg in the beginning of the last century. These narratives were Orientalizing the destination, connecting Oman with its colonial history in Zanzibar. In addition, she advised the tourists about sights of interest in the next destination of the cruise liner (Gutberlet, 2017). For example, she had praised Muscat as being the highlight of the journey. In order to witness the sunrise and the Omani coastline, she advised the tourists to get up early. A female tourist in her twenties, recalled with admiration her first actual sight of the imaginary country Oman and the bay of Muttrah (Gutberlet, 2017).

The travel imagery designed by the employees of the mega-cruise liner, produces a myth, a "fantasy parallel world inhabited by tourists" (MacCannell, 2011).

> *"Souq Muttrah can be already seen from the ship, whereas the other souqs on our itinerary in Manama (Bahrain) or in Dubai are located far away from the ports, ..."*

said an on-board cruise guide highlighting the close proximity of Souq Muttrah, next to the harbour of the ship. He recalled that upon arrival in the port, the German captain broadcast through a public address system on board an invitation to explore the most beautiful and most Oriental place of the entire cruise travel.

> *"Actually, we praise Muscat as a typical Oriental port. Dubai and Abu Dhabi are big cities with huge skyscrapers and tourist sites like Burj Khalifa or Burj Al Arab, which are not really associated with the 'Orient',"*

said the male on-board guide, referring to the modern and glamorous style of the Emirates and "the old and backward" imaginary of the Orient represented in The Sultanate of Oman. He continued saying that

> *many tourists travel to Muscat to experience an Oriental souq in Muttrah, which cannot be compared with the rather rebuilt and modern souqs in Abu Dhabi or Dubai.*

Cultural mediators on board the cruise ship directed the tourist gaze, shaping the tourists' imaginaries about Muscat as an Oriental and a "feminine destination" (Gutberlet, 2017). Moreover, German-speaking crew members advised the tourists to visit Souq Muttrah that is a traditional, Arabian souq and a "shopping destination" (Figure 5.3); therefore, promoting consumption practices that act as a means of freedom and as a way of communication with the other members of the society, while coding the members of the group (Baudrillard, 2017). Regardless of its cultural and heritage value, Souq Muttrah was promoted as an Oriental shopping experience, having a fairy-tale atmosphere (Elle Magazin, 2013).

Narratives in marketing brochures in English as well as in German mediate the tourists' sensuous imaginaries of a souq that is a historic, unchanged, timeless attraction (Echtner & Prasad, 2003) offering "a mysterious atmosphere, exotic smells and products" (AIDA, 2015/2016).

*Figure 5.3* The main entrance of Souq Muttrah with its tower at the Corniche road. The tower was built in the early 2000, prior to the arrival of mega ships

Source: Gutberlet (2013).

Smells are an essential element of the tourist experience in Souq Muttrah contributing to the well-being, the sense of place and feeling comfortable (Gutberlet, 2017). A German tour operator who participated in a professional workshop on board a cruise ship compared the smellscape in Souq Muttrah with Moroccan markets:

> "In Morocco the souq stinks because of the leather dyeing businesses. In Marrakech it can be dangerous, dark and unsafe with strange music. Here in Muscat the souq is safe and very clean," she said.

These features about Souq Muttrah "being safe and clean" were confirmed during my interviews with cultural mediators and tourists. It is not surprising that 77% of the mega-cruise tourists ($N = 719$) had very strong or fairly strong images of *colourful markets* in their minds (Gutberlet, 2017). A total of 70% of the mega-cruise tourists surveyed ($N = 706$) had strong or fairly strong images of frankincense in their minds (Gutberlet, 2017). These imaginaries were again misleading. Frankincense originates from the south of Oman. In the past, it was valued as a highly prized commodity like gold in the Roman Empire and in Greece (Vine, 1995). Official narratives were supported by Oriental imaginaries of a large, white frankincense burner, a monument that was labelled as representing "the symbol of the city" where in the surrounding landscape frankincense trees are planted (Mein Schiff, 2012/2013b). However, frankincense trees predominantly grow in the South of Oman. Such "collective narrative articulations" (Chronis, 2012) and imaginaries about the local culture, the landscape and frankincense were adjusted, transforming the destination into a commodity and a tourist attraction that suits stereotypical mass tourism expectations (Daye, 2005).

In social narratives in a promotional video of Oman, entitled '*Welcome to My Country*', Omani men and Western tourists were represented (Feighery, 2012). Expatriate male vendors, who dominate the space in Souq Muttrah as well as Omani women, who visit the souq as customers as well as the few women working in the souq, were excluded from visual representations in official narratives and imaginaries. This confirms Feighery (2012) and MacCannell (2011) who mentioned that different local peoples and "unseen layers of cultural or historic complexity" are often excluded in order to keep a flat and unified imagery.

## The tourist bubble

In the following sections, tourist imaginaries and embodied performances (Edensor, 1998) will be analysed along different stages of the tourist experience, during a city-tour by bus in Muscat.

Walking through the city is a self-directed everyday practice (Larsen et al., 2021), while being on a coach bus, the "tourist bubble" protects tourists from any geographical disorientation, from getting lost in an unknown environment as well as from excessive walking and physical exhaustion. They are travelling from one attraction to another by a Western-style cocooned sightseeing bus with air conditioning. Such mobile "tourist bubble" also shelters them from harsh weather like heat, rain and cold (Larsen et al., 2021).

From the beginning of the one-day excursions, which started in the morning at around 8.30 a.m. from the port in Muscat, the travel experience including the interpretation had to be rationalized, controlled and accelerated in time (Harvey, 1989; Urry, 1995). Enclosed, controlled "enclavic spaces" (Edensor, 2000) can enhance a feeling of being safe and the necessity to comply with a strict schedule and a belonging to an imaginary "cruise community", while restricting their freedom, placing individuals under pressure (Ryan, 2002).

Within the cruise excursion and its time-space compression, local labour processes had to be rationalized (Harvey, 1989). The drivers and the local guide had to be at the port in Muttrah before sunrise around 5 or 6 a.m. They worked more than 10–12 hours (Gutberlet, 2019a) similar to the long working hours on board a mega-cruise ship (Weaver, 2005c). The tight time-space compression confirmed a shift towards organizational disintegration and an increased sub-contracting of local employees (Harvey, 1989). To raise local profits, the Omani drivers were hired as freelancers. They had received little or no training in guiding German-speaking cruise tourists and in cross-cultural communication and their payment per day was little (Gutberlet, 2019b). Milano et al. (2019) noted that "the outsourcing of employment leads to precarious working conditions and the transformation of the commercial fabric of cities that undermine essential characteristics of places". The majority of the expatriate employees on a full-time contract guiding cruise tourists were hired on short, seasonal contracts of a few months duration with little pay for long working hours, which therefore magnifies their precarious employment conditions. They are often from Asia (India, Sri Lanka) but as well from Russia and Europe, confirming 'fluid social relations' within a liquid modernity (Bauman, 2000). Due to strict work regulations for expatriates in Oman, expatriate tour guides are not allowed to work as freelancers for several agencies, like, e.g. in Europe whereas Omani tour guides are allowed to work as freelance guides, creating an imbalance and discriminative practices between expatriates and Omani tour guides.

Capital accumulation is a priority of the mega-cruise ship.

> *"A cruise liner is a money machine. The more people on board the more money they can make. For example, this mega-cruise ship has 11 bars. You can get alcohol from morning 11 a.m. until after midnight. It's all-inclusive",*

said a senior manager from the local tour operator, referring to the high turnover of capital through services that are partially limited in the local destination.

> *"Nowadays, the cruise liner pricing is very attractive and affordable. They serve food 24 hours. Cruise tourists don't need a visa. They receive a daypass for each country visited. Taking a cruise is not a dream that cannot be reached anymore",*

said the general manager of one of the large shipping companies in Muscat during an interview. The cruise is demanding high-quality products, at a low cost and within very tight timelines (Lopes & Dredge, 2018). Due to the affordable pricing for the masses, for the local tour operator, it is a challenge to hire and to pay for knowledgeable multilingual tour guides, drivers and cars for one day, who cannot be hired for longer trips around Oman. For a Muscat city tour they paid around 50 Euros per person. According to local interviewees, the cruise ship usually keeps 50% or even up to 70% of the income of the excursion. There was little profit for the local tour operator, affirming the hierarchical power structures and the hegemony of a global network of cruise companies in the Global North (Gutberlet, 2019b; Jaakson, 2004a). This hegemony of the global cruise industry confirms an increasing lack of social responsibility towards local communities (Font et al. 2016; Klein, 2005; Lopes & Dredge 2018; Renaud, 2017) and an increasing dependence on cruise liner companies based in the Global North.

Due to the acceleration of time and space and the rationalized character of the excursion, the tourists were in a rush to leave the ship even without having time for having a small breakfast on board. Due to a large number of cruise tourists, they had to gather well in advance in the ship's theatre. From there they were distributed by on-board guides to a number of excursion buses and 4 × 4 cars. Outside the ship, they were seen rushing to board one of the vehicles waiting for them (Gutberlet, 2019b).

Descending the ship ramp at the port in Muttrah, the cruise tourists were photographed, sometimes along with a local "Other", representing a staged performance, directed by the cruise employees, similar to a Disneyland theme park. These photos were presented and sold on board, producing symbols of memories while shaping the tourists' imaginaries about the destination (Gutberlet, 2017).

One morning, cruise tourists were observed being photographed beside a female cruise employee wearing a black abaya (a long over-dress for women worn on the Arabian Peninsula), along with a black scarf and a black face veil. I asked a German cruise employee why they were staging a veiled woman at the ship ramp as their welcome to Muscat, although a face veil is rarely seen in Muscat.

I was told that this was a promotional joke. The German excursion manager from the cruise liner further explained to me that in a similar way, cruise tourists are welcomed by Mickey Mouse and Donald Duck in the United States, referring to the "commercial staging" in the United States, where mega-cruise tourism started in the last century. Hence, the local Omani culture with its narratives and performances was promoted in a stereotype version and as a postcolonial commodity (Chaney, 2002), while decontextualizing from local realities in the destination (Gutberlet, 2017). The intention of the cruise employees was to embody an "Oriental Other", misleading tourists and misrepresenting local (authentic) practices and representations, fuelling negative stereotypes as well as Western superiority about veiled females. Due to the misrepresentation of the "Oriental Other", seen "as a kind of ultimate Other of Western tourist consciousness", influenced by "collective memory" (MacCannell, 2012), it was not surprising that 86% of the mega-cruise tourists surveyed ($N = 729$) had strong or fairly strong images of veiled women in their minds (Gutberlet, 2017).

Having described the tourists' pre-arrival imaginaries and their experiences while descending the ship, in the following part, I will analyse the on-site tourist experiences and local reactions in Souq Muttrah.

## Performing, glancing and gazing in Muttrah

The tourists went on board their tourist buses, which drove them to different 'sights to see' in Muscat including the Sultan Qaboos Grand Mosque, one of the top cultural sights in Muscat, located on the opposite side of the city. This was a passive mobility (Larsen et al., 2021). The visit to the mosque was followed by a drive along the highway through the city of Muscat, a visit to one of the museums in Old Muscat and several short photo-stops. Then the tourists could capture a glimpse of a place and a visual memory of the site.

The souq in Muttrah was the last stop of the half-day city tour. Going on a city tour is a preferred practice, especially by middle-aged people. It is a comfortable way to move faster and to see more within a certain time. It is also a comfortable way of passively experiencing the place while overcoming the soaring temperatures outside. On board, the contemporary cruise liners, small, colourful pocket maps were distributed prior to the excursion. They can be unfolded easily while 'on the go', stressing on the time-space compression. However, these maps are not very precise, showing only the 'tourist bubble' in Muttrah with the harbour street, the souq and old Muscat, located in the next bay. Since many cruise tourists enjoy the element of surprise while on tour, precision is not important for the short stay in the city. Although these maps were free of charge, it was observed that tourists were not using them (Gutberlet, 2016a).

Referring to local tour operators and the local media, Souq Muttrah is the most popular tourist spot in Oman (Times of Oman, 2015a). According to Jaakson's (2004) analysis of the "tourist bubble", the core area of the bubble is the waterfront area with its Corniche road, the walking promenade, the residential area and Souq Muttrah (Figure 5.4). Along the Corniche road, there are ancient trading houses, built around 200 years ago. They are part of the residential walled district, the Sur Al-Lawatia. The area includes a Shia mosque with a blue dome and views of the surrounding mountain range. The walled district is a closed, private space, with extremely limited access for any outsiders of the community (Gutberlet, 2020). Along the Corniche road and in the souq there are many open spaces that offer beautiful views and some shaded benches to rest in. The place is an "open tourist bubble", a public space shared by locals, residents and tourists alike. The souq can be compared with a kind of "heterotopia", a place of mystery, a labyrinth with changing meanings, poignant memories and dark corners (Urry, 1995).

Often cruise tourists who want to explore the city on their own take a small shuttle bus to the gate of the port and then they take a taxi or they just walk on their own along the harbour street. Some tourists visit the fish, fruit and vegetable market next to the port and some venture towards the commercial business district of Muscat, Ruwi, and a few visit the ancient merchant house, the Bait Al Baranda Museum, a heritage museum. According to the director of the museum, only a few mega-cruise tourists pass by the museum in the morning hours. It is a hidden attraction. The large majority of the tourists walk in groups or individually like a male flâneur or a female "choraster" (Wearing & Foley, 2017). They stroll along the harbour street, where tourism shops sell souvenirs or jewellery and then enter the souq (Gutberlet, 2016a).

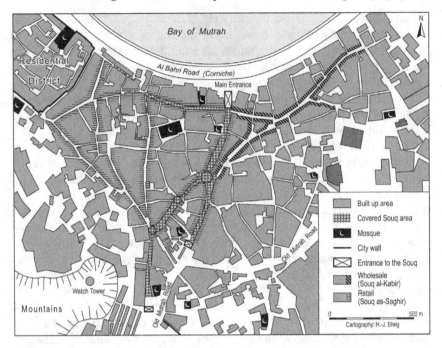

*Figure 5.4* Map of the Bay of Muttrah including its souq area and main tourist entrance as well as the residential district, Sur Al-Lawatia

Source: Ehrig, RWTH Aachen (2016).

In that area, small restaurants and coffee shops have opened since the arrival of cruise tourists. Through modification in the architecture, the souq has been modernized and homogenized for tourism purposes (Gutberlet, 2016a), representing a "staged authenticity" (Wels, 2004).

One morning, around 9 a.m., I observed a number of buses stopping in front of the souq. European tourists including Germans, Dutch, Austrians, French and Italians stepped out and flocked into the souq. They were in groups of 20–48 people, all of them had small white stickers, like name badges but indicating their bus numbers on their shirts (Figure 5.5).

The tourists entered the souq through the main entrance gate on the Corniche road, the replica watch tower, built just before the arrival of the mega-cruise liners. It marks the place as a tourist site. From there, the majority of the tourists were walking within "the tourist bubble", all having the same visual experience (Gutberlet, 2016a). From a Western perspective, strolling or walking is a major activity in urban tourism (Edensor, 2000). In Souq Muttrah, it is mainly performed within a group, linking together individuals (Chronis, 2015). The tourists were observed gazing at the shops, their outlets and the Asian vendors, giving them signs of "civil inattention" (Goffman, 1963). They were realizing their presence but without giving them a lot of attention, they just passed by in front of them (Figure 5.6). The vendors were clearly

*Figure 5.5* Tourists gather in front of the souq, Corniche road

Source: Gutberlet (2014).

*Figure 5.6* Cruise tourists walking along the main, colourful street of the souq, some vendors staring at them passing by

Source: Gutberlet (2014).

visible "in the front stage" compared to Omani vendors, who were often not visible. They were hidden in the "backstage" (Goffman, 1963), inside their shops. While the cruise tourists were strolling in small groups along the narrow streets of the "tourist bubble", male Asian shop vendors were standing in the street. They gazed at the tourists, realizing a "host gaze" and a "male gaze" (Maoz, 2006). They were praising their products.

I observed that they were staring intently at the Western tourists passing by, as if on a stage, appropriating the Western "Other", while the tourists were rather looking at the products on sale. From a Western point of view, staring is something that one does not ordinarily do to another person: "it seems to put the object stared at in a class apart" (Goffman, 1963, p. 1288), exercising power or even creating a power struggle over the space. Staring can be felt as an intrusion to privacy (ibid., 1963), in particular by females (Gutberlet, 2017).

## Staging Oriental imaginaries

Asian vendors were observed staging the *Orient* by approaching the tourists in an aggressive way, e.g. holding a pashmina scarf, a small bottle of safran or a fake *Amouage* perfume bottle (expensive designer perfume designed for Oman) in front of them, trying to sell their product in German or in another European language (Gutberlet, 2016a). The expatriate vendors were trying their utmost to sell Oriental "material imaginaries" (Chronis, 2015), materialized in the cheap, fake pashmina scarves, T-shirts, carpets and belly dancing costumes on display, as well as local frankincense or *bokhour*, a perfume mixture. The products on sale were mainly imported and showed little differentiation. A majority of 55% ($N = 771$) of the German-speaking cruise tourists surveyed liked the product range as well as the "light Oriental" features (Haldrup & Larsen, 2010) such as the architecture including the ceiling, the small open shops and the narrow streets. The cruise and group tourists interviewed mentioned that they enjoyed the tangible Oriental features such as the ethnic Omani dress, the dim light and the way of displaying the products in open shop stalls. These Oriental features were enhancing a direct contact and cultural exchange with the *Otherness* (Gutberlet, 2017), which is different to an encounter in a supermarket or in a mall. It was not surprising that tourists were searching for these Oriental features. An individual tourist, a pharmacist from Germany, who enjoyed the Oriental, cosy atmosphere of the souq said while walking along the small alleys of the souq:

> *"People in the souq are less pushy in their approach, compared to Morocco, where there are cyclists, motorcycles and donkeys walking along side by side with pedestrians. I love to observe the old people."* She had visited Oman several times, and for the first time in 1989. *"At that time, I was invited by the Minister of Education. We had dinner with gold plated cutlery"*, she remembered this special occasion with obvious pleasure and in detail. *"We were welcomed with rose water and we left with frankincense"*, she said remembering the fragrances. These experiences had a strong impact on her souvenirs about Oman.

*"Since that time, I dream about Oman. The country has changed totally. It's a different country". She continued saying: "You know, when I travel to a place I wish to connect with the local people. At that time, I took a number of photos. Now I wish to meet these people again and I wish to hand over their photo. I took photos of abaya vendors, Indian vendors and a kumma shop in Salalah",*

referring to her nostalgia about the first trip to Oman, which created an "interpersonal and existential authenticity" (Wang, 1999). The destination had transformed her towards the direction of the community and the local *"Other"* (MacCannell, 2011, p. 113), similar to volunteer tourism (Crossley, 2013) (Crossely, 2013). While re-visiting the place she became nostalgic, wishing to "return the moments she had taken from them in the past, captured in photos", having the expectation to receive and enact proximate care and gratitude from a usually distant "Other" (Crossley, 2013). Unlike other tourists, the tourist was already very familiar with the place. She even guided me to a halwa shop in the souq that I had never seen before. She promised to return to Oman the following year together with a group of 20 pharmacists. *"I will guide the group"*, she said. She had already prepared for the trip and written a specialized guidebook for her group. The book included detailed texts and colourful photos about the flora, fauna, history, society and traditions in Oman she had collected from various sources.

During our walk through the souq she took a photo of a henna-drawing on the left hand of one of the few females who are working at a grocery shop. The tourist asked the female Omani before taking the photo and respected her wish not to be seen in the photo, a "mutual respect" (Din, 1989) between the tourist and the local. It shows that the individual tourist had more "cosmopolitan empathy" towards the community (Crossley, 2013). The attraction, the souq, served as a vehicle or an agency to the "Oriental Other" (MacCannell, 2011, p. 113) and as a marker to communicate and get to know the community better (Figure 5.7). The attraction connected the individual and group tourists with the community. In contrast, the attraction does not connect the cruise tourist with the community.

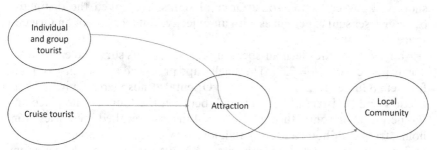

*Figure 5.7* The attraction connects the individual and the group tourist with the local community, whereas the cruise tourist is connected with the attraction only.

Source: Gutberlet (2021), adapted from MacCannell (2011).

## Frankincense smellscape

The frankincense shop located at the main street, inside the Souq, is one of the first shops that tourists often visit. It is a place where different senses are entangled with social narratives, olfaction and personal memories. One day, cruise tourists experienced a typical Omani "smellscape" (Edensor, 2000) of incense, burnt in two small clay pots at the open, elevated outlet of the small frankincense shop. Especially on the Arabian Peninsula, strong perfumes are important features in everyday life. It is important to be smelled by a person and to smell the other person (Rodaway, 2002).

A female German cruise tourist obviously enjoyed the smells, leaning over the frankincense burner and wafting the fumes towards her nose and her whole face. Through their senses, the tourists were connected with the place, while "making sense" of the space, engaging with their whole bodies. Olfaction is evocative of emotional responses (Rodaway, 2002), that differ from one person to another and one culture to another. The multi-sensory performances were reinforcing the dichotomy between "*home*" and being "*away*" in the Orient. It is not surprising that 80.2% ($N = 707$) of the mega-cruise tourists surveyed felt as if they were in a different world (Gutberlet, 2017). Hence, for 85% of the cruise tourists ($N = 732$), the souq represented a unique "Oriental experience". These strong perceptions were confirmed during my in-depth interviews with tourists.

Two young male Omanis in their 20s, wearing a long, white local dress (dishdasha) and a colourful turban with embroidery on their heads, embodying the *Oriental Other*, were standing in the tiny frankincense shop owned by a family from Salalah. They were selling frankincense and other perfume mixtures (bokhur). They were piled up to the ceiling in the back of the elevated shop without glass windows, showcasing *Oriental abundance*, realizing a typical Oriental shop (Figure 5.8).

"*We wanted to see Arabia*", said a male tourist highlighting that they wanted to experience a less modern place than Dubai. They visited Dubai the previous day. He was now gazing around in front of the frankincense shop, visually collecting some Oriental sights. He linked the distinctive olfactory, sensual experiences with an objective authenticity of an Oriental space.

About 68% of the German-speaking cruise tourists surveyed enjoyed the smells in the souq ($N = 722$). The smellscape produced a new sense of place for them (Gutberlet, 2017), creating an Oriental atmosphere, a spiritual connection and "existential authenticity" between the tourists, the place and the people. For some, the smell of frankincense recalled memories from home, from childhood and from religious services at the church.

For example, a male cruise tourist in his 60s remembered the ceremony at his church. He moved his right arm back and forth, imitating a catholic priest's movement with a frankincense burner during a religious ceremony.

*Figure 5.8* One of the first shops in the souq: the frankincense shop

Source: Gutberlet (2012).

In Souq Muttrah frankincense is stored, sold and consumed. Some cruise tourists were observed openly rejecting or avoiding the strong olfactory experience of frankincense, through their gestures: They turned their heads away from the fumes or they started to cough, whereas tourists with positive memories of frankincense stopped for a moment in front of the shop. They were curious about its application and usage in Oman. These tourists asked for additional interpretation (Gutberlet, 2017).

### Freezing a moment through photography

One day, while I was sitting inside the tiny frankincense shop, I was observing the scenery. A German-speaking Omani tour guide with his group of around 20 cruise tourists including a cameraman from the ship stopped at the shop staging and performing a "disciplined ritual". Cultural brokers like the tour guide and shop vendors are "stagers of sensations, they perform, play, enact and stage" (Urry & Larsen, 2011). The tourists were directed to the tourist site (Edensor, 2000), labelling the shop as a special place or a "marker" to see.

First, the guide climbed up a few steps to the frankincense shop, the stage, from where he was overlooking the crowd of German tourists. He was directing their performances and the tourist gaze, to realize a romantic or a "collective gaze" (Urry & Larsen, 2011). Hence, the tour guide was the director of the "disciplined ritual" (Edensor, 2000). A number of cruise tourists took out their cameras or mobile phones experiencing the place "through their lenses". They started taking photos while a cameraman from the cruise ship started to film the entire scene (Figure 5.9). They were preserving the scene for "future practices" (Crouch & Desforges, 2003) and for sharing with friends and family members. Ultimately, the frankincense shop turned into a stage set (MacCannell, 1999) showcasing "a mini-theatrical event" (Wu et al., 2014). Photography is an important ritual of vacationing (Gutberlet, 2016c), along with sightseeing and buying souvenirs, a "compulsion of the performance" (Edensor, 2000, p. 334).

Photography reflects a wish to arrest and freeze a magical moment in time (Bærenholdt et al., 2004, p. 117). The aim is to shoot the best photo for a holiday album, sharing with friends and colleagues lateron or with the public and the public instantaneously through the phone. Mobile photography is a part of everyday life. Selfies are frequently made 'on the go', nearly everywhere, while being shared on the tourist spot. Leisure has become an extension of our everyday lives and practices (Larsen, 2019). Photography is seen as a performance that "produces memories, social relations and places" (Larsen, 2019, p. 69). While recording their encounters and experiences at the frankincense shop as a video or taking photographs, they performed according to various scripts, roles, technologies, relations and places. The tourists transformed themselves from distanced spectators into active participants in the scene in form of directors and actors, producing "new realities", linking the destination Souq Muttrah with their everyday life at home. The on-board cameraman was recording the scene for a travel diary. Which is produced and sold by the ship. According to my survey, 80% of the cruise tourists ($N = 778$) used photography during their visit to the souq, which also confirmed the aesthetic value of their experiences.

*Figure 5.9* An Omani tour guide "staging" at the frankincense shop in front of his group of German-speaking cruise tourists

Source: Gutberlet (2012).

At the frankincense shop, many tourists took photos of the young Omani vendor, Amr (name changed), who represented an "Oriental Other" (Gutberlet, 2017). However, only a few tourists asked him for permission to do so, transforming the vendor into a passive object of the tourist gaze, while exercising power over him (Goffman, 1963). Amr did not understand German but he spoke some English. The Omani guide was the only one with whom the tourists interacted in their own language and culture. Moreover, the lack of signage on the products in the souq created a lack of interpretation for the tourists' understanding of the souq environment.

The Omani tour guide had to mediate between Amr and the German-speaking tourists, creating the gaze and affirming Oriental imaginaries that were sold to them in advance (Salazar, 2006), e.g. in marketing material through the cruise website, travel blogs, brochures, on-board daily newspapers and videos.

The frankincense shop is one of the few shops located at the entrance to the 'tourist bubble' catering to both tourists and the locals (Gutberlet, 2017). The local guide interpreted the attraction, the frankincense shop, on his own, replacing even the position of Amr, the vendor, while the tourists were observing and communicating in a dialogue with the guide. They were on an equal footing with each other, without appropriating the tour guide, the object of their gaze. As a consequence of the staging and a lack of his active involvement, the Omani vendor moved passively to the back of his shop, refilling frankincense and serving the local community. There, local Omani and other Arabic-speaking customers, e.g. from UAE or Yemen, bought frankincense often in large quantities from another window of his tiny shop. The shop has been owned by Amr's family since 2002; they originate from Salalah, where they own another business in the souq. Amr told me that Omani families buy frankincense from their shops in large quantities. They resell the incense in their villages in the interior of Oman.

In a separate interview later on, Amr told me that he sells around 30–50 kilograms of frankincense per day to the local community. The sale of frankincense in large quantities is predominantly handled on Thursdays, the end of the working week in Oman. Amr offers a variety of perfumes; he even sells frankincense with different flavours such as lemon, sandalwood or oud (Arabian wood) that is used to perfume clothes and the interior of homes and after meals, as a final sensual note.

In the scenery with the cruise tourists, the tourists were in a kind of "mystical place", adjusting the cultural production of frankincense to their German imaginary. From the tour guide in the frontstage of the shop, the tourists received interpretation and several stories (communicative staging), forming their own German interpretation of the tourist site.

The guide informed the tourists about the different qualities of frankincense and their prices. He said that the green frankincense is more expensive than the regular yellow one and continued explaining its everyday use. For example, frankincense can be used as a drink. The guide then opened a small box of frankincense. A few tourists took a piece of frankincense and tasted it. To show how Omanis perfume their clothes with frankincense, the guide placed the frankincense burner on the floor, underneath his dishdasha (Gutberlet, 2017). He continued saying:

> *"Myrrh is a gum; the best quality is from Salalah". "How do you burn frankincense?"* asked a female tourist. *"With charcoal"*, said the guide while pointing at a piece of charcoal and a colorful, small clay pot. *"This is a frankincense burner. You put the charcoal on top"*, he said.

He did not mention that the charcoal was an imported product from China. The tourist linked frankincense and myrrh with imaginaries derived from Biblical accounts of the three Holy Kings who offered gold, myrrh and frankincense to Jesus when he was born in Bethlehem. It becomes evident that people learn to associate certain images such as frankincense with meanings that are contextual (Banks & Zeitlyn, 2015). Within the guiding practices, the Omani guide was a key player in "localizing, folklorizing, ethnicizing and exoticizing" (Salazar, 2006) the frankincense shop. He connected the site and the tourists (Gutberlet, 2017).

The body of the Omani guide was used as a sign to communicate through embodiment and his social and cultural knowledge, while the personal display of the Omani cultural traditions became a cultural commodity (Hall & Tucker, 2004). The tourists from their side, seemed glad about all the "tourism tales" (Chronis, 2012; Salazar, 2006). They were framing the visit to the frankincense shop through the embodiment, with the smell, taste and their visual gaze of the products and the contacts with the tour guide and with the vendor, Amr, who represented the "Oriental Other". My questionnaire survey revealed that 58% of the cruise tourists very much liked or liked having contact with local people including cultural mediators like tour guides and drivers (Gutberlet, 2017). My findings correlate with research results of Wu et al. (2014) in the Silk market in Beijing, who highlighted that the social interaction is promoted through the mediation and social interaction with a local person. Such a mediator can often reduce a sense of threat or concern about buying an inferior quality. Because they felt reassured, and comforted by their "glocalised" guide (Salazar, 2005), they did not bargain and accepted the given prices. Besides frankincense, pashmina scarves and postcards were the most popular souvenirs for German-speaking megacruise tourists (Gutberlet, 2016a).

Due to the familiarization of the new Oriental environment through "transcultural frames" that translate the *Otherness* with an image known in the tourist culture (Salazar, 2010), a number of cruise tourists bought frankincense. I observed that especially the older tourists bought frankincense in order to create a certain olfactory environment at home, linked with their collective Christian identities and festivals. An Austrian woman said that she bought frankincense for her father because he enjoys perfuming his home with incense at Christmas. Other tourists bought frankincense for the pastor. The tourists aligned the holiday experience with their environments and their identities at home (Gutberlet, 2017). A male Yemeni tourist said in Arabic that he bought frankincense as a special gift from Muscat. Despite the fact that there are frankincense trees in Yemen, in the North and South of the country. An Omani male customer in his 40s from another district in Muscat said, he often goes shopping at the fish market and then to Souq Muttrah around two to three times per month. There he buys bokhur (a perfume mixture), which is used by females in the family to perfume their black abayas (overcoats), connecting family traditions and everyday practices (Gutberlet, 2017).

Other Omanis were buying textiles or household items. Among the local community and Arab tourists, the souq is an appreciated shopping place for frankincense, an original, objectively authentic product, reflecting their own identities and being used as an everyday perfume and medicine.

## Dressing up like an Oriental Other

Next to Amr's small frankincense shop in Souq Muttrah, one of the new Asian vendors who did not belong to the well-established Banyan trader community, showed a group of German tourists how to fold the traditional Omani turban, (headcover, in Arabic: *masar*). The vendor was engaging the German tourists in a playful way. The tourist looked like a local while having a picture taken, "entering a third frame" (MacCannell, 2011) staging and embodying an "Oriental Other".

Some male cruise tourists were observed wearing an Emirati headcover and a dishdasha (Gutberlet, 2017). The dress is like the Austrian or Bavarian leather trousers, said a male cruise tourist framing and localizing the Omani dress with a transcultural symbol from his home-country. Some female cruise tourists were observed wearing a black abaya, worn by most Omani and Muslim females, especially in the capital Muscat. It seemed the tourists wished to stage an Oriental female, but without wearing a headscarf. Some mega-cruise tourists who had bought an Omani dress mentioned that they kept the dress for an Oriental Carnival Night on board the mega-cruise ship. Hence, the holidays were seen as a search for individuality, freedom as well as a search for the *Oriental Other*. However, the way the cruise tourists tend to dress in a similar way reflects their wish for uniformity (Andrews, 2011) and belonging to an "imaginary community on board".

Another day, I observed a young Omani tour guide who was in his 20s. He was guiding a small group of mega-cruise tourists through the main street of the souq. At one shop he stopped and took a hair clip with a large plastic flower. Such a clip is used to elevate the shape of the headscarf of women. The Omani guide tried to fix a hair clip in a German tourist's black hair. The tourist in her 60s seemed very surprised about his spontaneous gesture. The majority of the tour group started laughing. Then one of the female on-board guides asked him for another flower clip. The tour guide chose another flower hair clip and handed it over to the on-board guide, like presenting a small gift flower. Both women seemed happy and they decided to buy the rose clips. The tour guide was an essential part of the tourist experience – interpreting and localizing the tourist setting. The tourists embodied experiences were important in grasping the sense of the place and its authenticity. A cruise tourist said the guide was "guiding them from his heart" through the souq and he was even reciting some Quranic verses for the group, creating an authentic, spiritual environment, connecting the tourists with the place and the people (Gutberlet, 2017).

Tour guides play an important role in familiarizing and de-exoticizing the tourist attraction, connecting the place and the people within time and space. A total of 85% of the mega-cruise tourists ($N = 732$) agreed in the survey that the souq is an exceptional Oriental experience.

The tourist's individual perception of an "objectively authentic" space with their embodied performances and narratives was realized according to the mediated Oriental pre-travel imaginaries. The tourists' connected imaginaries of an Oriental souq with old buildings, narrow streets, the smell of frankincense and other perfumes, tiny box-like shops, that displayed items for sale randomly, as well as dim lighting, and locals wearing non-Western dresses. A German cruise tourist in his forties commented that the souq is a valuable place to learn more about the history of a place and the exchange of cultures.

A German retired lawyer in his 70s whom I interviewed about his experience during a walk through the narrow side streets that were empty during mid-day, told me that he enjoyed the authenticity of the place. In particular, he liked its 'special life' its special life and to learn more about other mentalities, people and their trading. Hence, similar to the experience of group tourists, a walk through the souq created an appreciation of the diversity of cultures, the people and their trading practices (Gutberlet, 2017).

In the following part, I will describe the impacts of overcrowding on the multi-sensuous tourist experiences and the space in Souq Muttrah.

## Overcrowding: "*I need to get out here...*"

The increase in the number of cruise tourists has been impacting the social carrying capacity of the place, the people and its physical infrastructure (Gutberlet, 2020). Since the start of large-scale cruise tourism in Muscat in 2004, the business community in Souq Muttrah has noticed a sharp increase in tourist numbers. At the end of the cruise season in spring 2019, an Indian vendor in his 20s mentioned that sometimes more than 3,000 people pass in front of their shop within one day and another shop manager said on some days, there are so many tourists and it is difficult to walk (Gutberlet, 2020). A few years earlier, an Omani freelance tour guide said that the government should build another souq for tourists only, creating a separate 'bubble'. Compared to European destinations like Barcelona, Venice or Amsterdam that suffer from overtourism and where it is difficult to determine exactly the creators of disturbances for local communities (Koens et al., 2018, 2019; Milano et al., 2019), Western tourists in Oman are easy to differentiate from locals from their dress and open behaviours in public spaces.

One morning, around 11 a.m., the main street of Souq Muttrah was again crowded, creating a hot, sticky atmosphere. I was walking along the main street of the souq. People were trying to find their way out, somewhere pushing others in the back. On the edges of the main street, some people stopped to look at the souvenir shops.

*Suddenly an Austrian cruise tourist in her 60s screamed: "I need to get outside".* She started to panic in the crowd. Later on, outside the souq, she told me that she was afraid not to reach the shuttle bus back to the ship. For some people, overcrowding within the narrow streets of the souq created panic, confusion, disorientation and a lack of safety (Gutberlet, 2016a). On another occasion, I even witnessed a small fire, being quickly extinguished with a small fire extinguisher in one of the shops in the centre of the souq. I realized at that time that in case of any fire incidents or accidents, there is a lack of safety within the often crowded alleys of the souq. This confirmed the outcome of my questionnaire survey, where 88% of the German-speaking cruise tourists ($N = 721$) mentioned that the main street of the souq was too crowded, while 12% disagreed with the statement (Gutberlet, 2016a). The majority of the mega-cruise tourists surveyed stayed up to 30 minutes inside Souq Muttrah, which is a very short time for getting the essence of the space, immersing themselves and reaching the core or the heart of the place. Hence, most of them remained along the main street of the souq, where the shop vendors slowly adjusted to the taste of the crowds of mega-tourists who were passing by.

Those cruise tourists who have booked a Muscat sightseeing coach tour on board of the cruise liner visited the souq as part of their excursion. Regardless of the number of tourist buses that stop at the souq, the tour always followed the same itinerary including the Sultan Qaboos Grand Mosque, the fish market in Muttrah, one of the museums in Old Muscat and Souq Muttrah is the last stop before the return to the harbour. For the tourists' convenience, the buses drive along the one-lane Corniche street and stop in front of the entrance tower to the souq. I observed that there was a lack of coordination between the different tour itineraries and their buses, so that most tourist buses arrive between 11 and 12 noon at the main entrance of Souq Muttrah on the Corniche road. As soon as a group of tourists got in or out of their buses, the road was blocked to traffic entirely. In addition to the large tour buses, mini-buses and 4 × 4 cars queued for passengers along the street, creating further congestion and overcrowding of the space (Gutberlet, 2016a, 2020).

For many German-speaking individuals and group tourists interviewed, the crowding generated a negative experience. My manual counting on three Sunday mornings in January and February 2012, when two large contemporary cruise liners with a total of more than 4,000 tourists were in the port revealed that on average 1,371 tourists and 372 locals passed through the main entrance of Souq Muttrah, between 10 a.m. and 1 p.m., during a 15-minute count every hour. The number of tourists entering the souq exceeded the number of locals by 88%. The counting of tourists showed major crowding (Gutberlet, 2016a). The majority of the cruise tourists were from mega-cruise liners like AIDA, Costa Cruises, MSC or Royal Caribbean.

Two years later, on a Sunday in January 2014, when two mega-cruise ships (AIDA and Costa Cruises) were in the port, my participant observation at the entrance to Souq Muttrah showed continuous overcrowding of the space. Around noon, eight 40-seater buses stopped in front of the main entrance to the souq. At the same time, a large crowd of cruise tourists was waiting in the mid-day heat, to be picked up by their buses. This incident revealed a lack of crowd management, an inadequate tourist infrastructure including parking spaces and toilets for mass tourism as well as a lack of

*Figure 5.10* The main tourist street in Souq Muttrah when a mega-cruise liner was
in the port

Source: Gutberlet (April 2018).

coordination of the tourist buses to arrive at different timings (Figure 5.10).
Asked about their views, some locals raised their concerns.

> *"It's a shame, at Carrefour hypermarket in Muscat there is a lot of park-
> ing, but at the traditional souq there is no parking available"*, complained
> an Omani tour guide.

An Omani taxi driver said "*The buses cause a lot of traffic jams. We do not have any profit from tourism in Muttrah. Only the big companies like the tour operators benefit*", while another driver who was stationed close to the port said that around 10% of his customers were from the cruise liner.

Five years later, in March 2017, covered and open participant observation in Souq Muttrah, between 10 a.m. and 12 noon, when a mega-cruise liner was in the port, revealed again a similar situation. There was overcrowding along the "tourist bubble" of the souq, causing heavy traffic congestion with buses queuing in front of the main entrance while tourists were waiting for them in the mid-day heat. Moreover, I observed an aggressive selling behaviour and an increase in cheap, imported souvenirs (Gutberlet, 2020).

In January 2019, the Omani director of a public museum in Muttrah, whom I had already interviewed in 2012, mentioned that a few days earlier four large cruise liners arrived in the city the same day, leading to overcrowding along the Corniche road. The phenomenon of mega-cruise tourists staying overnight in Sultan Qaboos Port in Muttrah and ships embarking from there as a home port was new. This could reduce congestion within the space in Muttrah during the morning hours. The phenomenon was observed for the first time towards the end of 2018, highlighting the increasing role of cruise liners in the port of call Muscat.

## Social distinction: "We are 4-star not 5-star"

Inside the souq, different types of tourists meet in close proximity: mega-cruise tourists, individual and group tourists, as well as different Western nationalities. Some tourists distinguished themselves while pretending to have a higher cultural capital and habitus than the *Other* tourists from the mega-cruise ship (Bourdieu, 1984). Whereas mega-cruise tourists did not socially distinguish themselves from other types of travellers, especially individual tourists who wished to distance themselves, escape from the crowds of sometimes loudly chatting cruise tourists and venture on their own beyond "the tourist bubble" towards the periphery and the small alleys in the back of the souq.

Year by year, the souq became more inauthentic and staged. An individual German tourist who was travelling with his wife, complained about cheap imported souvenirs like fridge magnets, which meant less authenticity for him. He compared the souq and the items on display with Königswinter, a popular tourist attraction besides the river Rhine in Germany. He was pointing to shops filled with colourful, imported souvenirs. He therefore wished to distinguish himself, his class habitus (Bourdieu, 1984), his manners and attitudes from the crowd of German-speaking mega-cruise tourists in Souq Muttrah. He and his wife stayed in a different 'bubble on shore', the Shangri-la hotel resort, one of the luxury five-star resorts in Muscat. From there they had booked different day tours with a 4 × 4 car and a local tour guide, they stayed for one week (Gutberlet, 2016a, 2017). To avoid the crowds of cruise tourists in the souq, the tourist couple walked along the small alleys, at the back of the souq (periphery) where there are more local shops. They were accompanied by a female Russian, German-speaking tour guide (Gutberlet, 2016a). The tourist was carrying a sweatshirt and a camera over his shoulder.

> *"Originally, we wanted to visit Oman in 2001, but then we had to cancel our travel because of the 9/11 terror attacks"*, he said, referring to their adjusted travel plans due to increased geopolitical tensions.

During the walking interview, the tourist said that they liked the bustling atmosphere of a souq and that they had visited other colourful souqs in India and in Burma in previous years. In the previous five years, they had travelled to Asia, South America, Central America and India three times. They were the type of traveller defined by Jaakson (2004) as the "explorers", or "elite" and "off-beat" (Smith, 1976, 1989) who do their best to adapt fully or well to the local environment but who wished to distinguish themselves from the "Other" (Bourdieu, 1984).

A reaction of escape and social distinction (Bourdieu, 1984) as a consequence of crowding caused by cruise tourism was observed among most group and independent travellers. Another group tourist openly rejected the behaviour and language of the foreign "Other" cruise tourists who were loudly chatting, while being in favour of a more "familiar self" (Andrews, 2011). Another individual tourist, a retired medical doctor in her 60s said that she was shocked to see a large number of tourists inside the souq (Gutberlet, 2016a).

> *"It is awful. I feel sorry for the locals. They just enter the souq, they don't have a lot of time. They photograph everything and they even don't ask for permission"*, she said referring to the local community's tolerance level towards the large number of tourists and their rather intrusive behavior (Gutberlet, 2016a, 2017).

The tourist wished to distance herself, and her identity from the crowds of cruise tourists. Similarly, a female group tourist who was travelling with a group of friends, most of them were retired and from Vienna (Austria) said:

*"We are four-star tourists, not five-star"*, distinguishing herself from the luxury, elite tourists and the mega-cruise tourists, by using a star-categorization like a commodity.

Such categories of stars are commonly used for commodities, tourism products like hotels and resorts, but not for people. Referring to Goffman's (1963) categorization of stereotypes that stigmatize all members of the community in order to devalue the person, a group of German tour operators who were participating in a workshop on board a mega-ship said during a lunch break of a day-excursion:

> *"None of us likes mass tourism. I think we would not travel like that. We are here for work. We are attending a workshop throughout the entire travel."*

He stressed that they were travelling for work and not for pleasure, distinguishing himself from the Other cruise tourists.

## The tourist bubble expands

During the cruise winter season 2013/2014, along the Corniche road, I observed that additional, new tourist infrastructure was set-up including a few public toilets at the entrance of the souq, souvenir shops selling cheap items like magnets and textiles, and tourist restaurants with large colourful signboards, artificial grass carpets and wooden chairs. Even a small water fountain was set-up at a restaurant beside the Corniche road, where international food was served by expatriate waiters from Bangladesh or India. The new tourism infrastructure created a hyper-real, touristified space leading to more overconsumption. An accumulation of tourist facilities increases the scale of staging functions (Cohen, 1978, p. 221). As a result of overcrowding caused by mega-cruise liners along the core areas, the public sanitation facilities were not sufficient. Often a large number of tourists were queuing in front of only a few public toilets that were newly set-up by Muscat Municipality and located close to the Corniche road, the main tourist entrance to the souq. Some tourists were even using the facilities of a small hotel on the Corniche or the coffee shops along the harbour street. An Indian manager of a popular coffee shop beside the tourist bus parking said that sometimes more than 2,000 people were using one or two toilets only. As a result, he had introduced a 'toilet user fee', generating an additional small income for his business (Gutberlet, 2016a).

Through visual and infrastructural changes leading to a touristification and commodification of the place, the souq area became increasingly divided into a 'tourist bubble' with a "core tourist area" (Jaakson, 2004) and a 'local souq' at the backside and inside the narrow side streets. This periphery of the souq serves predominantly the Omani and expatriate communities (Gutberlet, 2016a).

In winter 2019, seven years since the start of my fieldwork, I observed that the souq had further developed into a 'tourist bubble' or a "tourist enclave", promoting a touristified, "hybrid space" with a "hybrid culture". Along the periphery of the 'tourist bubble' remained shops for the local Omani and Asian communities, tailoring abayas (local, female dress) by Asians, as well as selling jewellery, gold, shoes, perfumes, textile fabrics and household items (Gutberlet, 2016a, 2020). I observed that several elder Omani vendors along the "core tourist bubble" of Souq Muttrah had left their shops. The space had

*Figure 5.11* Tourist souvenir shops along the main street of the souq

Source: Gutberlet (2013).

changed, promoted by globalization and a capitalist economy, operationalized in a monoculture of shops where Asian vendors from Bangladesh, Pakistan and India were selling predominantly cheap, international tourist souvenirs like fake pashmina scarves, belly dancing costumes, carpets, fridge magnets and camel miniatures (Figure 5.11). Instead of locally produced handicrafts, food items for the local community or Omani coffee, there were cheap textiles from Asia, or commodified local puppets as salt and pepper dispensers, belly-dancing costumes and T-shirts (Gutberlet, 2020). The increase in the number of mega-cruise tourists has transformed Souq Muttrah into a homogenized, tourist site that aims to accumulate capital. Its operations were increasingly based on non-local capital as well as foreign practices, norms and values (Saarinen, 2004).

The first international fast food chain opened at the Corniche road, beginning of 2017 (Gutberlet, 2020). This shows an increased speed and, standardization of the food production within a neoliberal, globalized economy where there is little room for a conventional meal composed of local food and drinks. Under globalization, the local has to be constructed and reinvented continuously, while remaining meaningful to everyday life. The increased circulation of people, capital and information stimulates localization. The local destination and its culture have "multiple faces when globalizing" (Salazar, 2010).

*Figure 5.12* Tourist souvenirs, introduced on a larger scale in Souq Muttrah, with the arrival of more mega-cruise tourists from 2012 onwards.

Source: Gutberlet (2013).

Along with the change in the built identity of the place, materialized in fundamental changes in the interior design of the small shops, which were appreciated by the tourists, e.g. modern shop windows were inserted and wooden doors were now removed; thus the overall shop architecture changed. Moreover, the number of shops selling cheap, imported items had increased inside the 'tourist bubble' (Figure 5.12). An Omani tour guide complained that the souq became a 'textile souq' (Gutberlet, 2016a).

Beside the side-entrance to the Corniche road, a few young Omani shop-keepers from Salalah remained within the 'tourist bubble' along with their 'Asian helpers', who mainly served the customers. I observed that well-established shops such as a small antiquities shop in a narrow side street, owned by an elder Omani had shut down in recent years. The owner told me that he had sold many items to a museum. Other handicraft shops had changed the profile of their products to cater to the demand of mass-cruise tourists, omitting items, including traditional and local handicrafts, offered in the past (Gutberlet, 2020).

> *"We used to sell pottery and frankincense in the past, until about five years ago. But pottery is difficult for the tourists to transport, so not a lot is sold. So we switched to silver jewelry and Omani handmade khanjars"*, said Talal

(name changed) at the beginning of 2019. He is an Omani business-owner who co-owns a shop together with his brother (Gutberlet, 2020).

Similarly, another shop vendor mentioned that he had stopped selling Omani products and had switched to imported handicrafts. This can be interpreted as a growth-oriented, continuous, adjustment to a large number of cruise tourists. An Omani in his 40s, the owner of one of the most successful tourist souvenir shops in Muttrah, said that his family sold different items in the past while continuously adjusting to changing demand trends. After selling textiles for around 30 years, the family started selling handicraft 20 years ago (Gutberlet, 2020).

> *"Purchases by cruise passengers are negligible. Only five per cent of our customers are from cruise liners. They spend about one euro per visitor"*, he said when I interviewed him for the first time in 2012. *"The souq does not make any profit from them (the cruise tourists). They arrive by buses and they all walk with their tour guides through the main entrance…Only the main transportation companies profit from cruise tourism"*, he said

> Another Omani business owner who has a shop on the Corniche road commented that *around ninety-five per cent of the cruise tourists from mega ships just look and leave. I think they are just looking for cheap items* (Gutberlet, 2016a).

The vendors interviewed suggested a dispersion of the tourists through the entire souq and to other areas of the city, which is similar to the crowd management applied in European cities like Amsterdam and Barcelona (City in Balance 2019; Koens et al., 2018; Milano et al., 2019). An Indian business owner in the gold souq who was wearing an Omani dishdasha, expressing his belonging and a staged 'Omani identity' said that

> *Tourists come to the gold souq, but they do not purchase anything. Tourists only buy silver.* Stressing on the local ethnic identity, he said: *"We sell jewelry made in Muttrah and other items procured wholesale from Dubai"* (Gutberlet, 2016a).

As a consequence of the tourists' low spending behaviour, the vendor community has changed their selling approach and become more aggressive and pushy, which annoyed German-speaking groups and individual tourists.

> A female individual tourist in her 30s said that *vendors along the main street approached them* in a very aggressive way. They just felt that they wanted to escape.

It is known that Asian businessmen have a rather aggressive selling behaviour, whereas Omanis have a softer approach (Gutberlet, 2008).

German-speaking tourists were culturally unprepared to deal with a different selling behaviour and to negotiate a fair price (Gutberlet, 2016a).

Young Asian vendors who had worked from inside their shops along the 'tourist bubble' started employing additional salespeople in spring 2014. They were to hawk the products on the street, in front of the shop. Young Asian vendors called out in different languages including in German and Italian. Sometimes they were holding several products in their hands, e.g. a scarf along with a small perfume bottle or a small box of frankincense. They were calling the tourists with the slogans:

> "*Frankincense, saffron and perfume*" or even "*Saffran macht den Kuchen gelb*" (saffron makes the cake yello).

I observed throughout the years, that the rapid growth in the number of young Asian vendors in Souq Muttrah had led to increased social tensions and stereotyping. Omani vendors have been defending their passive, quiet selling approach. An Omani who owns a shop in the 'tourist bubble' said that if someone is interested in his shop and the products on display, he welcomes the person without pulling him inside his shop (Gutberlet, 2016a). Some German-speaking tourists who were guided through the souq appreciated the kind approach and gentle hospitality of the Omani vendor community. An individual traveller in his 50s mentioned that locals are very kind and less pushy, compared to Turkey, a popular tourist destination for Germans.

In spring 2014, I observed that shopkeepers were instructed by Muscat Municipality to remove their items from outside the shops, otherwise they would be fined. As a result of these instructions, I realized that expatriate vendors along the main 'tourist bubble' of the souq had adopted a passive selling approach (Gutberlet, 2016a). Moreover, to increase their sales, shops in Souq Muttrah had adjusted their currency to the Western tourist Euros or Dollars, indicating the prices in Euros and in US Dollars. The local currency, Omani Rials, is not available on board the cruise ships and there was just one exchange office located next to the souq. A newly established shop on the Corniche road displayed global currencies on their counter, creating a "hybrid monetary space" (Gutberlet, 2020) within the capitalist system of economic growth.

## Tour guiding: Speeding up in time and space

Tour guides contribute as local experts in shaping the tourists' imaginaries of the destination and their on-site experiences. During a Muscat city-tour cruise tourists have limited time for their visit, between 30 and 45 minutes (Gutberlet, 2016a). Most of the tour guides remained outside the souq area waiting in one of the coffee shops on the Corniche road. Consequently, cruise tourists received limited interpretation in the bus where the tour guide gave some information about the place, the products and the locals. Tour guides only guided individual tourists or small groups through the souq, offering them additional interpretation and insights.

*"From my experience with cruise tourism, everything has to be fast"*, said a German-speaking Indian tour guide in his late 20s referring to the speed of guiding and limited time in the destination.

Cruise tourists were observed descending the bus, and rushing to the souq entrance. Then, inside the souq, they slowed down and walked like "flâneurs" along the main street of the souq. Some were fearing getting lost inside the street labyrinth. Other cruise tourists said that they were unable to locate certain shops, such as those selling spices, herbs or even gold. These shops are located on the backside of the souq. A male German-speaking tour guide who was waiting for his group outside the souq, referred to the tourists' lack of geographical orientation.

*"Sometimes they do not find the spices. They have no orientation"*. Obviously, he did not feel responsible to support the tourists.

Moreover, due to a lack of orientation and time, many cruise tourists ventured along the main streets and bought from the product range offered within the "core tourist bubble".

*"They just do a tour and then they return to the cruise ship"*, said an expatriate shop owner expressing his disappointment about the lack of sales when a cruise liner is in the port.

Tour guides who were working with cruise tourists mentioned that they were instructed inofficially by the local tour operator, not to go along with their groups. They have been accused by well-established shopkeepers of demanding a commission, an unethical and prohibited practice (Gutberlet, 2020). This reveals a power struggle within the souq and a rather profit-oriented attitude of some tour guides and shopkeepers. It also shows a decrease in and a decrease in genuine, freely offered Omani hospitality that was prevalent in the past, before the sudden increase in mass tourism). As a result, megacruise tourists received less interpretation of the site. An Indian tour guide mentioned that Omanis can guide inside the souq, differentiating Omani and expatriate practices. This constrains the cruise tourists' (the targets') movements (Cheong & Miller, 2000) and the tourists' access to information about the attraction while marginalizing expatriate tour guides (Gutberlet, 2020). To overcome these guiding restrictions put in place, expatriate tour guides adjusted their practices. For instance, an Indian guide asked another Indian vendor from a coffee shop to buy souvenirs for his group, therefore creating a social bond with each other. Despite the restrictions, Indian tour guides were observed leading tourists to the inside of the souq.

*"Those of you who want to buy saffron and frankincense please come with me"*, said an Indian guide in German. A group of around ten cruise tourists followed him inside the souq.

A tour guide mentioned that problems with shopkeepers started when mega ships arrived in Muscat.

> *"The shop keepers think that we direct them to certain shops. We don't go inside the souq with the tourists, because we don't want to create any problems,"*

said a 24-year-old Indian tour guide, thus restricting the tourist experience. A few guides continued leading large groups to the frankincense shop (Gutberlet, 2017), from there they left them alone. As a result, the tourists often only got a glimpse of the souq, its heritage, local products and the people.

The cruise tourists gazed at the vendors and the vendors gazed at them (the host gaze). The tourists were observed taking photos, without receiving any permission from the locals, thereby objectifying them. Similar to the tourists' lack of knowledge about the local environment, I observed that tourists do not differentiate the nationality and social identity of vendors. Although Omani men wear a local white long dress (dishdasha) and Asian vendors from India, Pakistan or Bangladesh usually wear Western trousers and shirts, tourists perceived all shop vendors being 'local' Omani and Arab (Gutberlet, 2020). Some tourists were observed using a few Arabic words, e.g. greeting the shopkeepers with the Muslim greeting *salam wa aleikum*. Omani taxi drivers that I interviewed, who were standing in groups close to the main entrance to Souq Muttrah as well as next to the port in Muttrah, complained that the main profits of cruise liner tourism go to the tour operators, shipping agents and to the port authority. They also mentioned that mega-cruise tourists were not interested in taking a taxi. Some tourists experienced taxi drivers as being aggressive and expensive. Another challenge was a lack of communication and negotiation skills in English creating misunderstandings and a lack of trust between tourists and locals. Moreover, taxi drivers were not aware that Western tourists often like to explore a destination on foot. Cruise tourists ventured on their own along the Corniche road (Gutberlet, 2016a).

Inside the souq, tour guides transmitted distinctions and focused the tourist gaze regarding what the tourists can experience or not, creating sometimes stereotypes about the behaviour of expatriate Asian vendors (Gutberlet, 2020).

One day, in spring 2019, I observed an Omani tour guide, walking with a small group through the main alleyway of the souq, when a mega-cruise liner was in the port. The guide in his 50s said that this is a "traditional souq". The concept of "traditional" or "heritage souq" referred to being original and "authentic". However, it can also be seen as trivializing the local culture, which is a common method in "Orientalizing a destination and its people" (Causevic & Neal, 2019; Gutberlet, 2017). The term *traditional* referred to its *authenticity*, the age of the souq, its use by the local, indigenous community for shopping and trading, the remaining old architectural features such as the narrow, winding alleys and small shops without modern

*Figure 5.13* New colourful glass windows were inserted in the ceilings of the souq, within the 'main tourist bubble'

Source: Gutberlet (2014).

features like glass windows and air conditioners as well as the shop distribution according to specific products all grouped along one street. Shops selling gold, abayas, spices, textiles or handicrafts are grouped together in their own areas. New shops with modern features, e.g. windows have been set up along the main streets of the souq (see Figure 5.13), thus resembling a hybrid shopping street with a mix of products like anywhere else in the world (Gutberlet, 2020).

After a while, the Omani guide pointed to his right, saying that this was a mosque, but, no further explanations followed. It looked like a typical house, it had no visible minaret, just an entrance, small stairs and a door. Its representation was not obvious to a European, non-Muslim tourist. Without giving further details, he continued walking along the main street where he indicated that this was a gold shop, passing in front of an obviously new tourist shop with new Asian vendors, directing the tourist gaze to a staged attraction, but without giving further details. The souvenir shop was selling only a few jewellery items, while the actual traditional gold souq is located further inside the souq, on the periphery. The group was passing next to an Indian vendor who quickly opened a 'bokhor' (perfume) box and pushed it under the nostrils of the tourists which is a common selling practice that has increased since the arrival of cruise tourism and was repeated with cheap pashmina scarfs. The Omani tour guide was annoyed about the pushy sell-ing approach of the vendor. The Omani guide walked ahead mimicking the expatriate vendor and mocking his approach (Gutberlet, 2020).

## "They are tourists, but without money"

With the increase in mega-cruise ships and a decrease in the quality of the tourist experiences, the shop vendors have observed a change in the tourist spending.

> *"They are tourists, but they are not spending money"*, said a well-estab-lished Indian shop owner stereotyping the cruise tourists.

An Indian vendor from the harbour street complained in 2019 that those tourists who come by aeroplane were spending more money, categorizing the tourists according to their purchase and their mode of transportation. Shops located further inside the souq on the periphery of the 'tourist bubble', in the small narrow side streets of the souq, did not benefit as much from cruise tourism. Only the 'new vendors' from Asia, valued a large number of tourists as a commodity and a business opportunity, rather than as a threat to their values and the local culture (Hall & Rath, 2007, p. 18). They have adapted their product range to the taste and budget of the cruise customers.

A low spending behaviour among German-speaking mega-cruise tourists was confirmed in the questionnaire survey (Gutberlet, 2016a), which sup-ported the results of low-spending cruise tourists worldwide, discussed by Abassian et al. (2020), Henthorpe (2000), Klein (2011), Larsen et al. (2013), Milano et al. (2019) and Weaver (2005a). The low-spending behaviour was confirmed in my interviews:

> *"We have already bought a lot in Istanbul. We will not buy anything here"*, said a 30-year-old Austrian cruise tourist from a Costa cruise ship.

A total of 40% of the cruise tourists who responded ($N = 760$) did not spend anything in the souq and nearly 60% spent only little. About 33% spent less than 20 Euros, while just 2% spent more than 100 Euros (Gutberlet, 2016a). Cruise tourists were not primarily interested in buying local handicraft or luxury souvenirs such as a khanjar (local dagger worn by men on the Arabian Peninsula as a symbol of manhood) or jewellery. Besides the high value of a khanjar, the ship did not allow daggers on board. Typical Omani products purchased by tourists and that are bought by locals as well are: local clothes like dishdasha and turban (7%), gold and silver (7%), or Omani khanjars/daggers (2%), which were rarely purchased by the mega-cruise tourists surveyed ($N = 691$) (Gutberlet, 2016a).

My results confirm previous research such as Larsen et al. (2013) who found that cruise tourists in Scandinavia were low spenders compared to other tourists, e.g. individual and group tourists, who stay longer in the destination. Klein (2011, p. 67) and others stressed that the onshore spending of cruise tourists has decreased over the past decades (Gutberlet, 2016a). At the same time, the travel price for a cruise travel has dropped as well. In 2012, the lowest travel fare for the cruise travel-package travelling for one week in a small inside cabin was around 700–800 Euros. "The travel fare is sometimes less than staying at home", said an Indian shipping agent in Muscat joking about the mega-cruise travel. However, on board the cruise ship the tourists are under pressure to consume within a capitalist system. The holiday time spent on board the ship is an intense, relatively short-lived experience in which those who construct the tourist experience want to maximize their profits from the tourists within a minimum amount of time (Andrews, 2011; Weaver, 2005b).

In addition to contemporary mega-cruise tourists, I spoke to luxury cruise tourists about their experiences in Souq Muttrah. For example, a German couple in their 60s travelling with MS Europa luxury cruise liner had spent nearly 25,000 Euros for a one-week journey with the luxury cruise liner around the Arabian Peninsula. The travel included a helicopter flight over Dubai and a stay in the luxury Burj Al Arab hotel. In Muscat, they did an individual city tour very early so that they avoided the crowd of the "other cruise tourists". They wanted to distinguish themselves and their 'habitus' from the crowd of contemporary cruise tourists travelling with a mega-cruise ship. Through Muttrah, they ventured on their own, without any guidance. After the walk through the souq, they sat down in one of the coffee shops beside the entrance to the souq, having a cappuccino and a mango juice. In the souq, they bought frankincense, spending a total of around 24 Euros, which is more than the average spending of mega-cruise tourists. The couple mentioned that the shops were selling the same items as in Spain, one of the most popular German tourist destinations, highlighting globalization, the movement of products and people and the delocalization (Gutberlet, 2016a).

Mega-cruise tourists were consuming the place and the local culture visually. During the cruise season in early 2019, shop owners and sellers interviewed in Souq Muttrah expressed their disappointment about the increasing lack of profits within a fast cruise tourism development having a substantial impact on the culture and the people in the souq (Gutberlet, 2020). Six vendors interviewed within the 'tourist bubble' of the souq said:

> "*Mega-cruise tourists are not buying. They only look at the merchandise and leave*".

Vendors were stereotyping the tourists according to the profit made from them (Gutberlet, 2020). The vendors categorized cruise tourists as a commercial commodity according to their profitability. The natural, gentle and generous hospitality and cultural exchange between tourists and locals in Souq Muttrah that was prevalent in the past was increasingly missing (Gutberlet, 2020). The sociocultural exchange between tourists and locals was money-focused, focused on their consumption practices and the monetary value. With the increase in cruise tourism, there was a limited social exchange.

In this part, I have analysed tourist imaginaries and on-site experiences along with numerous impacts of mega-cruise tourism such as overcrowding in Souq Muttrah. In the next chapter, I will analyse further on-site experiences of tourists and community reactions as well as life-stories of the vendor community, their perceptions and their values along with tourist behaviours.

## References

Abbasian, S., Onn, G., & Arnautovic, D. (2020). Overtourism in Dubrovnik in the eyes of local tourism employees: A qualitative study. *Cogent Social Sciences*, 6(2), 1775944.

AIDA (2011/2012). AIDA Travel Catalogue. AIDA Cruises, Hamburg.

AIDA (2014). *Glanzvolle Feiertage im Orient*. Retrieved December 18, 2014, from http://www.aida.de/neue-generation/buchen.26 518.html#orient-1

AIDA (2015/2016). *Sehnsucht nach den schönsten Urlaubszielen der Welt*. November 2015 – Oktober 2016. AIDA Cruises.

Andersen, B. (2016). *Imagined community*. Reflections on the origin and spread of nationalism, Ebook for PC (revised ed.). Verso.

Andrews, H. (2011). The British on holiday. *Charter tourism, identity and consumption. tourism and cultural change*. Channel View Publications.

Bærenholdt, J. O., Haldrup, M., Larsen, J., & Urry, J. (2004). *Performing tourist places*. Ashgate Publishing.

Banks, M., & Zeitlyn, D. (2015). *Visual methods in social research* (2nd ed.). Sage Publications.

Baudrillard (2017). *The consumer society, myths and structures, theory, culture & society* (Revised ed.). Kindle Ebook. Sage Publishing.

Bauman, Z. (2000). *Liquid modernity*. Polity Press.

Bauman, Z. (2001). *Community. Seeking safety in an insecure world*. Ebook for PC. Polity.

Bauman, Z. (2004). *Identity. Conversations with Benedetto vecchi*. Ebook for PC. Polity Press.

Beeton, S., Bowen, H. E., & Santos, C. A. (2006). State of knowledge: Mass media and its relationship to perceptions of quality. In G. Jennings & N. Polovitz-Nickerson (Eds.), *Quality tourism experiences* (pp. 25–37). Elsevier Butterworth-Heinemann.

Bourdieu, P. (1984). Distinction. *A social critique of the judgment of taste*. Kindle Ebook for PC. Routledge.

Causevic, S., & Neal, M. (2019). The exotic veil: Managing tourist perceptions of national history and statehood in Oman. *Tourism Management*, 71, 504–517.

Chaney, D. (2002). The power of metaphors in tourism theory. In M. Crang & S. Coleman (Eds.), *Tourism between place and performance* (pp. 3867–4140), Kindle Ebook for PC. Berghahn Books.

Cheong, S.-M., & Miller, M. L. (2000). Power and tourism. A foucauldian observation. *Annals of Tourism Research*, 27(2), 371–390.

Chronis, A. (2012). Between place and story: Gettysburg as tourism imaginery. *Annals of Tourism Research*, 39(4), 1797–1816.

Chronis, A. (2015). Moving bodies and the staging of the tourist experience. *Annals of Tourism Research, 55*(1), 124–140.

City in Balance (2019). Retrieved October 25, 2019, from www.amsterdam.nl

Cohen, E. (1978). The impact of tourism on the physical environment. *Annals of Tourism Research, 5*(2), 215–237.

Crossley, E. (2013). Cosmopolitan empathy in volunteer tourism: A psychosocial perspective. *Tourism Recreation Research, 42*(2), 150–163.

Crouch, D., & Desforges, L. (2003). The sensuous in the tourist encounter. Introduction: The power of the body in tourist studies. *Tourist Studies, 3*(1), 5–22.

Daye, M. (2005). Mediating tourism. An analysis of the Caribbean holiday experience in the UK national press. In D. Crouch, R. Jackson, & F. Thompson (Eds.), *The media and the tourist imagination converging cultures* (pp. 14–25), Kindle Ebook for PC. Routledge.

Din, K. (1989). Islam and tourism. *Annals of Tourism Research, 16*, 542–563.

Echtner, C. M., & Prasad, P. (2003). The context of third world tourism marketing. *Annals of Tourism Research, 30*(3), 660–682.

Edensor, T. (Ed.). (1998). Tourists at the Taj. *Performance and meaning at a symbolic site*. Routledge.

Edensor, T. (2000). Staging tourism – tourists as performers. *Annals of Tourism Research, 27*(2), 322–344.

Elle Magazin (2013). *1001 Nacht: Der Oman zeigt sich von märchenhafter Seite.* German edition, April 2013, 329–332.

Feighery, W. (2012). Tourism and self-orientalism in Oman: A critical discourse analysis. *Critical Discourse Studies, 9*(3), 269–284.

Font, X., Guix, M., & Bonilla-Priego, M. J. (2016). Corporate social responsibility in cruising: Using materiality analysis to create shared value. *Tourism Management, 53*, 175–186.

Goffman, E. (1963): Behavior in public spaces. *Notes on the social organization of gatherings*. Kindle Ebook for PC. The Free Press.

Gössling, S. (2002). Human-environmental relations in tourism. *Annals of Tourism Research, 29*(2), 539–556.

Gutberlet, M. (2008). *Verhandeln mit Geschäftspartnern in Oman*. In H. Brenner (Ed.), *Praxishandbuch für Exportmanager* (pp. 1–16). Deutscher Wirtschaftsdienst.

Gutberlet, M. (2016a). Socio-cultural impacts of large-scale cruise tourism in Souq Muttrah. *Fennia, 194*(1), 46–63.

Gutberlet, M. (2016b). Cruise tourist dress behaviors and local-guest reactions in a Muslim country. *Tourism Culture & Communication, 16*, 15–32.

Gutberlet, M. (2016c). Tourist photography in a bazaar – Souq Mutrah/Sultanate of Oman. Proceedings of the VII international tourism congress, the image and sustainability of tourist destinations, December 2–4, 2014. Sultan Qaboos University, pp. 114–120.

Gutberlet, M. (2017). Staging the Oriental Other: Imaginaries and performances of German-speaking cruise tourists. Published online first and in 2019, *Tourist Studies, 19*(1), 110–137.

Gutberlet, M. (2019). In a rush: Time-space compression and its impacts on cruise excursions, *Tourist Studies, 19*(4), 1–29. Published online first, April.

Gutberlet, M. (2020). "They just buy a karak and leave" – Overtourism in Souq Muttrah, the Sultanate of Oman. *Zeitschrift für Tourismuswissenschaften*, De Gruyter Oldenburg, 13 October.

Gutberlet, M. (2021). Valuing social capital and a legacy: The old shops are the beauty of the place. In J. Saarinen & J. Richardson (Eds.), *Change in tourism/ tourism in change* (pp. 135–150). Routledge Publishing House.

Gutberlet, M. (2022a). Geopolitical imaginaries and cultural ecosystem services (CES) in the desert. *Tourism Geographies, 24*, 4–5.

Gutberlet, M. (2022b). Insight 288: Tourist bubbles and climate change in the GCC. COP 27 and Climate Action in the Middle East, Middle East Institute, National University of Singapore, October 24.

Haldrup, M., & Larsen, J. (2010). *Tourism, performance and the everyday: Consuming the orient.* Routledge.

Hall, C. M., & Tucker H. (2004). Tourism and postcolonialism. An introduction. In C. M. Hall & H. Tucker (Eds.), *Tourism and postcolonialism* (pp. 1–23). Kindle Ebook for PC. Routledge.

Hall, M., & Rath, J. (2007). Tourism, migration and place advantage in the global cultural economy. In J. Rath (Ed.), *Tourism, ethnic diversity and the city* (pp. 1–24). Routledge.

Harvey, D. (1989). *The condition of postmodernity.* Blackwell.

Henthorpe, T. (2000). An analysis of expenditures by cruise ship passengers in Jamaica. *Journal of Travel Research, 38*(3), 246–250.

Hirtz, N., & Cecil, A. K. (2008). Investigating the sustainability of cruise tourism: A case study of Key West. *Journal of Sustainable Tourism, 16*(2), 168–181.

Jaakson, R. (2004). Beyond the tourist bubble? Cruise ship passengers in port. *Annals of Tourism Research, 31*(1), 44–60.

Jaakson, R. (2004a). Globalisation and neocolonialist tourism. In M. Hall & H. Tucker (Eds.), *Tourism and postcolonialism. Contested discourses, identities and representations* (pp. 4482–4832), Kindle Ebook. Routledge.

Jansson, A. (2002). Spatial phantasmagoria: The mediatisation of tourism experience. *European Journal of Communication, 17*(4), 429–433.

Klein, R. A. (2005). *Cruise ship squeeze.* New Society Publishers.

Klein, R. A. (2011). Responsible cruise tourism: Issues of cruise tourism and sustainability. *Journal of Hospitality and Tourism Management, 18*, 107–116.

Koens, K., Postma, A., & Papp, B. (2018). Is overtourism overused? Understanding the impact of tourism in a city context. *Sustainability, 10*(12), 4384.

Koens, K., Postma, A., & Papp, B. (2019). Management strategies for overtourism – From adaptation to system change. In H. Pechlaner, E. Innerhofer, & G. Erschbamer (Eds.), *Overtourism, tourism management and solutions.* Routledge.

Larsen, J. (2019). Ordinary tourism and extraordinary everyday life: Re-thinking tourism and cities. In T. Frisch, N. Stors, L. Stoltenberg, & C. Sommer (Eds.), *Tourism and everyday life in the city.* Routledge.

Larsen, J., Gomes Bastos, M., Skovslund Hansen, L. I., Hevink, L. M., Jostova, K., & Smagurauskaite, D. (2021). Bubble-wrapped sightseeing mobilities: Hop on-off bus experiences in Copenhagen, *Tourist Studies, 6*, 1–17.

Larsen, S., Wolff, K., Marnburg, E., & Ogaard, T. (2013). Belly full purse closed. *Tourism Management Perspectives, 6*, 142–148.

Leite, N. (2014). Afterword. Locating imaginaries in the anthropology of tourism. In N. Salazar & N. Grabun (Eds.), *Tourism imaginaries. Anthropological approaches* (pp. 260–278). Berghahn Books.

Lopes, J. M., & Dredge, D. (2018). Cruise tourism shore excursions: Value for destinations?, *Journal of Tourism Planning and Development, 15*(6), 633–652.

MacCannell, D. (1999). *The tourist – A new theory of the leisure class*. University of California Press.

MacCannell, D. (2011). *The ethics of sightseeing*. University of California Press.

MacCannell, D. (2012). On the ethical stake in tourism research. *Tourism Geographies: An International Journal of Tourism Space, Place and Environment*, *14*(1), 183–194.

Maoz, D. (2006). The mutual gaze. *Annals of Tourism Research*, *33*, 221–239.

Mein Schiff (2012/2013a). Cruise guidebook, TUI Cruises.

Mein Schiff (2012/2013b). *Reiserouten – Dubai and Orient. Landausflüge, Reisezeitraum* 04.11.2012 - 24.03.2013, TUI Cruises.

Milano, C., Novelli, M., & Cheer, J. M. (2019). Overtourism and degrowth: A social movements perspective. *Journal of Sustainable Tourism*. https://doi.org/10.1080/09669582.2019.1650054

Morgan, N., & Pritchard, A. (1998). *Tourism promotion and power. Creating images, creating identities*. John Wiley and Sons.

Palmer, C. (1994). Tourism and colonialism. The experience of the Bahamas. *Annals of Tourism Research*, *21*(4), 792–811.

Rakić, T., & Chambers, D. (2012). Rethinking the consumption of places. *Annals of Tourism Research*, *39*(3), 1612–1633.

Renaud, L. (2017, July). Résister au débarquement: tourisme de croisière et dynamiques territoriales au Québec et dans la Caraïbe. *RITA* [online], N°10. http://revue-rita.com/thema/resister-au-debarquement-tourisme-de-croisiere-et-dynamiques-territoriales-quebec-caraibe.html

Rodaway, P. (2002). *Sensuous geographies: Body, Sense and place*. Kindle Ebook for PC. Taylor and Francis e-Library.

Rüte, E. (2004). *Memoiren einer arabischen Prinzessin*. Gallery Publications.

Ryan, C. (2002). The time of our lives' or time for our lives: An examination of time in holidaying. In C. Ryan (Ed.), *The tourist experience* (pp. 201–220). Thomson Learning.

Saarinen, J. (2004). Destinations in change. The transformation process of tourist destinations. *Tourist Studies*, *4*(2), 161–179.

Salazar, N. B. (2006). Touristifying Tanzania. Local guides, global discourse. *Annals of Tourism Research*, *33*(3), 833–852.

Salazar, N. B. (2010). *Envisioning Eden: Mobilizing imaginaries in tourism and beyond*. Berghahn Books.

Salazar, N. B. (2012). Community-based cultural tourism: Issues, threats and opportunities. *Journal of Sustainable Tourism*, *20*(1), 9–22.

Smith, V. L. (1976). Tourism and culture change. *Annals of Tourism Research*, *3*(3), 122–126.

Smith, V. L. (1989). Introduction. In V. Smith (Ed.), *Hosts and guests* (pp. 1–14). University of Pennsylvania Press.

Time Out Muscat (2012). *Muttrah Souk* (p. 36). ITP Executive Publishing.

Times of Oman (2015a, March 26). 8 most visited tourist places in Oman.

Urry, J. (1995). *Consuming places*. Routledge.

Urry, J., & Larsen, J. (Eds.). (2011). *The tourist gaze 3.0*. Sage Publications.

Vine, P. (1995). *The heritage of Oman*. Immel Publishing.

Vogel, M. P., & Oschmann, C. (2013). Cruising through liquid modernity. *Tourist Studies*, *13*(1), 62–80.

Wang, N. (1999). Rethinking authenticity in tourism experience. *Annals of Tourism Research, 26*(2), 340–370.

Wang, Y. (2007). Customized authenticity begins at home. *Annals of Tourism Research, 34*(3), 789–804.

Wearing, S. L., & Foley, C. (2017). Understanding the tourist experience of cities. *Annals of Tourism Research, 65,* 97–107.

Weaver, A. (2005a). The McDonaldization thesis and cruise tourism. *Annals of Tourism Research, 32*(2), 346–366.

Weaver, A. (2005b). Spaces of containment and revenue capture: 'Super-Sized' cruise ships as mobile tourism enclaves. *Tourism Geographies: An International Journal of Tourism Space, Place and Environment, 7*(2), 165–184.

Weaver, A. (2005c). Interactive service work and performative metaphors. The case of the cruise industry. *Tourist Studies, 5*(1), 5–27.

Wels, H. (2004). About romance and reality. Popular European imagery in postcolonial tourism in Southern Africa. In C. M. Hall & H. Tucker (Eds.), *Tourism and postcolonialism* (pp. 76–193), Kindle Ebook for PC. ELibrary.

Wu, M.-Y., Wall, G., & Pearce, L. (2014). Shopping experiences: International tourists in Bejings silk market. *Tourism Management, 41,* 96–106.

# 6 The local community and their silent resistance

## Tourist behaviours, culture clashes and the ethics of tourism

In this chapter, I will analyse the ethics of tourism conceptualized in current cruise tourist behaviours in public spaces and community reactions of a silent resistance linked with a laissez-faire attitude towards the increase in tourism. Moreover, I will outline some local values and identities through life-stories and narratives of Omanis and of the diaspora community in Souq Muttrah. Finally, I will highlight the social changes that developed because of 'undertourism', a phenomenon that evolved in Souq Muttrah due to the corona pandemic, between spring 2020 and autumn 2021.

### When the cruise liner arrived in Muscat it started with shorts

> … *Only when there is space for individual wishes, well-being starts.*
> (CEO of a mega-cruise brand, cruise brochure 2016/2017)

The arrival of mega-cruise ships in the port in Muttrah, in the Omani capital Muscat, marked a turning point in the tourist's overall *"care ethic"* for local customs and social values according to members of the long-established business community in Souq Muttrah. This phenomenon is conceptualized in a relaxed dress code reflecting a laissez-faire attitude of the cruise liner and cultural mediators on shore that have been promoting individual freedom and a rather borderless holiday spirit on board the ships (Gutberlet, 2016b; 2020).

Representatives of the tourism industry play an important role in shaping the holiday experience. They act as role models and cultural brokers. On-board guides especially mentioned that they remind the tourists about the dress code, but cannot 'force them to stick to it', which explains the spirit of freedom, individual and choice. On-board restrictions and rules are openly avoided, referring to the free dress code and a relaxed code of conduct on board a mega-cruise ship. It also shows a lack of accurate information provided by cruise employees (Klein, 2011) while some cruise employees did not adhere to the dress code either.

DOI: 10.4324/9780429424946-6

During the holidays, far away from home, the tourist acts and behaves within a physical, social and psychological environment. The visitor is not simply a passive consumer but a proactive contributor to the holiday experience (Hall & Lew, 2009), described as a liminal experience that occurs at the borders between places, situations, or social roles, leading the tourist to a new identity and sometimes more openness. Or it is covering the personal identity, transforming into a new identity called the "touristhood". The tourist may break social rules and excuse the behaviour of being a tourist. Therefore, not knowing better. However, this can lead to a self-realization that is possibly at the expense of other tourists and locals (Jafari, 1987).

Morality and ethics are important concerns for local communities, especially those suffering from overtourism. They are concerned about whether their local culture and heritage are treated respectfully by visitors (Klein, 2011). On the Arabian Peninsula, the local community is multicultural and rather conservative. The local social values and the dress code are homogenous, decent and rather traditional. Their appearance and dress behaviour are different from Western tourists in particular with respect to female dresses (Gutberlet, 2016b).

The local community in Souq Muttrah has recognized significant changes in the tourists' behaviour. Omanis have unwritten, transferred from one generation to the next and strictly followed social and cultural rules and practices that are linked to Islam, so-called *adat* (in Arabic). The values are similar to other religions and traditional communities in Asia such as, e.g. Kyrgyz (Kochkunov, 2010). Oman – and particularly its interior, show a resilience of forms and customs which have defied foreign influence over a long time (Al-Salimi et al., 2008).

In the 7th century, the Sultanate was one of the first countries to embrace Islam. The religion and its value system are deeply rooted in the Arabian Peninsula (Al-Salimi et al., 2008). Muslim societies have been immersed and influenced by the Western capitalistic economy so that the ideal expectations of an individual Muslim appear to be rather wishful (Din, 1989). Within the society, the individual has to adjust to the collective values of the community (Arabic: umma) and its patriarchal structure. The head of the extended family or tribe or even the head of a company (in Arabic *sheikh* for males or *sheikha* for females) exercises a moral authority.

In social impact studies, there has been a "moral turn", reflecting the relationship between ourselves and others and the responsibility we have for our environment (Caton, 2012). Ethics and an ethical behaviour in tourism are reflecting a series of responses to control an important issue within globalization, "liquid modernity" and a fast, consuming lifestyle (Bauman, 2004). Tourism with an open spirit and freedom, as it is widely practised in the West, can be seen as a result of increased freedom of expression, freedom of movement and as an essential contributor to the democratization of societies. However, international tourism can also be an educative process. It is suggested that cruise passengers who visit far places of the world and expect locals to have the same values and behaviours as the cruise passenger should be taught cultural sensitivity on board the ship and prior to the travel (Klein, 2010). This contrasts the "spirit of freedom" promoted on board of mega-cruise ships.

Social rules and cultural values are beliefs that regulate social behaviour (Pearce, 2010). Values refer to underlying qualities or features such as respect towards others, fairness, punctuality or the importance of things. The social representation theory includes values, beliefs, attitudes, explanations and it connects individuals to their social and cultural worlds (Pearce et al., 1996). These are preference elements of worldviews held by individuals or groups (Chan et al., 2010). Values, beliefs and attitudes can be either transformative or non-transformative.

Moral issues are collective in their character, whereas Western individualism, economic progress and rationality do not correspond well with social moral issues (Caton, 2012). In tourism, there has been an increased tension between self-actualization or self-gratification and social issues (ibid., p. 1917). Morality is about "how things should be" instead of "how things are" (ibid., p. 1907). Philosophically, tourism is seen as an ideal context for the "messy collision of Self and Other in life more generally". In preparation for a travel, the World Tourism Organization (UNWTO) advises that tourists should educate themselves in advance and take time. Tourists should learn as much as possible about the destinations visited and take enough time to understand local customs, norms and traditions while avoiding behaviour that could offend locals and other tourists (UNWTO, 2005). One possibility to develop such a tourist "care ethic" is to provide positive, authentic and memorable experiences through quality pre-travel information and quality interpretation tools throughout the travel. Such attractive information can give guidance for tourists, similar to medical information (Pearce, 2006). In order to create a more mindful behaviour, the ethics in tourism need to be promoted among all stakeholders. To openly welcome the 'unknown Other' is to admit the unknowability, and to honour its mystery (Caton, 2012).

On the Arabian Peninsula, Western tourists have great visibility and proclaim a difference through dress, speech and the overall manners. Similar to Pi-Sunyer (1989), who commented on the behaviour of tourists in a Spanish coastal town between the 1960s and 1980s, such negative incidents can be observed in Souq Muttrah.

In public spaces, Omani men and women are fully covered, from the ankles to the wrists. Omani males wear a small cap (in Arabic: *kumma*) along with a Kashmir turban (in Arabic: *masar*) carefully wrapped around the *kumma* and a wide long dress up to the ankles, a so-called *dishdasha*, which is officially white. Women wear a long, colourful flowing dress with embroidery and a trowser or a black abaya (dress) that cover the shape of the body along with a headscarf (in Arabic: *lihaf*). The Islamic dress code officially aims at protecting a person's dignity and modesty and giving them respect (Women in Islam, 1999).

*Figure 6.1* An Omani boy and his mother, in the periphery of Souq Muttrah, purchasing household items

Source: Own photography (December 2018).

For a conservative community the degree of mutual compatibility or similarity between the guests and hosts and the increase in the number of international tourists can result in less tolerance towards the *Other* (Saveriades, 2000). This can lead to a high level of irritation and culture shock situations, conceptualized in the social and cultural carrying capacity of the community (Hall & Lew, 2009). Hosts who belong to a different culture may experience culture shock situations when they are irritated by the open behaviour of visitors. This is especially the case when the number of tourists exceeds the "cultural carrying capacity" of the host community (ibid., 2009, p. 172) and when the social values of the tourists are different to the values of the host (Figure 6.1). To avoid culture shock situations destinations, the tourist and the local need to ensure that the individual behaviour is not only consistent with the authentic self, but also with the culture in which the tourist is interacting with (Fennell & Przeclawski, 2003). Communicating with people of a different value system and communication style can contribute to various "culture shock situations" (Pearce, 2010) or "culture confusion" (Hottola, 2004). Depending on the length of the time spent in a holiday destination, the type of tourist, and the cultural differences between the tourist and the resident, the overall intensity and duration of culture shock may vary (Carmichael, 2006). Culture shock situations can affect a normally competent person and turn the person into "a dazed and inept performer" (Carmichael, 2006, p. 131) or a "stigmatized person" (Moufakkir, 2015). Moufakkir (2015) called on the personal freedom of the tourist and adaptation of the host community towards the tourists' dress behaviour, in this case, the female veil of Muslim women. Such an acceptance of (physical) difference calls for respect, tolerance and an "unconditional hospitality" (p. 21). Well-established Indian shopkeepers in the souq mentioned that "it started with shorts, when the mega-cruise ships arrived in the port in Muscat". They recalled that this phenomenon started around 2001. Before that time, tourists were wearing more

> … *"respectful clothes,"* referring to a different, more carefree type of tourist. According to an Omani shop owner *"They (the tourists) do not care, when they visit the souq".*

Other shopkeepers and shop owners confirmed that sociocultural changes appeared around 2006/2007, along with a sharp increase in the number of mega-cruise liners. Between 2005 and 2014, the number of ships arriving in Muscat increased fivefold (Gutberlet, 2016b). However, it is essential to highlight that an increasingly open dress code has been observed not only in Muttrah but as well in other public places and "enclosed bubbles" such as shopping malls in Muscat where expatriates were observed in revealing clothes. This can be seen as a result of globalization, time-space compression and the influence of social media as well as a "spill-over effect" from neighbouring countries like Dubai, indicating that a Western lifestyle is slowly imposing itself on the rather conservative values of the local community (Gutberlet, 2016b). However, there are differences among the countries on the Arabian Peninsula.

> *"In Dubai and Bahrain it is ok to walk around in T-shirt and shorts, in Bahrain as well, but in Abu Dhabi the locals are stricter,"* said a male Omani government employee.

An Omani sheikh (community leader) from the interior of the country stressed that he wished that tourists would dress 'respectfully', which implies that tourists should cover the entire bodies similar to the local dresses. Asked about their views of the tourist dress code in Souq Muttrah, the male-dominated business community (a total of 12 shopkeepers responded), mentioning that the tourists' dress was not respectful, while eight shopkeepers said the tourists' dress conforms to local customs.

> Elder Omani members of the well-established business community described the female dress as being too *revealing, open, or even similar to a night dress,* adding that the dress behaviour will harm the image of Oman and the cultural values of the local community.

The dress is a very important feature on the Arabian Peninsula. It is a part of the local identity (Gutberlet, 2016b). Arab societies are collective societies, that depend on in-groups and on power figures while having a larger power distance (Hofstede et al., 2010). In Islam, religious values guide the host-guest relation and they also forbid excessive display of wealth through the dress and material possessions. Moreover, traditional social values and norms often restrict women's individual movements in public spaces including exercising certain leisure activities together with men and individual travels. Travel is often limited to travelling with family members or other acceptable companions and for religious travel, such as a pilgrimage to Mecca (Apostolopoulos & Sönmez, 2001). Along with a woman's jewellery and a man's khanjar, it is a symbol for the tribal, regional and national affiliation and self-expression (Dörr & Richardson, 2003).

To stress the importance of respecting the traditional male Omani dress, the *dishdasha* and *masar* (turban) or *kumma* in public. The Oman Chamber of Commerce and Industry has even issued a warning to companies who do not stick to the official dress code (Oman Daily Observer, 2014). An Omani government employee who works at the port said that often tourists seem to be uninformed about the local values.

> *"When you go to Venice nobody talks about the dress code, but here it is a cultural part"*, said the director of a museum in Muttrah while comparing values in public places.

In his view, the cruise tourists do not care about the local culture. They just wear a top and hot-pants when they are leaving the ship.

Tourists who travel to a destination with a Muslim-dominated population are expected to adjust their behaviour and manners. Especially the behaviour in public spaces including the dress code, the prohibition of drinking alcohol and showing affection should be known and respected.

> *"We were not aware about the strict dress code and that it is not allowed to drink alcohol in public. We received some information on board the ship but we did not attend the info evenings,"* said a male German in his 50s, who was travelling along with his wife with the same mega-cruise liner for the third time. Tourists who are away from their everyday lives often change their identities.

Referring to the carefree attitude of mega-cruise tourists, a male German on-board guide said that

> *"Tourists do not really read instructions given to them. They wish to relax and take things as they come, without reflection. They do not want to get over-involved in the country."*

The guide concluded while adding that tourists gaze at the destination but they do not understand the local culture and the people (Gutberlet, 2016b). This can be due to a lack of attractive interpretation and pre-travel preparation leading to a lack of overall travel knowledge and skills. The cruise tourist wished to stay in the well-known comfort zone using the destination as an "ego-enforcement". The carefree type of tourist is in contrast to luxury ships that usually carry a different category of travellers, referring to the tourists' higher cultural capital and habitus (Bourdieu, 1984).

## Mindfulness and mutual respect

The concept of "mindfulness" versus "mindlessness" introduced by Moscardo (1999) describes the awareness and the behaviour of a tourist to minimize negative impacts while visiting a destination. Mindful tourists proactively think about where they are and what they are doing. An essential feature of mindful tourists is that they are more open-minded, they adapt easily to new environments, and therefore they are more likely to learn, change their behaviour pattern, and enjoy their holidays within local communities (Moscardo, 1999). They are also more "emancipated tourists" (Krippendorf, 1987). This is in line with Heidegger's (2010) thoughts about creating awareness of the environment and a fulfilment of being alive and of "being-in-the-world".

A "mindless tourist" is using his old routine, paying little attention to the setting, having little or no interest in new information (Pearce, 2006, p. 151) while doing rather "irrational things" that are not acceptable in the destination, such as getting drunk (Ryan, 2002a). Mindless tourists often express an attitude of cool indifference, remaining in a "cocoon of their own cultural beliefs and standards of behaviours" (MacCannell, 2011). For Turner and Ash (1975), Jafari (1987), Krippendorf (1987), and Grabun (1989), the travel motivation is often ego-centric and self-oriented. A carefree tourist behaviour arises because tourists are under-skilled, and underprepared for challenges they may face (Pearce, 2006). Their on-site experiences may create potential for behaviour that would not occur at home (Ryan, 2002). While on holidays tourists wish to behave and being treated differently, like a 'king' or a 'queen'. They are especially interested in the aesthetics of the natural and built environment. "The people living in the destination are almost irrelevant" (Krippendorf, 1987). The tourists' individual social behaviour conflicts with the morals, values, and the behaviour of the host community. A change in the nature of tourism would have to be preceded by a fundamental change in the attitudes and behaviours of tourists visiting a place and their neurosis (Turner & Ash, 1975).

Within a phenomenology for tourist experiences, Cohen (1978) categorized these tourists as "recreational and diversionary tourists", according to the tourist's own understanding of the world and the spiritual centre.

To what extent does the local community need to adjust to a deviant tourists' behaviour? Din (1989, p. 555) has classified attitudes of Muslim destinations towards tourism in three stages: *"discouraging"* and *"laissez-faire"* attitudes, *"accommodating"* and as *"isolating"* tourism from the local community (Figure 6.2). The Irridex model (Doxey, 1976) describes four stages of the resident's reaction to tourism development: Euphoria, apathy, annoyance and antagonism.

To avoid culture shock situations, several experienced Omani and expatriate tour guides that I interviewed said that *they proactively take responsibility, educate and communicate* with the tourists prior to a tour. They said that they "check, inform and prepare the tourists" for the tour. If they wear shorts, they are asked to return to the ship and change (Gutberlet, 2016b). An Omani freelance tour guide referred to mutual respect and cultural

*Figure 6.2* A cruise tourist wearing revealing clothes and other tourist wearing a
local dishdasha and turban in the main street of Souq Muttrah

Source: Own photography, March 2019.

empathy towards the local community and their conservative values in public spaces.

> *"…When you see Omanis wearing a nice dress, you have to behave like them. You have to respect them. This is the most important,"*

As Said mentioned (Said, 1989, p. 619), Western attitudes of cultural superiority can reinforce an alien system of values and accelerate the displacement of already weakened Islamic cultural norms. Hence, there is a need for a more religious, Islamic-centred development.

> *"Our religion tells us in public we need to follow certain rules …When we show respect for other people, we are also respected,"* said a sheikh (the head of a family tribe) in the oasis.

Some male guides argued that a strict dress code applies to the visit of a religious place like the Grand Mosque in Muscat only while other guides complained that female tourists were obviously ignoring their cultural values. This can be seen as a defensive reaction towards the cultural differences of the host community (Hottola, 2004), realizing their own selves.

## Travel preparation and unconditional hospitality

Male Omani and expatriate tour guides and drivers were not trained at all in cross-cultural communication in order to inform the German tourists about the dress code in a direct way. Moreover, tour guiding is male dominated on the Arabian Peninsula. There were only a few female tour guides who could communicate and approach female tourists differently. Young, male Asian and Arab tour guides who were in their 20s felt shy to address Western tourists. An Indian, German-speaking tour guide in his late 20s, said that

> *"it is too direct to approach the tourists about their dress, it is a taboo. Tourists have to inform themselves. The cruise ship should ensure that tourists are covered during their tour on shore".*

The guide referred to an essential feature of Asian cultures, the concept of *"mutual respect"* for other cultures and *"reciprocal hospitality"* (Din, 1989). Mutual respect is opposed to a Western spirit of individual freedom. During one of the day excursions by bus, a male, German on-board protestant pastor from Hamburg, who was accompanying mega-cruise tourists, openly reminded the tourists via the microphone to adhere to a *"a conservative dress code while on tour"*. Consequently, several female tourists checked whether they were dressed according to the local values. Although the announcement was late during the tour, he wished to openly created awareness about the mutual respect and empathy, enhancing a "care ethic" towards the local community and their values (Gutberlet, 2016b).

He said that compared to Germany, Oman has a very different society. The "umma" (in English: community) is very important and not the individual. A Muslim knows that he is part of the religious community and there are certain rules to observe. He added that, due to an increasing lack of social and moral values in the West, negative individual values have increased, reflected in the individual tourist behaviour, a lack of openness towards other cultures, values and new learning experiences. European tourists travel from an individual, gender-mixed, democratic environment to a collectivist, male-dominated society where the collective values are largely followed in public. This can create potential for tension and culture shock stresses for both the locals and the tourists (Gutberlet, 2016b). Sheikh Kahlan, Assistant Grand Mufti of Oman, the second religious' leader in the Sultanate said that local Muslims feel offended, especially when women are *"half dressed in public"*. He argued that non-Muslims and females in particular need to be informed and show respect towards the local culture, the religion, the family and their values without rejecting their own values and traditions (Gutberlet, 2016b).

Different awareness campaigns were conducted by the Ministry of Religious Affairs and Awqaf, including a conference on *Values and Ethics* held in 2014 and weekly live interviews with the Grand Mufti or Assistant Grand Mufti were broadcast on Oman TV in order to highlight the importance of the Sultanate's Islamic values and to strengthen them within the local community in Oman (Gutberlet, 2016b). One way for local stakeholders to enhance a more mindful behaviour in tourism is a clear structure of the pre-travel communication and the on-site interpretation, corresponding to what visitors already know (Moscardo, 1999). To inform the tourists, pre-arrival information was communicated in various steps by the shipping agency: through information brochures, by the local tour operator, the cruise brochure, the website as well as on-board communication (Gutberlet, 2016b). Members of Arab cultures tend to use high-context communication styles, where participants are not outspoken to others and meaning has to be interpreted. This is in contrast to low-context, direct communication styles used in Northern Europe. Moreover, there is more individualistic behaviour with low power distance. Hence, people behave more independent from other group members and powerful others (Hofstede et al., 2010, p. 104). Visitors should care about the destination visited; they need to be aware of the impact of their behaviours (Moscardo, 1999). The tourists' behaviour is rule-forming, and "engaged in creating categories and distinctions" (Ryan, 2002c). If the communication is clear for visitors, then learning, understanding and an overall satisfaction could be the outcome (Moscardo, 1999). Cruise tourists were informed in several stages about the destination. On board the ship, tourists received information through an evening presentation, a daily newsletter and an on-board TV programme. A slide or video presentation about day excursions is given by on-board tour guides in the main theatre of the ship just before the arrival in Muscat.

During the presentation, the Golden Rules are communicated, including the local dress code. The on-board guides advise the tourists to dress modestly on the Arabian Peninsula. An on-board swimming pool for nudists on one cruise liner was closed during the entire travel highlighting that the ship had adjusted and closed facilities according to local social values (Gutberlet, 2016b). Moreover, an excursion brochure distributed stated on one of its last pages that tourists should cover their shoulders and knees. The excursion brochure of the second cruise ship surveyed conveyed a rather indirect, misleading visual information. In tourist brochures the physical body is a referent for both the tourist and the local, so that "tourists and locals are placed on the same biopolitical plain" (Minca, 2012), showcasing a misleading assumption of individual freedom. In the introduction, the cruise brochure showed a full-page photo of a tourist couple that was taken in a Mediterranean setting. The female tourist pictured wears knee-length shorts and a semi-transparent, sleeveless top with a deep cleavage. The male tourist wears a non-transparent T-shirt and trousers. He was hugging the female tourist (Gutberlet, 2016b). Later on, the same excursion brochure mentioned some further recommendations including that "*women should be covered and short skirts, crop tops, tight shorts and tight clothes should be avoided because they may offend the local religious and cultural values*". The visual information confirms often misleading narratives and imaginaries created in cruise brochures. Female tourists are requested to cover their bodies; they do not need to wear an *abaya* (wide, long and usually black overcoat) like local females. Among local male stakeholders in tourism, there were various views about the dress code. An Omani tour guide said that females should cover their entire bodies, except the face and their hands.

In line with the concept of "unconditional hospitality", neither the official website of the Ministry of Tourism nor any of the various marketing brochures explicitly mentioned a female dress code for travellers.

To emphasize on the female dress code during the Muscat city-tour and the guidelines inside the Grand Mosque in Muscat, a cruise ship excursion ticket stipulated that women should wear long sleeves and trousers as well as awn scarf. However, further guidelines for female travellers in other public spaces are not given. A separate 1-page leaflet *Tourism Guidelines* was freely available inside the port building in 2013, mentioned the following (Gutberlet, 2016b):

> "*Men and women should cover knees and shoulders*" and "*respect local codes of behavior and traditions of dress.*"
>
> (Ministry of Tourism, 2012)

The leaflet, was not seen to be distributed to cruise tourists (Gutberlet, 2016b). In 2020, a leaflet 'General Guidelines' was on display at the Ministry of Tourism in Muscat, mentioning right on top of the list a general guideline:

> *Dressing conservatively is appreciated. Clothing that covers knees and shoulders are required for men and women.*
>
> (Ministry of Tourism, experienceoman.om 2020)

Expatriate tour operators in Oman use vague language when dealing with their European counterparts. A male Indian manager said:

> "*We mention not to wear transparent, revealing clothes.*"

Moreover, a male senior manager from a shipping agency argued that so-called common sense should be applied and women do not need to wear a scarf but respect the local culture and wear a decent dress. Tourists can also go to the beach and sunbathe (Gutberlet, 2016b). When I asked him what *decent* means, he responded that it should be known and that nobody needs to explain.

Referring to Hofstede et al. (2010), people who belong to a collectivist culture, such as in Asian countries including the Middle East, use high-context communication styles where participants have to interpret the meaning. Similarly, local travel magazines published in English are vague in their travel advice where *inappropriate clothing* was mentioned being most likely considered offensive (Scott, 2012).

Hence, written travel advice in marketing material uses adjectives like *modestly, conservative, decent, revealing, inappropriate* and *offensive,* to describe the dress code. For a European tourist who travels to Oman for the first time, these guidelines assume mindfulness and pre-travel knowledge about the culture and its values.

Local community members feel that the instructions regarding tourist behaviour were stricter and that tourists behaved more responsibly in the past. However, for the tourist, the consumption of 'Oriental holiday experiences' has been linked with freedom and well-being. Having an imaginary Oriental country in their minds while promoting a spirit of freedom on board, the cruise tourists were visiting different tourist sites including Souq Muttrah.

An expatriate shop owner said that especially local men are sensitive and react to physical exposure. This was confirmed one day when three tourists entered the souq. One was wearing a miniskirt and a sleeveless top with deep cleavage. "*Look at those girls,*" said a young Omani vendor, addressing his friend. They both stared at other females passing close by, realizing a "male gaze" staring at them and objectifying the women. Within the local, Omani culture, this is a behaviour that is socially not acceptable. Men are in particular requested to lower their views and not to gaze at a woman. This behaviour shift was also observed in other public places such as shopping malls where young males gazed at females.

Local community members working in tourism, having economic benefits were in favour of a rather laissez-faire attitude towards the tourists' dress behaviour (Gutberlet, 2016b). In-depth interviews with male locals in Souq Muttrah revealed that 50% of the 40 shopkeepers and shop owners of different nationalities preferred not to comment on the way tourists dress (Gutberlet, 2016b). In particular, the well-established Omani and Indian shopkeepers of the wholesale market as well as the elder Omanis, who were working in the souq for many decades and generations, did not wanted to share any critical thoughts about visitors. "The souq is a man's world," said a former male resident of Muttrah highlighting the dominance of male vendors in public space. There were only a few female vendors in the souq who were rather hidden in the backside. Female shoppers visiting the souq are usually accompanied by males, while female Western tourists were often observed visiting the souq on their own.

The dress code was a taboo that one should not comment on out of respect for the 'Other', the tourist from the Global North, or because they were afraid of expressing a critical view towards the Western tourist. As a male Omani said that Islam obliges them to respect everybody (Gutberlet, 2016b).

The need to encourage and accommodate tourists from other cultures has resulted in a "laid-back", "laissez-faire attitude" which has been observed in other tourist destinations in the Middle East, in Malaysia or North Africa (Din, 1989) as well as a lack of reinforced guidelines. As a result, the possibility of an aggression against tourists is now feared. Translated into Doxey's Irridex, well-established shopkeepers expressed their annoyance (Gutberlet, 2016b) and their concerns regarding an "imitation effect" and the adoption of the tourist behaviour by the younger generation. An Omani shop owner told me in Arabic that he recalled watching tourists kissing each other openly, which is not accepted in a public space. He added that if tourists were not respectful it is harmful for the reputation of Oman. He was shocked about the behaviour and felt powerless about the open behavior. Similarly, an Indian shopkeeper recalled an incident that created a culture shock situation. A female tourist who wanted to try one of his t-shirt in his shop, removed her shirt in front of him.

The female tourist may have felt empowered by the anonymity of a "liminoid tourist space" where she could move beyond the social and ethical boundaries (Berdychevsky et al., 2013). This can be seen as an act of harassment, away from any peer-group pressure and social control, the tourists acted mindlessly or intentionally to attract the locals' attention with a "carefree holiday spirit" (Gutberlet, 2016b). However, removing clothes in public is not morally acceptable in Europe either.

Locals expressed their anger and fear about a depreciation of their place. Some vendors feared that with an influx of inconsiderate tourists, local customers especially from the Interior of Oman may stay away (Gutberlet, 2016b). Shopkeepers expressed feelings of rejection and an increase in the stereotyping of tourists. This confirms culture shock situations and earlier research (Din, 1989; Saveriades, 2000). With the increase of mega-cruise tourism in Oman, stereotypes may be applied to all tourists without a corrective factors that were normally applicable when there were few tourists (Pi-Sunyer, 1989). Hence, the increase in the number of mindless tourists who do not care for their dress behaviour has exceeded the social and cultural carrying capacity (Hall & Lew, 2009), the level of acceptable tolerance of the local community towards the visitors. This has created "culture shock stresses" for locals (Gutberlet, 2017).

Stereotyping or stigmatization is more likely to occur when the length of the tourist stay is short and the number of visitors is high, which applies to German-speaking mega-cruise tourists arriving on the Arabian Peninsula (Gutberlet, 2016a).

A male on-board guide in his 20s mentioned during an interview that the local community should adapt and accept the "tourist culture". As a result of an increased "laissez-faire attitude" in UAE, two female Emiratis launched a social media campaign on twitter for the protection of the community values and a conservative dress code (Agence France-Presse, 2012). The women activists suggested that anybody who does not follow the dress code should pay a fine.

*Figure 6.3* Tourists along the main street. Male cruise tourists in shorts and a loosely wrapped turban, staging an 'Oriental Other' at the entrance to the souq

Source: Gutberlet (March 2013).

My questionnaire showed that mega-cruise tourists seemed well-informed about the local dress code and other behaviours in public (Figure 6.3).

Out of 830 German-speaking mega-cruise tourists surveyed in Souq Muttrah, 85% mentioned that they were informed about the dress code in Oman ($N = 235$), 87% said they were well informed about the code of conduct not to show affection in public while 12% said they were only partially informed. Despite their knowledge about the dress code, only 57% ($N = 229$) of the cruise tourists surveyed mentioned they were informed about the prohibition of drinking alcohol in public in Oman.

> "We have read a travel guide book before our travel. Onboard the ship we have a ship newspaper that informs about how to dress and what to be careful about in each destination," said a female tourist in her late 20s.

About 33% of the tourists surveyed ($N = 236$) were informed about the travel through guidebooks and 26% through the cruise brochure (Gutberlet, 2016b). Despite these various pre-travel information, the mega-cruise ship is seen as the main travel destination. The ship has the power to dictate its own rules to destinations, promoting a rather carefree holiday spirit, according to the motto: "freedom, individual and choice" that accompanies the economic system of late capitalism (Andrews, 2011).

An Omani highlighted in an interview the increasing influence of globalization on the changes in the values of the Omani society. This also confirms mutual respect and the acceptance of different behaviours. It is evident that increased economic benefits from tourism can promote the acceptance of a loss of cultural values, care and sensitivity towards the protection of the local heritage which confirms the results of Saveriades (2000). A high-ranking government official suggested raising the number of "good tourists" from luxury cruise liners, where in his view knowledge is transferred so that young Omanis can learn from them (Gutberlet, 2016b). Luxury, small-scale tourism and social capital were connected with increased respect and value for the community. As a consequence of extensive tourism development within the several Integrated Tourism Developments, I observed in 'Al Mouj' that the dress code was increasingly "relaxed" and "open". Western expatriates walk around in shorts and miniskirts and nobody seems to be critical or offended (Gutberlet, 2016b). This phenomenon is currently restricted to certain "enclosed Westernized tourist bubbles" that are designed for high-end consumption.

### Reengineering the tourist behaviour

Referring to the cruise sector, all stakeholders "need to recognize and identify that the tourist behaviour creates a problem for locals" (Pearce et al., 1996). Neocolonialist relationships should not be reinforced by imposing a Western dress and behaviours (Timothy, 2001). According to Hofstede et al. (2010) for low-context cultures, the information needs to be direct, clear and precise and the context should be explained. Through active personal intervention, so-called re-engineering, the tourist behaviour can be influenced positively (Pearce, 2010). In addition, more interpretation such as visual signboards as well as sociocultural training should be given on board the cruise liner and quality pre-travel information with images (Pearce, 2010). As a consequence of a relaxed Western dress behaviour, a number of signboards were set up in different parts of Muscat. However, these signboards conveyed again a vague message, promoting a "respectful and conservative dress behaviour" (Gutberlet, 2016b). The Royal Opera House Muscat has introduced an Omani dress rental service and a dress control. A written formal dress code stipulated on the back of each opera ticket and a "dress check" at the main entrance doors of the Opera House offer a good example. Similarly, tour operators and their tour guides could hand out *abayas* to those female cruise tourists who are not dressed according to the local dress code.

I agree there is no ready-made formula to achieve the goal of an "ideal Muslim host" (Din, 1989) and of an "ideal non-Muslim visitor" either. Hence, an agreement should be reached by the local community in Oman regarding their social carrying capacity, what is acceptable for the tourists' dress. The degree of deviation from local cultural norms that can be tolerated by the hosts should be clarified and communicated (Gutberlet, 2016b). It seems, newly developed tourist spaces or 'tourist bubbles' like in Souq Muttrah tend to rather reinforce the ego of tourists.

In the following, I will analyse the reactions of local stakeholders of the community towards tourism development in Souq Muttrah.

## A silent community resistance

> We certainly do not encourage tourism in its general unrestricted sense. When I was in Spain last year I met the King of Spain – he came to dinner – and he asked me 'What is the tourist situation in your country?' I told him: 'We have begun to open up the country.' He said 'Be careful.' Be extremely careful that you do not make the same mistakes that we did. I replied 'We have absolutely no intention of making the same mistakes you did.' Tourism has a positive side and a negative side and we are concentrating on the positive side. We thank God that there are many positive aspects and they have started to produce beneficial results, which, God willing, will have a positive impact in providing employment for our sons and daughters (and our daughters and sons) in the hotel sector and in a wide range of other sectors.
>
> (Late His Majesty Sultan Qaboos' address to students,
> Sultan Qaboos University, May 2, 2000, p. 280)

Referring to the increase in tourism development and Late His Majesty Sultan Qaboos' statement in the year 2000, he expressed his wish to develop tourism for the benefit of the Omani population. I observed that the well-established Omani and expatriate business community in Muttrah have developed a *silent resistance* and a *passive attitude* towards mass tourism and its impacts within their community. Most members of the former Omani resident community living around Souq Muttrah had relocated to other neighbourhoods in Muscat long before the arrival of mega-cruise ships, from the 1970s and 1980s onwards. The place became a heritage site and a 'tourist bubble'. Locals only come to their family homes that now serve as second homes in Muttrah on weekends and for family gatherings. I was told that especially the young, Omani generation is rarely seen in Souq Muttrah, only for weddings or other family gatherings. Instead, expatriate vendors are a predominant presence in the souq with cruise tourists *invading* coffee shops where they are served by Indian or Bangladeshi waiters. Those coffee shops have adjusted to an international taste, managed by Indian businessmen (Gutberlet, 2020). Shops that cater for Omanis and their product range of groceries, embroideries, halwa (Omani sweets), dishdasha (Omani male clothing), kummas (male cap), masar (turban) and other accessories are relocating from the main street to the narrow alleys in the interior of the souq, the periphery of the 'tourist bubble'. This phenomenon was observed at the entrance to the main street, where a local shop owner selling perfumes, textiles and embroideries for the local community for the past 40 years moved to the inside of the souq in 2014. The shop converted into a tourist shop (Figure 6.4), selling imported, cheap pashmina scarves, Indian textiles, postcards, carpets and belly dancing costumes (Gutberlet, 2016a). The Indian vendor, who has been working in Muttrah in the second generation continues selling items to local customers from his shop inside the souq.

Similarly, in the same year another Omani shop on the main street selling khanjars and locally produced items, was converted into a shop selling imported pashmina scarves. In addition, the Omani owner and vendor left his shop and several expatriate vendors took over the space (Figure 6.5).

The change in the social structure has been described as a continuous, slow process. An Omani in his 60s, the owner of a traditional halwa shop reflected on that change:

> "*Before 1970, the shopkeepers were all Omani. That has changed, now less than five per cent are Omanis, the majority are foreigners.*"
>
> (Gutberlet, 2016a)

An Omani herbal and spice shop that had traded in the centre of Souq Muttrah for several generations, over 150–200 years, closed down in 2013. That shop had been popular among Western tourists and locals, due to its authentic (old) interior where tourists were transported *back in time* to a time when there was no air conditioning and no electricity in the souq. Wooden boxes displayed a variety of local and regional items like spices, rose petals, oils and medical herbal remedies from India. It was renovated at the beginning of 2014 and the shop was offered for rent for banking ATM machines. "*We have to move on*", said the owner, thus stressing the need to transform the souq into a modern shopping street (Gutberlet, 2021). Two years earlier, the same shopkeeper had mentioned in an interview that the shops and their identity in Souq Muttrah need to be protected. However, among the local community and Muscat Municipality there has been no consensus about regulations regarding the sale of products in the souq. With an increase in the number of tourists visiting an Omani souq, a high-ranking government official claimed in an interview an increased loss of authenticity:

> "*If foreigners (he means international tourists) go to the local souq, they will kill it,*" referring to the loss of the collective identity due to a tourist influx.

This reflects the fear of being overwhelmed by the large number of tourists and of losing the cultural and social identity. Referring to the local identity, a shop owner of the long-established Indian trader community asked one day

*How the community would cope with an influx of tourism in the coming years? He pointed out that they were already struggling with more than a hundred ships visiting during the winter months.*

*Figure 6.4* An Omani shop selling items from Africa and Oman along the main street until 2014. One year later the shop converted into a tourist shop

Source: Gutberlet (2015).

*Figure 6.5* The Omani shop was converted into a tourist shop in 2014

Source: Gutberlet (2016a).

Due to overcrowding along the main streets of the souq and a lack of parking space, local Omani and expatriate customers who used to go shopping in Souq Muttrah now avoid the area when a mega-cruise ship is in the port (Gutberlet, 2016a). Translated in Doxey's (1976) irritation index, the local community shows a wish to escape and a high degree of irritation. In addition, there has been a decrease in the number of shops selling products for the local community. The 'tourist bubble' has extended. The attitudes of the local, well-established business community who own the shops reflect their views towards getting the greatest financial benefits out of tourism development. Such deep transformation of businesses had already occurred in the past in Souq Muttrah. Scholz (1990) mentioned that local food products and turbans were still sold in Muttrah during the early 1970s, but also recorded the rapid economic and social changes that occurred from the 1970s onwards, with the increasing demand for new, imported products by the expatriate community. To ease congestion of the public space in Muttrah, an official measure was the setting up of a large, red signboard by Muscat Municipality in front of the souq at the Corniche road, just before the tourist season 2013/2014. The signboard prohibits local vendors and customers from loading and unloading trucks during the peak tourist timings in the mornings and in the afternoons. Thus, prioritizing the flow of tourists while restricting the timing and the purchases of local customers who often buy in large quantities, limiting the local flow of everyday life (Gutberlet, 2016a).

### Setting-up boundaries

To protect themselves from the large number of tourists walking in front of their houses, some residents have created physical and social boundaries. The old residential, walled district opposite the cruise terminal, Sur Al-Lawatia, featured in tourism advertisements, has an Asian guard sitting beside the entrance gates, on the Corniche road and at the rear of the Souq. The guard refuses access to all outsiders, those who do not belong to the community, including other Omanis, expatriate residents and tourists. However, the entrance from the rear of the souq where Omanis and others can enter and exit the district has no guard (Gutberlet, 2016a). Beside the entrance gate, a new signboard "*Residential Area*" was installed, indicating that entry is highly restricted, even for Omanis who are not part of the resident community. During the annual religious month of Al Muharram, celebrated by the resident Muslim Shia community in Muttrah, which has occurred during the cruise season in winter 2013/2014. The community had set up a wall in front of the entrance gate. They wished to protect their privacy and themselves from curious people. This observation of creating additional boundaries was reinforced whenever I entered the place. I was asked several times to leave the place and told that it is a residential place. The shops are located on the next streets, further away, indicated an Omani lady, refusing to have non-sightseers inside the historic, walled district (Gutberlet, 2016a). The rejection of the *Other* was confirmed by male Omanis who do not belong to the residential community. They said that they are unwelcome inside the district (Gutberlet, 2016a). To prevent non-residents and tourists from entering the residential area and non-Muslims from entering the mosque, four signboards in English were set up beside the entrance of the mosque and the entrance to the residential district. These borders indicate further limitations. They push back the tourists and others within the limits of an urban experience (MacCannell, 2012). One day, I was asked by a male Omani resident who owns shops in Souq Muttrah to cover my hair when entering the district. However, covering the hair is not an explicit obligation for Omani women and especially not for expatriate females in Oman. The reaction indicates a limited access to highly gendered, secluded spaces, a conservative attitude and a reinforcement of the community's social values. The families living in the district are more religious-oriented and not interested in tourism, explained a senior member of the community, indicating that there is no interest in opening the district to the world and for outsiders.

Hence, the community has clearly defined a distinction and draws additional borders between residents, "insiders" of the extended family and the "outsiders" or the Others of the resident community – non-resident Omanis and expatriates as well as international tourists alike (Gutberlet, 2021). These identities were reinforced during the corona pandemic when the entire district was locked. I will further analyse the situation later on.

In the following part, I will elaborate on other sociocultural changes that have impacted the community, their identities and local governance.

## Disrupted sociocultural identities

Due to globalization and the increase in mega-cruise tourism in Souq Muttrah, the product range for tourists has increased while the product range for the local community had decreased (Gutberlet, 2021). Moreover, face-to-face interaction has become less important. They were handled increasingly online or by Asian expatriates who are aggressively approaching customers, giving Souq Muttrah the character of a rather "transitional neighbourhood" (Colic-Peisker & Robertson, 2015). Souq Muttrah can be consumed by the masses, the largely uncritical consumers within a sanitized and unified tourist attraction or 'tourist bubble', similar to a Disneyland theme park (Gutberlet, 2020), disconnected from the local environment.

> *"For the cruises the destination is only commercial, they do not care about the place and the people,"* said a former government official in January 2020 adding that Oman has a weak position, compared to European destinations facing increased power struggle. *"Venice can set up conditions, Barcelona can as well, but Oman is not in the position to put conditions,"* he said, stressing the dominant global, neoliberal economic system and its power relations.

He mentioned that on-board lecturers should inform about the destination visited and special shops could sell Omani handicrafts in order to increase the income for locals (Gutberlet, 2021). Similarly, a high-ranking employee from the Ministry of Tourism said about tourism development in Souq Muttrah and a lack of cooperation between government institutions:

> *"In Souq Muttrah, we cannot change the situation. It's the responsibility of the Municipality. The government could buy all the shops,"* expressing hope for increased governmental control over the neoliberal, uncontrolled economic situation in Souq Muttrah changing the urban lifestyle and local identities throughout time. *"In the seventies and eighties, Muttrah and the Corniche were the place to be in the evenings, now it is 'Al Mouj' (The Wave), and before that, it was 'Shatti Al Qurum' and 'Sabco Centre',"* he said referring to the authenticity of the space compared to "newer, themed spaces" in Muscat. The new, urban areas are valued more for being *modern* compared to an old, traditional, marketplace (Gutberlet, 2020).

> *... In Dubai there is the City Mall, and in other parts in Europe you can walk along a river. We need to construct such new places. Where do you go in the evening in Muscat?*

he said, questioning the authenticity of existing tourist sites in Muscat and the demand for a "constructed authenticity", themed, enclosed "tourist

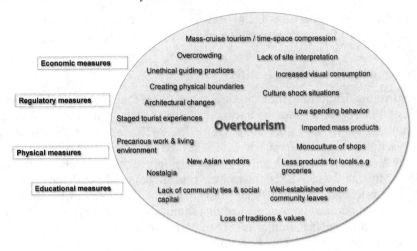

*Figure 6.6* Dimensions of overtourism and local governance in Souq Muttrah

Source: Adapted from Gutberlet (2020).

bubbles" to be consumed and for the tourist gaze. Figure 6.6 shows dimensions of overtourism and local governance in Souq Muttrah.

In the following part, I will outline some local identities through life-stories and narratives of Omanis and of the diaspora community in Souq Muttrah.

### Omani kahwa shaping local identities

With the increase in tourist numbers, the well-established vendor community became nostalgic about the past, their attachment to the place and social bonding with the other members of their ethnic, kin-based community network (Gutberlet, 2020). For example, they remembered the Omani coffee seller in Souq Muttrah. Omani black coffee with cardamom is part of the natural, genuine Omani hospitality and the community spirit, originally offered free-of-charge, shaping identities (Gutberlet, 2021). However, cruise tourists have been consuming tea in Souq Muttrah, sold in one of the small coffee shops or take-away food stalls.

"*They buy a small cup of karak tea and then they quickly leave the souq,*" said an Omani in his mid-50s stereotyping the mega-cruise tourists according to their purchase behaviour on shore, referring to the Indian black tea with milk and spices. Karak tea is a hybrid product that has replaced the traditional Omani coffee sold in Souq Muttrah in the past. The tea is sold in a small cup for 100 baiza only, (around 15 cents). Unlike in the past, karak tea is sold in disposable cups that cannot be reused (Gutberlet, 2020), creating more waste. The tea is cheap, mass consumed and adjusted to the liquid times and modern consumer within a throw-away society.

Here, authenticity is fluid and depends on the present circumstances in which it is represented (Park, 2014). Many houses including the shops in Souq

Muttrah are owned by members of the Al-Lawati business community. They have nostalgic memories about the souq and their community ties. They shared memories about the past when Omani coffee sellers like Mr Khamis shaped the image of Souq Muttrah. One of the elder community members of the Al-Lawatia family remembered that the male community met every morning at the coffee shop at the corner, Mr Khamis was the owner of the coffee shop. All men were sitting there, having a cup of tea with milk, exchanging information. At prayer time, they would all go together to the mosque. Therefore, he was connecting the place, with the culture and the old Omani coffee seller, creating an objective and 'interpersonal authenticity' (Wang, 1999). An Indian pharmacist in Souq Muttrah remembered the deep-rooted kahwa tradition and Salim the coffee seller during an interview in 2013 (Gutberlet, 2020).

> *He said that he used to sit in the court, inside Souq Muttrah. However, now he is sick. He always sold his kahwa (coffee) to tourists and locals. He made some sounds with his fingers, clinking the cups and then he attracted the tourists. I think tourists want something original… If you give a tourist a cup of Nescafe, he will say we have that in our country,*

and laughed, referring to the genuine originality and objective authenticity of an Omani coffee, served in small porcelain cups. In an interview for a local magazine (Black & White, 2010), the kahwa maker Salim explained that he makes Omani kahwa with 'Salini coffee beans', rosewater, spices and herbs.

> *"We belong to a different era. We grew up with certain traditions, food and a certain routine. My life is not complete without the traditional kahwa,"* he said.

Salim sold three kettles of kahwa per day, around 200 cups, for 50 baisas each. He remembered the old times of the souq when there was no ceiling. At that time, he was selling the cup for one baisa, then for 5 baisa, 10 baisas and now for 50 baisas.

> *"Making kahwa and selling it has become my life. Every cup I pour out to a customer is sheer bliss for me. I cannot think of a day I am doing something else. Everyone in this souq are like members of my family,"* said Salim.

(Black & White, 2010)

The Omani coffee seller connected the local people, representing Omani natural hospitality, community life and a slower, gentler lifestyle, having time for inter-personal relations within a coffee break and an exchange of news, stressing modernity and the changes towards a modern, faster and comfortable lifestyle and communications within modernity and globalization (Gutberlet, 2020). A vendor from the well-established Indian, Banyan trading community said in 2013 that there were several coffee sellers in the souq:

> *"There was a coffee seller, he was our helper and his main business was to sell fresh coffee to the community in the souq. In the past there were several coffee sellers in the souq. They worked from morning until evening and they sat here. Especially people from the Interior enjoyed the coffee,"* he said.
>
> (Gutberlet, 2020)

In 2021, the original lifestyle with an Omani coffee seller has vanished from the souq. There is no Omani coffee seller who preserves a slow way of life and the authenticity of the local 'kahwa tradition', creating a valuable social capital of the community. Instant coffee like 'Nescafe' and Indian karak tea (spicy milk tea) are now sold in glass or paper cups in several coffee shops, operated by Asians at the Corniche street and inside the souq.

## A legacy was built in the souq: It was a tradition to work there

The souq has witnessed continuous physical and social changes, creating resilience and a legacy in the place (Figure 6.7). An older member of the Al-Lawatia community in Souq Muttrah sees the hardship of the past in a positive way and in contrast to the pace of modernity and development. The 'Banyan' community, the Omani Balushi community and the Al-Lawatia community created a sense of mutual bonding social capital (Soulard et al., 2018), similar to African-Americans in the United States. The community seemed closer to each other in the past (Gutberlet, 2021).

*Figure 6.7* A shop of the well-established trader community in Souq Muttrah

Source: Gutberlet (2013).

Expatriates and Omanis are working together in the souq, forming an important local place for informal community development and exchange (Colic-Peisker & Robertson, 2015).

> *"In the past all men worked in the souq. It was a tradition. Our fathers and grandfathers worked in the souq. They had their shops in the souq. In the mornings they went to the souq, before their prayers. The old generation were working for example as carpenters. The new generation wants to work for the government."*
>
> (Gutberlet, 2021)

Forty years ago, people travelled for days to the souq for trade and shopping. Well-established community members retain fond memories of their simple lifestyle and trade. For instance, the Omani halwa maker in Souq Muttrah remembers the architecture and the social importance of the souq:

> He said that the souq has changed several times since the 1970s. At that time, the souq was roofed with palm branches and the Corniche road did not exist. There was no Corniche road. People came with a camel, a donkey or a horse. It sometimes took them two weeks to travel from Nizwa to Muscat. They sold local dried dates, dried fish, cooking oil and even mishkak (meat-sticks).

With economic development and modernity, the interest in manual work decreased. Nowadays, office jobs with more comfort, regular office hours and air conditioning are more valued by the young generation. Consequently, the majority of the Al-Lawatia community members and other families have left the souq. Their large business cooperations are dispersed in Muscat, owning monopolies, instead of bridging their knowledge with the souq, where they seem to be unwilling to continue the legacies of their families.

> *"The young who live in Muscat are not keen to work in the souq. The government programmes to support SMEs need a direction from everybody, a push to encourage them ... They see the Bengalis earning a lot of money,"*

said an Omani business owner who stressed the importance of setting up a small business and of bridging social capital with the government. An older Omani halwa maker remarked that salaries and living standards are very low for those who work in the souq (Gutberlet, 2020).

> *"Here in Muttrah the salaries are only 100-150 RO. In Muttrah five expatriates live in one room, maybe sometimes 15 or more live in one apartment. They don't stay at home, they work the whole day."*

To increase the attractiveness of the place and to raise the working and living conditions for Omanis, he suggested governmental control and restrictions, enhanced through the creation of law and financial incentives. With an increase in modernity and tourism development, changes in local practices and the flow of everyday life occurred.

*"In the past, the souq closed its doors at sunset. Everybody slept at 8 p.m. Each area had large doors that were closed around 6 p.m. You could then only pass through small doors with a secret password,"* remembers an Omani shop owner.

Sanjay (not his real name), who is around 70 years old, is a small, thin person without a beard. I had met him already when I worked as a tour guide. He relocated his small shop from the entrance to the inside of the souq in 2013, where he worked along with his son (Gutberlet, where he worked along with his son (Gutberlet, 2016a). In his old shop close to the Corniche road, I interviewed him several times. One day he told me that his father had opened the shop in 1922. Sanjay then took over about 40 years ago. "Since that time, everything has changed", he said. In the 1950s and 1960s there was no road on the Corniche in Muttrah. The seawater sometimes reached the outside of his shop. There were no cars and everybody arrived on a camel or on a donkey. Since tourism development started from the 1980s onwards and around 2004, tourists have been visiting the souq in larger numbers.

He described the changing use of the space, from a traditional trading place, where hardship and a slow life prevailed, developing into a commodified fast place where many visitors come only once and stay for a short time, reflecting on the development and modernization of the surrounding built environment, the infrastructure, the mobilities of people and the ethnic diversity (Gutberlet, 2021).

*"In the past the souq was multi-cultural. Indian traders, ancestors of the Khimji and Bahwan families brought food and electrical items to Oman,"* said an Omani tour guide.

In official marketing brochures, the souq is promoted as a traditional, Omani destination (Gutberlet, 2016a), diversity and a lack of representation of ethnic minorities. Due to an influx of newly arrived expatriate vendors from Asia, the bonding social capital through reciprocity decreased (Colic-Peisker & Robertson, 2015) in the past years.

Another well-established vendor said, *in the past only Omani and Banyan men worked in the souq. Omani customers trusted their quality and only bought from certain shops*, confirming a bonding and bridging social capital between the customer and the shop vendor (Gutberlet, 2021).

*"...all my customers come from the interior of Oman. Tourists buy different items. Tourists buy pashmina scarves and caps,"* said Sanjay with a smile, stressing the differentiation between his products for the local community and the rest of the "tourist souq" that caters to the international tourists. During the interview, an Omani woman and her son enter Sanjay's shop. She sits down on a small chair and tries some Arabian oud perfume (a local perfume) on her wrist. They decide to buy "oud" and "bokhoor" that are used to perfume clothes and homes. They leave and carry a number of plastic bags with them. Another Omani customer arrives to pay for his

purchase. Sanjay does his accounting manually, inside a small book, placed on a cupboard. There is no technology involved in the process. Another Omani buys a package of sea shells and packages of bokhoor (local perfume used at homes). Here, the authenticity of the place goes deep beyond the commercial purpose and the surface appearance. It is an emotional exchange and bonding social capital between the customer and the business owner (Gutberlet, 2021). In 2013, Sanjay's perfume shop closed down. It was renovated, adjusted to mass tourism and turned into a pashmina shop. Moreover, I observed that new vendors from India were selling with little storytelling, emotional exchange and bonding involved (Gutberlet, 2016a).

In 2021, one year after the COVID-19 pandemic had struck international tourism, I spoke to the Asian pashmina seller in Sanjay's shop located at the entrance to the souq. He was frustrated about the decrease in sales. He said that they may need to close down and return to Bangladesh. Compared to those shops that catered already to the local community, e.g. the frankincense shop or Sanjay's original perfume shop, for the pashmina shop it was difficult to adapt to the new situation and a lack of tourists. These observations were also evident in other tourist shops along the 'tourist bubble'.

## A legacy vanishes – stories about Arabia

Similar to Sanjay's shop, Akshay has inherited a family business that has been existing in the souq for several generations. Akshay (name changed) and his family are selling herbs, a large variety of products on display in a small space in the souq, in a small grocery and traditional herbal shop, located in the centre of the souq. They are selling dried limes, nutmegs, dried dates, tea, spices, dry ginger, henna leaves, rose water, herbal medicine, as well as herbal beauty products from Oman and India. He is even selling rock salt, soaps and rose petals from the Omani Jebel al Akhdar mountains. In summer during the date season, he sells fresh dates from their own farm in Al Batinah region, outside Muscat. In his tiny shop, the items are displayed naturally, in open wooden boxes, like in the past. The shop has no entrance door or glass window. It also does not have any air conditioner, only a fan, preserving its old character. There are very few remaining simple grocery shops like that inside the souq.

> *The shop remained the same as it was in the seventies, including its furniture and the doors. The only change is the electric signboard.*

Akshay who is in his 30s works together with his father, an elderly man sitting in the back of the shop, seems like a passive observer of the scenery. In June 2013, he tells me about his family history and the inherited shop. This ancient family shop was established already around 250 years ago. Originally, the family was a Sindhi from the South of Pakistan, a "diaspora community" (Timothy, 2011). Akshay grew up in Oman and in the souq. He told me that he was playing in the souq since childhood and since the age of 12, the souq and the family shop have been an essential part of his everyday life.

The first traders from India and Pakistan came to Oman about 600 years ago. They are a marginal community, belonging to early traders, around 79 families still exist in Oman, 12–15 families still work in Muttrah. They established a business in the city of Sohar and then they moved to Musannah and then to Muttrah.

One day he told me that the Banyan community was the main reason why the Portuguese traders gave nuts the name '*Muscat nuts*' (Gutberlet, 2021). Akshay was always engaging with his environment. Often he acted as a creative storyteller for tourists. He had the talent to transform the elevated shop into a *theatre stage*. He quickly attracted an interested crowd of listeners, who were attentively listening to his tales about Arabia. They were mesmerized while listening to his stories and recipes. For example, he explained the use of neem seeds that strengthen the immune system.

> "*Soak them for 24 hours, squeeze the seeds, boil them over low fire for 3 hours, strain and fill a bottle, remaining seeds for half a litre. Take a teaspoon per day for 40 days.*"

In an interview in 2014, he said that many vendors have become more profit-oriented in the souq and less social. In the past, joint everyday activities had created a bond or a cohesion between community members:

> "*You don't see people playing cards or sitting together while having a kahwa coffee. This is modernization…. I wish the community here could find a balance between modernization and our culture,*" he told me in 2014.

He referred to the modernization of the souq, linked with a neoliberal, capitalism-based development lacking the slower encounters between people which were a characteristic of the place. For Akshay, the social transformation of the souq occurred at the expense of social values, traditions creating and tight community ties, which were more prevalent in the past (Gutberlet, 2021).

> He argued that tourism is money-based. "*You can no longer see the original culture of the souq, that has been lost. Nowadays capitalism is dominating the souq.*"

By "culture", he meant especially the intangible features of local traditions, the everyday flow of everyday life and their values, which were not money-based, such as community trust, support, networks and cooperation within the legacy of his shop. Through such "bonding social capital", his family was connected with the community network which secured their survival. Similar to the other Omani shops, Akshay's shop vanished from Souq Muttrah during the course of my field research. It closed at the end of 2013, when his father became sick and was not able to return to the souq, to his workspace. I then interviewed Akshay again in 2014 (Gutberlet, 2021).

He told me that *he went through hell, explaining that he had to throw all his products into the sea and the shop boxes were dumped into the garbage.* He was mourning the loss of the past, his attachment to the souq and his fond memories of the family shop.

Akshay wanted to leave the past behind and set up a new business. He had invested Omani Rials 10,000 (around Euro 22,000) and was waiting for a reply from a bank. One day, he complained that nobody wants to invest in the souq. *The shopkeepers are more aggressive than two to three years ago.* In the past, there was no problem of sales, there were too many restrictions referring to the economic slowdown, a lack of social stability and community cohesion within the souq and modern society.

Then suddenly, Akshay installed an ATM money machine in his inherited family shop, adjusting to the capitalist development. It was the first ATM installed inside the souq. In 2016, the shop turned into a flashy pashmina, textile tourist shop with windows, selling imported textiles by vendors from Bangladesh (Figure 6.8). Akshay left behind family traditions and a legacy (Gutberlet, 2021).

Since the transformation of the shop, Akshay was not seen again in the narrow streets of Souq Muttrah. He told me over the phone that he left the souq and opened up another business elsewhere in Oman. This loss shows an essential loss of bonding and bridging social capital through a lack of cooperation and community trust. It developed along with a shift from a traditional long-term attachment to the souq towards liquid modernity and an infinite series of short-term projects and episodes (Bauman, 2000).

*Figure 6.8* Akshay's shop turned into a flashy textile, tourist shop with windows and an air conditioner, from 2016 onwards.

Source: Gutberlet (2019).

Old customers were replaced with new customers from mega-cruise liners, enhancing the sale of hybrid, global products and a loss of local knowledge (Gutberlet, 2021).

> *"In future, the sale of tourist items will grow until all shops sell similar items,"* predicted an elder Omani of the Sur Al-Lawatia resident community already in 2013. "These products are Omani products made by Pakistanis or Indians," he said referring to the authenticity of the local products and the Asian labour market, where handicraft skills can be acquired for much lower wages compared to Omani salaries.

During an interview in March 2013, an American heritage expert from the Ministry of Heritage highlighted the long-standing predominance of Banyan artisans from India and Pakistan. Their skilled social capital was already famous in the 19th century in Zanzibar skilled social capital in the 19th century in Zanzibar (Gutberlet, 2021).

Another local store for the community is located in the periphery of the souq, in the small side street leading to the gold souq. Abdul (name changed) from India has been working in the souq for a long time. I interviewed him on a hot summer day in June.

I have to climb up a few stairs to reach Abdul's shop. As flood protection, many shops are elevated in Souq Muttrah. Inside this tiny shop, there is a smell of washing powder. A small plastic curtain at the door protects the inside of the shop from the soaring heat. Inside, the air conditioner is running flat-out, but it seems time has come to a standstill. Abdul's shop has been in existence for around forty to fifty years. I sit down on a small bench opposite his small table where he sits as a cashier, located just beside the entrance. The tiny space is filled to the ceiling with household items like washing powder, Chlorox floor cleaner, shampoo, herbal toothpaste, cigarettes and coconut oil or olive oil. Abdul does not understand English, so we speak Arabic.

He recalls his arrival by ship in the mid-1970s. *"I arrived with the Akbar Line in Muscat".*

He arrived along with his brother who had worked as an engineer for an Austrian Engineering company in Muscat. At that time Muttrah harbour did not exist and the ship had to anchor far away from the bay of Muttrah. They were then brought in with a small boat.

Previously, Abdul had assisted his father in a grocery shop in Mumbai, India. Abdul recalls the development of the area next to his shop.

> *"In the past, there was a vegetable shop next to my shop and on the other side there was a barber shop and a cafeteria. There were as well some Indian restaurants nearby. There were no abaya shops here. Muttrah was the main business district at that time. People travelled from the Interior of Oman with a donkey for shopping in Muttrah,"* he said.

He becomes nostalgic about the past, highlighting the simple lifestyle and the high importance of the place Souq Muttrah for their livelihoods, connecting the community and its trade. Nowadays, Omanis, Pakistanis, Indians and Bangladeshis who live in Muttrah are his customers.

> *"Sometimes a tourist comes in and buys a toothpaste or cigarettes,"* he says smiling.

One of his long-term customers, a female Omani in her 40s, dressed in black abaya (a black overcoat) enters the shop and sits down on the small bench. She tells me that she always comes for shopping at this shop. Here she can buy exactly what she needs and not expensive. Her experience is different is different from shopping at a large hypermarket like Lulu (a popular hypermarket chain on the Arabian Peninsula).

Abdul tells me that he works together with a supermarket close by, outside the souq area. From there he buys all fresh products. They deliver the grocery to the customer's home; thus he offers an individualized customer service and an additional value for the local resident community (Gutberlet, 2021).

Due to the increase in mass tourism, well-established shop owners like Saleh, Sanjay and Akshay have left their shops in Souq Muttrah in recent years, decreasing the social capital (Gutberlet, 2021). Hence, with the increase in mass tourism, there has been a loss of "bonding social capital" through an increased ethnic fragmentation in Souq Muttrah. This has resulted in a lack of trust and the loss of networks, aggravated by a shift from local customers with a long-term attachment to the place and the people to a large number of short-term, international visitors who have no connection with the place, its local products or the people.

As a soft measure to counteract the disappearance of traditional shops inside the souq, the Omani Handicraft Authority had set-up a small, mobile Omani handicraft kiosk close to the main entrance of the souq, thus mitigating any conflict with new Asian vendors. However, the small handicraft kiosk vanished in 2018 and was not seen again. I observed that in January 2019 only a few remaining original shops were open while along the main street of the souq well-established vendors had left their shops to expatriates, further enhancing a staged authenticity.

One month later, in February 2019, I noticed that more well-established shop owners who were selling Omani heritage items had shifted their businesses to the "hidden backstage" of their shops, the inner areas, where they were not directly in contact with tourists. From the back they were doing business with selected customers in person and via phone calls or social media. Others continued selling in person, during certain times only, online or via phone. In the front of their shops, newly arrived Asian vendors continued rather aggressively selling cheap, imported global souvenirs.

The space had changed, promoted by globalization and operationalized in a monoculture of shops where Asian vendors from Bangladesh and

India were selling cheap, international tourist souvenirs like fake pashmina scarves, belly dancing costumes, fridge magnets and camel miniatures. Instead of locally produced handicrafts, food items for the local community or Omani coffee, there were cheap textiles from Asia or commodified local puppets such as salt and pepper dispensers, belly-dancing costumes and T-shirts (Gutberlet, 2020). Hence, the face-to-face interaction became less important and handled by Asian expatriates who were approaching the tourists in English, German, French or Italian and rather "catching" them from the street. This selling attitude has turned Souq Muttrah into a hybrid space, having a rather 'transitional and disruptive identity' (Figure 6.9).

Tourism development in Souq Muttrah has increased a division and disruption in Souq Muttrah and disrupted, disrupting the well-established multi-ethnic community, their products, their generations, their legacy, their bonding social capital and their ethnic backgrounds. The souq has developed into a staged, commodified place. Newly arrived Asian vendors are at the front stage. The older generation of well-established vendors and owners including those from diaspora communities and their legacy have taken a rather passive back seat in the backstage. They seem to avoid direct face-to-face involvement in mass tourism, avoiding any possible cultural clashes (Gutberlet, 2021).

In 2019, an Omani from the Sur Al-Lawatia resident community that had restricted tourist access mentioned, that there are wishes to open up the district on the one hand and on the other hand to preserve and protect its charm for insiders of the community and the remaining residents only. However, a local residential house transformed into a boutique hotel is planned to open in close proximity to the walled district (Gutberlet, 2020). Some well-established Asian vendors told me in 2019 that they felt being excluded from the official tourism planning. They did not give any further explanations. Moreover, I realized that they were excluded from a governmental *Muttrah Tourism Committee*, formed several years ago. The tourism committee seemed to gather an elite business and government circle of male Omanis, excluding members of the expatriate trader community.

### Neoliberal tourism development

The high political, social and cultural importance of my research has become evident, highlighted through the continuous media coverage on neoliberal, growth-oriented tourism development. Along with the increase in mega-cruise tourism, construction work on the US$2 billion integrated tourist port and lifestyle destination Mina Sultan Qaboos Waterfront project was scheduled to begin in November 2019 (Muscat Daily, 2019), transforming the entire port and Corniche area into a modern, hybrid place. A few years earlier, there was a plan to convert and redevelop Muttrah into a more modern, pedestrian-friendly and "Smart City" with a digital infrastructure. This could improve the attractiveness and acceptance of Souq Muttrah as a local heritage place for the local community as well as improve the

| | High bonding & bridging social capital | Low bonding & bridging social capital |
|---|---|---|
| **Handicraft:** | Locally made | Ready-made, global |
| **Shops:** | Kin-based, owned and operated by a family, handed over from one generation (Omani and non-Omani) to the next one - promoting continuity | Sold or operated by new expatriates - lack of continuity |
| **Government intervention:** | Little, social mix | High, e.g. Omanisation quota |
| **Lifestyle in the Souq:** | Simple, sharing the flow of everyday lives, networking, doing business, playing cards | Modernization, little sharing of everyday lives, anonymity, grocery shops and coffeemaker vanished, sales-oriented behavior |
| **Networks:** | Kin-based, tight, local mutual bonding between vendors and vendors and with customers, based on trust, reciprocity and collaboration | Loose global networks, social mobility Capitalist-driven development, low work conditions and cheap labor, little trust, cooperation and involvement, isolation |
| **Customers:** | Predominantly local (residents and expats), emotional exchange and people-focused (the storyteller) | International tourists, superficial, money-focused and online exchange |
| **Community resilience** | Community resilience | Little community resilience |
| | 'Loci of informal community development' / cohesion | 'Transitional neighborhood' / disruptive identity |

*Figure 6.9* Framework of the dimensions of bonding and bridging social capital leading to a transnational community in Souq Muttrah

Source: Adapted from Gutberlet (2021).

tourists' geographical orientation. It may facilitate walking, hiking, biking or other "slow tours" such as scooter tours through Muttrah. Due to budget constraints, the development was put on hold and transferred to the Omani government and its development company Omran as main developer in 2020.

According to official plans in 2019, the place was designed similar to other tourism developments elsewhere around the world, e.g. the Waterfront project in Cape Town, South Africa, or the Walk Dubai. The redevelopment plan envisions the establishment of a themed, luxury "simulacra" space (Baudrillard, 1994) within a new cruise port area. This will promote an increased consumption of Oriental signs and themed Oriental environments for the tourist gaze (Urry, 1995), including a seven-star "Heritage Hotel", a protected old house that was transformed into a hotel. Such hotels are a common sight in other other modernized heritage souqs in the Arabian Gulf. For example, in Souq Waqif in Qatar and Souq Al Seef in Dubai luxury hotels are a core feature of the retail souqs. The tourism development plans can be seen as a continuation of the transformation of the hybrid space of Souq Muttrah within neoliberal tourism development. These plans are adjusting to the needs of a local urban elite and international tourists, mainly from mega-cruise liners as well as the ships' corporate needs, instead of focusing on the well-being of the local community and their everyday needs and wishes (Gutberlet, 2020). Within the community, there was the wish to have a joint, participatory vision and a tourism development strategy connecting different stakeholders in Souq Muttrah. The majority of the multi-ethnic interviewees of the business and vendor community mentioned being in favour of the planned cruise liner port, but on a smaller scale. For instance, welcoming three large cruise liners per week, not per day in Oman, were suggested (Gutberlet, 2016a).

For a public event in Souq Muttrah held at the Bait Al Baranda Museum, which belongs to Muscat Municipality, in March 2019, I invited different stakeholders from the local community. I wanted to initiate and create a platform for discussion on urban development in Souq Muttrah. However, none of the well-established Omani and expatriate vendors and owners attended the event, compared to a number of government representatives. This may again translate into a lack of trust and reciprocity regarding the establishment of an equal and participatory platform, fostering a constructive exchange and a continuous discussion and involvement, a bridging and bonding social capital between different stakeholders of the multi-ethnic community (Gutberlet, 2021).

In the following part, I will highlight the social changes that developed because of "undertourism", caused by the corona pandemic. The phenomenon evolved in Souq Muttrah between March 2020 and autumn 2021.

## Empty spaces, undertourism and uncertainties

Between the end of March and mid-June 2020, Souq Muttrah was completely locked down as one of the hotspots of the corona pandemic (Gutberlet, 2021). Souq Muttrah was one of the first spaces where COVID-19 infections were detected in Oman in mid-2020. The souq symbolizes a narrow, confined meeting space where people interact in close proximity to each other, and social distancing is difficult to realize there. Governments had imposed restrictions to keep citizens 'in' and travellers from abroad 'out' from spring 2020 onwards

(Lew et al., 2020). At the same time, the economy slowed down worldwide, all activities came to a standstill, all land borders were closed and travel restrictions imposed in spring 2020. The entire district of Muttrah, where the majority of workers of the souq live, was locked up for five months in 2020. People were not allowed to move. Compared to other districts in Muscat, the movement of people in Muttrah was highly restricted. All businesses had to shut down and people had no income at all, although they had to pay their rents and their living expenses. Governmental emergency funding was not available to the multi-ethnic community. Hence, a valorization of the diverse social capital within tourism development faced a more than uncertain future.

In May 2021, the souq and all businesses were closed again for one week. Until the end of July 2021, several night lockdowns followed including a full lockdown over the Eid Al-Adha holidays in July 2021.

In a highly mobile place where people had got used to mobilities, border crossings and tourism and where they become dependent on the tourism system, the complete standstill in many business operations and the immobility of people has damaged the quality of life of the place and its communities (Milano & Koens, 2021).

In spring 2021, one year after the start of the COVID-19 pandemic, an Omani vendor along with several expatriate vendors that I had interviewed in previous years had left their shops. They had returned to their home countries in Asia, mainly India and Bangladesh. Vendors in the souq mentioned a lack of business opportunities from the standstill of mega-cruise tourism, their economic situation also compounded by the fall in oil prices and the higher exchange rate with the Euro. At that time, I spoke to six established vendors and businessmen in the souq whom I had already interviewed in 2013. I had the opportunity to conduct informal conversations during successive years until 2021.

The worldwide pandemic could develop further as a result of the increased time-space compression on our planet (Harvey, 2020). According to a report by the UN Development Programme, the corona pandemic overlapped and interacted with other ongoing global tensions: between people and technology, between people and nature and between the haves and the have-nots – which were already shaping a new generation of inequalities (UNDP, 2020, p. 22). During the COVID-19 pandemic, the economic situation in Oman as well as social tensions worldwide were severely aggravated. The United Nations Development Programme (UNDP) has called the crisis a systemic crisis, affecting economies and societies in unprecedented ways (UNDP, 2020). People from the Global South especially and from low-income groups worldwide are vulnerable to the effects of the pandemic since they lack the ability to come up with emergency funds (UNDP, 2020, p. 21).

During several visits in April 2021 in the morning hours, I only encounter one individual female and a European couple, walking along the Corniche road, towards the souq. She is wearing a knee-length dress and he is wearing jeans. Two weeks later, on the Corniche road more cars are parked, especially around the Lawatia district. It is Ramadan time. I observe Omanis walking along the Corniche carrying bags filled with textiles, most probably for Eid

*Figure 6.10* In front of Souq Muttrah – an empty square where tourists gathered in the past.

Source: Gutberlet (April 2021).

celebrations, the festival after Ramadan. There are no tourists in the area. The souq belongs to the locals again who can go shopping without meeting large crowds of tourists. However, vendors complain about a lack of sales and income. There is undertourism in a previously overcrowded tourist destination (Figure 6.10).

With the outbreak of the new Coronavirus (Delta variant) in May 2021, flights from many countries in Asia including India, Bangladesh, Pakistan, Philippines and all Gulf countries were suspended and not relaunched until mid-August, which included as well supply chains for the souq being disrupted. Moreover, low-cost flights were cancelled, which had a major impact on the mobilities, especially of low-income workers. Up to the autumn 2021, the future seemed uncertain in Oman and in particular in the souq that has developed into a "tourist bubble" in the past years. Physical and social encounters are an essential feature of a marketplace. However, due to Corona restrictions, the area has recently experienced a real dearth of customers, and social distancing has increased the pressure on the site.

(*My observations*) Walking along the Corniche road towards Souq Muttrah is like walking through a beautiful but empty space beneath a bright, blue sky. Usually, this is a time when many Western tourists walk along this area, chatting in different languages.

*"Since last year we have not had any tourists coming to our shop, only a few residents. I don't know if we can survive this year. If this continues, maybe we all need to leave and go home by end of the year,"* said a Bangladeshi vendor whom I have known for many years at the beginning of April 2021.

This again confirms uncertainties within "fluid social relations", liquid modernity (Bauman & Vecchi, 2000) promoting a precarious situation for the workers, unlike in European countries where SMEs have been largely supported with financial aid during the pandemic, from 2020 onwards. In Oman, there was initially no government support for SMEs in place. End of 2020 and in 2021, financial aid was given to Omani business owners only, expatriates in Souq Muttrah were excluded from the financial aid programme.

## "The souq is a bit tired"

During the pandemic, I observed further tangible and intangible changes within the cultural heritage of Souq Muttrah. One of the last remaining grocery shops owned by a member of the Banyan community, who had managed the shop for generations, closed down and was sold. The shop that was located on the main street in the souq, turned into a tourist silver jewellery shop. The Indian (Banyan) owner invested in a new family business outside the souq.

One day, close to the entrance, in a corner shop, the Omani frankincense vendor whom I had interviewed many times throughout the past years, sits on the floor, filling small plastic boxes with Arabian oud (perfume). When he sees me, he smiles and gives me a box with incense, and says in Arabic:

*"It is for clothes and for the house".* I thank him for the gift and ask about the work situation in the souq. He replies: *"The souq is a bit tired or stressed"*, which means, the souq is not as it was.

People are tired of the continuous restrictions and social distancing. Within the Omani culture of communicating with each other especially, the narrow alleys of the souq and the proximity of the shops being next to each other prevent social distancing in times of the Coronavirus. That day, several Omanis stop in front of the frankincense shop. They look around the shelves with curiosity but they don't buy anything. I am surprised and think, they are similar to the tourists who are just looking at the product range, consuming the place visually. However, I realize that some were comparing the prices and the quality. The frankincense vendor continues filling the small boxes. We have a small chat about the family. He tells me that they have started selling 'frankincense oil' from Salalah, a new local product. I imagine that some tourists from Europe would love to buy such an authentic product.

I continue my walk along the main street, where a number of shops have adapted their product range to the local customers.

*"Those shops that offer products for the local community are in a better situation. Maybe we need to change our products,"*

says another Asian vendor. One young vendor on the Corniche road, an engineer, who is currently supporting his father's business mentions that he has started to post their products, mainly handwoven Kashmiri scarves used for the Omani turban (*masar*), on Instagram. He seems very engaged to increase sales in these times of uncertainty, shifting the sales online, towards home delivery in Muscat, keeping the health regulations and social distance with customers. Hence, the young generation seems more innovative and engaged with the community through sales via social media while the older generation of business people sticks to their old direct face-to-face selling practices.

Another morning, while walking along the main tourist street, I am the only European. The vendors try to praise and sell their products aggressively:

> *"Look! Perfume, pashmina, frankincense, silver,"* they say. *"Please have a look, come inside"* … said another young Asian vendor.

I want to escape like the German tourists I interviewed in the past … now the products they want to sell are unimportant. I explain to them that I am not a regular tourist and that I have been living in Muscat for a long time while doing field research. I think they just think that I am a white European female and a tourist and I have money to buy things … I return to the Corniche road … it is really empty along the street, only a few Omani shoppers where usually crowds of people pass by. At the entrance, I take a photo of the empty square where usually people stand and wait. The sightseeing *'Big Bus'* stop is still there, waiting for tourists to hop on and off, as well as the restaurants with juices and sandwiches. I was told that one of the restaurants had to close some months ago. It is a sad picture. I remember an elderly Omani from the community in Sur Al-Lawatia whom I interviewed around eight years ago. At that time, he told me during a walk through the souq:

> *"Tourism in the souq is a blessing, we need it. If the tourist items had not taken over, the souq would have disappeared a long time ago. It would have become a ghost souq."*

In times of corona, it seems that the tourists have become a "blessing", safeguarding the heritage and the sociocultural identity of the souq within modernity.

In summer 2021, while visiting the souq, it looks empty like a ghost souq. The Sultanate had not yet recovered from the various shocks of the COVID-19 pandemic. In another district, away from the old district of Muttrah, the Mall of Oman, a huge modern shopping mall, an 'enclosed bubble,' developed by Al Futtaim Group from Dubai was inaugurated and attracted many young Omani residents.

In Souq Muttrah, it has become clear that the power that was there in the past to act locally within the area has been transferred to a larger, global and more powerful level, while politics and local decision-making have been bound to the local level. The concepts of community and inter-human bonds become more vague and temporary (Bauman, 2007, p. 1f.), while modern society as such is perceived as "a network of random connections and disconnections".

For the recovery of tourism in Souq Muttrah, there is a need for a more participatory approach and an appreciation of the available social capital. UNWTO (2020) and OECD (2020) have stressed the importance of a responsible recovery from the COVID-19 crisis placing people, social inclusion, public health, circular economy, biodiversity, finance and governance at its heart. However, let us hope that the pandemic is forcing an expansion in human consciousness that may make humankind better able to address other future global challenges (Galvani et al., 2020) such as other pandemics and climate change and therefore focus towards a people-oriented and more equal or "just tourism" (Higgins-Desbiolles, 2021; Ioannides & Gyimóthy, 2020; Jamal & Higham, 2021; Lew et al., 2020). My research is especially relevant for future tourism development within the political and social planning towards more just and people-focused tourism within an emerging tourist destination that has been promoting the construction of "enclosed tourist bubbles" on land (Gutberlet 2019, 2020).

In the past two chapters, I have highlighted tourist imaginaries and on-site experiences in an emerging urban destination on the Arabian Peninsula, along with impacts of large-scale cruise tourism and local community perceptions towards overtourism and tourist behaviours. Finally, I highlighted the sudden lack of tourism caused by the global COVID-19 pandemic, challenging the multi-ethnic community and their identities.

In the following chapter, I will analyse German-speaking tourist imaginaries and experiences during a 4 × 4 tour to the interior of Oman, the Sharqiyah Sands desert and an oasis, and connect them to the ethics of tourism and slow tourism. Slow tourism is a way of engaging in-depth, slowing down time within the environment, valuing the community and intangible Cultural Ecosystem Services (CES) that the landscape provides human beings with.

## References

Agence France-Presse (2012). *Two Emirati women begin online campaign against skimpy dress.* Apex Media: Muscat Daily, 26 May.

Al-Salimi, A., Gaube, A., & Korn, H. (2008). *Islamic art in Oman.* Mazoon Printing, Publishing and Advertising.

Andrews, H. (2011). The British on holiday. *Charter tourism, identity and consumption. tourism and cultural change.* Channel View Publications.

Apostolopoulos, Y., & Sönmez, S. (2001). Working producers, leisured consumers: Women's experiences in developing regions. In Y. Apostolopoulos, S. Sönmez, & D. J. Timothy (Eds.), *Women as producers and consumers of tourism in developing regions* (pp. 3–17). Praeger.

Baudrillard, J. (1994). *Simulacra and simulation* (trans. S. F. Glaser). University of Michigan Press.

Bauman, Z. (2000). *Liquid modernity*. Polity Press.

Bauman, Z. (2004). *Identity. Conversations with Benedetto Vecchi*. Ebook for PC. Polity Press.

Bauman, Z. (2007). *Liquid times. Living in an age of uncertainty*. Ebook for PC. Polity Press.

Bauman, Z., & Vecchi, B. (2004). *Identity*. Polity Press.

Berdychevsky, L., Gibson, H., & Poria, Y. (2013). Women's sexual behavior in tourism: Loosening the bridle. *Annals of Tourism Research*, *42*, 65–85.

Black & White (2010). *Kahwa, anyone?*, June 21–July 6, Volume *1*, 28–35, Black & White Magazine.

Bourdieu, P. (1984). Distinction. *A social critique of the judgment of taste*. Kindle Ebook for PC. Routledge.

Carmichael, B. (2006). Linking quality tourism experiences, resident's quality of life, and quality experiences for tourists. In G. Jennings & N. Polovitz-Nickerson (Eds.), *Quality tourism experiences* (pp. 113–131). Elsevier Butterworth-Heinemann.

Caton, K. (2012). Taking the moral turn in tourism studies. *Annals of Tourism Research*, *39*, 1906–1928.

Chan, K.M.A; Satterfield, T., & Goldstein, J. (2012). Rethinking cultural ecoservice systems to better address and navigate cultural values. *Ecological Economics*, 74, 8–18.

Cohen, E. (1978). The impact of tourism on the physical environment. *Annals of Tourism Research*, *5*(2), 215–237.

Colic-Peisker, V., & Robertson, S. (2015). Social change and community cohesion: An ethnographic study of two Melbourne suburbs, *Ethnic and Racial Studies*, *38*(1), 75–91.

Din, K. (1989). Islam and tourism. *Annals of Tourism Research*, 16, 542–563.

Doerr, M., & Richardson, N. (2003a). Context and Influences. In His Highness Seyyid Shihab bin Tariq Al Said (Ed.), *The craft heritage of Oman* (Vol. 1, pp. 11–31). Motivate Publishing for the Omani Craft Heritage Documentation Project.

Doerr, M., & Richardson, N. (2003b). Beyond tradition. In His Highness Seyyid Shihab bin Tariq Al Said (Ed.), *The craft heritage of Oman* (Vol. 2, pp. 512–523). Motivate Publishing for the Omani Craft Heritage Documentation Project.

Doxey, G. (1976). When enough's enough: The natives are restless in old Niagra. *Heritage Canada*, *2*(2), 26–27.

Galvani, A., Lew, A. A., & Maria Sotelo Perez. (2020). COVID-19 is expanding global consciousness and the sustainability of travel and tourism. *Tourism Geographies*, *22*(3), 567–576. https://doi.org/10.1080/14616688.2020.1760924

Fennell, D. A. & Przeclawski, K. (2003). Generating Goodwill in Tourism through Ethical Stakeholder Interactions. In: Singh, S., Timothy, D. J. and Dowling, R. K. (eds). *Tourism in Destination Communities*. Oxon: Cabi Publishing, 135–152.

Grabun, N. H. H. (1989). Tourism: The sacred journey. In V. L. Smith (Ed.), *Hosts and guests: The Anthropology of Tourism* (2nd ed., pp. 21–36). University of Pennsylvania Press.

Gutberlet, M. (2016a). Socio-cultural impacts of large-scale cruise tourism in Souq Muttrah. *Fennia*, *194*(1), 46–63.

Gutberlet, M. (2016b). Cruise tourist dress behaviors and local-guest reactions in a Muslim country. *Tourism Culture & Communication*, *16*, 15–32.

Gutberlet, M. (2017). Staging the Oriental Other: Imaginaries and performances of German-speaking cruise tourists. Published online first and in 2019 *in. Tourist Studies*, *19*(1), 110–137.

Gutberlet, M. (2019, April). In a rush: Time-space compression and its impacts on cruise excursions. *Tourist Studies*, 19(1), 1–29.

Gutberlet, M. (2020). "They just buy a karak and leave" – Overtourism in Souq Muttrah, the Sultanate of Oman. *Zeitschrift für Tourismuswissenschaften*, De Gruyter Oldenburg, 13 October.

Gutberlet, M. (2021). Valuing social capital and a legacy: "The old shops are the beauty of the place. In J. Saarinen & J. Richardson (Eds.), *Change in tourism/tourism in change* (pp. 135–150). Routledge Publishing House.

Gutberlet, M. (2022a). Geopolitical imaginaries and cultural ecosystem services (CES) in the desert. *Tourism Geographies, 24*, 4–5.

Gutberlet, M. (2022b). Insight 288: Tourist bubbles and climate change in the GCC. COP 27 and Climate Action in the Middle East, Middle East Institute, National University of Singapore, 24 October.

Hall, M., & Lew, A. (Eds.). (2009). *Understanding and managing tourism impacts: An integrated approach*. Routledge.

Harvey, D. (2020). *Paris, capital and modernity*. Routledge.

Higgins-Desbiolles, F. (2021). The "war over tourism": Challenges to sustainable tourism in the tourism academy after COVID-19. *Journal of Sustainable Tourism, 29*(4), 551–569.

Hofstede, G., Hofstede, G. J., & Minkov, M. (Eds.). (2010). *Cultures and organizations, software of the mind, intercultural cooperation and its importance for survival*. The McGraw Hill Companies.

Hottola, P. (2004). Culture confusion. *Annals of Tourism Research, 31*(2), 447–466.

Ioannides, I., & Gyimóthy, S. (2020). The COVID-19 crisis as an opportunity for escaping the unsustainable global tourism path. *Tourism Geographies, 22*(3), 624–632. https://doi.org/10.1080/14616688.2020.1763445

Jafari, J. (1987). Tourism models: The sociocultural aspects. *Tourism Management, 8*(2), 151–159.

Jamal, T., & Higham, J. (2021). Justice and ethics: Towards a new platform for tourism and sustainability. *Journal of Sustainable Tourism, 29*(2–3), 143–157.

Klein, R. A. (2011). Responsible cruise tourism: Issues of cruise tourism and sustainability. *Journal of Hospitality and Tourism Management, 18*, 107–116.

Kochkunov, A. (2010). The ritual of hospitality in traditional and modern Kyrgyz culture. *Berghahn Journals Anthropology of the Middle East, 5*(2), 36–58.

Lew, A., Cheer, J. M., Haywood, M., Brouder, P., & Salazar, N. B. (2020). Visions of travel and tourism after the global COVID-19 transformation of 2020. *Tourism Geographies, 22*(3), 455–466. https://doi.org/10.1080/14616688.2020.1770326

MacCannell, D. (2011). *The ethics of sightseeing*. University of California Press.

MacCannell, D. (2012). On the ethical stake in tourism research. *Tourism Geographies: An International Journal of Tourism Space, Place and Environment, 14*(1), 183–194.

Milano, C., & Koens, K. (2021). The paradox of tourism extremes. Excesses and restraints in times of COVID-19. *Current Issues in Tourism*. https://doi.org/10.1080/13683500.2021.1908967

Minca, C. (2012). No country for old men. In C. Minca & T. Oakes (Eds.), *Real tourism: Practice, care and politics in contemporary travel culture, contemporary geographies of leisure* (pp. 478–1045). Tourism and Mobility.

Ministry of Tourism (2012). *Cruise liner arrivals in Muscat*. Statistics from the Directorate General for Planning, Follow-up and Information. Muscat.

Moscardo, G. (Ed.). (1999). Making visitors mindful, principles for creating sustainable visitor experiences through effective communication. *Advances in tourism applications series 2*. Sagamore Publishing.

Moufakkir, O. (2015). The stigmatized tourist. *Annals of Tourism Research, 53*, 17–30.

Muscat Daily (2019). *Work on $2 bn Mina al Sultan Qaboos project to begin in Nov.* Muscat Daily. Apex Media Publication.

OECD (2020). Rebuilding tourism for the future: COVID-19 policy responses and recovery. Tackling Coronavirus (COVID-19) Contributing to a Global Effort. 14 December 2020.

Park, H. (2014). *Heritage tourism.* Routledge.

Pearce, P. L. (2010). Tourist behaviour – Themes and conceptual schemes. In *Aspects of tourism.* Viva Books.

Pearce, P. L., Moscardo, G., & Ross, G. F. (1996). *Tourism community relationships.* Elsevier.

Pi-Sunyer, O. (1989). Changing perceptions of tourism and tourists in a Catalan resort town. In V. Smith (Ed.), *Hosts and guests* (pp. 187–202). University of Pennsylvania Press.

Ryan, C. (2002). The time of our lives' or time for our lives: An examination of time in holidaying. In C. Ryan (Ed.), *The tourist experience* (pp. 201–220). Thomson Learning.

Ryan, C. (2002c). From motivation to assessment. In C. Ryan (Ed.), *The tourist experience* (pp. 58–77). Thomson Learning.

Said, A. A. (1989). The paradox of development in the Middle East. *Futures,* 619–627.

Saveriades, A. (2000). Establishing the social tourism carrying capacity for the tourist resorts of the east coast of the Republic of Cyprus. *Tourism Management, 21*(2), 147–156.

Scholz, F. (1990). *Muscat. Sultanat Oman. Geographische Skizze einer einmaligen arabischen Stadt.* Das Arabische Buch.

Scott, B. (2012). *Meet Oman 2012 magazine.* Nicolas Publishing International.

Soulard, J., Knollenberg, W., Boley, B. B., & Perdue, R. R. (2018). Social capital and destination strategic planning. *Tourism Management, 69,* 189–200.

Timothy, D. J. (2001). Gender relations in tourism: Revisiting patriarchy and underdevelopment. In Y. Apostolopoulos, S. Sönmez, & D. Timothy (Eds.), *Women as producers and consumers of tourism in developing regions* (pp. 235–248). Praeger.

Timothy, D. J. (2011). *Cultural heritage and tourism/an introduction.* Kindle eBook. Channel View Publications.

Turner, L., & Ash, J. (1975). The golden hordes. *International tourism and the pleasure periphery.* Constable and Company Limited.

Urry, J. (1995). *Consuming places.* Routledge.

UNDP (United Nations Development Programme). (2020). Human development perspectives, COVID-19 and human development: Assessing the crisis, envisioning the recovery, United Nations Development Programme. UNDP.

UNWTO (United Nations World Tourism Organization). (2005). *Responsible tourist and traveler.* Retrieved July 25, 2014, from http://ethics.unwto.org/en/content/responsible-tourist

Wang, N. (1999). Rethinking authenticity in tourism experience. *Annals of Tourism Research, 26*(2), 340–370.

Women in Islam (1999). *25 Frequently asked questions.* Discover Islam Publishing.

# 7 Fast and slow experiences in the desert and an oasis

In this chapter, on-site tourist experiences within "enclosed tourist bubbles" in the periphery and local community reactions will be explored. This will be done according to the travel phases, the pre-travel preparation and the on-site experiences in an oasis and in the Sharqiyah Sands desert. I trace the tourists' views and their paths throughout an excursion (Gutberlet, 2019, 2022a). I analyse the German tourists' imaginaries and experiences (Gutberlet, 2017) and the main features that create the spiritual and aesthetic value of the desert, influencing the tourists themselves and their identity creation within the space (Gutberlet, 2022a). These experiences are embedded in community views about the ethics of tourism and local social values towards tourism activities, tourist behaviours and tourism development. As such, the text is structured as a flow of the tourist's activities and experiences during a full-day-tour – from the beginning at the port in Muscat until the end of the tour upon their return to the cruise ship (Figure 7.1).

Time-space compression has impacted the experience of tourists and locals alike. Here, I will first explore the ethics of tourism, slow travel and Cultural Ecosystem Services (CES) that enhance a self-transformation and authentic experiences in natural environments. Spiritual conceptions affirm a oneness of humans with nature, a deep connectedness and well-being (Cooper et al., 2016; De Lacey & Shakleton, 2017).

## Transformative experiences

A more responsible, "just tourism" and the ethics of tourism can offer a potential for radical change in tourism, "when it is free of moralistic precepts and coupled with post-humanist affirmative ethics and political responsibility while solidarity and advocacy are complementary principles" (Jamal & Higham, 2021). Social justice refers to the fair distribution of societal goods (Britton 1982), using appropriate institutional structures. Such institutional rules should reduce inequalities or guarantee that inequalities favour the most disadvantaged (Rawls, 1971 quoted by Jamal & Higham, 2021). Concepts like just tourism (Hultsman, 1995), the ethics of tourism (Fennell, 2015; Fennell & Malloy, 2007; Fennell & Przeclawski, 2003; MacCannell,

DOI: 10.4324/9780429424946-7

*Figure 7.1* German-speaking cruise tourists leaving a mega-ship one early morning in Muscat

Source: Gutberlet (2013).

2012) responsible tourism (Goodwin, 2011; Grimwood et al., 2015), mindful tourism (Moscardo, 1999), hopeful tourism (Caton, 2018), the moral economy (Su et al., 2013) as well as slow tourism (Lumsdon & McGrath, 2011) have emerged in response to increased inequalities, injustice and the degradation of the resources on our planet Earth.

An indigenous, Arab proverb that I learnt while studying Arabic says:

> *Where there is haste there is regret, but there is peace and safety where there is time and care.*

Slowness and slow, spiritual travel are part of the Arab and Muslim culture while admiring pure nature on our planet Earth. In most Muslim countries time is largely oriented according to the five daily prayers. This spiritual 'time-off', automatically slows down everyday life. Time-space compression and the overall speed of mass tourism impacts the concept of time in destination communities.

Travelling with a slower pace is the opposite of fast mobilities (Lumsdon & McGrath, 2011). The key aspects of having slow experiences are time and stillness: A person is fully absorbed in the experience, without any external disturbances (Lumsdon & McGrath, 2011, p. 274). This is in contrast to "liquid life" (Bauman, 2005) where life and society cannot stand still. Hence, it is not enough to gaze upon and consume tourist sites and the people, tourists must experience travel and the places deeply, in order for it to be meaningful, mindful and authentic. Slow travel involves quality experiences compared to a large quantity of experiences promoted by modern mobilities. The main features of slow travel are the value of time, locality, tourist activities, the mode of transportation, the travel experience and an environmental consciousness. Slow travel leads to a deeper travel experience and a deeper sense of place (Bauman, 2005). Slow travel means involving less driving time, being less energy intensive, allowing tourists to enjoy on-site experiences by valuing socialization with each other and the local community and diverse landscapes (Singh, 2012), increasing local benefits for communities (Conway & Timms, 2012). Slow travel can enhance a physical and mental well-being through more meaningful experiences (Kay Smith & Diekmann, 2017). It promotes the creation of a new identity through "reflection, renewal and growth" (Tengberg et al., 2012). Furthermore, slow travel enhances 'liminal spaces', that are outside our everyday lives and the daily routine (Duignan et al., 2017).

In the West, slow travel started with the Romantics and Transcendentalists (Howard, 2012). In the 18th and 19th centuries, famous European writers like Goethe and Rousseau appreciated their solitary nature walks, which enhanced their creativity (Howard, 2012, p. 16).

Aesthetic, natural environments are linked with nostalgia, heritage, community and the pure, which allow visitors to find their roots within a hectic and a rather rootless world (Tresidder, 1999). In the Nordic and German context, the concept of a *landscape* includes the interactions between people and place, whereas from an Anglophone perspective landscape is understood and perceived from the visual character of a place (Tengberg et al., 2012) and as being an Other (Hill et al., 2014). Within cultural landscapes, individuals have different aesthetic preferences (Daniel et al., 2012, p. 8813) and their perceptual capacities vary from one individual and one culture to another (Cauvin Verner 2007; Urry, 1995). Nevertheless, there is a *social authoring* or collective imaginary of the meaning of spaces, their actions and the belief systems (Belhassen et al., 2008). For example, pilgrimages are socially constructed as being sacred. A pilgrimage means leaving home in order to recreate a certain meaning within another specific place. Hence, authenticity emerges during the pilgrimage (Belhassen et al., 2008). The concept of *geopiety* defines a cognitive and emotional attachment to a sacred place, e.g. during a pilgrimage, based on the visitor's faith or values (Belhassen et al., 2008, p. 684). Visiting religious spaces like Medina and Mekka in Saudi Arabia or Santiago de Compostela in Spain or Nazareth in Israel, people often experience powerful, spiritual reactions towards the environment (Belhassen et al., 2008; Howard, 2012).

The speed of modern tourism impacts the concept of time and the appreciation of non-material benefits of the natural environment (MEA, 2005), conceptualized in the aesthetic, educational and cultural values, the

Cultural Ecosystem Services (CES). They are products of different experiences associated with ecosystems including contemplation of organisms, natural processes and natural sites (Chan et al., 2012). CES are changing rapidly. CES and their essential value for human beings is a concept that will be explored in the following paragraphs.

## Cultural Ecosystem Services and belonging

Globally, CES have decreased in the past decades. They are defined as a change in the ecosystem features, which have diminished the cultural benefits provided by the ecosystem (MEA, 2005). Similar to pilgrimage experiences, CES are shaped by individual and community values as well as belief systems. They are enhancing a holistic understanding of the human-environment relationship. The dimensions of values and their implications for benefits are important for policy and decision-making. Due to increasing leisure time worldwide, the demand for CES is expected to increase (Milcu et al., 2013).

Wilderness and nature seen as unspoilt, virgin and unpolluted are important, features, that are advertised and used for branding tourist destinations like The Sultanate of Oman. The concept of Ecosystem Services applies to ecological systems that are used to extract relevant services that benefit people. At the same time, they protect the ecosystem by continuing to maintain its functions and the capacity to provide services for tourists (Lew & Wu, 2018). Many Ecosystem Services have benefits for people. For example, fishing is linked with recreation as well as with inspirational services. Moreover, as food, fishing has a provisioning service and it is a source of income for many people (Chan et al., 2012). Dryland ecosystem services like sand deserts have provisioning services as well as regulating services. Moreover, they provide support services that maintain the conditions for life on our planet and non-material cultural services. Wide, empty landscapes like deserts and green urban spaces (Daniel et al., 2012) like parcs and church gardens provide spiritual, sacred spaces to visitors (De Lacy & Shackleton, 2017). Visitors benefit socially and psychologically, e.g. through spiritual and aesthetic inspirations, cultural heritage values, cultural identity, diversity and indigenous knowledge systems (MEA, 2005).

Analysing CES is important to understand their high value for human beings and the ecological challenges such as climate change and health pandemics faced worldwide. To include CES in valuations and to highlight their importance for individuals can reverse the focus on material, quantifiable benefits of ecosystems (Hirons et al., 2016). CES stress the importance of social values, belonging and community with natural environments and with people. Creating a unity between emotions and the natural environment can enhance a deep connection, happiness and overall individual well-being (Hill et al., 2014). Some cultural services can be assessed in terms of the number of people affected (Schaich et al., 2010). CES and especially spiritual ecosystem services provided by vast, natural, empty spaces like deserts have not been analysed in tourism research (Gutberlet, 2019; 2022a). They require an analysis because they have become degraded in recent decades (MEA, 2005).

CES are often not obvious, existing 'mixed in' with other ecosystem services while often being managed for different objectives, mainly for the purpose of tourism development including expanding the built infrastructure, as a business and for financial gain. The assessment of ecosystem services is important for different stakeholders, in order to protect and restore natural ecosystems while establishing clear links between nature conservation and the well-being of humans (Brancalion et al., 2014). Payments for ecosystem services (PES), e.g. through entrance fees to natural parks, are used to manage and maintain the physical quality of ecosystem services (Lew & Wu, 2018).

Values can be transformative or non-transformative (Schaich et al., 2010). Intangible values that enhance the individual and community well-being are often seen as a contradiction to economic values (Chan et al., 2012, p. 9). An advance to change that was made by Chan et al. (2012) who proposed a framework regarding the valuation of cultural services and the decision-making that affects them. It is difficult to define a uniform scale or metrics of a service or benefit provision of a cultural service (p. 15). For example, aesthetic values of landscapes can be enjoyed by viewing a single tree, or a vast empty landscape like a forest or a desert (Schaich et al., 2010).

## The desert

The search for authentic experiences in nature, beyond the modern material world, evokes feelings of peace and belonging. The liminality of tourist sites encourages a reflexivity of the self and a construction and deconstruction of the landscape. Such "cognitive reflexive actions" link our own knowledge and memories with the tourist destination and an "individual refiguring of hegemonic discourses" (Tresidder, 1999).

CES, geopolitical narratives (Mostafanezhad & Norum, 2016) and imaginaries associated with the sand desert often reflect a "colonial dream" linked with an admiration among Western societies for authority over the Orient (Said, 2003). Tourists wish to explore and reconnect with a world and a simple lifestyle that has disappeared in many parts of the world (Graulund, 2009). Hence, people need to create landscapes that are located "outside their time and space" in order to spend and consume more *sacred time* highlighting the power of each person "to redefine landscape in a constantly shifting world" (Tresidder, 1999).

The desert has been imagined as a pristine and deserted space by all but a few desert tribes. It is believed to be the furthest removed from a state of 'normal' or Western everyday life (Graulund, 2009). Similarly, travelling to the North Cape in Europe can evoke a deep connection, and a feeling of belonging and of being at home in the destination (Tresidder, 1999). The natural, vast environment delivers a spiritual and cultural service where tourists feel spiritually and physically refreshed. Tourists visiting a desert park in Morocco experienced a feeling of authenticity within a controlled space, an artificial "tourist bubble" (Wagner & Minca, 2016).

Similar to the tourist experience in natural environments in Australia (Hill et al., 2014), Norway (Birkeland, 1999), the United States (Chronis, 2015) or Morocco, tourist experiences in Oman are influenced by a set of pre-defined, geopolitical or *Oriental imaginaries* (Wagner & Minca, 2016).

Desert landscapes provide a setting for contemplating the sun, creating a different inner self, which is in contrast to Western philosophy, e.g. Kant or Descartes separated humans from the natural environment (Holden, 2008). This idea leads to the analysis of tourist behaviours and experiences in a "tourist bubble" within the Omani desert landscape in the interior of Oman. In the following, I will analyse the paths of German-speaking cruise tourists and group tourists on their excursions to the Sharqiyah Sands desert and to an oasis. Depending on the mode of transportation, the tourists' movement can be highly controlled, e.g. during 4 × 4 safaris, or slightly controlled while hiking, walking through the desert sands or sitting and contemplating a sunset.

### Tourist bubbles and hurried on-site experiences

One sunny morning around 8.30 a.m. in January, at Port Sultan Qaboos in Muscat, a group of 48 German-speaking cruise tourists left the mega-ship that had docked around two hours earlier in the port in Muttrah. The tourists walked along a small ramp and were then distributed by on-board guides between twelve 4 × 4 vehicles, plus a lead car. Families and friends were sitting in groups together in cars. The lead car was reserved for the Omani, English-speaking guide, the German cruise guide and a male German cruise photographer (Gutberlet, 2019b).

According to the excursion manager from the ship, a total of 1,100 cruise passengers had booked a half-day or a full-day tour that day. This was a large number of visitors and cars that drove in a convoy through Muscat and then through the countryside, having the capacity to congest the roads, impacting and damaging the environment. That day there was no time for an introduction to the environment. Moreover, local cultural mediators were not skilled in cross-cultural communication and in giving in-depth information in German. The female cruise guide in the front car remarked with some humour, that the tourists do not really know where they are heading to and the Omani drivers do not speak any German. She referred to a highly controlled and pressure-loaded work environment on board and during the excursion on shore (Weaver, 2006a). The overall behaviour of cruise employees is homogenized and that of cruise tourists as well.

The on-board guide acted as a parent, treating cruise tourists like children who need to be instructed and controlled by a more experienced, senior person (Gutberlet, 2019).

> *"Where there are many people together in one place, they often behave like children"*, said the cruise photographer smiling.

He was accompanying the group along with the on-board guide. The guide said that they usually gather all tourists in the theatre of the ship at 8 a.m. and they distribute stickers to each one of them. For a better orientation on shore and to remind them about their car or bus number, the tourists get stickers of the car number on their shirts treating them like commodities (Shepherd, 2015).

The guide was holding up a white small signboard with the car number and escorting the group from an assembly point to their mobile tourist bubble on-shore, a comfortable 4 × 4 car (Gutberlet, 2019b). Such scripted behaviour can be seen at tourist sites around the world, where cruise tourists are distributed to "enclosed bubbles" like buses or cars.

The timing of the onshore excursion was planned by the tour operator in Muscat and by the cruise company in Germany; thereby empowering foreign interests and capital, creating a dependency between the Global North and the South (here Oman) as well as between the capital Muscat and the periphery where the oasis and the desert are located (Britton, 1982; London & Lohmann, 2014). The local tour agency and its employees were under enormous pressure "to maximize the serviceability" of the demand (Ljubica & Dulcic, 2012) in order to provide a high-quality excursion (Lopes & Dredge, 2018).

> While driving along the main Sultan Qaboos highway in Muscat, the Omani guide in his 30s explained that this *was a 15-minute trip: They stayed 15 minutes in the first stop, then they drive for 15 minutes to the oasis and it will take another 15 minutes to drive to the desert.*

If there was any delay, the entire departure of the cruise ship would be delayed, leaving few opportunities for a slower involvement in the destination. Moreover, the cruise tourists might complain and ask for compensation. Such financial consequences can be compared with a standardized production of McDonald's fast food (Weaver, 2006a). The lead driver sped up to more than 100 km/h along the narrow, winding mountain road between the capital Muscat and the Eastern region, although the speed limit was 80 km/h, leading to compromises on safety while driving. A cruise tourist said that their driver was driving too fast, while the landscape was passing quickly behind the car windows. Along the winding road, there was little time to engage with the environment, consisting of a "series of passing panoramas" (Urry, 1995).

A cruise tourist, who was in his 50s, questioned the environmental sustainability of the excursion. The tight schedule puts enormous time pressure on local drivers and tour guides. Given the Omani culture, and the hot climate, locals would follow a rather slower time schedule including more breaks from driving. An Omani lead driver said that they are "in a rush" all the time during the excursion. He preferred a much slower travel mode so that he can offer additional value to the excursion (Gutberlet, 2019).

### Slowing down time: Visiting an oasis and the desert

During a pause in a small motel, which symbolized another "enclosed tourist bubble" or a 'non-place' (Augé, 2010) similar to an airport, the local tour guide addressed the cruise group for the first time in English while the female German cruise guide was asked to translate the information to the group. The 4 × 4 convoy stopped just a few kilometres away from the oasis. The tour guide located the tourist gaze while highlighting the historic importance of one of many watchtowers along the road. The cultural brokers prepared the tourists for their visit to the oasis, focusing on the qualities of the landscape, within time-space compression and its high abstraction of space. In the cruise excursion brochures (2012/2013), the oasis is socially constructed in the past, as an imaginary village. It seems time had "come to a standstill", creating an imaginary space without time, representing a "symbolic authenticity" (Wang, 1999), which is in contrast to modern urban life and the overall speed of the excursion. In reality, the oasis is not timeless, surrounded by walls and closed entrance gates restricting the view and access for outsiders. The imaginary open spaces are used as private gardens. During the day a number of male Asian workers can be observed working in the oasis, but local Omanis are rarely seen. However, Asian workers are not mentioned in tourism narratives; they are obviously absent.

A cruise brochure (2016) as well as a small brochure from the Ministry of Tourism advertise the Omani oases within a nostalgic, romantic image of "traditional Omani villages" and of publicly open and accessible oasis gardens with roses, apricots and pomegranates that are watered by a *falaj* irrigation system, communal underground channels (Ministry of Tourism, 2016). When I asked the tourists about their perception of an oasis, the cruise tourists had a nostalgic image from the media in their minds, expressing a dichotomy between old and new, and a space that is empty, without people. A female tourist in her 20s said that she read about the old Omani mudbrick houses in guidebooks. She said, that she likes to experience old buildings in Oman, compared to modern cities in the United Arab Emirates.

She expressed her appeal about the built environment, creating nostalgia as an escape away from urban places and modern lifestyles. Similarly, a male cruise lecturer in his 50s observed the landscape passing by the window with nostalgia.

> He said, *"being a European, this is something we are searching for – the 'Old Orient'. It was now replaced by new buildings. I think the Old Orient only remains alive in Yemen."*

Upon arrival in the old centre of the oasis town, the group of cruise tourists gathered at the marketplace underneath a large, indigenous acacia tree. The group was standing next to an old multi-storey mudbrick building. Moreover, the Heritage Museum and some remains of mudbrick shop boxes, the old irrigation system (falaj) and the oasis greenery behind tall walls was also next to them (Gutberlet, 2019).

The Omani tour guide, his "local memory" (Gutberlet, 2019, p. 166) and his narratives about history, the place and the people were important to the tourists' authentically performed experiences, reliant on his interpretation and the stories told. He was drawing a rather nostalgic picture of the date palm tree and its usage, as conveyed by the cruise brochure, depicting the palm tree in the past creating nostalgia, when palm trees were commonly used as sustainable building materials. Some Bedouins still use palm fronds to construct easily set up so-called *barasti huts* for their homes and as shelter for their camels and goats in the desert (Keohane, 2011). In the oasis, the reality is that the traditional construction material called *sarooj* had been entirely replaced with concrete, a cheaper, non-sustainable, highly polluting and heat-absorbing building material (Gutberlet, 2019). The use of cement instead of a traditional building material reflects a quick, short-term instead of a long-term sustainability of the local, tangible and intangible heritage.

At midday the marketplace was empty, and the shops were closed. Some tourists questioned the authenticity of the place, referring to city centres in Northern Europe, filled with people as a symbol of everyday life and mobility. I explained that residents, in particular women, avoid the heat. They often do not leave their homes during the day. Instead, they gather outside in their courtyards or they go around by car in the late afternoons and evenings. However, I avoided mentioning male Asian workers from the oases who live in simple accommodation buildings. They do not have cars. Workers are a very common sight while walking or cycling through the area during the day.

## Slow experiences

To slow down the tourists' movements in time and to welcome them to an Omani oasis, within a quiet place, under the shade of an indigenous, large tree, Omani 'unconditional hospitality' within the bubble of 'the cruise communitas' were simulated. Hospitality towards strangers has a high-social value in the Arab world, in Asia and in many parts of the Global South.

> *"Hospitality is one of the main customs and traditions that we are obliged to preserve and pass on to new generations"*,

explained Sheikh Kahlan bin Nabhan Al Kharousi, Assistant Deputy Mufti of Oman, Ministry of Awqaf and Religious Affairs, during an interview in 2013.

The German cruise brochure advertised the oasis as an authentic setting where the tourist is transformed through the taste and smell of an imaginary Omani coffee and fresh dates, picked from the oasis palm trees (cruise brochure 2012/13).

Another brochure exaggerated the social representation of a multi-sensuous "royal coffee ceremony" within the oasis setting. The taste of coffee, transporting the tourists back in time and space, to the times *when spices were transported with camel caravans through the desert*" (cruise brochure 2015/16: 135).

In reality, tourism employees created a "constructed authenticity" and a staged, 'pseudo-event' (Boorstin, 1961), underneath the indigenous tree, on a white plastic table covered with a plastic tablecloth. This can be compared with a picnic break beside the road. Tourism providers were staging open hospitality, the naturalness of the Omani hospitality to the visitors, the mega-cruise tourists, in addition to the underlying belief that outsiders deserve a special welcome and hospitality with coffee and dates, usually free-of-charge. To authenticate the coffee break, an elder Omani who worked at a hotel in the next city, acted as a "coffee man" together with the Omani tour guide and two young male Omani helpers (Figure 7.2). They distributed to each tourist some coffee in small porcelain cups, along with a

*Figure 7.2* The constructed coffee break in the oasis.

Source: Gutberlet (January 2013).

white plastic plate and a spoon with one dry date and a spoon full of halwa for each tourist (Gutberlet, 2019).

The authenticity of the place was influenced by the imaginary Oriental myths and by the Omani hosts themselves. The tour guide explained that Omanis receive guests at their homes or in their offices. They serve them coffee, dates and *halwa*, which is a locally made, very sweet, sticky and spicy pudding. Through Oriental imaginaries time is slowed down. The tourists transform their own identities in a different version of themselves (Gutberlet, 2019).

Traditionally, offering Omani hospitality means taking some time, like a pause, having Omani coffee with spices that is often given free-of-charge along with dates. It is a time to slow down, to sit, relax and socialize with others, exchange news, a kind of slow tourism. The coffee break created for the tourists was a planned, staged "pseudo-event" (Boorstin, 1961). Due to the tight time schedule, the staged coffee break was rationalized and speeded up in time and space. Coffee was served only once, which is uncommon. Moreover, most tourists were standing while having coffee, which is uncommon as well. Here they were welcomed in the market square, where men still gather in the cooler evening hours. Typically, visitors are seated on cushions on the floor or on a sofa at a private home, a majlis area, or in a courtyard. The local etiquette was not explained – there was no time for it. Some explanations could have enhanced awareness and mindfulness towards the local culture. Halwa is usually served from a bowl. Traditionally, older people are served first. Everybody serves himself with a spoon and with the right hand only. The Omani sweets were standardized mass products with little taste. I observed that most cruise tourists did not try the *halwa*. This may be due to a lack of time and interpretation by the tour guide, mixed with a lack of curiosity, cultural capital and travel knowledge. A male tourist in his 20s compared the sweets with an international sweet spread, familiar to him at home, *Nutella*. Although I was told that date farms and a date factory are close by these sweets did not originate from the oasis. Fresh dates are harvested during the hot summer months in June or July when there are a few international tourists in Oman (Gutberlet, 2019). Cruise tourists and other international tourists visit the oasis in winter when only dry dates are available.

During his introduction, the Omani tour guide briefly explained the importance of date palm trees within the Omani heritage and culture. Dates are part of every household in Oman. He mentioned that there are male and female date trees and that the palm trunks are used for building houses.

Two male tourists were joking. One of them said "*Which ones are the male and female dates? The other tourist replied: The ones that are beautiful are the females*".

Telling a joke about the gender of the palm tree may create lasting memories of the place in the tourist's minds. For other tourists, the place, the people, the funny narratives and the local food were part of an activity-related "existential authentic" experience (Gutberlet, 2019). This confirms that tourist sites are activated through multi-sensory immersion, the vision and the taste (Everett, 2008). During the coffee break, the German tourists gathered in small groups, exchanging their thoughts. The guide and drivers were having an authentic picnic, sitting far from the group on a picnic mat and having a pot of halwa and coffee in front of them. They were chatting in Arabic and laughing, sometimes gazing at the tourists on the other side. Several tourists were taking photos of them, but without asking for their permission. The intercultural and social exchange between drivers and tourists remained visual and distanced, confirming the tourist gaze (Urry, 1995) and the cruise tourist "communitas" (Yarnal & Kerstetter, 2005). Both sides remained within their social groups, realizing an "inter-personal authenticity" within the German "cruise communitas" or local "guide/driver communitas" (Wang, 1999).

For the tourist, a good tour can be characterized by being "pleasurably sidetracked and detained while maintaining a comfortable distance from the sites" (MacCannell, 2011) as well as from the people that appear in front of them. Within their German tourist group, they asked the on-board guide or the researcher about everyday life in Oman. Omanis are very communicative and like to converse with others in Arabic, English or another language, e.g. Swahili. The coffee man said in an interview that he usually does not speak with tourists, only sometimes (Gutberlet, 2019). Although he worked at a hotel, his English language skills were limited and I observed that he was not at ease communicating with the tourists. Similarly, most of the drivers were quiet with the cruise tourists and rather low-skilled in English (Gutberlet, 2019). The lack of interpretation for tourists and a lack of soft skills and openness towards the European "Other", influenced the tourists' perception of the drivers and their overall travel experiences. Several tourists told me that they received hardly any interpretation along the road. This confirms earlier research on unskilled cruise tourism employees promoting a lack of interpretation on shore (Klein, 2011). The tourists' perception of the local drivers created a structural pressure on the people working in tourism, to live up to the branding image of the place (Büscher & Fletcher, 2017).

Because of the communication gap and the long driving time between Muscat and the oasis, the tourists' perception of the country was built on their visual, fast-passing glances, a "travel glance" (Larsen et al., 2021) from their windows, similar to a video or TV-screen showcasing Oriental place-myths. One of the cruise brochures promised an exceptional landscape that can be enjoyed comfortably from the seat of the jeep (cruise brochure, 2011/2012). The jeep refers to the 4 × 4 car brand; however, in Oman most of the cars used in tourism were Asian brands. Mobility changes the aesthetic appreciation of landscapes and societies (Urry, 1995). As a result of time-space compression, some tourists lost their orientation and could not capture the places visited.

Following the introduction about the oasis by the Omani tour guide, tourists walked alone or in groups. They were disoriented and even lost within the place, looking for familiar representations of "home". Some tourists walked along the irrigation system that is used for irrigating fields. This made them feel at *home* (Wang, 1999). Some females walked through the water of the falaj system, which was filled with small fish, swimming on the bottom of the falaj.

Referring to the global "fish spa" brand a female tourist said that it looks like the wellness brand. Some tourists discovered discarded metal ring-pulls and small fish, a symbol for a throwaway society (Gutberlet, 2019). A male tourist reflected about the environmental behaviour at home: "*In Germany we had them everywhere in the 1970s*" remembering the environmental challenges faced in modernity. Nowadays, cans with ring pulls are not sold anymore in Germany. Other tourists were observed taking a photo of the old houses from one of the old watch towers. One tourist couple was observed posing for a photo in front of a black garbage bin as their backdrop. Another couple was hugging each other openly and holding hands. It seemed, they were not informed and not aware that intimate, affective gestures are considered culturally inappropriate in a public space (Gutberlet, 2019).

The most important element was the tourist's individualization and their habitus or social reputation within a customized environment. Tourists realized an existential, intra-personal authenticity and a staging of the communitas through photography (Bærenholdt et al., 2004). Moreover, cruise tourists were observed wearing shorts or transparent, revealing clothes. They were obviously not instructed about the local dress code. In the oasis town, the number of visitors is much lower and the direct contact is very limited, due to a lack of touristic sites compared to the capital and in Souq Muttrah, where tourists were pedestrians most of the time and seen as potential consumers of souvenirs.

In the oasis, residents observed the tourists as passers-by, sitting in the car or walking through the small roads of the oasis, with little or no social contact and exchange between the tourists and the locals (Gutberlet, 2016b). Authenticity was personal, visual or tactile and a subjective immersion in the tourist destination (Mordue, 2005). Although there was a small privately owned museum located at the market square, the cruise tourists never visited it (Figure 7.3). I observed that the community in the oasis had no financial income from the cruise excursion.

After a one-hour break in the oasis, the tour continued through the narrow streets of the lush oases greenery. Tourists could gaze from their car windows passing by the date palm trees as well as banana, papaya and mango trees along with colourful bougainvillea flowers, most of them hidden behind the walls. They were glancing at the passing landscape.

*Figure 7.3* Cruise tourists immerse themselves in the oasis.

Source: Gutberlet (2013).

One tourist in his 80s, who was one of the oldest in the group, reflected on the visual experience:

> "*It is interesting to see the Orient. When we stopped and had dates and saw the Oriental*",

he said, gazing at and objectifying the male, local 'Other'. The Omani drivers in their 20s and the guide, wearing the *dishdasha* and *kumma* (the local male dress and a small cap), they were seen as an exotic, "Oriental Other" and as a visual attraction.

While driving through the narrow alleys of the oasis, along the walls of the oasis gardens. A male cruise photographer in his 20s said that he would like to bicycle through the oasis, wishing to experience the environment slower and with all his senses. Cycling through the oasis is less polluting. It also shows a less materialistic, being socially equal to an expatriate workers on a bike, being close to the natural environment and at a slower pace of transportation, outside the car, their enclosed safe travel 'cocoon' or 'mobile bubble' (Gutberlet, 2019). A female tourist in her 60s said about the speed of travel that she prefers to travel individually and slowly instead of "hurried" within the group. She thought they would drive through an oasis, meet with local Bedouins and drive through the sand desert. This reflects the lack of time and opportunities for the tourists having a more mindful exchange with locals, beyond the material and enclosed tourist bubbles.

Nevertheless, my results show that German-speaking mega-cruise tourists were satisfied with experiencing the oasis, being a strange but safe, staged and hence customized environment, a "material space of exception", an 'enclosed tourist bubble', within a constructed authenticity (Wang, 2007). During the lunch break in a luxury desert camp hotel, another "material space of exception" (Büscher & Fletcher, 2017), both communitas, tourists and guides/drivers, were eating separately – this time from an international buffet, served by Asian waiters. This was another customized enclosure, a 'closed tourist bubble', showcasing a staged, safe and heat-proof setting within a harsh desert environment, where the temperature outside is around 40 degrees at lunchtime. I was informed that the guides were instructed by their employer not to engage with the tourists. Traditionally, Omanis sit on the floor and eat with their hands from one large plate, enhancing a feeling of belonging and communitas.

*"During round trips the guides and drivers eat together with the tourists, enhancing a feeling of togetherness; but when they travel with cruise tourists they are separated,"* explained a young Omani driver.

Due to the construction of mobile tourist bubbles and special "spaces of exception", some tourists questioned the authenticity of the tourist camp.

With this in mind, the former Minister of Tourism Ahmed bin Nasser Al Mahrzi said during an interview (in 2012) that they are planning to transform the old villages in the Interior of Oman, into so-called 'show-villages', similar to Moroccan heritage villages. Hence, the government was planning to customize the tourist experience (Gutberlet, 2019). Their objective was to brand several villages through stories about the place and the people, creating "material spaces of exception" (Büscher & Fletcher, 2017) or "marked tourist sites". Such changes lead to a simulated, artificial village, in which locals will not actually live in. It is another kind of "pseudo-event" (Boorstin, 1961) within a customized "tourist bubble" that is easy to consume visually, like a "dreamscape" (Urry, 1995). As my research shows, it is important to highlight and differentiate the variety of on-site experiences within one group of cruise tourists.

## The desert – An imaginary, liminoid sandscape

In marketing brochures of the government, the desert is promoted as an imaginary, "wild environment" with high aesthetic value. The desert is featured as a beautiful place, without any borders, nor the hardship or danger encountered by visitors. The desert is characterized as a natural environment that has an extensive biodiversity and diverse indigenous knowledge systems (Ministry of Tourism, 2014).

However, during their visit, the tourists do not encounter a large number of animals and indigenous people. A few Bedouin houses are still located in the desert, incorporating a tangible and intangible heritage value. A German cruise guidebook (2012) promises that there is an incredibly wide range of plants and animals. Hundreds of camels and thousands of goats that belong to Bedouin families.

For German-speaking cruise tourists who stay around two hours in the desert, the place remains an imaginary, mythical space that is difficult to grasp within a short time. Tourists and cultural brokers visiting the desert mentioned the experience being very different to any place they had ever experienced before. An on-board tour guide said that the Omani desert is unique compared to other deserts in the Arabian Gulf region:

> "*The Omani desert is the most attractive desert of the entire trip. The sand is reddish and there are lots of small bushes. In Abu Dhabi and in Dubai there is absolutely no greenery and the sand is yellow. The red sand in Oman looks very beautiful and special,*" he said.

For the majority of the German-speaking cruise tourists, 65% ($N = 233$), it was their first trip to the desert. Prior to their travel, 92% ($N = 235$) had informed themselves about the destination (Gutberlet, 2022a). Tourists had booked the desert tour from home or on-board the ship. While preparing for their journey within the pre-liminal phase, their imaginaries were formed (Di Giovine, 2014). On-board presentations, videos and the social media influenced the tourists' perceptions of the destination.

Through a one-hour presentation, given by on-board tour guides and a video shown in the cabins, tourists were prepared for the destination, framing their geopolitical imaginaries (Gutberlet, 2022a). Their fantasies can be conceptualized like pre-existing stereotypes or "as a kind of ultimate Other of Western tourist consciousness" (MacCannell, 2011, p. 108) about their relationship with the local environment. Fantasies or stereotypes shaped their views about the Orient and the Oriental Other in Western societies, linking the Orient with a nostalgic, "colonial dream" and the mysterious "Oriental Other" (Said, 2003; Yeğenogluğ, 1998) while connecting the tourists with a simpler, more authentic lifestyle that has vanished in the Western lifestyle (Gutberlet, 2022a).

Reflecting on the social distance and dichotomy between life in Europe and in the Orient, a female cruise tourist in her 20s said that the Arabian Peninsula represented an Orient style.

> Another female cruise tourist in her sixties who was travelling with her husband, indicated her search for an 'unexplored', 'untouched' destination, representing a myth of the European elite to conquer a destination, similar to life in the TV-series 'The dream ship' (in German: Das Traumschiff) that was broadcast in German representing dream holidays, travelling within a safe travel mode around the world.

Other cruise tourists recalled that they had imaginaries of a fairy-tale country of '1001 Nights' in their minds linking Oman with romanticism and narratives like Aladdin's lamp from the stories of *1001 Nights*, "beautiful, veiled women", symbolizing the mythical and unknown female 'Oriental Other'. Results of my questionnaire revealed that the cruise tourists imagined Oman being less a country of the stories of '1001 Nights' and of Bedouins but more a desert country with a sand desert (94%, $N = 222$), camels (89%, $N = 221$), oil reserves (75%, $N = 202$) and a Sultan (74%, $N = 204$). (Gutberlet, 2022a). The intensity of the tourists' fantasies was influenced by their prior experiences in the destination.

## Wildlife and authenticities

Inside the sand desert, while dune driving, the tourists' personal stories and images were influenced and mediated by their on-site experiences and the encounter with other tourists, cultural mediators and the natural environment (Chronis, 2015). To promote the visual Oriental imaginary and the production of an Oriental experience of the desert, the $4 \times 4$ cars stopped for a photo in front of a group of camels. These were not wild camels; their Bedouin owner was beside them.

The German female on-board guide said that the tourists will love this photo-stop with camels, representing 'exotic' animals they may encounter for the first time in their lives. It was an embodied encounter with a unique, natural and human environment, similar to the authenticity created during a wildlife and rainforest viewing (Hill et al., 2014). To describe the reality and diverse forms of otherness, tour guides often use a language that has different "registers" including Orientalism and primitiveness (Salazar, 2010).

In the Omani desert, the encounter with the camels was not planned or staged. However, due to the overall planning of the entire excursion, some tourists thought it was staged for them. The tour guide or the drivers did not explain the context of the photo-stop.

Often camels are seen moving around freely in the Omani desert. Here the camel was kept on a rope, customized and objectified for the "tourist gaze" and for a staged photo souvenir that preserves the moment in future. A young tourist couple realized the staged character of the scenery. They said that it would be more authentic to observe a camel passing next to the car instead of a camel being attached and the legs bound together.

> *If we would see a camel walking around in the desert, it would be more authentic than a camel that is just there for the tourists and for a photo. The difference here is that you don't pay money for nature, like what we experienced in Thailand. There you pay to sit on an elephant, said a male tourist in his twenties, giving his view of an inauthentic, commercialized setting for tourists.*

Demonstrating the visual realization of the Oriental space, giving an identity and attachment to the desert a total of 93% of the cruise tourists took photos of sand dunes and 76% took photos of camels ($N = 235$) (Gutberlet, 2019), processing the tourists' Oriental imaginaries.

Similar to other slow encounters, e.g. in an urban space (Pink, 2008) or in a rainforest (Hill et al., 2014), the tourists in the desert expressed their experiences with nature as being "sensuous and embodied". Tourists found spiritual, aesthetic and inspirational benefits in the landscape, which transformed into a liminoid space outside their everyday lives, away from the normal routine, similar to other nature experiences (De Lacy & Shackleton, 2017). My questionnaire survey showed that 74% ($N = 225$) very strongly or strongly felt they were in a different, unfamiliar and an even strange environment or a *strange world* (in German: eine fremde Welt) (Gutberlet, 2022a).

Memorizing and transporting the experience, a female tourist in his late 20s bent down to collect some sand in a small bottle.

She told me that she would keep half of the sand as a souvenir from Oman and she would offer the rest to a friend who collects desert sand from all over the world and fills them in bottles. The tourist wished to preserve an objective, authentic souvenir of the desert (Gutberlet, 2019). The top spiritual and aesthetic benefits of the cultural ecosystem were the sand that had an immaterial, aesthetic value for the tourist as well as the sensuous experience of driving through the sand (97%, $N = 226$), and the aesthetic fascination for an open, wide landscape. In addition, the knowledge of the guide and the interpretation contributed to a positive desert experience whereas the luxury desert camp, the wildlife and the contact with locals (58%, $N = 143$) were less important for the tourists. Hence, CES including spiritual and place values within deserts are products of these diverse experiences linked with the ecosystem (Gutberlet, 2022a). A female cruise tourist, in her mid-50s, who was travelling with her husband, said that she wished to visually, emotionally and bodily immerse herself in the desertscape.

The tourist wanted to experience the place, so that she can "claim to have seen it with her own eyes" (MacCannell, 2011), which also implies a rather superficial experience within time constraints.

The tourist experience in the desert can be seen as a pause to stop, taking a break from the fast speed of their travel and to experience and to preserve some memories. The immersion in the desert instils an embodied, slow experience that can incorporate a "deep personal reflection" (Howard, 2012) and a spiritual value (Chan et al., 2012). However, these experiences are only possible when there is enough time, a key feature for slow travel.

## Fast mobilities and a community spirit

Further into the desert, dune driving was the main attraction and seen as an adventure. For many cruise tourists interviewed, the desert was the highlight of the day tour, similar to a 'roller coaster' (Gutberlet, 2022a), reinforcing on the one hand an authentic selfhood and the ego and on the other hand a community spirit with others on board – their friends, partners or colleagues. An official marketing brochure of the Ministry of Tourism promises fantastic fun in the desert while learning how Bedouins drive through the dunes (Ministry of Tourism, 2016).

The geopolitical narratives of tourism marketing about the desert, as a vast, empty space, without physical borders or ownership and with little human interference created an impression of a "space of freedom and fun". The cruise tourists wished to enjoy and dash down the dunes through the sand, experiencing the speed of the $4 \times 4$ drive. The luxury $4 \times 4$ cars protected them from the heat and the harsh desert landscape. The majority of the cruise group was waiting in the soaring, midday heat, gazing at the cars and taking photos of the staged performance and of each other. The time in the desert and along with friends and family is seen as a time, realizing an "existential, intra-personal authenticity" (Wang, 1999). A group photo materializes the memories of the tourist site and their *cruise communitas*. The tourists gathered in pairs or in the entire group for a photo shoot, realizing an "intra-personal experience" (Shepherd, 2015) within a group or a couple (Gutberlet, 2019).

> A German male tourist said before the dune driving that he wished to have *"an adrenaline shock"*.
>
> (Gutberlet, 2022a)

Such an intense search for authenticity, self-transformation and ego-enhancement (MacCannell, 2011) within a sense of belonging is common in different ecoservice systems. The description shows an implicit spiritual value of the place (Cooper et al., 2016). Dune driving becomes something personal, having an embodied, quick, powerful effect, like a drug. Standing in the sand dunes beside a group of cruise tourists in the midday heat, I observe five 4 × 4 cars. They drive to the top of the dunes. There, they stop for a moment. Some tourists clap their hands cheerfully for the drivers' performances. The drivers showcase their driving skills while the tourists take photos. Some drivers raise the volume of their pop music within the space of silence. They then speed and drive along the dunes, sand whips around their cars. It seemed like a staged event, a show rally and a competition among the Omani drivers. The sand dunes turned into a wide, open adventure zone, a liminoid space without any limitations that exist in everyday life and within an imaginary, Oriental backdrop (Gutberlet, 2022a).

### Getting stuck in the sand desert

Suddenly, some cars got stuck in the fine desert sand. This can put the passengers' health at risk and the drivers under pressure to perform well. The other cars helped quickly and pulled out the cars. For the tourists, who believed that all male Omani drivers are well-skilled, getting stuck in the sand seemed to be part of the adventure experience and excitement. A special driving license for the desert sand driving should be necessary but it is not required. An Omani driver confirmed that he was visiting the desert for the first time, like the tourists. It seemed they themselves enjoyed being outside and on tour with their *driver communita*, escaping their everyday lives and family obligations in Muscat, being in a wide desert environment.

> *"It's like a journey for us"*, said a driver in his 20s who usually works for the government in Muscat.

Then, one car arrived back from a dune drive. The doors of the 4 × 4 car opened. Four tourists get out and four tourists get inside the white 4 × 4 car. The scenery was similar to a theme park like Disneyland, characterized by repetition and control (Wagner & Minca, 2016). Some women hesitated to get into the cars, while a male tourist encouraged his wife to be part of a staged imaginary event, a TV movie, Hence, for tourists and tourism providers, the desert tour was treated like an "occasion for retreat, or deep regression into the imaginary" (MacCannell, 2011).

One tourist shouted happily, comparing the power of the event with the impact of a mechanical tool, a 'hammer'. The tourist was travelling with a group of friends, who captured the moment with their cameras. These were implicit statements of spiritual value (Cooper et al., 2016) and "excitement or thrill" which is felt by participants in a wildlife environment (Hill et al., 2014) (Figure 7.4). One female tourist in her 60s observed the scene, cars stopped on the edge of a dune and one drove backwards down the hill. The drive through the dunes was similar to a roller coaster event but without safety instructions and without any direct payment involved. Similar to the desert experience in the Moroccan desert, it represents a theme park within

*Figure 7.4* Fast experiences in the desert landscape that transforms into a liminoid zone

Source: Gutberlet (2013).

powerful discourses and as a geographical European dream of conquest, a projection of space without borders (Wagner & Minca, 2016).

The desert space being transformed into a liminal zone, removed from any social norms and structures (Howard, 2012, p. 20). A female tourist even wished to relocate to Oman so that she could drive through the dunes every day (Gutberlet, 2022a). The gliding through the sands and the sounds of the music contributed to feelings of being in a different world, a spiritual and multi-sensory experience. These experiences were shaping the tourists' own selves, just as an *authentic selfhood*, similar to a spiritual experience that is shaped during a religious pilgrimage (Belhassen et al., 2008).

The majority of the cruise tourists, 97% ($N = 226$), mentioned in the questionnaire survey that they *very much enjoyed* or *enjoyed* the drive through the dunes and 26% of the tourists said they wished to experience nature during the tour (Gutberlet, 2022a).

The dune driving had an existential, transformative impact on the tourist's identity. Some tourists described the dune driving as being exciting, an emotional "shock event" that can be compared to other adrenalin-rush adventure activities such as ski racing, parachuting, bungee jumping or wildlife watching in a rainforest (Hill et al., 2014). The desert transformed into a liminoid space for tourism providers as well as tourists (Gutberlet, 2022a).

## Liminoid behaviours

Gender relations influence the way women and men construct their tourist experiences. Female tourist experiences are often influenced and more vulnerable by the gendered nature of society (Berdychevsky et al., 2013), creating challenges. Within this spirit of freedom and fun while driving through the dunes, some tourists had less positive encounters with gendered power relations.

> *(My observations): Once, a car arrived back from the dune drive, music was turned on high volume. "Who wants to go next now?" asked an Omani driver. A female, middle-aged tourist screamed "yes, me" running to the open door of the 4 × 4 car. The middle-aged, Omani driver immediately slapped her on the backside and smiled. She showed no reaction. She sat in the back of the 4 × 4 car and the driver slammed the door behind her.*

I myself was shocked by this sexual harassment that I had never witnessed before in public in Oman. Therefore, I rushed to the male lead tour guide who had witnessed the scene. He showed no reaction and did not want to intervene. Later on, during the lunch break, the guide spoke to the driver. He told me that the female tourist had slapped the Omani man earlier and he wanted to "revenge her attack". The unique social atmosphere of the "enclosed bubble" and the "tourist communitas" promoting a spirit of "freedom and thrill" may have encouraged such misbehaviour. There seemed to be no cultural barriers, defending the sexual harassment. The voice of the female who was attacked was not heard either at the time or later on. The tour guide did not speak to her.

Tourism can be seen as a unique social, liminoid activity within "tourist bubbles". However, it often takes place in anonymity, fewer constraints in general and also with respect to sexual advances (Berdychevsky et al., 2013). In an Oriental context, Western white females are often stereotyped and imagined as being "easy-going" and "easy-to-be with" compared to Middle Eastern and Asian women who are more socially restricted in public. Moreover, people of opposite sex and outside the family, do not mix easily and avoid showing any affection in public. Hence, it seems that neither the Omani man nor the female German tourist had been informed by the tour agency, the cruise liner or a cultural mediator about the cross-cultural and behavioural differences (Wilson & Little, 2011).

## Degrading Cultural Ecosystem Services

As another result of limitless dune driving within a liminoid space, several cruise tourists raised environmental concerns, regarding the care-ethics towards the protection of the natural ecosystem.

Due to the large number of people passing through the desert, it is raising environmental concerns. The tourists and camp owners interviewed felt "empathy" for the environment.

A male tourist in his late 20s stressed the importance of pleasure, self-enhancement and the monetary profits of tourism while compromising on the environmental protection. He said that while driving through the dunes there may be some oil leakages and that environmental restrictions seem to be stricter in Germany (Gutberlet, 2022a). Tourists observed plastic garbage and cans dumped in the desert dunes, drifting away.

Beside the tourists, residents of the oasis nearby and camp owners have raised their concerns about the waste management and noise pollution, especially during weekends and holidays. They remarked that the environment has changed over the years and adjusted to business interests and the increasing demands of business owners, tour operators and mass tourists.

> *"In the past there was no water in the desert. Now there are even swimming pools in the desert"*, said the owner of one of the first eco-friendly desert camps about the luxury camping sites, so-called glamping, in the desert.

Moreover, noise pollution has increased in recent years. During weekends, especially there are traffic, music, shouting and noise from people chatting loudly, thereby disturbing the naturally silent, empty desert space. Consequently, some locals wish to have less crowding of people that affect their livelihoods and the tangible heritage value of the desert and its CES.

> The Bedouin owner of a camp complained that he has stopped conducting longer camel trips with groups of tourists, due to the number of cars driving through the desert, causing noise and waste, which harms and scares away goats and camels.

He wished that more regulations were implemented regarding the movement of people and the environmental and wildlife protection. Moreover, a tarmac road was built through the desert, linking an oasis with one of the camps. To further protect the ecosystem, the ecological science advisor of *UNESCO* Arab region, Dr. Benno Boer (interviewed in 2013), said that he suggested to introduce a special bio-reserve and zoning, including a "core zone", "buffer zones" with eco-lodges and "transition areas", limiting the carrying capacity of the desert. In his view, only drivers with dedicated licenses should be able to drive through the dunes, thus limiting their accessibility and increasing their environmental protection (Gutberlet, 2022a). It is clear that the commodification of the desert space and the imposition of nostalgic imaginaries has had negative impacts on local people (Büscher & Fletcher, 2017), their local identities as Omanis, as Bedouins and on their environments.

Some cruise tourists expressed their desire for slower, deeper experiences with the natural environment and the local community, away from the "tourist bubble".

A female traveller in her mid-30s wished to slow down from the time-space compression and experience the details of the desertscape and the oasis visited during the tour.

> *"We did not learn a lot about the desert. We should come back to Oman, after these 'floods (large number) of impressions' about everything here",* said the female tourist who collected sand in the desert.

As a result of scripted and choreographed cruise excursion schedules that meet the ship's sailing times, a "grazing behaviour" through tight time-space compression is evident. This is the result of a rapid increase in cruise passenger volumes, being transported and processed from one place to another while travelling with a mega-ship (Gutberlet, 2022a, 2019).

Another tourist was disappointed with the standardized tour. She wished to learn and know more about the identity of the country while travelling slowly, engaging with the environment. The tourist was searching for the unexpected, a deeper spiritual meaning and encounter beyond the excursion and outside the "enclosed tourist bubble" (Gutberlet, 2019).

Upon their return to the harbour in Muscat, at around 5.30 p.m., I observed tourists leaving the car in a hurry. Many of them without even saying goodbye to the Omani tour guide. They were hastening to the gangway, where they then had to wait in a long queue. Some received cold soft drinks and they took hand sanitizer from a dispenser to welcome them back on board, to their temporary "floating home". The tourists then disappeared inside the mega-ship to proceed to their rooms on board. Dinner would be served at different restaurants on board, where they could reflect on their experiences.

Reflecting on the proliferation of choice in tourism (Urry, 1995) and the tourists' continuous over-consumption and "grazing" of tourist destinations as commodities, an on-board guide remarked that only around 10% of the cruise tourists that visited Oman for one day might return for a longer holiday another time. A total of 70% ($N = 232$) of the cruise tourists surveyed mentioned in the questionnaire survey that their pre-travel expectations were met with their actual on-site experiences in the desert, while 30% mentioned they were met only partially (Gutberlet, 2019). The cruise tourists' multi-sensory experiences of the desert through the aesthetic and cultural ecosystem contribute to the ranking of its symbolic and physical features (Rickly-Boyd, 2010). In addition to its spiritual and cultural value for individuals, a desert is ecologically diverse, in terms of biocomplexity (Gutberlet, 2022a). Hence, spiritual and place values are products of different experiences associated with the ecosystem, including contemplation of the natural site (Chan et al., 2012), the fine desert sand, the fast drive through the sand and the contemplation of a wide, natural and open landscape (Gutberlet, 2022a). In the following, I will describe the tourist experience of group tourists within the vast desert landscape.

## Spiritual group experiences: "Moments of flow"

Compared to the fast desert experience of mega-cruise tourists, group tourists experienced the place at a slower pace. They had an overnight stay in the desert. As part of a slower travel, they were searching for a multi-sensory, immersion and an "attachment to the place" (Hill et al., 2014); a "geopiety" (Belhassen et al., 2008).

The group tourists arrived in the camp in the late afternoon. One group comprised of tourists who were all above 55 years old listened to stories of 1001 Nights, read by their German tour guide just before the sunset. These narratives confirmed Oriental imaginaries and a journey back in time and space (Gutberlet, 2017a). They were influenced by similar imaginaries as those of mega-cruise tourists (Gutberlet, 2019, 2022a).

Later on the tourists observed the sunset from the top of the dunes. The drivers drove them with $4 \times 4$ cars to the dunes, to an observation point. Compared to cruise tourists, only a few people were observed taking photos of each other, which may indicate that they struggled to take possession of the large landscape (Bærenholdt et al., 2004). They were aware that the actual views from the dunes were richer than the pictures they take with their cameras. The tourists experienced the desert within "moments of solitude", creating a deep spiritual connection, belonging within the space, apart from the other group members and at their own pace. They experienced the desert in more multi-sensory ways, despite the fact that they were restricted in time and space.

> A female tourist in her mid-sixties contemplated on her own the structure of the sand. *"… These different colors, the playing of colors on the sand. I am fascinated by the wind and how the desert has been formed. These drawings in the desert,* she said, comparing the desert experience with a drawing and another empty open space, the sea, expressing her spiritual connection with nature through its CES in the desertscape.

The group tourists wished to fully immerse themselves with all their senses. Without any boundaries in mind, some tourists laid down in the reddish desert sand, like children playing in the winter snow in Europe. CES of the desert environment created ties between people and the desert environment, feeling 'at home', united and relaxed. A female tourist in her 50s, who travelled alone within the group, described a sensuous experience which involved her entire body. She enjoyed the sand, the warm temperatures, the wind and the empty landscape. The natural features of the desert environment played an essential role in immersing themselves, creating a feeling of being at "at home" (Schaich et al., 2010).

One female tourist was overwhelmed physically and emotionally by her experience in the sand dunes. She felt like floating on the sea, similar to an open water dive (Cooper et al., 2016; Gutberlet, 2022a).

### The sunset in the desert: 'An edge of the modern world'

In addition to the sand, the sunset in the desert is another spiritual, silent encounter with nature, affirming another multi-sensory immersion (Hill et al., 2014) and oneness of the tourist with the vast, natural environment. With the other German group members and their German guide, it produced a "bonding social capital" (Gutberlet, 2022a; Heimtun, 2007). For a photo of the sunset, the tourists positioned themselves in small groups or alone on a sand dune. It was quiet. There was only the wind: No car noise or people chatting with each other. Within this spiritual silence, a female tourist in her mid-50s remarked with admiration that the sun was disappearing slowly on the horizon. *"...soon we can capture her"*, highlighting her wish to physically take possession of the sun through the act of capturing a photo. She then took a few photos, while the sun disappeared over the horizon. It seemed time came to a standstill, within a liminoid space (Figure 7.5). Immersing herself into nature felt like a long time (Gutberlet, 2022a).

*Figure 7.5* A spiritual communion with nature, memorizing the sunset

Source: Gutberlet (2013).

The pace of the experience in the desert was in contrast to the high speed of their travel through the North of the Sultanate by 4 × 4 cars. The tourists' experiences were similar to watching the sunset at the North Cape, forming "a spiritual community" (Mazumdar & Mazumdar, 2009) with nature or with the other group members. The mutual contemplation of the sun and the waiting for the sun to set can be compared with a pilgrimage enhancing an attachment and a self-transformation, a "geopiety" (Belhassen et al., 2008). Moreover, the moment can be compared to wildlife watching, where "moments of flow" are created to promote the tourist's spirit (Hill et al., 2014). The sunset at the North Cape is described as "an edge of the modern world" (Birkeland, 1999, p. 18) and as the origin of self-transformation. The desert in Oman can be seen as another "edge of the modern world" and a "birthplace", where a part of humanity and Islam were formed on the Arabian Peninsula (Gutberlet, 2022a).

To experience solitude, allowing a self-immersion into the desert while distancing himself physically from the other group members including his parents, a male tourist in his 40s walked through the sand, around one kilometre away from the group. He wished to find a separate place for observing the sunset and to find sand dunes that are more pure and 'natural', away from modern life and any signs of civilization such as electricity lines or streets. Such places have become rare on Earth (Gutberlet, 2022a).

The tourist was searching for a 'pure nature experience' on foot through a rather unmanaged wide ecosystem, similar to close wildlife watching. Compared to nature watching by 4 × 4 cars, such a desert experience is more likely to produce a sense of immersion for the individual and the group (Hill et al., 2014).

## A sky full of stars & stories of 1001 Nights

At night, the star and moon gazing represented another spiritual encounter with nature. A German tour leader, a pharmacist, said these are the "1001 stars in the sky" referring to Oriental imaginaries of 1001 Nights, which in her view were the most authentic features of the desert camp rooms that had an open ceiling in the bathroom. She was fascinated by the open sky views from their rooms and the closeness to nature, a spiritual and metaphysical value of the desert. The dark sky and the stars that can be viewed in large numbers in the desert, a place that was undisturbed by sounds and city lights, although most of the camps were equipped with artificial lights and an electricity generator.

Some tourists were disappointed with the luxury desert camp, an enclosed "tourist bubble" with many facilities. In their view, the camp was "a bit decadent", too comfortable and modern within a wild, natural environment. There was a reception area, a restaurant, a pool as well as many other hotel amenities like an international dinner buffet, small paved ways leading to the rooms and trolleys for the tourists' suitcases. The tourist camp was a 4-star hotel in the desert wilderness, a visual experience (Urry, 1995). It was a "glamorous camping place" or "glamping" creating an artificial, material space of exception through a comfortable, "sanitized tourist bubble". It was less about multi-sensory tourist experiences within the CES of the desert environment and more about placing the tourists outside the natural and social context of the desert environment (Büscher & Fletcher, 2017).

A German couple in their 70s mentioned during their breakfast in the restaurant that they were disappointed by the speed of the tour that affected their appreciation of the aesthetics of the cultural ecosystem. The couple reflected on the large number of stars seen the previous night in the desert, thereby, mentioning the increased urbanization in Europe resulting in degrading CES and little pure nature experiences. For them, apart from experiencing the desert during dune driving and star gazing, there was not enough time, thus slowness, to engage themselves completely and immersing themselves in the desert environment. They had already visited other deserts in Africa and they thought that their visit would be "closer to nature" while leaving behind "no or little material waste".

Hence, having less impact on the natural environment and its ecosystem services. This demonstrated her wish for more simplicity and nostalgia. She wished to be close and immerse herself into an indigenous way of life, away from any comfort, similar to early desert explorers like Wilfred Thesiger.

However, the "leave no waste behind", or Leave No Trace (LNT) ethic rather 'greenwashes' and hides the amount of waste produced (Büscher & Fletcher, 2017) and the overall social and environmental impacts of outdoor activities (Mullins, 2018). Other tourists of the group associated an open campfire with a simple, more authentic desert feeling, linked with the imaginary, indigenous Bedouin way of life and a nostalgic Wilfred Thesinger adventure.

The campfire was even paid (10 Euros), it had been commodified and lost its cultural value for the tourist. Some tourists felt the camp was too modern, too large and less authentic while enjoying comfort with beds and equipped bathrooms like in a hotel. Moreover, the camp had a small swimming pool with green water, a lot of noise due to the electricity generator as well as noisy pest control spraying that was conducted in the camp and in their rooms in the presence of tourists in the afternoon. Its main purpose was to remove unwanted insects like mosquitos and scorpions, natural features of the desert, creating further "material spaces of exception" (Büscher & Fletcher, 2017), removing the camp setting from nature and a simple, Oriental lifestyle. Moreover, overcrowding of space by too many tourists around the camp was observed.

As a consequence of "the creation of material spaces of exception" (Büscher & Fletcher, 2017) in the desert landscape, for group tourists interviewed the spiritual, religious and aesthetic values, such as the unique silence in the desert, the simplicity of the lifestyle and immersion in the desert (Hill et al., 2014), have become degraded (Gutberlet, 2022).

During midday, on their drive out of the desert, the tourist group stopped beside a sand dune. The tourists gathered beside the dune. They decorated the sand desert with Easter eggs from Europe and they took photos of the arrangement. Thereby transforming the desert into a hybrid space (Duignan et al., 2017), similar to a garden in Germany. They wished to memorize the special visit to the desert and the unique moment, visually linking it to a religious Christian celebration and their actual home in Germany. The convoy of 4 × 4 cars then continued their drive to the main road and along the Eastern coastline back to Muscat.

In 2020 and 2021, due to the COVID-19 travel restrictions, the Sharqiyah Sands tourism operations shifted to local and regional tourism in close proximity to home. Consequently, residents especially from Muscat used the desert for extensive dune bashing in groups, wild camping and some rented rooms in luxury desert camps. According to local camp owners, those desert camps that had been targeting international visitors were suffering from a lack of international tourism, similar to Souq Muttrah, causing "undertourism" and increased uncertainties about the future of their business. Some expatriate employees who had been working in these camps for many years had to return with uncertainties and without any job security to their families in their home countries in Asia.

In this chapter, I have focused on analysing the cruise and group tourists' travel to the interior of the Sultanate, the periphery, the desert and an oasis. German-speaking group and cruise tourists were searching for Oriental imaginaries and enjoyment and spirituality in the desert, linked with a self-transformation. Some experiences of the tourists in the desert such as contemplating the sunset can be compared with a pilgrimage (Belhassen et al., 2008; Howard, 2012), forming the core of the tourist experience with its existential authenticity and identity creation (Figure 7.6 below).

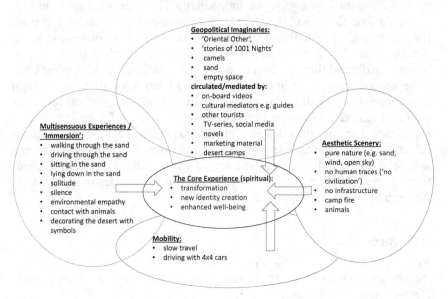

*Figure 7.6* Framework of aesthetic and spiritual ecosystem services in the desert and their importance for creating a new identity (for German-speaking tourists)

Source: Gutberlet (2021), adapted from Gutberlet (2022a).

The spiritual, pilgrimage-like, transformative tourist experience in the desert is created initially through geopolitical imaginaries, e.g. by stories of 1001 Nights circulated through tour guides or branding material. Secondly, the tourist experience is promoted through the aesthetic and biophysical scenery characterized by some tourists as pure nature, implying wildlife, and a lack of human interference, noise and infrastructure such as roads or electricity and telegraph poles. Moreover, it is enhanced through a slow travel mode such as walking or sand dune driving and an on-site experience through multi-sensory immersion, concentrating on being or "being-in-the-world", transforming the tourists into a "new self" within a core spiritual experience outside their everyday lives. This self-transformation can be enhanced through solitude and community with others and certain embodied activities (Gutberlet, 2019, 2022a).

My results show that mega-cruise tourism with its extreme time-space compression creates another "space of exception" through tourist bubbles. This means for the tourists, being in a certain natural environment while actually not really being there (Büscher & Fletcher, 2017). Time-space compression promotes the formation of staged authenticities within "spaces of exceptions" or "enclosed tourist bubbles". A slower mode of travel, away from the mainstream of the cruise or group communitas, leads towards enhanced spiritually tourist experiences. The tourist experiences are enhanced by CES that nature provides us with through the aesthetic scenery, mobilities as well as stillness and contemplation. Pure, empty nature has to be experienced within the "communitas" of a group or individually. However, such moments are rare to find on Earth and therefore have an intangible, high value and price tag. As shown, CES are threatened through increased tourism development, "the creation of material spaces of exception". Overcrowding and noise pollution contributed through operations of fast mobilities to decreasing CES. Time-space compression in cruise excursions leads not only to fast tourist experiences but as well to an overuse of labour and local natural resources with its negative impacts on local communities, their CES and the tourist experience. Quality, thus deeper, valuable experiences and more meaningful and beneficial exchange with local communities is enhanced through slowness. In the following two chapters, I will highlight recommendations towards creating long-term responsible tourism in both destinations on the Arabian Peninsula along with my conclusions.

# References

Augé, M. (2010). *Nicht-orte*. Verlag C.H. Beck.

Bærenholdt, J. O., Haldrup, M., Larsen, J., & Urry, J. (2004). *Performing tourist places*. Ashgate Publishing.

Bauman, Z. (2005). *Liquid life*. Ebook for PC. Polity Press.

Belhassen, Y., Caton, K., & Stewart, W. P. (2008). The search for authenticity in the pilgrim experience. *Annals of Tourism Research*, *35*(3), 668–689.

Berdychevsky, L., Gibson, H., & Poria, Y. (2013). Women's sexual behavior in tourism: Loosening the bridle. *Annals of Tourism Research, 42*, 65–85.

Birkeland, I. (1999). Mytho-poetic in northern travel. In D. Crouch (Ed.), *Leisure/Tourism geographies. Practices and geographical knowledge* (pp. 17–33). Routledge.

Boorstin, D. J. (1961). *The image: A guide to pseudo-events in America.* Harper and Row.

Brancalion, P. H. S., Villarroel Cardozo, I., Camatta, A., Aronson, J., & Rodrigues, R. R. (2014). Cultural ecosystem services and popular perceptions of the benefits of an ecological restoration project in the Brazilian Atlantic forest. *Restauration Ecology, 22*(1), 65–71.

Britton (1982). The political economy of tourism in the third world. *Annals of Tourism Research,* 9, 331–358.

Büscher, B., & Fletcher, R. (2017). Destructive creation: Capital accumulation and the structural violence of tourism. *Journal of Sustainable Tourism, 25*(5), 651–667.

Caton, K. (2018). Conclusion. In the forest. In B. S. R. Grimwood, K. Caton, & L. Cooke (Eds.), *New moral natures in tourism* (pp. 194–205). Routledge Ethics in Tourism.

Chan, K. M. A., Satterfield, T., & Goldstein, J. (2012). Rethinking cultural ecoservice systems to better address and navigate cultural values. *Ecological Economics, 74*, 8–18.

Chronis, A. (2015). Moving bodies and the staging of the tourist experience. *Annals of Tourism Research, 55*(1), 124–140.

Cooper, N., Bradley, E., Steen, H., & Bryce, R. (2016). Aesthetic and spiritual values of ecosystems: Recognising the ontological and axiological plurality of cultural ecosystem 'services'. *Ecosystem Services, 21*, 218–229.

Conway, D., & Timms, B. F. (2012). Are slow travel and slow tourism misfits, compadres or different genres. In T. V. Singh (Ed.), *Critical debates in tourism* (pp. 363–373). Kindle Ebook for PC. Channel View Publications.

Cauvin Verner, C. (2007). *Au désert. une anthropologie du tourisme dans le sud marocain.* L'Harmattan.

Daher, R. F. (2007). Reconceptualising tourism in the Middle East: Place, heritage, mobility and competitiveness. In R. F. Daher (Ed.), *Tourism in the Middle East. Continuity, change and transformation* (Vol. 9, pp. 1–69). Channel View Publications.

Daniel, T. C., Muhar, A., Arnberger, A., Aznar, O., Boyd, J. W., Chan, K. M. A., Costanza, R., Elmqvist, T., Flint, C. G., Gobster, P. H., Gret-Regamey, A., Lave, R., Muhar, S., Penker, M., Ribe, R. G., Schauppenlehner, T., Sikor, T., Soloviiy, I., Spierenburg, M., … von der Dunk, A. (2012). Contributions of cultural services to the ecosystem services agenda. *Proceedings of the National Academy of Sciences of the United States of America (PNAS), 109*(23), 8812–8819.

De Lacey, P., & Shakleton, C. (2017). Aesthetic and spiritual ecosystem services provided by urban sacred sites. *Sustainability, 9*, 1628.

Di Giovine, M. A. (2014). The imaginarie dialectic and the refashioning of pietrelcina. In N. B. Salazar & N. H. Grabun (Eds.), *Tourism imaginaries anthropological approaches* (pp. 147–172). Berghahn Books.

Duignan, M., Everett, S., Walsh, L., & Cade, N. (2017). Leveraging physical and digital liminoidal spaces: The case of #EATCambridge festival. *Tourism Geographies.*

Everett, S. (2008). Beyond the visual gaze? The pursuit of an embodied experience through food tourism. *Tourist Studies, 8*(3), 337–358.

Fennell, D. A., & Przeclawski, K. (2003). Generating goodwill in tourism through ethical stakeholder interactions. In S. Singh, D. J. Timothy, & R. K. Dowling (Eds.), *Tourism in destination communities* (pp. 135–152). Cabi Publishing.

Fennell, D. A. (2015). *Ecotourism* (4th ed.). Routledge.

Fennell, D. A., & Malloy, D. C. (2007). *Codes of ethics in tourism, practice, theory, synthesis.* Kindle Ebook for PC. Channel View Publications.

Goodwin, H. (2011). *Taking responsibility for tourism.* Goodfellow Publishers Limited.

Graulund, R. (2009). From (b)edouin to (A)borigine: The myth of the desert noble savage. *History of the Human Sciences, 2*(1), 79–104.

Grimwood, B. S. R., Yudina, O., Muldoon, M., & Qiu, J. (2015). Responsibility in tourism: A discursive analysis. *Annals of Tourism Research, 50*, 22–38.

Gutberlet, M. (2016b). Cruise tourist dress behaviors and local-guest reactions in a muslim country. *Tourism Culture & Communication, 16*, 15–32.

Gutberlet, M. (2017). Staging the Oriental Other: Imaginaries and performances of German-speaking cruise tourists. *Tourist Studies, 19*(1), 110–137.

Gutberlet, M. (2019). In a rush: Time-space compression and its impacts on cruise excursions. *Tourist Studies, 19*(4), 1–29. Published online first, April.

Gutberlet, M. (2021). Valuing social capital and a legacy: "The old shops are the beauty of the place". In J. Saarinen & J. Richardson (Eds.), *Change in tourism/ tourism in change* (pp. 135–150). Routledge Publishing House.

Gutberlet, M. (2022a). Geopolitical Imaginaries and cultural ecosystem services (CES) in the desert. *Tourism Geographies, 24*, 4–5.

Gutberlet, M. (2022b). Insight 288: Tourist bubbles and climate change in the GCC. COP 27 and Climate Action in the Middle East, Middle East Institute, National University of Singapore, October 24.

Heimtun, B. (2007). Depathologizing the tourist syndrome. Tourism as social capital production. *Tourist Studies, 7*, 271–293.

Hill, J., Curtin, S., & Gough, G. (2014). Understanding tourist encounters with nature: A thematic framework. *Tourism Geographies, 16*(1), 68–87.

Hirons, M., Comberti, C., & Dunford, R. (2016). Valuing cultural ecosystem services. *Annual Review of Environment and Resources, 41*, 545–574.

Holden, A. (2008). *Environment and tourism*, Routledge Introductions in Environment Series, (2nd ed.). Routledge.

Howard, C. (2012). Speeding up and slowing down: Pilgrimage and slow travel through time. In S. Fullagar, K. Markwell, & E. Wilson (Eds.), *Slow tourism. Experiences and mobilities.* Channel View Publications.

Hultsman, J. (1995). Just tourism – an ethical framework. *Annals of Tourism Research, 22*(3), 553–567.

Jamal, T., & Higham, J. (2021). Justice and ethics: Towards a new platform for tourism and sustainability. *Journal of Sustainable Tourism, 29*(2–3), 143–157.

Kay Smith, M., & Diekmann, A. (2017). Tourism and wellbeing. *Annals of Tourism Research, 66*, 1–13.

Keohane, A. (2011). *Bedouin nomads of the desert.* Kyle Books.

Klein, R. A. (2011). Responsible cruise tourism: Issues of cruise tourism and sustainability. *Journal of Hospitality and Tourism Management, 18*, 107–116.

Larsen, J., Gomes Bastos, M., Skovslund Hansen, L. I., Hevink, L. M., Jostova, K., & Smagurauskaite, D. (2021). Bubble-wrapped sightseeing mobilities: Hop on-off bus experiences in Copenhagen. *Tourist Studies, 21*(3), 1–17.

Lew, A. A., & Wu, T. C. (2018). Cultural ecosystem services, tourism and community resilience in coastal wetland conservation in Taiwan. In A. Lew & A. Cheer (Eds.), *Tourism resilience and adaptation to environmental change. Definitions and frameworks* (pp. 102–155). Routledge.

Ljubica, J., & Dulcic, Z. (2012). Megaships and developing cultural tourism in Dubrovnik. In A. Papathanassis, T. Lukovic, & M. Vogel (Eds.), *Cruise tourism and society* (pp. 17–28). Springer Verlag.

London, W. R., & Lohmann, G. (2014). Power in the context of cruise destination stakeholders' interrelationships. *Research in Transportation Business & Management*, *13*, 24–35.

Lopes, J. M., & Dredge, D. (2018). Cruise tourism shore excursions: Value for destinations?. *Journal of Tourism Planning and Development 16*(6), 633–652.

Lumsdon, L. M., & McGrath, P. (2011). Developing a conceptual framework for slow travel: A grounded theory approach. *Journal of Sustainable Tourism, 19*(3), 265–279.

MacCannell, D. (2011). *The ethics of sightseeing.* University of California Press.

MacCannell, D. (2012). On the ethical stake in tourism research. *Tourism Geographies: An International Journal of Tourism Space, Place and Environment, 14*(1), 183–194.

Mazumdar, S., & Mazumdar, S. (2009). Religious placemaking and community building in diaspora. *Environment and Behavior, 41*(3), 307–337.

MEA (2005). *Millenium ecosystem assessment. ecosystems and human well-being: Desertification synthesis*, World Resources Institute. www.milleniumecosystem.assessment.com

Milcu, A. I., Hanspach, J., Abson, D., & Fischer, J. (2013). Cultural ecosystem services: A literature review and prospects for future research. *Ecology and Society, 18*(3), 44.

Ministry of Tourism (2014). *Marhaba Oman.* Ministry of Tourism.

Ministry of Tourism (2016). *Marhaba Oman.* Ministry of Tourism.

Mordue, T. (2005). Tourism, performance and social exclusion in Olde York. *Annals of Tourism Research, 32*(1), 179–198.

Moscardo, G. (Ed.). (1999). Making visitors mindful, principles for creating sustainable visitor experiences through effective communication. *Advances in tourism applications series 2.* Sagamore Publishing.

Mostafanezhad, M., & Norum, R. (2016). Towards a geopolitics of tourism. *Annals of Tourism Research, 61*, 226–228.

Mullins, P. F. (2018). Toward a participatory ecological ethic for outdoor activities. In B. S. R. Grimwood, K. Caton, & L. Cooke (Eds.), *New moral natures in tourism* (pp. 149–164). Routledge.

Pink, S. (2008). An urban tour. The sensory sociality of ethnography place-making, *Ethnography, 9*(2), 175–196.

Rickly-Boyd, J. M. (2010). The tourist narrative. *Tourist Studies, 9*(3), 259–280.

Said, E. (2003). *Orientalism.* Modern Classics Penguin Books.

Salazar, N. B. (2010). *Envisioning Eden: Mobilizing imaginaries in tourism and beyond.* Berghahn Books.

Schaich, H., Bieling, C., & Plieninger, T. (2010). Linking ecosystem services with cultural landscape research. *GAIA, 19*(4), 269–277.

Shepherd, R. J. (2015). Why Heidegger did not travel: Existential angst, authenticity, and tourist experiences. *Annals of Tourism Research, 52*, 60–71.

Singh, S. (2012). Slow travel and Indian culture: Philosophical and practical aspects. In K. Fullagar, K. Markwell, & E. Wilson (Eds.), *Slow tourism. Experiences and mobilities* (pp. 5895–6215). Kindle Ebook for PC. Channel View Publications.

Su, X., Wang, H., & Wen, T. (2013). Profit, responsibility, and the moral economy of tourism. *Annals of Tourism Research, 43*, 231–250.

Tengberg, A., Fredholm, S., Eliasson, I., Knez, I., Saltzman, K., & Wetterberg, O. (2012). Ecosystem services. *Ecosystem Services, 2*, 14–26.

Tresidder, R. (1999). Tourism and sacred landscapes. In D. Crouch (Ed.), *Leisure/Tourism geographies. Practices and geographical knowledge* (pp. 137–148). Routledge.

Urry, J. (1995). *Consuming places.* Routledge.

Wagner, L., & Minca, C. (2016). Topographies of the Kasbah route: Hardening of a heritage trail, *Tourist Studies, 17*(2), 1–27.

Wang, N. (1999). Rethinking authenticity in tourism experience. *Annals of Tourism Research, 26*(2), 340–370.

Wang, Y. (2007). Customized authenticity begins at home. *Annals of Tourism Research, 34*(3), 789–804.

Weaver, A. (2006a). The McDonaldization thesis and cruise tourism. *Annals of Tourism Research, 32*(2), 346–366.

Wilson, E., & Little, D. E. (2011). The solo female travel experience: Exploring the geography of women's fear. *Current Issues in Tourism, 11*(2), 167–186.

Yarnal, C. M., & Kerstetter, D. (2005). Casting off – An exploration of cruise ship space, group behavior and social interaction. *Journal of Travel Research, 43*, 268–379.

Yeğenogluğ, M. (1998). *Colonial fantasies. Towards a feminist reading of orientalism.* Cambridge University Press.

# 8 Management and planning implications

## Rethinking tourism: Towards more community and an ethics of care

In the previous chapters, I have discussed the rapid pace and the large scale of cruise tourism resulting in degrading tourist experiences and various conflicts between tourists and locals and their well-being, impacting the sustainability of the social, cultural and natural environment in Souq Muttrah and in the oasis and the desert in Oman.

In the Sultanate of Oman, a Western approach of sociocultural sustainability is realized within hierarchical, patriarchal and tribal structures of the society. While there seem to be good intentions from the Omani government to include different aspects of sustainability in large-scale tourism development, problems are noticeable. Here, the sociocultural sustainability is closely related to the scale of tourism and its ethical operations. The local communities in the souq, in the oasis and the desert seem to be in constant struggle within "liquid modernity" (Bauman, 2000, 2004, 2005) over their identities, access to social networks, knowledge and the distribution of resources. A resource-based tradition of sustainability that boosts the economy has been prevalent. It aims at an exploitative, continuous quantitative growth, overexploiting natural, physical, cultural and social resources within time-space compression and its forces. Originally, the concept of sustainability derives from livestock studies that relate to the maximum number of grazing animals that is sustainable without damage to the stock or grazing resources (Dasmann et al., 1974). Since tourism is a dynamic activity that is in constant change *liquid*, always causing negative impacts within "liquid modernity", such a resource-based idea is difficult to achieve for the tourism industry and its development.

### The power of tourism politics

For a sustainable tourism development, a pluralistic approach to tourism planning and development is necessary. It is imperative to collaborate with different stakeholders on implementing and monitoring a responsible,

DOI: 10.4324/9780429424946-8

ethical use of the natural and cultural environment and its resources. A responsible tourism planning should foster dignity and responsibility, including stakeholders of the government and the multi-ethnic community within its diversity – women, expatriates, the youth and the elderly should be part of the planning and implementation process. Such an approach also includes controlling the carrying capacity and the development of the local production of goods by supporting independent, local businesses.

For instance, the souq could be rebranded as a historic heritage site for trading and a multi-ethnic place for the resident community. Local festivals as well as ethnic grocery shops, ethnic clothes, textiles and book shops could be set-up.

A holistic approach towards tourism development aims to consider the needs of the local community as well as the tourists, while at the same time protecting the tangible and intangible heritage, enhancing opportunities for future generations (UNWTO, 2020, 2021). The setting-up of "limits to growth" (Meadows et al., 2004) is necessary through active negotiations, participation and regulations within the community.

Since a positive support of tourism increases with the community's benefits, trust in government institutions and policies, such a community-based approach aims to empower first the host community. Such a Western perspective of a "participatory community approach" can provide a possibility that the importance to consult over the use of shared resources and the needs of neighbours opens an opportunity for solving conflicts in tourism (Hall, 2003). The aim is that tourism benefits all, not only the elite, wealthy and those community members with access to knowledge and power, often geographically located in the capital. It ideally promotes a better quality of life for communities and a protection of resources for future generations (United Nations, 2019). Such community-based tourism often inhabits a kind of "romantic" or "naïve" view that everyone has equal access to power and representation, which is often not the case due to limited access to influential networks, financial resources, expertise, public relations, media and time. A one-dimensional view of power in communities suggests that the decision-making process is at least visible. Hence, some groups and individuals often have more influence than others (Hall, 2003).

As for mega-cruise tourism, in both case studies the power and capital distribution were found to be centred on the mega-cruise company, the local government and international and national tour operators, shipping agents and other tourism-related businesses. The local residents and business owners were little or not at all considered and consulted in tourism planning and development.

It has been argued that a "true" form of sustainable tourism, one that is holistic, equitable and future-oriented is difficult to achieve or even unachievable within a capitalist economic system. The main reasons are the current extractive, imperialistic and dependent nature of the global North-South (centre-periphery) tourism production, the consumer-centred promotion and the large-scale consumption of tourism, which do not fit into an endogenous, small-scale, community-led development (Sharpley, 2000). Hence, only when the entire tourism industry and its suppliers from the North to the South accept, respect and act according to a more responsible, sustainable utilization of all natural, social and economic resources, according to the United Nations Sustainable Development goals (2019), can a form of sustainable tourism be achieved. Cave and Dredge (2020, p. 506) called for a "diverse economies framework", conceptualizing "the co-existence of capitalist, alternative capitalist and non-capitalist practices" that provide an alternative towards more resilient, regenerative practices in tourism. These practices should be incorporated into a collaborative economy with alternative economic transactions like "gifting and sharing" where the individual benefit is not the goal; e.g. neighbourhood initiatives, indigenous and small-scale female businesses. Hence, any informal work in community-based tourism needs to be recognized, formalized and paid. Women's participation in community-based tourism is high worldwide. These businesses owned and managed by women could bring even more benefits to their families and communities if they were more empowered and entitled to social and legal protection.

Within the community, the main goal should be a stronger, resilient connection and community bonds supporting the "moral economy" away from "profit-obsessed consumer markets and their fights" towards an ideal "mutual care and help, living for the other, weaving the tissue of human commitments, fastening and servicing inter-human bonds, translating rights into obligations, sharing responsibility for everyone's fortune and welfare" (Bauman, 2004, p. 74). Moreover, "voluntary acts of kindness" can play an important role in shaping the experiences on both sides, locals and tourists (Filep et al., 2017). It is about an equal, just involvement and distribution of space and power for local residents and other stakeholders, their various ethnic backgrounds, cultural values and beliefs. Thus, it is not only about enlarging the tourism infrastructure, building roads and airports along with modernization and economic development. Critical, alternative development strategies can support small, emerging tourist destinations on the Arabian Peninsula to become less reliant on tourism and instead more sustainable, equitable and less vulnerable to sudden shock events like pandemics or climate change (Sheller, 2021). Moreover, everybody who is a tourist has a share and responsibility for our planet. This may imply showing self-restraint and considering staying and consuming local. By reducing the consumption including the amount of petrol used for travel, "staycations" are one way to limit the carbon footprint (Fyall, 2019).

### *Slow is respectful and beautiful*

A positive relationship with the destination and the people depends largely upon the scale of tourism and the planning of the destination including the typology of the tourists, their travel motivation and on-site behaviours.

Cultural mediators play a major role in engineering the behaviour of tourists. My deep concern is that as long as there is a dominating perception that public spaces in natural environments such as the desert are free-of-charge and unlimited, it will be difficult to promote a more ethical use of space. I agree with Milano et al. (2019) and Seraphin et al. (2019), the political and operational strategies put in place to maintain the well-being of the local community need to focus on de-growth and de-marketing of mega-cruise tourism and large-scale tourism.

I agree with MacNeill and Wozniak (2008), suggesting that regulatory measures should be put in place and strictly monitored (Gutberlet, 2016a, 2020). There is some hope for more social responsibility and justice in cruise tourism operations. The Global Sustainable Tourism Council has recently conducted a sustainability assessment of the Mediterranean city of Dubrovnik, funded by CLIA. Other destinations in Greece may follow (CLIA, 2021). However, funding by the cruise industry can impact a transparent outcome of the assessment. Such funding can be seen as a veiling or greenwashing of negative impacts on communities.

To ease the pressure of overtourism on the local community and their environments, I suggest to introduce and monitor continuously economic, physical, regulatory and educational measures (Figure 8.1). Locals should not only be informed but also be included as active voices and members, e.g. within regular Tourism Committee meetings and decision-making. A social, cultural and economic empowerment of the entire multi-ethnic community inclusive of all stakeholders could be realized through the

| Strategy | Initiatives (facilitated through stakeholder involvement & continuous monitoring) |
|---|---|
| physical | • On-site management towards more quality experiences<br>• On-site design towards the protection and maintenance of the local tangible heritage |
| regulatory | • Limit mass tourism / quota / zoning<br>• Limit tourist numbers in one place / dispersion of tourists<br>• Restrict access to private areas |
| economic | • Fees for cruise liners & tourists;<br>• taxes, local heritage fund<br>• Eco-certification |
| educational | • Awareness campaign on board and within the local community<br>• Tourism education at schools<br>• Printed info-material on board<br>• Signboards at the site, a visitor centre<br>• Guided, educational walks in small groups |

*Figure 8.1* Management implications for emerging cruise destinations

Source: Gutberlet (2021).

creation of a special group the "Muttrah Tourism Committee" (Gutberlet, 2016a) and the "Sharqiyah Tourism Committee" as well as a local "Cruise Committee" (Hull & Milne, 2010) and further enhanced through continuous participatory workshops (Bertella et al., 2021). Such committees should include representatives of The Port Authority, the Municipality, the Ministry of Transportation and Communication, The Royal Oman Police, the Ministry of Heritage and Tourism, the Ministry of Regional Municipalities, the Ministry of Environment and Water Resources, the Public Authority for Handicrafts, the local Women's Association, the Ministry of Religious Affairs and Awqaf, local shipping agents, tour operators, local male, female Omani and expatriate tour guides, business owners, residents and vendors in Muttrah. Such committees should not be limited to a certain group but include representatives of all stakeholder groups, regardless of age, gender and social background. Through open participation and independent guidance, these committees should develop a set of sustainable tourism development indicators (Torres-Delgado & Saarinen, 2014), reflecting the various needs of the local community, including, e.g.: the number of cruise tourist arrivals per day, the ratio of tourists/locals (residents and expatriates), the sale of locally made products and the employment rate, reflecting the historic ethnic diversity of the place.

To ensure valuable, positive results for the community, it is necessary for the indicators to be implemented and monitored continuously by an impartial government watchdog and an independent, private body. I think within the current capitalist, extractive system of tourism development, a long-term sustainable development cannot be reinforced unless there are strict regulations, laws and fines in place. In the following, I will further explain my vision for both destinations.

I fully agree, stakeholders in the tourism business and the tourists themselves should compensate negative effects on the community and for the damage caused to the natural and built environment (Jafari, 1987). This could be done through an environmental and economic accounting and auditing (Fyall, 2019), which should include a sociocultural accounting as well. Consequently, mitigating the carbon and "social footprint" caused including impacts like culture shock situations. Tourists and cruise companies should get financially involved by contributing to taxes and/or heritage funds that benefit all stakeholders of the community. For example, a daily tourist tax for cruise tourists should be charged, e.g. 10–15 Euro (approx. 5–8 R.O.) per person and per day. The amount could be then reinvested into local community development and the preservation of their natural assets (Gutberlet, 2016a). Until today, the problem of increased tourist numbers is solved by industrial methods, leading to a "MacDonaldization" and a rather "dehumanizing" experience (Ritzer & Liska, 1997) through standardization, mass production of souvenirs, food and the overall setting-up of high-capacity facilities and infrastructure through the touristification of places like Souq Muttrah or the oasis and the desert as well as day excursions.

Management tools to mitigate and deal with the impacts of overtourism (Milano et al., 2019) focus on different forms of community-based tourism or niche tourism such as "creative tourism" and "adventure tourism". Creative tourism entails the active involvement of locals and tourists in 'slower', creative activities, e.g. festivals, language or cooking courses, art workshops, nature walks etc. creating "intrinsic value" (skills, respect, appreciation for the tourists) and "instrumental value" through additional financial income for communities (Richards, 2021). Moreover, de-seasonalization, decentralization and a dispersion of tourists to other areas and attractions should be considered as well as an overall "slower", more responsible tourism. Furthermore, a local supply chain for food products increases the value for the community. As for cruise excursions, the duration or distance of travel may offer opportunities for the tourists to be part of the local "flow of life" in the destination. The tourists could adapt gradually to the new environment and climate, facilitating their geographical orientation while at the same time increasing the time for interpretation and benefits for locals (Gutberlet, 2019b).

Slow tourism can be seen as an essential process for the tourists and the branding of the community. However, "slowness" should be valued and branded in a positive way. "Slow" indicates more respect for our planet and for future generations. Slowness also stands for an enhanced appreciation of time, the local culture and nature, which should be of the utmost importance for all stakeholders.

Similar to other emerging cruise destinations on the Arabian Peninsula, the aim should be a tourism industry where the social capital and "ethnic distinctions" are addressed, in order to develop a more socially harmonious multi-ethnic environment (Stephenson & Ali-Knight, 2010). Currently, the majority of the labour force in tourism operations in the desert and the oasis and in Souq Muttrah rely on expatriates from Asia and increasingly from Africa, thus fostering historic ties to some former Omani territories (Gutberlet, 2017), while reducing and dumping labour costs. Hence, equal labour regulations should apply to expatriates and for Omanis alike.

At the same time, tourism is an educative tool. In order to achieve more just and sustainable tourism, locals should be educated about more responsible tourism from an early age onwards, at school. The local community should have the right to choose their vision for tourism. An international certification or eco-labelling of the destination Oman and each individual destination would enhance the branding efforts of Oman, being an emerging, sustainable and responsible destination that respects and protects its rich, diverse social, cultural and natural heritage (Gutberlet, 2020, 2021). The ultimate aims should be the "readiness" and broad approval of the community, within their culture and environment, and that tourists behave ethically and respectfully. Moreover, indicators for sustainable tourism could

be introduced as guidelines and to be promoted, monitored and realized as responsible tourism practices. These indicators are valuable for tourists, local and, international stakeholders alike, e.g. the Kuoni Code of Conduct (Kuoni, 2014) or UNWTO indicators (2004) or others (Torres-Delgado & Saarinen, 2014) along with an international destination certification according to social, environmental and cultural sustainability indicators, rating or eco-labelling system. In the following, I will outline recommendations for the souq in Muttrah as well as the oasis and the Sharqiyah Sands desert.

### The souq

Souq Muttrah is the ancient heart of a fast-growing city and an inspiration for current and future generations. It should be marketed as a multi-ethnic, heritage and trading space with its rich social capital and legacy. Souq Muttrah constitutes a valuable place to unite and present the rich, diverse and little discussed, veiled trading history including its dark hidden sides to the people (Gutberlet, 2021). Similar to the arrival of cruise liners in the Caribbean, Jaakson (2004) described the view from the shore, locals in Oman may reflect similar way.

> The cruise ship is gleaming white and larger than any other structure in the harbor (of Muttrah). Most of the cruise tourists are white... To a worker gazing at the cruise ship and taking some photos may not be different from what it would have been some 200 years ago when gazing at a large sailing ship that arrived from the mother-country on shore at a colony with flags flying and officers on board dressed in imperial costumes.
>
> (Jaakson, 2004, p. 4702)

Considering the impacts of mega-cruise tourism, its costs and benefits for the local community and tourists within the overall sociocultural structure, my analysis suggests that the Omani government and all private stakeholders in tourism should limit day mega-cruise tourism in the small bay of Muttrah. To avoid overcrowding, only small cruise ships should be allowed to anchor while restricting the number of mega-cruise tourists through a quota (Gutberlet, 2016a). In addition, cruises should be encouraged to stay overnight while "giving back" to the community in a responsible way. To enhance the quality of life of locals and to slow down the tourist experience, the number of cars needs to be considered as well as the duration of the excursion. In Muttrah, more low-impact transportation should be offered and set-up, e.g. electric shuttle buses, e-scooters, bicycles or e-bikes and cycle rickshaws. Moreover, safe, walkable, shaded areas where there is no car traffic as well as shaded biking and scooter pathways should be designed along the Corniche road in Souq Muttrah. Large trees could provide the necessary shade while reducing air pollution. Slower modes of transportation should be available for small groups and within close proximity to the port. This would create more space for tourists and locals to enjoy the scenery and reduce the noise and air pollution (Gutberlet, 2019a). Through the introduction of slower and more responsible modes of travel, the Omani culture and people can be understood better and negative impacts on the community and the tourist experience can be mitigated. Visits of large groups of tourists to Souq Muttrah should be avoided and numbers continuously monitored, e.g. at the entrance to the souq (Gutberlet, 2016a). The tourism planning in Amsterdam, "City in Balance" (2019), suggests the dispersion of tourists to alternative sites in the city area to encourage them to visit less crowded areas, while the introduction of regulations for tourist shops is another tool.

Commercial pressure has dominated tourism development in Souq Muttrah. It has resulted in a commodified space, "a tourist bubble", changing the product range, and contributing to a loss of local heritage and social capital (Gutberlet, 2016a, 2016b, 2017). These losses should be avoided through a holistic management plan. Such a plan should resist the artificial creation of a fully "Omanized tourist bubble" as well as any partnership with an international shipping company. It seems the planned mega-infrastructure project, the Waterfront in Muttrah, will create a simulacrum Disney park-like "tourist bubble", where tourists consume signs and experiences within Integrated Tourism Projects (ITCs). Such "tourist bubble" shields tourists (and others) from culture-shock situations and ensures a standardized, safe experience without novelties. As a result, local well-established residents and businesses may become more alienated as its local identity with its sense of place is transformed into an increasingly homogenous "tourist bubble", focusing on the needs of outsiders (Gutberlet, 2016a). As part of the Waterfront project in Muttrah, a special Tourist Souq has been planned to be set-up inside the port. A high-ranking official suggested a semi-privatization of the souq that is currently managed by Muscat Municipality. In his view, one of the biggest tour operators should buy and run certain shops in Souq Muttrah, thereby reducing the number of expatriates and promoting Omanis and their identities within a semi-governmental supervision (Gutberlet, 2021). The idea is similar to artificial islands in the Caribbean owned by the shipping company. This would create another power struggle and an artificially, staged "bubble" for the tourists and their demands. In my view, a local "Community Souq Initiative" is recommended similar to the "Souq al Sabt", a Saturday market, an open-air community market for the public, set-up in a pedestrian street in Al Mouj district in Muscat. Such a market should be established, where the diverse local community, individuals, SMEs and minorities can sell innovative ideas, home-made food, handicrafts, clothes etc. Some of them have already set-up their own businesses in various parts of Muscat, even on the Corniche in Muttrah. Such local grassroots, participatory initiatives can support innovative SMEs to be established in a prime tourist attraction. Unfortunately, triggered by COVID-19 and the lack of tourists along with a lack of financial emergency support, a number of SMEs had to close down in 2021. For their survival, government support or the setting-up of a private fund managed by an independent, impartial body is necessary.

Innovative ideas and bonding social capital including trust, involvement of the local community and cooperation between the private and public sectors are necessary to unite and present the heritage and its multi-ethnic community (Gutberlet, 2021). Strong social capital can promote community resilience and the ability of the community to resist and adapt to sudden, future disruptions caused, e.g. exogenous factors such as health pandemics and climate change.

### The desert and the oasis

The news that one of the mega-cruise liners surveyed had cancelled its excursion to the desert and the oasis during the cruise season in 2019 was welcomed. Currently, there is a conflict of interest between locals who complain about losing their livelihoods and animals as well as group and individual tourists who seek quiet, empty spaces and cruise tourists who wish to experience an adrenaline thrill driving through the dunes. Infrastructural development and overcrowding currently resulting in a decrease in Cultural Ecosystem Services (CES) while preventing tourists searching for an identity creation, "geopiety" (Belhassen et al., 2008) and the transformative value of travelling to the desert.

To preserve the natural and cultural resources, it is important to control, monitor and sanction disturbing and destructive activities in order to protect especially CES in the fragile desert environment, while at the same time giving space to and protecting wild spaces with their high intangible CES value (Gutberlet, 2019a). Since the number of tourists visiting natural environments is increasing year by year, it is advisable to introduce a managed bioreserve in Sharqiyah Sands. In other words, a fenced enclosure, a park in the desert with a "no-go" core zone that enhances the visitors' search for self-transformation and where an entrance fee per person should be charged. The income from these fees could serve the management of the bioreserve that should include the setting-up of a desert visitor education centre. In addition, a "buffer zone" with infrastructure as well as a special area for 'dune fun driving' should be created. Moreover, the number of tourist camps should be limited, controlled by law, and overseen and enforced by an independent body. A propos, the former Minister of Tourism mentioned during a personal conversation in May 2018 that zoning is planned in the Sharqiyah Sands desert (Gutberlet, 2019b).

### Shaping imaginaries and a mindful behaviour

I agree with Larsen (2019) that "much tourism is strikingly ordinary, while everyday life in eventful and multicultural cities is full of extraordinary moments and encounters". However, these need time and space. I would

218 *Management and planning implications*

like to expand this line of thoughts on wide, natural environments like vast deserts that offer extraordinary moments, transforming and shaping identities through CES. The tourist imaginaries impact on how the individual cares about the place and the natural, social and physical environment. They also impact on how far the person is willing to respect the local community, its values, traditions and the natural environment. Tourists need to respect and be aware that they do not visit a liminal zone or a living museum but a place of everyday life, where visitors need to "fit in" (Larsen, 2019) rather than disturb the quality of life of the local community. Through a process of re-engineering "imagineering" (Daher, 2007) of geographical spaces and discourses through new, modern imaginaries, so-called "counter-imaginaries" (Leite, 2014) new and more equal relations between Europe and the "new Orient" should be disseminated while recognizing their historical linkages. Due to the current empowerment of the tourists and the engineering of space and culture by outsiders, it is important to involve the local community and their understanding of the destination, thereby reshaping the power of Oriental imaginaries according to their understanding of the identity, culture, history and today's space (Gutberlet, 2017, 2019a).

To transform tourists into more mindful human beings, it is recommended that stakeholders in tourism take responsibility and action to educate and inform mega-cruise tourists during their travel, not only prior to their travel but also on board the ship and while on tour. The introduction of an *ethical code of conduct* is suggested, including even the signing of a code of conduct agreement for stakeholders working in tourism so that they inform the tourists correctly (Gutberlet, 2016b). Every tourist and every local should be educated thoroughly prior to the arrival on the Arabian Peninsula, not just about health and safety issues but about the social and cultural fabric of the destination and responsible tourism practices, while avoiding belittling certain behaviours (Larsen et al., 2021). The Iceland Academy inspired by the Iceland pledge (2021) calls for a responsible tourist behaviour. It offers a diploma for a responsible preparation of tourists planning to visit Iceland (VisitIceland, 2021). This is a forward-looking role model for promoting values and ethics in tourism within a more responsible, mindful travel behaviour on an individual basis.

Values can be transformative or non-transformative for tourists. Similar to the Iceland pledge, Mullins (2018) suggests codes of conduct that guide outdoor practices using a participatory ecological approach while engaging the community in the tourist experience, fostering relations that leave positive traces on our humanity and environments.

Participatory, ecological ethics for outdoor activities enhancing learning and empathy for the environment (ibid.: 158f.) should be applied for tourism in the desert. For example, the following guidelines could be promoted and mediatized by governments through social media, influencers, cruise companies and tour operators who are planning and offering excursions to their clients abroad and to cultural brokers on board the ship, who are mediating the tourist's travel:

1 Remember you are not the first or only one here, you won't be the last. Learn from and respect those you meet.
2 Choose carefully the stories that motivate and shape your trips and that you tell about your trips and their settings.
3 Learn and use ecologically responsive and responsible techniques to travel along environmental flows, through diverse landscapes, across park boundaries.
4 Learn to attend your surroundings rather than your devices. Use tools and technologies as ways of learning and engaging further with places, processes and issues.
5 Fuel your journey responsibly; you consume; you are not human powered.
6 Use economies to positively impact communities in and around your route.
7 Support engage, and improve social, environmental and activity-related stewardship and justice.
8 Reduce consumption and increase accessibility by sharing equipment and clothing. (Mullins, 2018, pp. 158–160).

These principles are part of the concept of "slow tourism" that encapsulates five key dimensions, fostering a 'conscious travel' (Caffyn, 2012):

• Place (locality, distinctiveness, landscape, heritage, environment, produce)
• People (community, culture, local enterprise, cuisine, hospitality, authenticity)
• Time (pace, relaxation, unhurried, more in-depth)
• Travel (distance, speed, mode, low carbon) and
• the Personal (well-being, pleasure, recreation, conviviality, learning, meaning, enjoyment, understanding)

The more elements are integrated into the travel, the more sustainable the travel experience (ibid.: 80). Hence, there is more value and a win-win situation for tourists and the local community, contributing more benefits to the community and destination while achieving a more satisfying tourist experience.

In this chapter, I have given some recommendations for a more sustainable, people and nature-centred tourism planning and management in two emerging cruise destinations. Within the current capitalist, extractive system of tourism operations in *liquid modernity* (Bauman, 2000, 2004, 2005), sustainability is hard to be reinforced. However, I think unless there are strict regulations, laws and fines in place promoting responsibility and ethics in tourism including an ethical behaviour and consumption as well as a participatory approach towards tourism development, sustainability can be achieved in the long term. Due to the fast pace of the tourism development in both places, it would be necessary to record the changes through continuous monitoring and fieldwork. The current body of research has focused on two locations, which it is hoped will inform more sustainable planning and development. Souq Muttrah has a high intangible and tangible value for the memory and identity of the community and the sand desert and oasis ecosystem have great aesthetic and spiritual value being equally important as a source of transformation and regeneration for tourists and urban-base locals and expatriates alike. In the following chapter, I will elaborate on my final thoughts and conclusions.

## References

Bauman, Z. (2000). *Liquid modernity.* Polity Press.

Bauman, Z. (2001). *Community. Seeking safety in an insecure world.* Ebook for PC, Polity Press.

Bauman, Z. (2004). *Identity. Conversations with Benedetto Vecchi.* Ebook for PC. Polity Press.

Bauman, Z. (2005). *Liquid life.* Ebook for PC. Polity Press.

Belhassen, Y., Caton, K., & Stewart, W. P. (2008). The search for authenticity in the pilgrim experience. *Annals of Tourism Research, 35*(3), 668–689.

Bertella, G., Lupini, S., Romanelli, C. R., & Font, X. (2021). Workshop methodology design: Innovation-oriented participatory processes for sustainability, *Annals of Tourism Research, 89,* 103251.

Caffyn, A. (2012). Advocating and implementing slow tourism. *Tourism Recreation Research, 37*(1), 77–80. https://doi.org/10.1080/02508281.2012.11081690

Daher, R. F. (2007). Reconceptualising Tourism in the Middle East: Place, Heritage, Mobility and Competitiveness. In: Daher, R. F. (ed.). *Tourism in the Middle East. Continuity, Change and Transformation. Tourism and Cultural Change 9.* Clevedon: Channel View Publications, 1–69.

Dasmann, R. F., Milton, J. P., & Freeman, P. H. (1974). *Ecological principals for economic development.* John Wiley.

Cave, J., & Dredge, D. (2020). Regenerative tourism needs diverse economic practices. *Tourism Geographies, 22*(3), 503–513.

CLIA (Cruise Lines International Association) (2021). *State of the cruise industry outlook.* CLIA Cruise Line International Association. Retrieved July 12, from http://www.cruising.org/about-the-industry/press-room/press-releases/pr/state-of-the-cruise-industry-outlook

Filep, S., Macnaugton, J., & Glover, T. (2017). Tourism and gratitude: Valuing acts of kindness. *Annals of Tourism Research, 66,* 26–36.

Fyall, A. (2019). Too many tourists? The problem of Overtourism – and how to solve it, summer 2019, Pegasus, The magazine of the University of Central Florida. Retrieved November 13, from https://www.ucf.edu/pegasus/too-many-tourists/

Gutberlet, M. (2016a). Socio-cultural impacts of large-scale cruise tourism in Souq Muttrah. *Fennia, 194*(1), 46–63.

Gutberlet, M. (2016b). Cruise tourist dress behaviors and local-guest reactions in a Muslim country. *Tourism Culture & Communication, 16,* 15–32.

Gutberlet, M. (2017). Staging the Oriental Other: Imaginaries and performances of German-speaking cruise tourists. *Tourist Studies, 19*(1), 110–137.

Gutberlet, M. (2019). In a rush: Time-space compression and its impacts on cruise excursions, *Tourist Studies*, *19*(4), 1–29. Published online first, April.

Gutberlet, M. (2020). "They just buy a karak and leave" – Overtourism in Souq Muttrah, The Sultanate of Oman, *Zeitschrift für Tourismuswissenschaften*, De Gruyter Oldenburg, 13 October. https://doi.org/10.1515/tw-2020-0004

Gutberlet, M. (2021). Valuing social capital and a legacy: The old shops are the beauty of the place. In J. Saarinen & J. Richardson (Eds.), *Change in tourism/ tourism in change*. Routledge Publishing House.

Gutberlet, M. (2022a). Geopolitical imaginaries and cultural ecosystem services (CES) in the desert. *Tourism Geographies*, *24*, 4–5.

Gutberlet, M. (2022b). Insight 288: Tourist bubbles and climate change in the GCC. COP 27 and Climate Action in the Middle East, Middle East Institute, National University of Singapore, October 24.

Hall, M. C. (2003). Politics and place: An analysis of power in tourism communities. In S. Sing, D. J. Timothy, & R. K. Dowling, *Tourism in destination communities*. CABI Publishing.

Hull, J. S., & Milne, S. (2010). Port readiness planning in the arctic: Building community support. In M. Lück, P. T. Maher, & E. J. Stewart (Eds.), *Cruise tourism in Polar Regions. Promoting environmental and social sustainability* (pp. 181–204). Earthscan.

Jaakson, R. (2004). Beyond the tourist bubble? Cruise ship passengers in port. *Annals of Tourism Research*, *31*(1), 44–60.

Jafari, J. (1987). Tourism models: The sociocultural aspects. *Tourism Management*, *8*(2), 151–159.

Kuoni Travel Holding (2014). Assessing human rights impacts. *India project report. Corporate social responsibility*. Kuoni. Retrieved September 2015, from https://business-humanrights.org/en/kuoni-assessing-human-rights-impacts-india-project-report

Larsen, J. (2019). Ordinary tourism and extraordinary everyday life: Re-thinking tourism and cities. In T. Frisch, N. Stors, L. Stoltenberg, & C. Sommer (Eds.), *Tourism and everyday life in the city*. Routledge.

Larsen, J., Gomes Bastos, M., Skovslund, Hansen, L. I., Hevink, L. M., Jostova, K., & Smagurauskaite, D. (2021). Bubble-wrapped sightseeing mobilities: Hop on-off bus experiences in Copenhagen, *Tourist Studies*, 21(3), 1–17.

Leite, N. (2014). Afterword. Locating imaginaries in the anthropology of tourism. In N. Salazar & N. Grabun (Eds.), *Tourism imaginaries. Anthropological approaches* (pp. 260–278). Berghahn Books.

MacNeill, T., & Wozniak, D. (2008). The economic, social and environmental impacts of cruise tourism. *Tourism Management*, *66*, 387–404.

Meadows, D., Randers, J., & Meadows, D. (2004). *Limits to growth, the 30-year update*. Chelsea Green Publishing.

Milano, C., Novelli, M., & Cheer, J. M. (2019). Overtourism and degrowth: A social movements perspective. *Journal of Sustainable Tourism*. https://doi.org/10.1080/09669582.2019.1650054

Mullins, P. F. (2018). Toward a participatory ecological ethic for outdoor activities. In B. S. R. Grimwood, K. Caton, & L. Cooke (Eds.), *New moral natures in tourism* (pp. 149–164). Routledge.

Richards, G. (2021). Business models for creative tourism, *Journal of Hospitality and Tourism Management*. www.johat.org

Ritzer, G., & Liska, A. (1997). 'McDisneyzation' and 'Post-Tourism' – Complementary perspectives on contemporary tourism. In C. Royek & J. Urry (Eds.), *Touring cultures. Transformation of travel and theory* (pp. 98–109). Routledge.

Séraphin, H.; Zaman, M.; Olver, S.; Bourliataux-Lajoinie; Dosquet, F. (2019). Destination branding and overtourism. *Journal of Hospitality and Tourism Management, 38,* 1–4.

Sharpley, R. (2000). Tourism and sustainable development: Exploring the theoretical divide. *Journal of Sustainable Tourism, 8*(1), 1–19.

Sheller, M. (2021). Reconstructing tourism in the Caribbean: Connecting pandemic recovery, climate resilience and sustainable tourism through mobility justice. *Journal of Sustainable Tourism, 29*(9), 1436–1449.

Stephenson, M., & Ali-Knight, J. (2010). Dubai's tourism industry and its societal impact: Social implications and sustainable challenges. *Journal of Tourism and Cultural Change, 8*(4), 278–292.

Torres-Delgado, A., & Saarinen, J. (2014). Using indicators to assess sustainable tourism development: A review. *Tourism Geographies: An International Journal of Tourism Space, Place and Environment, 16*(1), 31–47.

United Nations (2019). Sustainable development goals. http://www.undp.org/content/undp/en/home/sustainable-development-goals.html

UNWTO (2020). *One planet vision for a responsible recovery of the tourism sector. One planet sustainable tourism programme.* World Tourism Organization.

UNWTO (2021). Inclusive recovery guide – Sociocultural impacts of Covid-19, Issue 3: *Women in tourism* (p. 4), UNWTO.

VisitIceland (2021). Visit Iceland, Iceland Academy. Enrol in the academy. Retrieved July 17, from https://visiticeland.com/iceland-academy

# 9 Conclusions

Throughout the book, it becomes evident that globalization, large-scale cruise tourism and the occurrence of overtourism enhance the formation of *tourist bubbles* on the Arabian Peninsula. These are linked to negative impacts for the local community and for tourists alike. Such tourist bubbles disconnect social relations, the history of the place and they cause a decrease in social stability and bonding capital for locals. For the tourists, travelling with a mega-cruise liner means travelling comfortably through an *imaginary Orient*. On board and on land, the tourists move within customized bubbles (Gutberlet, 2017, 2019). However, for governments, it is imperative to slow down the race for increasing tourist numbers. Tourism is a dynamic process and can be a tool to diversify the economy, create jobs while enhancing peace and understanding between people, supporting specific places, diverse communities, their local environments and cultures. The main goal should be to create a kind of tourism that is less extractive, supporting communities and local supply chains, according to the United Nations Sustainable Development Goals (2021), Goals 8 (Decent work and Economic Growth), 10 (Reduced Inequality), 11 (Sustainable Cities and Communities) and 12 (Responsible Consumption and Production). Mass tourism should involve less overconsumption and less egocentric, "ticking off" boxes of special attractions. It should be about quality experiences instead of quantity and a more conscious way of "being in the world" with a global awareness and compassion for our planet and for other people and cultures.

The discussion of this book and the theory presented have been analysed through a lens of critical tourism scholarship and the sociology of tourism within globalization, mobilities and time-space compression. This was conceptualized in mega-cruise tourism causing overtourism in emerging destinations on the Arabian Peninsula. Overtourism has resulted in various sociocultural impacts for the local community as well as tourists, their imaginaries, embodied experiences and changing authenticities within the destination. Moreover, a loss of social values and social capital in particular in Souq Muttrah, are seen to outweigh the economic and social benefits of mass-cruise tourism (Gutberlet, 2016b, 2017, 2019, 2021, 2022a).

DOI: 10.4324/9780429424946-9

*Figure 9.1* A mega-cruise liner arriving in Muscat

Source: Gutberlet (2019).

In my research in the periphery, in the desert and in an oasis, I have especially focused on space and time-space compression, spirituality and identity creation linked with geopolitical imaginaries that frame the tourist's experience within Cultural Ecosystem Services (CES) (Gutberlet, 2022a). My research is based on a new emerging phenomenon that had not previously been researched on the Arabian Peninsula. It is timely and calls for a sustainable transition of tourism. It started during a period of dramatic increase in mega-cruise tourism (Figure 9.1) reaching its historical peak in Oman in 2012/2013 and another peak in 2019, just before the outbreak of the corona pandemic. Sociocultural impacts of COVID-19 on tourism in Souq Muttrah were also analysed and included in this book. My findings presented serve for academics, students, policymakers and decision-makers in sustainable tourism as well as for regional and urban planning and destination management organizations.

Mega-cruise tourism on the Arabian Peninsula and, in particular, in the Sultanate of Oman has been restructuring the local economy from an oil-based towards a more service-based economy, creating potential business and job opportunities, in particular for the Omani. Similar to small emerging destinations like Greenland (Ionnides, 2019), Oman is not immune from the impacts of mass tourism if development is encouraged without setting limits. My results have shown that the development of mega-cruise tourism entails the governing and restructuring of local environments through capital and increased fast mobilities within time-space compression (Harvey, 1989). This has implications for the commodification of the tourist experience, the well-being of local communities, their social capital and the natural and cultural environment, as well as equal access to local resources. There is a lack of access in particular to financial, human and natural resources. Hence, the absence of consensus and a joint political control over the growth of mega-cruise tourism makes international mega-cruise liners an important "source of uncertainty" for local communities. Within the destinations, it appears very difficult to disentangle and disrupt power structures that have developed. Currently, it is preferred to avoid a participatory discussion and a confrontation with the "veiled" past, e.g. in Souq Muttrah and its sociocultural context (Gutberlet, 2017, 2020, 2021).

Both destinations discussed in this book are full of valuable human and social capital, history and stories including well-hidden, dark sides. In particular, social capital can be seen as an important tool to promote equal, inclusive and sustainable tourism and to analyse the social cohesion of the community. According to community members interviewed in Souq Muttrah, everyday life in the souq created a bond between families, which has decreased over time (Gutberlet, 2021). This was due to a lack of trust, consultation and communication within the community regarding tourism development, decreasing the bonding social capital, creating feelings of exclusion, being left out of the development process. It seems that in the past there was more attachment to the place and to other members of the ethnic, "kin-based community network", creating a sense of "mutual social capital" (Gutberlet, 2021; Soulard et al., 2018).

Local and tourist authenticities remain diverse while adjusting to the shift from small-scale tourism to mass tourism. I have also argued that the cultural and aesthetic values of the vast empty desert benefit recreational and self-transformative tourist experiences as well as environmental awareness. As such, individual spiritual and aesthetic value systems influenced by geopolitical narratives and tourism marketing create the impression of a hybrid desert "space of freedom" (Gutberlet, 2019a).

My research has emphasized various tendencies in mega-cruise tourism within space, society and time. It responds to calls to investigate the sociocultural sustainability and value creation of cruise tourism in specific destinations around the globe (Klein, 2011; Lopes & Dredge, 2018; MacNeill & Wozniak, 2008; Renaud, 2017, 2020). Wilkinson (1999) explicitly called already for research on the "cruise inauthenticity", emphasizing that local stakeholders should enhance their dialogue to create more environmental and sociocultural responsible cruise tourism including their excursions on land (Gutberlet, 2016a). It seems, even more than 20 years later, a lot has to be done for the sustainability in destinations. My research also fills a gap on tourism operations and development in the Middle East, in particular with regard to mega-cruise tourism, overtourism and the authenticity of tourist experiences "in situ". It is a valuable addition of applied research to the current body of research around the world (Abbasian et al., 2020; Cheer et al., 2019; Ionnides, 2019; Johnson, 2006; Koens et al., 2019; Larsen et al., 2021; Lopes & Dredge, 2018; MacNeill & Wozniak, 2008; Milano et al., 2019;

Papathanassis, 2012, 2017; Renaud, 2020; Vogel & Oschmann, 2013; Weaver, 2005a; Wilkinson, 1999; Yarnal & Kerstetter, 2005). In the following paragraphs, I will highlight the different concluding ideas of my analysis.

First, I have shown that mass-cruise tourism has commodified local hospitality and cultures within "liquid modernity" (Bauman, 2000). Throughout history, Omanis like other Arab populations have practised genuine, open hospitality towards visitors, especially from the West/Global North. Such hospitality has been unconditional, free-of-charge by virtue and by religious belief. Up to now, this has been a common, traditional practice on a small scale and at private homes, especially outside the urban centres and in the countryside where visitors are warmly welcomed for an Omani coffee with cardamom and dates. Hence, such hospitality has been "objectively authentic" (Wang, 2007). However, latterly tourism has been marketed as a commodity which is part of a capitalist system of producers, suppliers and intermediaries. In the desert and the oasis, only a small number of local stakeholders are involved in tourism and profit from it. As a result, the perception of a genuine Omani hospitality has changed within the pace of the tourism development. It has developed into "staged bubbles", associated with the allocation and distribution of benefits materialized in the access to money, knowledge and networks. This has caused power struggles between the centre and the periphery as well as among different stakeholders in tourism and their knowledge networks, resulting in winners, losers and rivalries.

> *"Many people eat from the cake – the Bedouins, the camp owners, the car rental services, the petrol stations. Tourism is like that for the community"*, said an Omani camp owner in the Sharqiyah Sands desert who complained about the increased competition among tourist camps.

Similar to Göreme in Turkey (Tucker & Akama, 2010), in Souq Muttrah and in the desert, the multi-ethnic community and their cultures have been commodified through tourism-as-capital (Büscher & Fletcher, 2016). Only a small section of the local, well-established multi-ethnic community is able to benefit economically from cruise tourism (Gutberlet, 2020, 2021).

Second, travelling with a mega-cruise liner means travelling comfortably through the "imaginary Orient". On board and on land, the tourists move within customized "enclosed tourist bubbles". In these bubbles, tourists are disconnected from the local, natural and sociocultural environment (Gutberlet, 2019). In Souq Muttrah, it seems much easier to construct a new space with new vendors from Asia and little social capital (Gutberlet, 2017, 2019b, 2021), while in Sharqiyah Sands desert new luxury, large campsites are established (Gutberlet, 2019, 2022a). The power of tourism stakeholders like camps and tour operators with extensive networks to the Global North dominates the tourism setting along with local tourists, 'outsiders from the capital'. In terms of Bauman's (2001) concept, the social capital transforms into "liquid social capital" within a disruptive identity in a "transitional place" and "enclosed tourist bubbles" (Gutberlet, 2021, 2022a), while the circulation of goods, services and images through mass tourism promotes a continuous "global miniaturization" and "disembedment" of space (Harvey, 1989; Urry, 1995). Hence, the tourists are increasingly disoriented – there is a lack of interpretation, the tourist experiences become unreal and less sustainable within the social, cultural and natural environment of the destination. The intercultural exchange remains superficial. Cruise tourists move around within a customized, "luxury, mobile tourist bubble" that protects them like a social shell or shield. It controls the tourists as well as their tourism providers (Gutberlet, 2019). For the tourists, tourist bubbles are safe enclosures. Given a large number of mega-cruise tourists, an "enclosed tourist bubble" may relieve social pressure on the host community and their culture (Gutberlet, 2019; Williams & Lew, 2015) while providing comfort and safety for tourists. Here, I agree with Urry (1995) who argued that the visual consumption and therefore the aestheticized lifestyle has led to an end of tourism experiences through time-space compression within disorganized capitalism. People are tourists most of the time, whether they move or only experience simulated mobility through various signs and electronic images (Urry, 1995, p. 148).

Third, within the fast pace of globalization and liquid modernity (Bauman, 2001), the concept of community or "communitas" has been changing continuously and the concept of "inter-human bonds" becomes vague and temporary within liquid modernity (Bauman, 2007). A community reflects a search or longing for *dwelling*, being an integral part of an *imaginary local community* which stands for a warm, cosy, comfortable place (Bauman, 2001). A place outside everyday life. "Whatever has been left of the dreams of a better life shared with better neighbours all following better rules of cohabitation" (Bauman, 2000, p. 92). Mega-cruise tourists form a separate "communitas" (Gutberlet, 2019). They are actively involved in the creation and consumption of a hybrid, mobile, tourist culture, which means, being part of an 'imaginary community' on land. Cruise excursions are customized mass-products that are accelerated in time and space within a staged "community". The practices are adapted to the fast speed of the overall cruise travel that aims at visually consuming, collecting or grazing on as many places and images as possible within one week while simultaneously reducing the authenticity of space (Gutberlet, 2019). The most important travel motivation for the tourists is to *overconsume*, experiencing visually as many places, people and cultures as possible while realizing an activity-related "existential authenticity" (Wang, 1999). On the other hand, their emotional connection with the place leads to an "ideological reinforcement", shaping a group identity within a *cruise communitas* (Gutberlet, 2017, 2019, 2022a). While on tour, the tourists experience their own selves. The authentic 'we' within the tourist "communitas" is reinforced on board the cruise ship and during a visit on shore. My findings reveal that also due to a lack of information and time-space compression during the travel, mega-cruise tourists show limited interest and openness towards the "local Other", their values and ethical norms. From the local community, an "accommodationist", "laissez-faire attitude" (Din, 1989) or an "unconditional hospitality" that supports and fully adjusts to the behaviour of the "Other" is prioritized, abandoning local social identities, values and customs (Gutberlet, 2016b, 2020).

Fourth, mega-cruise tourism development as experienced in the emerging destinations in the Sultanate of Oman creates divisions and inequalities. It mainly attracts and accumulates capital for an urban elite, forcing the local population in Souq Muttrah, in the oasis and in the desert to adjust and to compromise with natural and social resources. This is especially evident in Souq Muttrah, where local Omanis and well-established expatriates are confronted with a neoliberal tourism development that fragments and divides the society and their cultures according to their nationality, social status, networks and wealth. The culture in Souq Muttrah is transformed into new configurations of diversity, where the concept of identity within a homogenous Omani culture and community is continuously redefined (Amoamo, 2011). Nevertheless, local actors like Omani and expatriate shop vendors and expatriate tour guides are not passive observers but actors and co-creators (Causevic & Neal, 2019) in a process of adjusting their narratives and everyday lives to mega-cruise tourism development, which is experienced as a growing number of tourists and their demands for a staged authenticity in Souq Muttrah and in Sharqiyah Sands. For most interviewees in my research, Souq Muttrah is now about participating in an ongoing dynamic cultural and historical process or an "Orientalized legacy", while struggling to protect their own multi-ethnic identities within time and space (Gutberlet, 2017, 2021).

My research reveals diverse experiences and views about overtourism and the development of a staged authenticity that is enhanced by "Oriental imaginaries" within the formation of commercialized, touristified spaces, "tourist bubbles" (Gutberlet, 2019b, 2020). A neoliberal cruise tourism development has commodified, touristified and framed the urban tourist destination Souq Muttrah as a top tourist site while promoting the formation of hybrid, commodified spaces or bubbles including a "core tourist bubble" along the main streets (see Chapters 5 and 6). In the desert, luxury desert camps form "enclosed luxury bubbles" (see Chapter 7). It becomes evident that globalization, large-scale tourism and the occurrence of overtourism enhance a "deterritorialisation of capital, labor and touristic place itself" (Wood, 2000). This disconnects social relations, the history of the place and causes a decrease in social stability and bonding capital for the local community (Gutberlet, 2021). Such a "tourist bubble" is linked to negative impacts for the local community and for tourists.

As a result of these fast global changes and mobilities, imaginaries shape travel experiences and identities. Referring to Foucault's (1980) concepts of knowledge and power, knowledge is disseminated through the distribution, extraction or retention of ideas. Oriental imaginaries frame the identity of tourist places. Souq Muttrah, Sharqiyah Sands desert and the oasis have been marketed as traditional, mystical places and as being authentic and "Oriental" (Gutberlet, 2017). Hence, the destinations are transformed into 'stages' for performances where imaginaries of the "Oriental Other", frankincense, colourful markets, an "Oriental oasis" and a pure, empty desert are created within a multi-sensuous experience. The local tour guides and drivers turn into the main actors in "localizing" and exoticizing the place, a kind of "authentic stage play" in which tourists participate and reflect the concept of an Orientalized Arabian Disneyland (Gutberlet, 2017, 2019, 2022a). It is the place narrative, discourse (communicative staging), the materiality, its architectural characteristics and the products that are sold to the tourists (material staging) (Chronis, 2012, 2015). Hence, the local guide's mediation is essential towards the reconstruction and manipulation of the tourist performance (Gutberlet, 2017, 2019, 2020, 2022a). Through the tourists' imaginaries, they wish to discover Oman in the same way they were instructed to do so through different media. These exotic imaginaries of German-speaking mega-cruise tourists are similar to exotic imaginaries of visitors, e.g. in Indonesia, Tanzania (Salazar, 2010), Göreme/Turkey (Tucker & Akama, 2010), the Taj Mahal (Edensor, 1998) or the Egyptian Sinai (Haldrup & Larsen, 2010). Geopolitical imaginaries about the desertscape Sharqiyah Sands create a sense of meaning and attachment to the place. The "in situ" tourist experience is framed by the cruise company, the media and cultural brokers (Chapter 7). Analysing the cultural processes and narratives that influence geopolitical imaginaries shaping the tourist experience and power relations is imperative in order to understand the importance of local heritage and nature with respect to future challenges like climate change and increased desertification faced worldwide. Imaginaries of a fairy-tale, Oriental country of "The Arabian Nights" are defined and they label Omanis as "embodied Oriental Other" within unequal, postcolonial, power relations about "us" (the West/Global North) and "them", "museumizing" the local community, creating superiority over the "Oriental Other" (Gutberlet, 2017, 2019, 2022a). I agree, that this can lead to an "indirect form of imperialism" (Daher, 2007, p. 9) while there is also a self-promoted "self-Orientalization" from the Omani side (Feighery, 2012). These imaginaries are not connected with the modern everyday reality in Oman but they create stereotype ideas. With the increase in mega-cruise tourism and the extension of the cruise terminal in Muscat, it will be important to create and circulate new images and discourses about "the Orient" (Gutberlet, 2017, 2019, 2022a).

Furthermore, the sociocultural impacts of overtourism and "tourist bubbles" are challenging the local community, tourists and their authenticities in both locations (Figure 9.2). Locals mentioned that the number of annual visitors should be limited. Their accepted level of tolerance and "perceived social carrying capacity" has been reached. According to the majority of the community and the tourists surveyed, there is no more space for more tourists (Gutberlet, 2021). It is obvious, the local community is escaping from the "core tourist bubble" in Souq Muttrah when a mega-cruise ship is

*Figure 9.2* A local, expatriate tour guide explains the souq and its heritage to a small
group of German tourists, at the frankincense shop in Souq Muttrah

Source: Gutberlet (2013).

in the port, protecting themselves and their identities from curious onlook-
ers. Some residents have set up physical borders (Gutberlet, 2016a) while in
Sharqiyah Sands Bedouin camp owners have stopped conducting long camel
trips and they protect their animals from the crowds of people (Chapter 7).
In addition to the physical carrying capacity, the increasing presence of
cruise tourists is experienced as a threat to the Omani and expat identity.
Local authenticities are comprised of different objectives and interpersonal
elements, such as being able to purchase the necessities of everyday life in
the souq as well as sharing Omani coffee (Chapter 6). These activities facilitate interacting with others as a way of creating community ties and social
bonding as well as an easy access to the physical space and the preservation
of its historic features (Gutberlet, 2016b, 2017, 2019, 2021, 2022a).

Locals in both places critically observe their behaviours, especially in the
oasis, where the community is rather conservative and where women primarily remain inside their homes, there is no or very little exchange with
the tourists. In the oasis, local residents experience tourists as "passers-by"
(Chapter 7). I agree that local people often have little economic choice but to
accept and to adapt to "touristified identities, spaces and cultural views that
are created for them" (Salazar, 2005, p. 836). I believe that tourism can be

an essential force for peace and understanding as well as for positive social change and justice (Büscher & Fletcher, 2016). In Souq Muttrah especially, social exclusion is a feature of an accelerated neoliberal tourism development. Women as well as the well-established Asian community and the older male Omani community (those above 45 years) are missing in the creation of these imaginaries and embodied on-site experiences of mega-cruise tourists (Gutberlet, 2017). This tendency has been reinforced during the corona pandemic. It is important to further study the relationships between social capital, race, identity and community-based tourism that benefit local actors.

Overall, my study used data collected from Omani and expatriate stakeholders as well as German-speaking tourists. As such my findings may have limited applicability to other societies; however, they act as a reference to other tourist destinations in the region as well as to other places in emerging destinations that have turned into commodified tourist sites within a short time. The different stakeholders involved in the planning and management of emerging destinations should protect, preserve and promote especially the intangible heritage value, the soul and the spirit of the place (Gutberlet, 2021, 2022a).

## My final thoughts: Well-th (wealth) and community redefined

My book has demonstrated the increased importance of transformations in tourism within space. Mega-cruise tourism is reshaping spaces, local communities and their well-being in time. Moreover, mobilities in time-space compression have transformed tourist experiences. I have provided some insights into understanding the nature of large-scale cruise consumption on shore and particularly during day-excursions with their time-space compression. They promote fast travel and the formation of standardized, "closed tourist bubbles" on land and multiple authenticities. Moreover, I have highlighted the importance of integrated tourism planning and urban social studies as tourism increasingly makes and remakes the everyday lives of people and cultures. Tourism is a very dynamic phenomenon impacting destinations. When analysing various tourist experiences and behaviours as well as local reactions, patronizing individual behaviours should be avoided.

Tourism should involve more mindful consumption and less ticking off boxes of spectacular attractions for selfies. Also governments should slow down in the race for increasing tourist numbers and bed-nights. Tourism can be an active commitment towards peace while supporting specific places, peoples and their local environments and struggles (Büscher & Fletcher, 2016). It should be about quality experiences instead of quantity and a more conscious way of living and "being in the world" (Heidegger, 2010); impacting the well-being of communities, promoting long-term connections between people and places instead of fast, fading ones.

Despite the contributions of my long-term, empathic research, there are limitations such as the number of stakeholders interviewed and the focus on German-speaking tourists. Nevertheless, it represents a unique, detailed, long-term perspective. It is my hope that my research will contribute to the creation of awareness and understanding of the fast social and cultural changes influenced by 'liquid modernity' and capitalism. I wish to enhance responsible, far-reaching political, economic, regulatory and physical measures. I agree, there is some hope that local communities will have the chance to decide about the future of tourism and a return to the "old normal" (Sheller, 2021) or business "as usual" through more active participation. There should be a transition in local, regional and international governance and decision-making from prioritizing *growth for development* to *degrowth for livability*, for the "future of our planet' linked with more social equality. Local communities and their multiple stakeholders on the Arabian Peninsula should decide what is best for them instead of having decisions imposed on them by mass tourism companies (Renaud, 2020) or governments. To facilitate change, strategic participatory community workshops including all stakeholders could be held (Bertella et al., 2021), promoting a common mission and vision for the destination while enhancing and building networks, trust and innovation within the local community. I am sure, this will need time and effort and will be a challenge and difficult to realize within highly fragmented communities (Gutberlet, 2020, 2021, 2022a).

The overall management and planning goal should be a *substantial transformation*: "A re-organization phase of innovation and creativity, which is necessary for our human system to transform itself to adapt to the new context of the planet we inhabit" (Lew et al., 2020, p. 456). The ideal is a different economic system that promotes a more sustainable, ethical and just form of tourism, and which protects natural and cultural resources for future generations (Crossley, 2020; Higgins-Desbiolles, 2021; Jamal & Higham, 2021; Lew et al., 2020) as well as a redefinition of "wealth", social equality and the well-being of our planet. In indigenous terms, wealth is defined as "a social, physical and mindful well-being within the social structure of the tribe" (Cave & Dredge, 2020), which could be applied to the social structures and cultural values that exist on the Arabian Peninsula.

Nature-based tourism in deserts can play an important role in reconnecting people with our planet, with humanity and with themselves. It can enhance empathy for the natural environment, while creating individual well-being (Gutberlet 2022a, 2022b). Following previous research on the aesthetic and spiritual value of ecosystem services (Cooper et al., 2016; Daniel et al., 2012; De Lacy & Shackleton, 2017; Hill et al., 2014; MEA 2005; Milcu et al., 2013; Mullins, 2018; Wang & Lyu, 2019), my research has shown the high importance of these CES for the human-environment relationship and empathy for our natural and sociocultural environment. Taking into account the differences in aesthetic preferences between individuals, ethnicities and different cultures, my research has highlighted imaginaries and on-site tourist experiences from the perspective of German-speaking tourists as well as perceptions and reactions of local communities.

Regarding future studies in fragile desert environments, it would be valuable to analyse how the local GCC and expatriate community value and benefit from the place with its CES (Gutberlet, 2019). It should be imperative to monitor the sociocultural impacts on the community in the region and the diverse tourist behaviours, their imaginaries and the tourist experiences within space and in a continuous manner. In addition to climate change (Gutberlet 2022b), there are interesting research topics to explore, e.g. post-pandemic tourism operations, sociocultural impacts on a tourist hotspot, the local Friday animal market in the interior of Oman, female tourist experiences in male-dominated spaces, the environmental impacts of day-cruise tourism as well as the social and emotional stress for local residents. Mega-cruise tourism in a cross-cultural context is an emerging topic that requires further passionate research involvements, while considering the historical links between the Arabian Peninsula and other countries in Africa and in Asia.

The overall challenge is to maintain a sustainable approach to large-scale tourism while balancing economic benefits and negative impacts on the local community and their current and future natural resources. It is necessary to preserve the cultural and natural beauty of Oman – a country with a long coastline that is highly prone to the negative effects of global climate change similar to the rest of the Arabian Peninsula. Although attempts are made in the Gulf countries on the Arabian Peninsula to manipulate the climate and trigger artificial rain through 'cloud sourcing' in the UAE (Duncan, 2021), bordering Oman, extreme weather events such as heat waves, droughts, storms, cyclones, desertification and flooding have obviously increased in scale and strength throughout the past 15 years highly impacting livelihoods. In July 2007, Oman was hit by tropical cyclone *Gonu* and in October 2021, the coastline was hit by another heavy tropical storm *Shaheen*, both events caused severe flooding in many areas in the North of the Sultanate, resulting in casualties and devastated homes and infrastructure. According to the latest report of the Intergovernmental Panel on Climate Change (IPCC), in many parts of the world including in Asia "adverse impacts from tropical cyclones, with related losses and damages, have increased due to sea level rise and the increase in heavy precipitation (medium confidence)" (ICPP, 2022).

Along with global warming, the rise of inequality is one of the principal challenges confronting the world today (Piketty, 2020, p. 656). Hence, social capital and social justice need to be highly considered in future tourism planning, development and operations along with applied social research (Gutberlet 2022b).

Ultimately, the goal is to create a kind of tourism that is less extractive, supporting local supply chains – fishermen, farmers and renewable energy micro-grids, reducing the amount of energy and waste generated. The environmental impacts of tourism on fragile marine and desert environments should be considered, as well as the impacts of climate change. The heavy fossil-fuel consumption linked with long-haul flights, the marine diesel consumed by mega-cruise ships, seawater pollution, coral bleaching and the overall use of cars, air-conditioning, electricity and energy-consuming buildings places a heavy burden on the local infrastructure of emerging destinations while reinforcing the conditions of an unequal exposure to climate change risks in the Global South compared to the North (Sheller, 2021). Tourism generates a hidden fossil fuel consumption related to the importation and consumption of non-local food, goods and services linked with a disproportionate use of water, a resource that is extremely scarce on the Arabian Peninsula (Gutberlet 2022b).

Moreover, the worldwide COVID-19 pandemic has shown high impacts in the Middle East region and in tourism, with no definite end in sight. No accurate prediction is possible regarding its overall economic and social damage (Fotiadis et al., 2021). On the one hand, the world has witnessed a soft opening of regional travel in Europe, North America and the UAE, where a large majority of the population has received a vaccine. For example, the UAE have opened the EXPO 2020 in October 2021, and in Scotland a cruise ban was lifted while in Seattle the first cruise ship was welcomed after 18 months of total suspension, launching the Alaska cruise season (Cruise Adviser, 2021). On the other hand, in countries like Oman or South Africa where the vaccination campaign had a slow start, a series of new restrictions and lockdowns were put in place in July 2021 and flights to Asian countries were suspended. A social divide between the vaccination in the Global North and the Global South and between the rich and the poor became obvious. The COVID-19 pandemic has caused a significant collapse of the social and economic systems on our planet (United Nations Development Programme [UNDP], 2020). "Shocks have long-lasting consequences on human development and can be passed to subsequent generations. Even after an epidemic ends or economic growth returns, the impacts of a shock can leave lasting damage" (UNDP, 2020, p. 11).

The concept of mobility justice (Sheller, 2021) is a concept of power and inequality impacting the governance and control of movement, as experienced during the corona pandemic worldwide and in particular in tourism in small, emerging destinations in the Global South. "Mobility justice reveals travel and tourism as mobility regimes that have deep historical roots in colonial racial capitalism having ongoing connections to the reproduction of vulnerability" (Sheller, 2021, p. 1442).

In the long run, I hope that the diverse, multi-ethnic communities in both destinations in Oman as well as in other emerging destinations on the Arabian Peninsula will be able to find a balance. Such a balance will be imperative in order to protect the charm and the sense of place while limiting or even banning large numbers of mass-tourists passing through, such as Venice suffers from. There resident activists have shown that their local voices are not just heard and recognized in decision-making (Giuffrida, 2021), but are supported globally through social media by UNESCO in Paris. This gives hope for the empowerment and well-being of communities, their environments and our planet. Throughout a neoliberal development where every city aspires to have a glamorous waterfront and a fascinating heritage, ethnicity and social problems like unemployment or the relocation of residents are seldom considered (Selby, 2004). A silencing or a "veiling" of critical views (Causevic & Neal, 2019) is typical to capitalist, growth-oriented tourism planning and place marketing in many parts of the world. Tourism should be a living-part of the local community (Veijola, 2018). It would be advisable to reconstruct the paradise-like imaginaries of Oman according to modern, inclusive imaginaries, similar to the reconstruction projects of community-based grassroots movements in the Caribbean (Sheller, 2021). I also believe that a more community-focused, ethical, less egocentric and less intra-personal approach to travel can promote more "acts of kindness" (Filep et al., 2017), personal involvement and genuine experiences in tourism, reshaping, transforming and even activating a new "global consciousness through tourism" (Galvani et al., 2020).

As the Swiss tourism researcher Krippendorf (1987) mentioned a long time back, a process of substantial change should be enhanced through tourism education. Sustainable tourism and leisure education should be taught globally at schools from an early age onwards. The overarching process of change within the destructive capitalist creation that is the basis for current tourism development is key for a more equal and just tourism (Büscher & Fletcher, 2016). Ultimately, this could lead towards a more human and personally connected world and peace. Intangible values that promote the well-being of communities are often seen as a contradiction to business interests and economic values, but this valuation needs to change (Gutberlet, 2019).

The COVID-19 pandemic could open new opportunities for applying innovation, beyond business as usual and promote social justice (Higgins-Desbiolles, 2020) and human-nature connections. For instance, new forms of economic practices with greater involvement of the community and towards more protection of the natural environment with their indigenous knowledge that can lead towards a more ethical, fair trade of transactions (Cave & Dredge, 2020). Effective efforts should be made "to make the big better" (Singh, 2012), which entails to make mega-cruise tourism more sustainable and beneficial for the people, through more active involvement. This could be done, through "volunteer tourism", "compassion tourism" and "creative tourism" (Richards, 2021) while reducing its scale and social, cultural and environmental impacts. Time is very limited, and the number of cruise tourists will continue to increase, as soon as it is safe again to travel, borders are open for everybody and people are fully vaccinated. Until autumn 2021, the Omani government and in particular the Ministry of Health was restricting mega-cruise tourism due to health safety, while the Ministry of Tourism wishes to start the winter cruise season on time in order to continue with the business "as usual". By October 2021, cruise liners were not yet allowed to arrive in Oman though borders had opened for international tourists on 1 September 2021. In November 2021, mega-cruise tourism restarted in the

Sultanate of Oman. Due to health and safety protocols on board, mega-ships were travelling with a lower passenger load, therefore limiting the risk of overtourism at the destination.

On a final note, I think no research can be complete. There is always space for more thoughts and more analysis. Any errors, misunderstandings or mis-interpretations are mine. I wish that my research will be the start of something more and that it will inspire discussions on participatory tourism planning and more sustainable tourism on the Arabian Peninsula. Responsible, par-ticipatory community planning, marketing, and on-site management can do much to foster the well-being of multi-ethnic communities not just in the Sultanate of Oman but elsewhere around the world. Thinking about future generations, I hope that my empathetic research will contribute to more criti-cal thoughts, research and concrete actions regarding solving the urging topic of overtourism and overconsumption leading to an overaccumulation of peo-ple, places and services as commodities in our *liquid times*.

## References

Abbasian, S., Onn, G., & Arnautovic, D. (2020). Overtourism in Dubrovnik in the eyes of local tourism employees: A qualitative study. *Cogent Social Sciences*, 6(2), 1775944.
Amoamo, M. (2011). Tourism and hybridity: Revisiting Bhabha's third space. *Annals of Tourism Research*, 38(4), 1254–1273.
Bauman, Z. (2000). *Liquid modernity*. Polity Press.
Bauman, Z. (2001). *Community. Seeking safety in an insecure world*. Ebook for PC. Polity Press.
Bauman, Z. (2007). *Liquid times. Living in an age of uncertainty*. Ebook for PC. Polity Press.
Bertella, G., Lupini, S., Romanelli, C. R., & Font, X. (2021). Workshop method-ology design: Innovation-oriented participatory processes for sustainability, *Annals of Tourism Research*, 89, 103251.
Causevic, S., & Neal, M. (2019). The exotic veil: Managing tourist perceptions of national history and statehood in Oman. *Tourism Management*, 71, 504–517.
Cave, J., & Dredge, D. (2020). Regenerative tourism needs diverse economic prac-tices. *Tourism Geographies*, 22(3), 503–513.
Cheer, J., Milano, C., & Novelli, M. (Eds.). (2019). Afterword: Over overtourism or just the beginning? *Overtourism: Excesses, discontent and measures in travel and tourism* (pp. 227–232). CABI.
Chronis, A. (2012). Between place and story: Gettysburg as tourism imaginery. *Annals of Tourism Research*, 39(4), 1797–1816.
Chronis, A. (2015). Moving bodies and the staging of the tourist experience. *Annals of Tourism Research*, 55(1), 124–140.
Cooper, N., Bradey, E., Steen, H., & Bryce, R. (2016). Aesthetic and spiritual values of ecosystems: Recognising the ontological and axiological plurality of cultural ecosystem 'services'. *Ecosystem Services*, 21, 218–229.
Crossley, E. (2020). Ecological grief generates desire for environmental healing in tourism after COVID-19. *Tourism Geographies*, 22(3), 536–546.

Cruise Adviser (2021). Seattle marks restart of Alaska cruise season. Retrieved July 21, from https://cruise-adviser.com/seattle-marks-restart-of-alaska-cruise-season/

Daher, R. F. (2007). Reconceptualising tourism in the Middle East: Place, heritage, mobility and competitiveness. In R. Daher (Ed.), Tourism and Cultural Change 9. *Tourism in the Middle East. Continuity, change and transformation* (pp. 1–69). Channel View Publications.

Daniel, T. C., Muhar, A., Arnberger, A., Aznar, O., Boyd, J. W., Chan, K. M. A., Costanza, R., Elmqvist, T., Flint, C. G., Gobster, P. H., Gret-Regamey, A., Lave, R., Muhar, S., Penker, M., Ribe, R. G., Schauppenlehner, T., Sikor, T., Soloviiy, I., Spierenburg, M., ... von der Dunk, A. (2012). Contributions of cultural services to the ecosystem services agenda. *Proceedings of the National Academy of Sciences of the United States of America (PNAS)*, *109*(23), 8812–8819.

Din, K. (1989). Islam and tourism. *Annals of Tourism Research*, *16*, 542–563.

Duncan, G. (2021). How does cloud-seeding in the UAE work? The national, 28 January. Retrieved July 20, from https//www.thenationalnews.com/uae/environment/how-does-cloud-seeding in the-uae-work.1.911961

Edensor, T. (Ed.). (1998). Tourists at the taj. *Performance and meaning at a symbolic site*. Routledge.

Feighery, W. (2012). Tourism and self-orientalism in Oman: A critical discourse analysis. *Critical Discourse Studies*, *9*(3), 269–284.

Filep, S., Macnaugton, J., & Glover, T. (2017). Tourism and gratitude: Valuing acts of kindness. *Annals of Tourism Research*, *66*, 26–36.

Foucault, M. (1980). Power/Knowledge: Selected interviews and other writing 1972–1977. In C. Colin Gordon (Ed.), *Knowledge and strategies* (pp. 134–146). Vintage Books.

Fotiadis, A. K., Woodside, A. G., Del Chiappa, G., Séraphin, H., & Hansen, H. O. (2021). Novel coronavirus and tourism: coping, recovery, and regeneration issues. *Tourism Recreation Research*, *46*(2), 144–147.

Galvani, A., Lew, A. A., & Sotelo Perez, M. (2020). COVID-19 is expanding global consciousness and the sustainability of travel and tourism. *Tourism Geographies*, *22*(3), 567–576. https://doi.org/10.1080/14616688.2020.1760924

Giuffrida, A. (2021). Monsters or a must? Venice tussles with return of cruise shops. *The Guardian*. Retrieved June 14, from ttps://www.theguardian.com/world/2021/jun/14/monsters-or-a-must-venice-tussles-with-return-of-cruise-ships

Gutberlet, M. (2016a). Socio-cultural impacts of large-scale cruise tourism in Souq Muttrah. *Fennia*, *194*(1), 46–63.

Gutberlet, M. (2016b). Cruise tourist dress behaviors and local-guest reactions in a Muslim country. *Tourism Culture & Communication*, *16*, 15–32.

Gutberlet, M. (2017). Staging the Oriental Other: Imaginaries and performances of German-speaking cruise tourists. Published online first and in 2019 *Tourist Studies*, *19*(1), 110–137.

Gutberlet, M. (2019). In a rush: Time-space compression and its impacts on cruise excursions. *Tourist Studies*, *19*(4), 1–29.

Gutberlet, M. (2020). "They just buy a karak and leave" – Overtourism in Souq Muttrah, The Sultanate of Oman, *Zeitschrift für Tourismuswissenschaften*, De Gruyter Oldenburg, 13 October.

Gutberlet, M. (2021). Valuing social capital and a legacy: "The old shops are the beauty of the place. In J. Saarinen & J. Richardson (Eds.), *Change in tourism/ tourism in change* (pp. 135–150). Routledge Publishing House.

Gutberlet, M. (2022a). Geopolitical imaginaries and cultural ecosystem services (CES) in the desert. *Tourism Geographies, 24*, 4–5.

Gutberlet, M. (2022b). Insight 288: Tourist bubbles and climate change in the GCC. COP 27 and Climate Action in the Middle East, Middle East Institute, National University of Singapore, October 24.

Haldrup, M., & Larsen, J. (2010). *Tourism, performance and the everyday: Consuming the orient.* Routledge.

Harvey, D. (1989). *The condition of postmodernity.* Blackwell.

Heidegger, M. (2010). *Being and time.* Translated by Joan Stambaugh. State University of New York Press.

Higgins-Desbiolles, F. (2020). Socialising tourism for social and ecological justice after COVID-19. *Tourism Geographies: An International Journal of Tourism Space, Place and Environment, 22*(3), 610–623. https://doi.org/10.1080/14616688.2020.1757748

Higgins-Desbiolles, F. (2021). The "war over tourism": Challenges to sustainable tourism in the tourism academy after COVID-19. *Journal of Sustainable Tourism 29, 21, 4, 551–569.*

Intergovernmental Panel on Climate Change (ICPP) (2022). Climate Change 2022. Impacts, Adaptation and Vulnerability. Summary for Policymakers, Working Group II, Contribution to the Sixth Assessment Report of the Intergovernmental Panel on Climate Change, WMO and UNEP. ICPP.

Ionnides, D. (2019). Greenland's tourism policy making and the risk of overtourism. In C. Milano, J. Cheer, & M. Novelli (Eds.), *Overtourism: Excesses, discontent and measures in travel and tourism* (pp. 209–223). CABI.

Jamal, T., & Higham, J. (2021). Justice and ethics: Towards a new platform for tourism and sustainability. *Journal of Sustainable Tourism, 29*(2–3), 143–157.

Johnson, D. (2006). Providing ecotourism excursions for cruise passengers. *Journal of Sustainable Tourism, 14*(1), 43–54.

Klein, R. A. (2011). Responsible cruise tourism: Issues of cruise tourism and sustainability. *Journal of Hospitality and Tourism Management, 18*, 107–116.

Koens, K., Postma, A., & Papp, B. (2019). Management strategies for overtourism – From adaptation to system change. In H. Pechlaner, E. Innerhofer, & G. Erschbamer (Eds.), *Overtourism, tourism management and solutions.* Routledge.

Krippendorf, J. (1987). *The holiday makers.* Heinemann.

Larsen, J., Gomes Bastos, M., Skovslund Hansen, L. I., Hevink, L. M., Jostova, K., & Smagurauskaite, D. (2021). Bubble-wrapped sightseeing mobilities: Hop on-off bus experiences in Copenhagen, *Tourist Studies 6*, 1–17.

Lew, A, Cheer, J. M., Haywood, M., Brouder P., & Salazar, N. B. (2020). Visions of travel and tourism after the global COVID-19 transformation of 2020. *Tourism Geographies, 22*(3), 455–466,

Lopes, J. M., & Dredge, D. (2018). Cruise tourism shore excursions: Value for destinations? *Journal of Tourism Planning and Development,* 16(6), 633–652.

MacNeill, T., & Wozniak, D. (2008). The economic, social and environmental impacts of cruise tourism. *Tourism Management, 66*, 387–404.

MEA (2005). *Millenium ecosystem assessment. Ecosystems and human well-being: Desertification synthesis.* World Resources Institute. www.milleniumecosystem.assessment.com

Milano, C.; Novelli, M. & Cheer, J.M. (2019): Overtourism and degrowth: a social movements perspective. *Journal of Sustainable Tourism*, DOI: 10.1080/09669582.2019.1650054.

Milcu, A. I., Hanspach, J., Abson, D., & Fischer, J. (2013). Cultural ecosystem services: A literature review and prospects for future research. *Ecology and Society*, *18*(3), 44.

Mullins, P. F. (2018). Toward a participatory ecological ethic for outdoor activities In B. S. R. Grimwood, K. Caton, & L. Cooke (Eds.), *New moral natures in tourism* (pp. 149–164). Routledge.

Papathanassis, A. (2017). Cruise tourism management: State of the art. *Tourism Review*, *72*(1), 104–119. https://doi.org/10.1108/TR-01-2017-0003

Papathanassis, G. (2012). Guest-to-guest interaction on board cruise ships: Exploring social dynamics and the role of situational factors. *Tourism Management*, *33*(5), 1148–1158.

Piketty, T. (2020). *Capital and ideology* (Kindle ed.). Harvard University Press.

Renaud, L. (2017). "Résister au débarquement: tourisme de croisière et dynamiques territoriales au Québec et dans la Caraïbe", *RITA* [online], N°10. Retrieved July 2017, from http://revue-rita.com/thema/resister-au-debarquement-tourisme-de-croisiere-et-dynamiques-territoriales-quebec-caraibe.html

Renaud, L. (2020). Reconsidering global mobility – Distancing from mass cruise tourism in the aftermath of COVID-19. *Tourism Geographies*. https://doi.org/10.1080/14616688.2020.176211

Richards, G. (2021). Making places through creative tourism? In N. Duxbury (Ed.), *Cultural sustainability, tourism and development: (Re)articulations in tourism contexts* (pp. 36–48). Routledge.

Salazar, N. B. (2005). Tourism and glocalisation "Local" tour guiding. *Annals of Tourism Research*, *32*(3), 628–646.

Salazar, N. B. (2010). *Envisioning Eden: Mobilizing imaginaries in tourism and beyond*. Berghahn Books.

Selby, M. (2004). *Understanding urban tourism: Image, culture & experience*. I.B. Tauris.

Séraphin, H.; Zaman, M.; Olver, S.; Bourliataux-Lajoinie; Dosquet, F. (2019). Destination branding and overtourism. *Journal of Hospitality and Tourism Management* 38, 1–4.

Sheller, M. (2021). Reconstructing tourism in the Caribbean: Connecting pandemic recovery, climate resilience and sustainable tourism through mobility justice. *Journal of Sustainable Tourism*, *29*(9), 1436–1449.

Singh, T. V. (Ed.). (2012). *Critical debates in tourism. Introduction*, 316–398. Kindle Ebook for PC. Channel View Publications.

Soulard, J., Knollenberg, W., Boley, B. B., & Perdue, R. R. (2018). Social capital and destination strategic planning. *Tourism Management*, *69*, 189–200.

Tucker, H., & Akama, J. (2010). Tourism as postcolonialism. In T. Jamal & M. Robinson (Eds.), *The handbook of tourism studies* (pp. 504–520). Sage.

United Nations Development Programme (2020). *Human development perspectives, COVID-19 and human development: Assessing the crisis, envisioning the recovery*. United Nations Development Programme.

United Nations Sustainable Development Goals (2021). Department of Economic and Social Affairs Sustainable Development, Sustainable Development Goals. https://sdgs.un.org/goals

Urry, J. (1995). *Consuming places*. Routledge.

Veijola, S. (2018). Afterword. In B. S. R. Grimwood, K. Caton, & L. Cooke (Eds.), *New moral natures in tourism* (pp. 206–209). Routledge Ethics of Tourism. Routledge.

Vogel, M. P., & Oschmann, C. (2013). Cruising through liquid modernity. *Tourist Studies, 13*(1), 62–80.

Wang, N. (1999). Rethinking authenticity in tourism experience. *Annals of Tourism Research, 26*(2), 340–370.

Wang, L., & Lyu, J. (2019). Inspiring awe through tourism and its consequences. *Annals of Tourism Research, 77,* 106–116.

Wang, Y. (2007). Customized authenticity begins at home. *Annals of Tourism Research, 34*(3), 789–804.

Weaver, A. (2005a). The McDonaldization thesis and cruise tourism. *Annals of Tourism Research, 32*(2), 346–366.

Wilkinson, P. F. (1999). Caribbean cruise tourism: Delusion? Illusion? *Tourism Geographies: An International Journal of Tourism Space, Place and Environment, 1*(3), 261–282.

Williams, S., & Lew, A. A. (Eds.). (2015). *Tourism geography. Critical understandings of place, space and experience* (3rd ed.). Routledge.

Wood, R. (2000). Caribbean cruise tourism: Globalization at sea. *Annals of Tourism Research, 27*(2), 345–370.

Yarnal, C. M., & Kerstetter, D. (2005). Casting off – An exploration of cruise ship space, group behavior and social interaction. *Journal of Travel Research, 43,* 268–379.

# Index

Abend, L. 30, 31
action research 7
AIDA 93, 97, 114; AIDAblu 64–65,
    73, 74
Airbnb 29
Al Jazeera 49
Al Lawatia family 155; Al-Lawatia,
    Sur 101, 170; Al Lawati community
    155–171
Al-Monitor 59
Al Muthairib 55
Al Shaibany, S. 60
Amoamo, M. 228
Andrews, H. 146
Arabia 106; Aladdins lamp 191; Jewel
    of Arabia 49; 1001 Nights 191,
    201–203, 229
The Arabian Nights 11, 39, 74, 93–95, 229
Arabian Peninsula X, 7, 12, 126, 127,
    135, 200, 204, 233, 236
Arabic 78, 186
Assistant Deputy Mufti of Oman
    76, 183
Augé, M. 10, 182
authenticity 20–21, 187; authentic
    selfhood 195; 200–204; authentic
    souvenir 192; constructed
    authenticity 11, 184; customized
    authenticity 11; existential
    authenticity 186; inter-personal
    authenticity 186; intra-personal
    authenticity 193; staged
    authenticity 36

Baerenholdt, J.O. 21, 187, 199
Bahrain 63, 137
Bait al Baranda Museum 166
Baluchistan 51
Barasti huts 183

Barcelona 29, 30
Baudrillard 96, 133
Bauman, Z. 1, 18, 22, 90, 134, 169, 171,
    177, 209, 211
Bedouin 39–40, 51, 54, 190–197
Belhassen 177, 195, 202, 217
Berdychevsky, L. 195–196
Berlin 30
Bertella, G. 213
Bourdieu, P. 116, 138
Brilliance of the Seas 74
Bruner, E. 20, 39
Burj: al Arab and Burj Khalifa 96
Büscher, B. 28, 32, 186, 201,
    202, 231
business monoculture 31

camels 37–40, 190–192
Cape Town 62, 166
capital 33; bonding and bridging social
    capital 159–165, 199; capital accumu-
    lation 99; cultural capital 3; foreign
    capital 181, 225; social capital 32–34,
    85, 159–166, 223–227
capitalism 1, 7, 18, 32, 160, 210
Caribbean 27, 65
carrying capacity 3, 23, 210; cultural
    carrying capacity and social carrying
    capacity 136
Caton, K. 135
Causevic 124
Cauvin Verner, C. 39, 80, 177
Cave, J. 211, 232
Chambers, D. 89
Chan, K.M.A. 179, 198
Cheer, J. 18, 29, 225
Chronis, A. 35, 89, 98, 103, 180
city-tour 98
Cohen, E. 139

community 22, 70, 210–215, 231–236;
Banyan community 169; community-
based tourism 211; community
network 161; cruise communita
11; driver communita 194; group
communita 204; host community
141; local community 76–85, 133–164,
148–171; multi-ethnic community 51,
212, 234, 236; participatory community approach 210, 236; tourist
communitas 186, 193, 196
community-based tourism IX, 33,
210–220
consciousness 6, 235; conscious travel 219
consumption of places 22; mass
consumption 25
Cooper, N. 175, 199
Corniche Road in Muttrah 77
Costa Cruises 71, 114
COVID-19 pandemic 4, 32, 57, 71, 78,
159, 167–169, 170–171, 202, 224, 234
Crouch, D. 21, 34
Cruise Alliance 8; cruise ships 5, 89, 98
cruise destinations 3
Cruise Lines International Association
(CLIA) 23–24, 65, 212
cruise operations 5, 65
cruise passengers XI, 4–6, 63–65,
89–128, 175–204
cruise tourism X, 23–23, 223–236; contemporary cruise tourists 127; cruise
hegemony 99; large-scale cruise tourism 63; luxury cruise tourism 127
Cultural Ecosystem Services 171–204
cultural mediators 22, 180–196; 212
culture 161; culture clashes 133–138; culture confusion 136; tourist culture 146

De Botton, A. 38
De Certeau, 2
degrowth 6, 232
De Lacey, P. 175
de-marketing 6
desert 78–82; desert experience 179–204
destination: feminine destination 96;
Oriental destination 70
development, economic 59
Di Giovine, M.A. 34
Din, 145, 228
Doxey, G. 139, 151
Dredge, D. 211
dress code 137–148
Dubai 62, 65, 92, 121, 137, 154, 166,
171, 190

Dubrovnik 32, 212
Duignan, M. 202

Echtner, C.M. 38
Edensor, T. 21, 22, 106, 108, 229
Eid Al-Adha 167
emerging destinations XI, 69
ethics in tourism 11, 70, 133–148; care
ethic 135, 138–141, 209–215
ethnography 69, 72, 76
event, pseudo-event 185, 189
excursion 79
expatriates, Asian 153, 183
experience; fast and slow experiences
182–204; spiritual experiences
198–204; tourist experiences 10,
98–113, 175–203; transformative
experiences 175–204

falaj system 81, 183–189
Fayall, A. 29, 211
Feighery, W. 98
Fennell, D. 136, 175
Filep, S. 211
Font, X. 28
Foucault, M. 228
frankincense burner 110; frankincense
shop 75, 77, 106–111

gaze, gazing 100; collective gaze 108;
male gaze 69, 104; tourist gaze
191–192
gendered spaces 69; enclavic spaces 98,
spiritual spaces 39
German-speaking culture 89; German
passenger 5; German-speaking tourists 67, 121, 180–204
globalization IX, 19, 28, 127, 153, 223
Global North 99
Global South 12
Goethe, J.W. 38
Goffmann, E. 103, 117
Goodwin, H. 176
Gössliing, 92
Graulund, R. 40, 179
grazing behavior 197; grazing
destinations 91
Grimwood, B. 176
Gulf Cooperation Council (GCC)
57, 65

habitus 91, 127
Haldrup, M. 74
Hall, M. 145, 210

halwa 77, 84, 148, 185–186; halwa
  maker 157
Harvey, D. 1, 19, 98, 167, 224
Heidegger, M. 22, 139
Heimtun, B. 199
heritage: local 183; tangible heritage 197
Higgins-Desbiolles, F. 18, 29, 32, 171,
  232, 235
Hill, J. 178; 194; 195, 198, 201, 202
His Majesty Sultan Haitham bin Tarik
  Al Said 50
His Majesty Sultan Qaboos bin Said al
  Said 50, 148
Hofstede, G. 142, 144
Holden, A. 39, 180
home-port 31
hospitality 183–185; unconditional hos-
  pitality 136; reciprocal hospitality 141
Howard, C. 177
hypercapitalism 18

Iceland 31, 218
imaginaries 10; collective imaginaries 177; counter-imaginaries 218;
  geopolitical imaginaries 34–40, 229;
  imaginary community 227; Oriental
  imaginaries 37–40, 89–98, 104, 109,
  180; 183–189, 191, 196–199, 201, 223;
  postcolonial imaginaries 89, 196;
  tourism imaginaries 34–40, 72,
  231–236
interviews: walking interviews 74–82, 144
Ionnides, D. 10, 224
Islam 200

Jaakson, R. 10, 18, 28, 101, 117, 215
Jafari, J. 213
Jamal, T. 6, 175
Justice, social 175

kahwa (coffee): Omani 155–156, 184
karak tea 84, 154–156
Kay, M. 28
Klein, R. A. 22, 29, 126, 186
Koens, K. 29, 167, 225
Krippendorf, J. 35, 139, 235
Kuoni 215

labelling 35, 95
Larsen, J. 67, 98, 186, 217
Leite, N. 38, 218
Lew, A. 18, 179, 232
liminal zone 194; liminoid space
  190–200

liquid life 23, 91
liquid modernity 2, 4, 5, 99, 209, 219, 232
local community 10; local dress 95;
  local elites 28; local flow of life 77;
  local identities 7
London, W.R. 181
Lopes J.M, 181
Lüdeling, E. 54
Lumsdon, L. 176

MacCannell, D. 36, 96, 105, 109, 112,
  152, 186, 190
MacNeill, T. 212
Manama 79
market 97
mass tourism IX, 6, 20, 118
Mazumdar, S. 200
Meadows, D. 210
mega-cruise tourism 10, 49, 231, 235;
  mega-cruise ships 62, 72; mega-cruise
  tourists 92, 127; mega-projects 61–65
Mein Schiff 71, 94
Milano, C. 18, 29, 99, 126, 167, 212,
  214, 227
Milcu, A. 178
Millennium Ecosystem Assessment
  (MEA) 178–179
Minca, C. 27
mindfulness, mindlessness 138–147
Ministry of Heritage and Tourism 64
Ministry of Tourism 57, 143
mobilities 1, 18–20, 193–194; mobility
  justice 234
Mordue 22, 187
Morocco 56, 97
Moscardo, G. 142, 176
Moufakkir, O. 136
Mowforth, M. 19
Mullins, P.F. 202, 232
Muscat Daily 8, 62–63, 164
Muttrah: harbor 162; Muttrah Tourism
  Committee 164; Souq Muttrah
  89–171, 215–217

National Centre for Statistics and
  Information (NCSI) 51, 83
North America 5

Oman Daily Observer 62, 137
Omanisation 57
Orient 35, 94, 104, 179; Oriental
  abundance 106; Oriental country
  144; Oriental experience 106–113;
  Orientalizing 95; Oriental Other 100,

105–113, 187–229; Orientalism 28;
Oriental space 192, 229
Other: exotic XI, 35; Otherness 104,
105, 111
overaccumulation 3
overconsumption 89, 118, 198, 227, 236
overcrowding IX, 31, 113–119, 204
overtourism IX, 3–6, 28–30, 236
Oxford Business Group 57, 61

Palmer, A. 93
Pearce, P.L. 135, 136, 139, 147
performance 21
photography 72, 108–11, 193, 199
Piketty, T. 1, 18, 233
Pink, S. 75, 80, 81
playscape 4, 26
pleasure IX
public spaces 67

Qatar 49, 57, 63, 166
questionnaire survey 72

rebound 4
regenerative tourism 6
relationship human-environment 178
Renaud, L. 3, 18, 225
research locations 85
Richards, G 214
Rickley-Boyd, J.M. 74, 198
Ritzer, G. 20, 26, 213
Rodaway, P. 106
Royal Caribbean 26, 71, 114

Saarinen, J. 10, 119
saaroj 183
Said, E. 36, 179, 190, 191
Salazar, N. 22, 95, 109, 111, 191,
229, 230
Santos, P.A.
Saveriades, A. 145
Schaich, H. 179, 199
Scholz, F. 52, 151
self-transformation 21, 82
Séraphin, H. 3, 212
sexual harassment 196
Sharqiyah Sands desert 53, 78–82, 171,
179–203, 217, 228, 230; desert camp
56, 230; Sharquiyah Sands region
53–57
Sheller, M. 7, 211, 232, 234
Shepherd, R.J. 181
Sindbad 95

Singh, T.V. 235
smellscape 106; bokhur 125, 159; myrrh
110; saffron 112
Smith, V. 23, 30
social constructivist 8
social distinction 116–118
social exchange 127, 186
social exclusion 231
social identity 33, 124, 228;
sociocultural identities 153
social values 134–138; Islamic social
values 141; individual values 141
Soulard, J. 33, 225
Souq Muttrah 8–10, 39–40, 49,
51–53, 63, 71–78, 98–128; 133–171,
207–220, 223
Space of freedom 10; empty spaces 167;
hybrid space 118, 122, 202; spaces of
exception 2, 189, 204
staging 21; backstage 164;
communicative staging 110;
frontstage 110
stakeholders 69, 179, 209
Statista 2
Stephenson, M. 214
The Sultanate of Oman 2, 49–65, 70,
209; desert 78–82; Muscat, 64, 79;
port Khasab 63; port Salalah
63–64
Sultan Qaboos University 59, 148
sunset 199
sustainability 209, 223; sustainable
tourism 5, 221–223
Swahili 186

theoplacity 21, 194–197
Thesiger, W. 202
Times News Service 58, 61
Times of Oman 101
Time-space compression 28, 82,
180–194, 197–204, 209
Timothy, D. X–XI; 147
Torres-Delgado, A. 215
tour guide 81, 180–196; in the desert
183–204; tour guiding 108–113; 122–126
tourism development 33, 56–59, 210,
235; tourism planning 216; tourism
destination branding 178; tourism
infrastructure 57
tourismphobia 30–31
tourist behaviors 133–148, reeingi-
neering tourist behaviors 147; dress
behavior 134

tourist bubble 4, 24, 27, 98–104, 118–122, 126, 148, 180–203, 216, 223, 228–231; enclosed tourist bubbles 11, 65, 147–152, 189, 196, 198–204, 231; mobile bubble 189, 227; sanitized tourist bubble 201
tourist gaze XI, 100–104; 192–196
tourist police 31
transportation 50; mode of transportation 180
Trell, E.-M. 75
Tresidder, R. 179
Trexit-measures 32
Tucker, H. 195, 229

undertourism 5, 32, 166
United Arab Emirates 49, 63, 70, 110, 146, 233–234
United Nations Development Programme (UNDP) 167, 234
United Nations Organization for Education, Science and Culture (UNESCO) 81, 197, 234

United Nations World Tourism Organisation (UNWTO) 57, 73, 135, 171, 210, 215
urban destination 1
Urry, J. 19, 28, 101, 166, 181, 186, 198

values: transformative and non-transformative 179
Venice 4, 28, 30, 137
Visit Iceland 218
Vogel 19, 24

Wagner, L. 56, 180
Wali of Muttrah 76
Wall, G. 23
Wang, Y. 11, 20, 187
Weaver, A. 7, 126, 180
Weeden, C. 7
wellbeing 33, 179, 209, 231
wildlife 190–193
Wilkinson, P.F. 23, 29
Wilson, E. 67, 68
Wood, 27

Printed in the United States
by Baker & Taylor Publisher Services